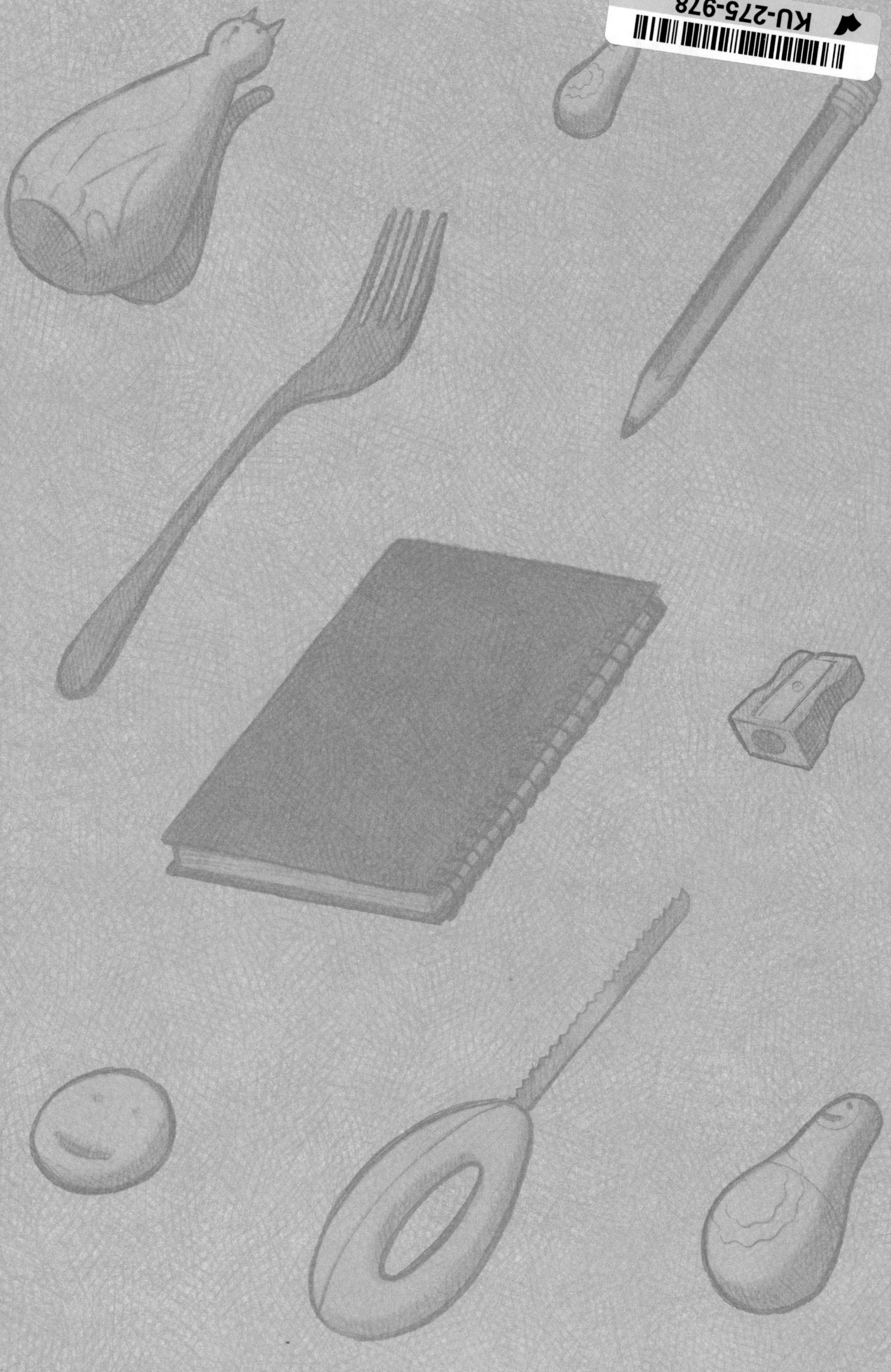

THE GIGANTIC BEARD THAT WAS EVIL

THE GIGANTIC BEARD THAT WAS EVIL

Stephen Collins

JONATHAN CAPE
LONDON

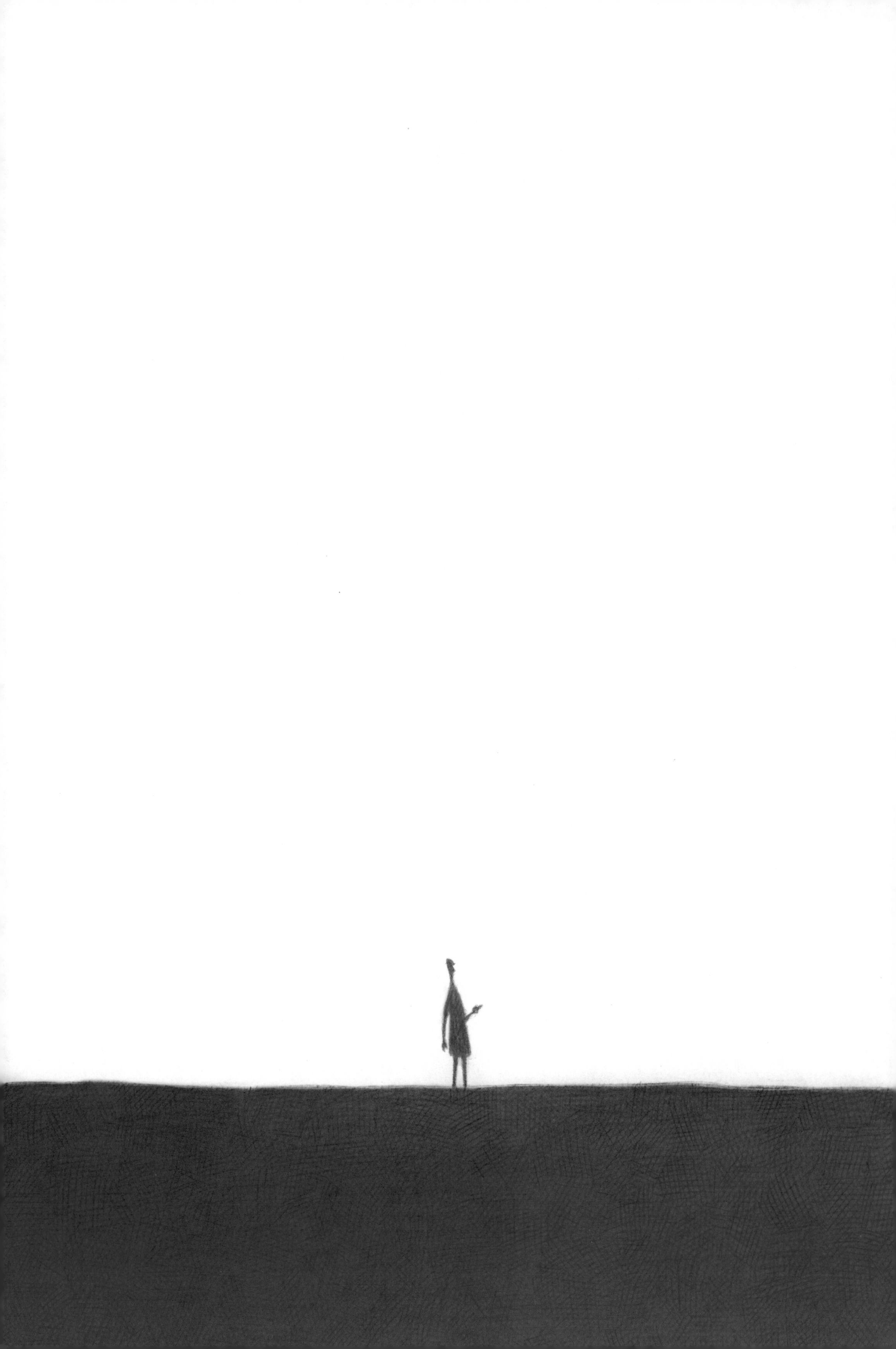

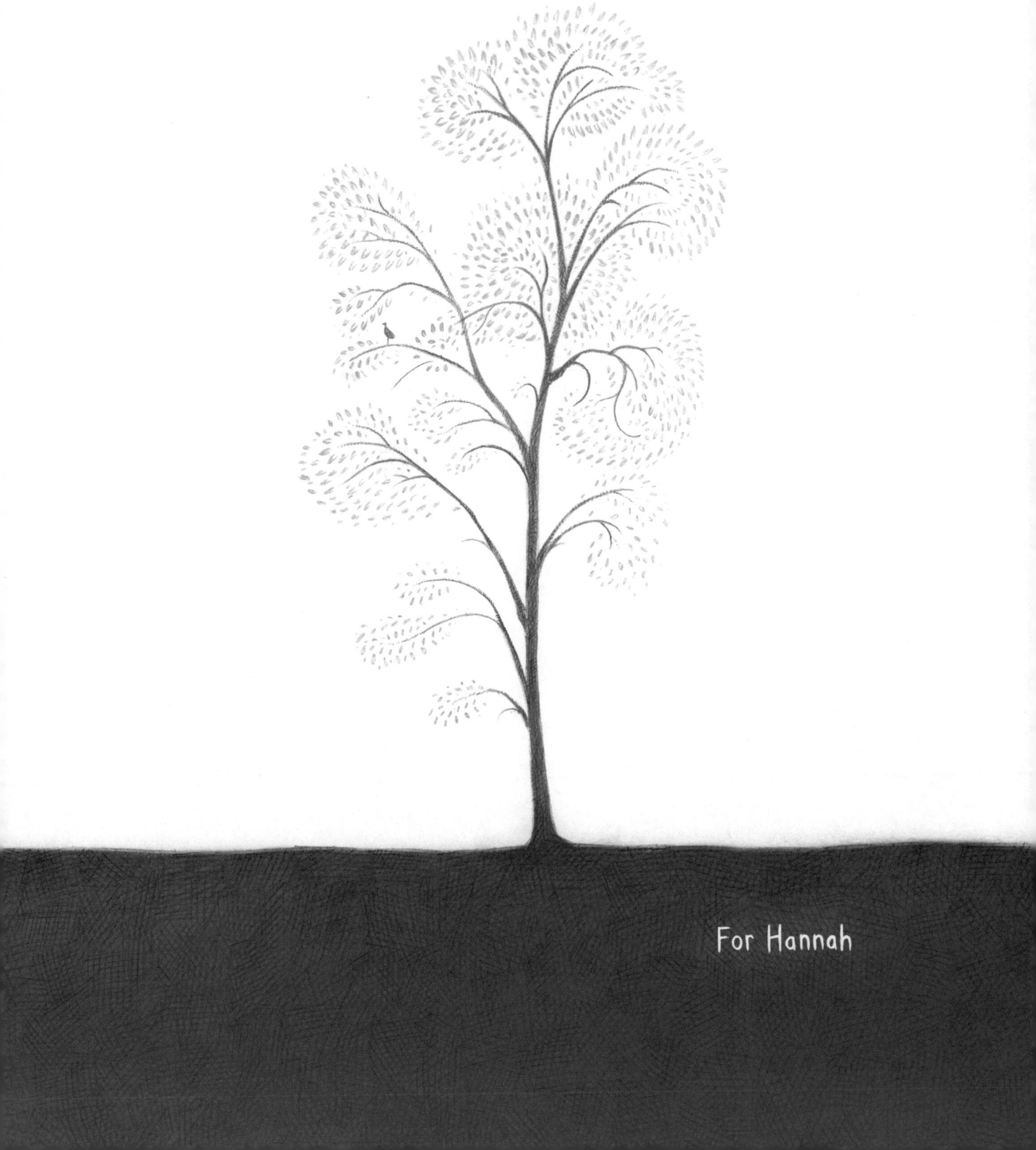

For Hannah

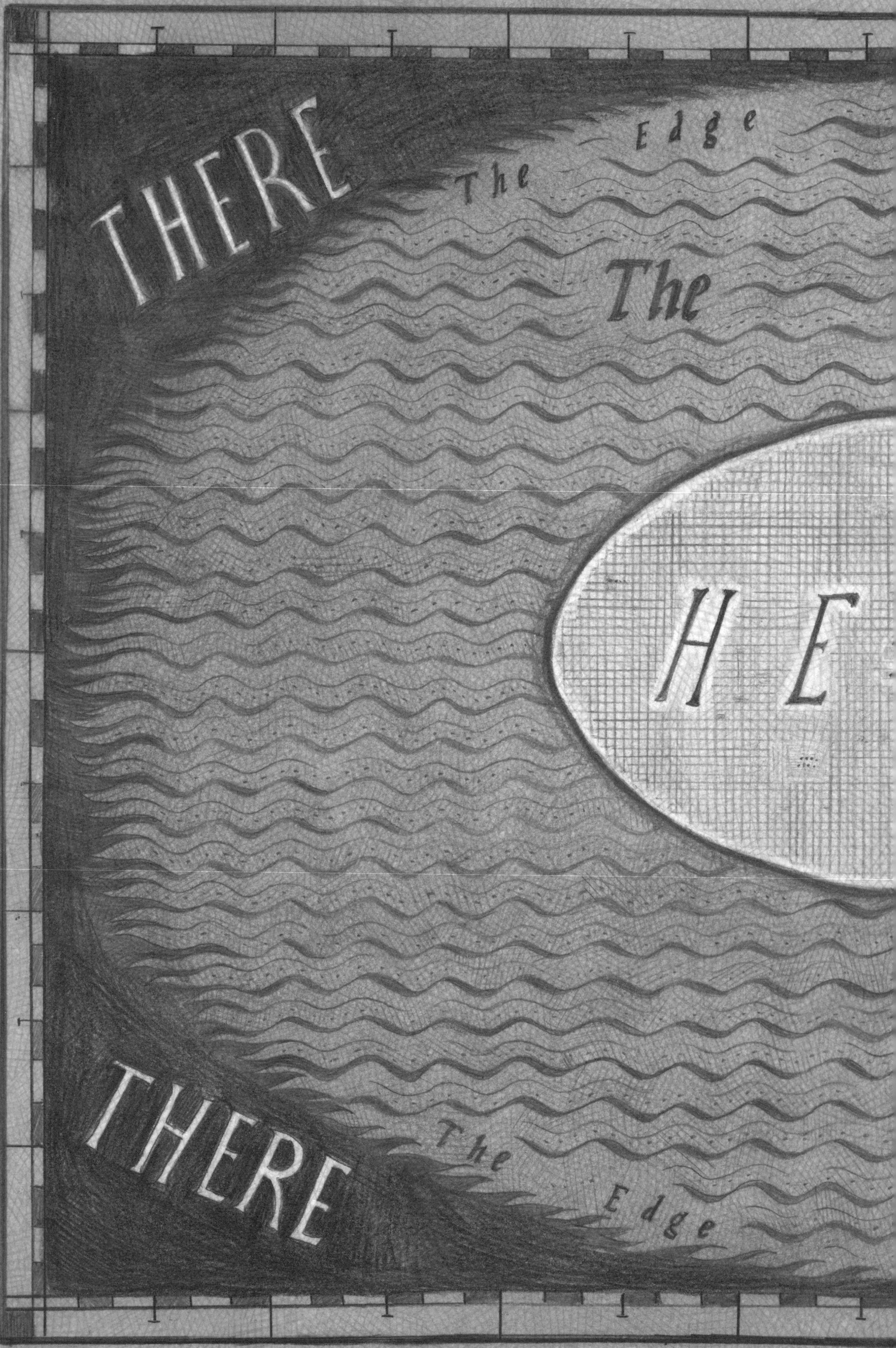
THERE
The Edge
The
HE
THERE
The Edge

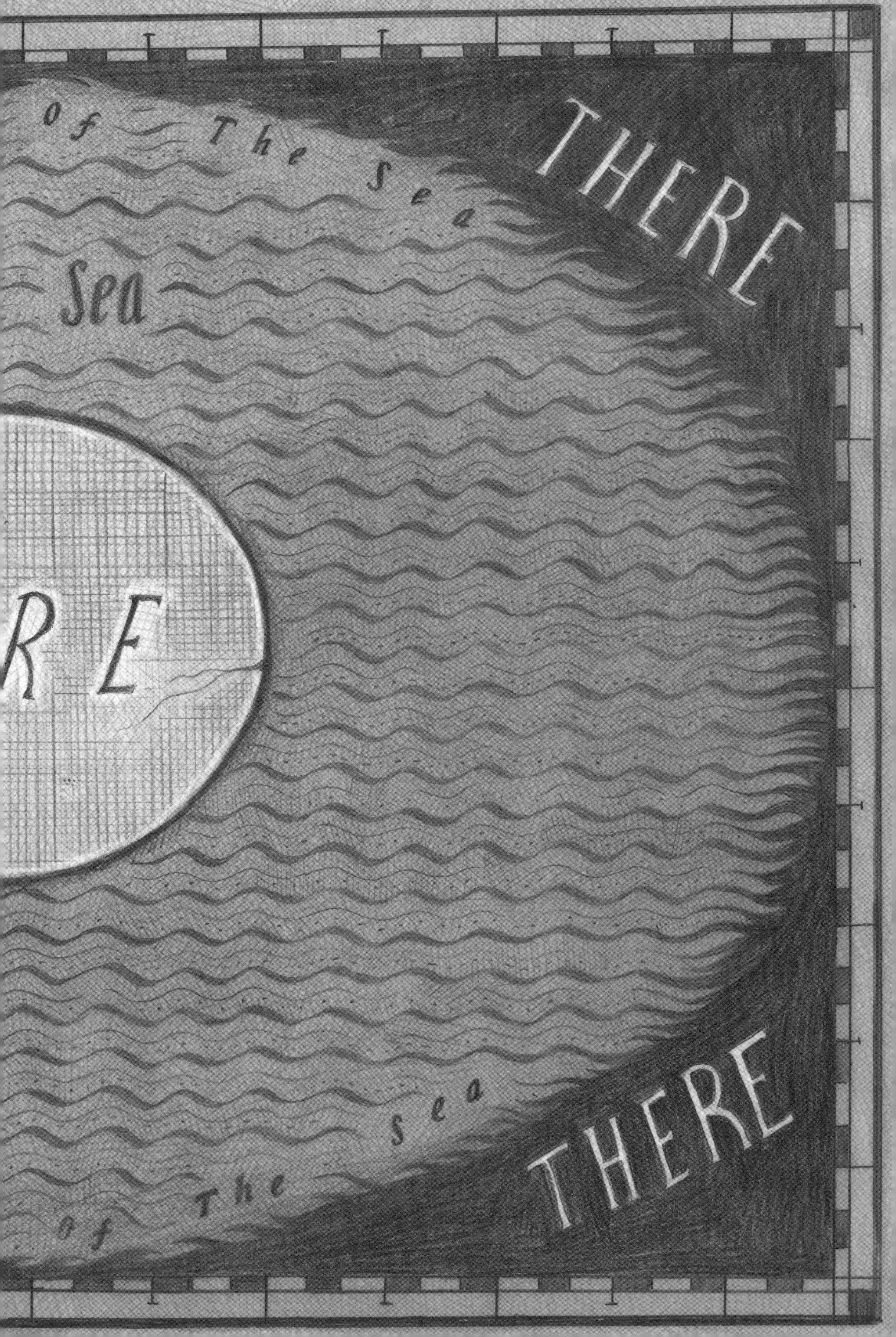
of The Sea
THERE
Sea
RE
Sea
of The sea
THERE

1.

HERE

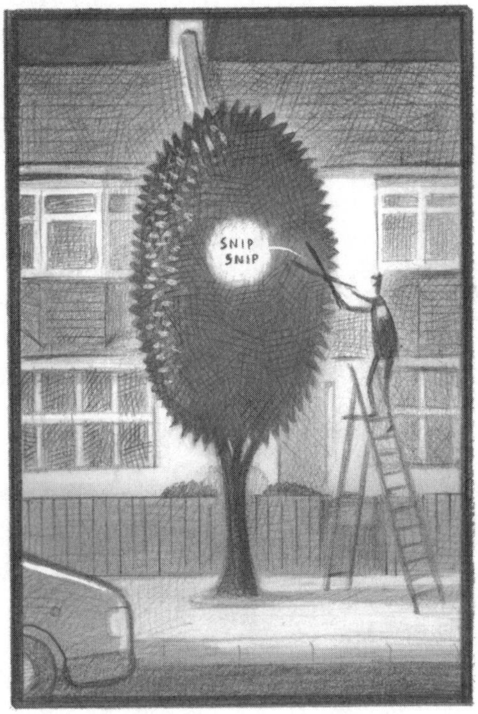
SNIP
SNIP

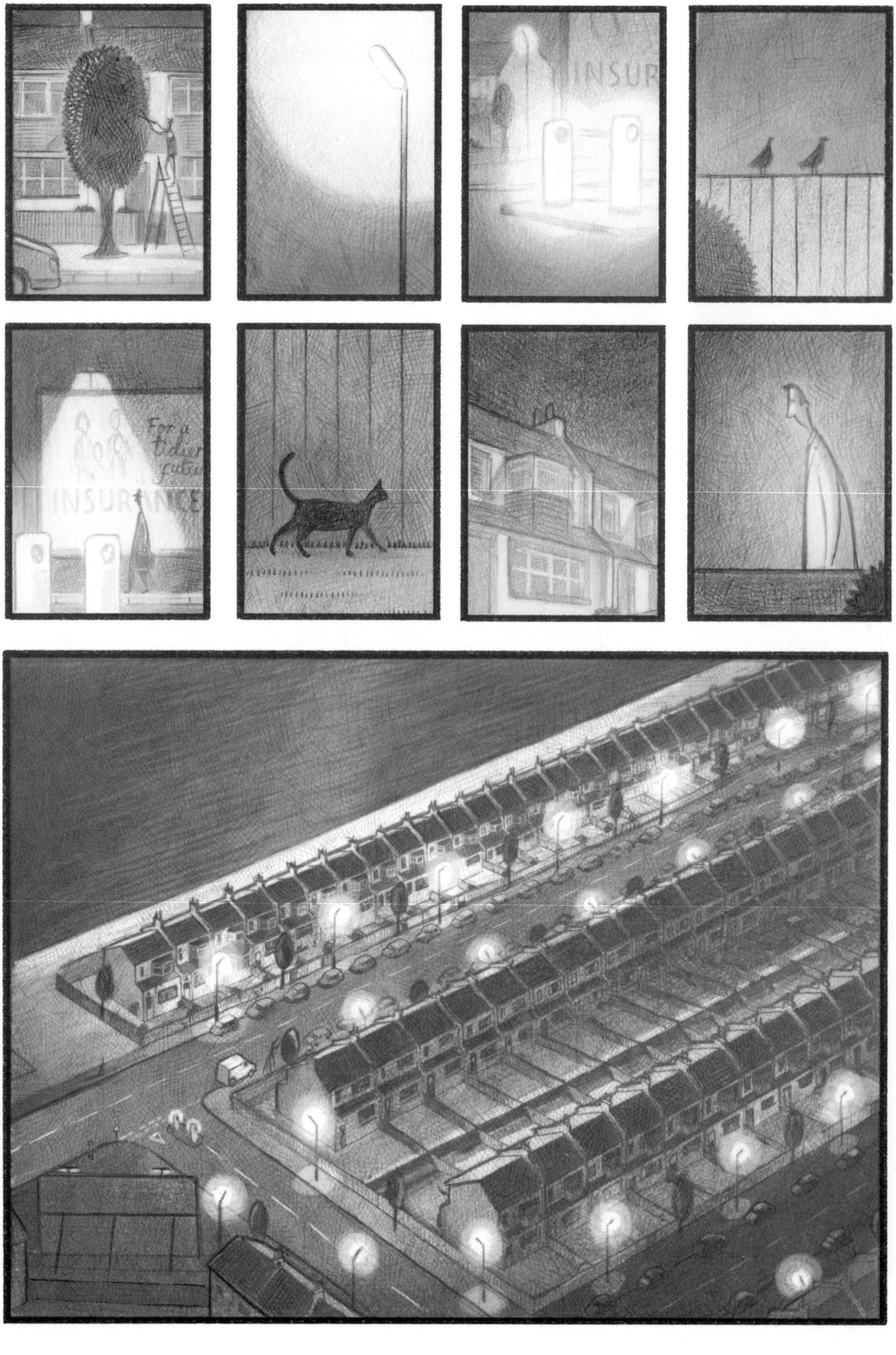
INSUR
For a
INSURANCE

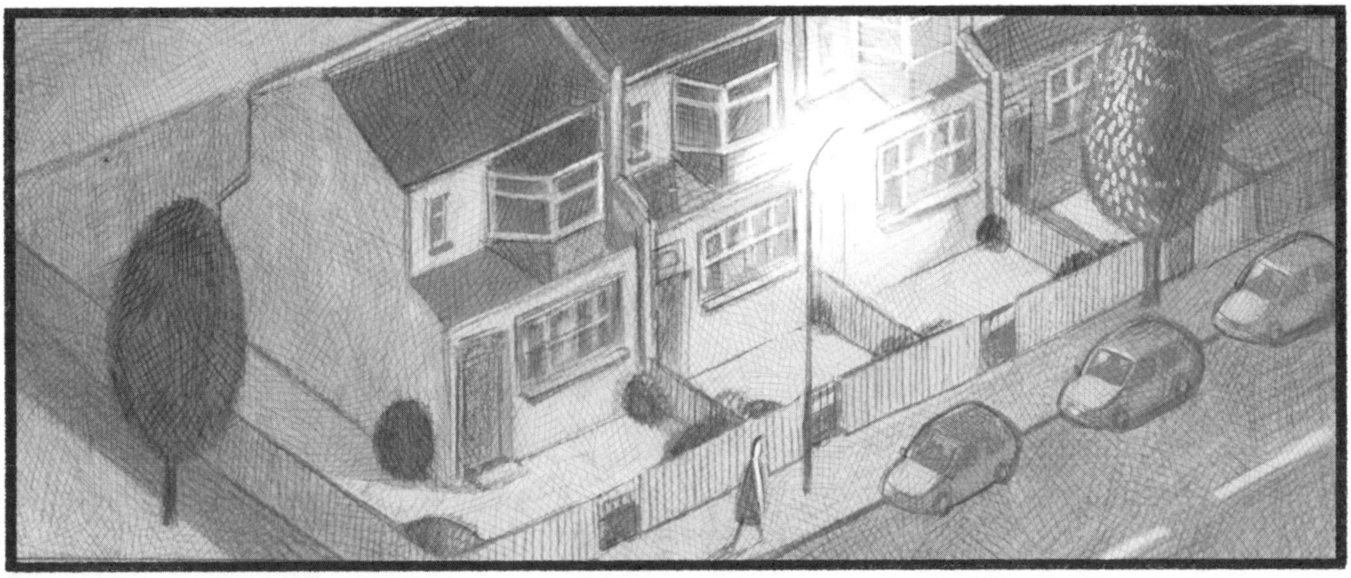

Beneath the skin

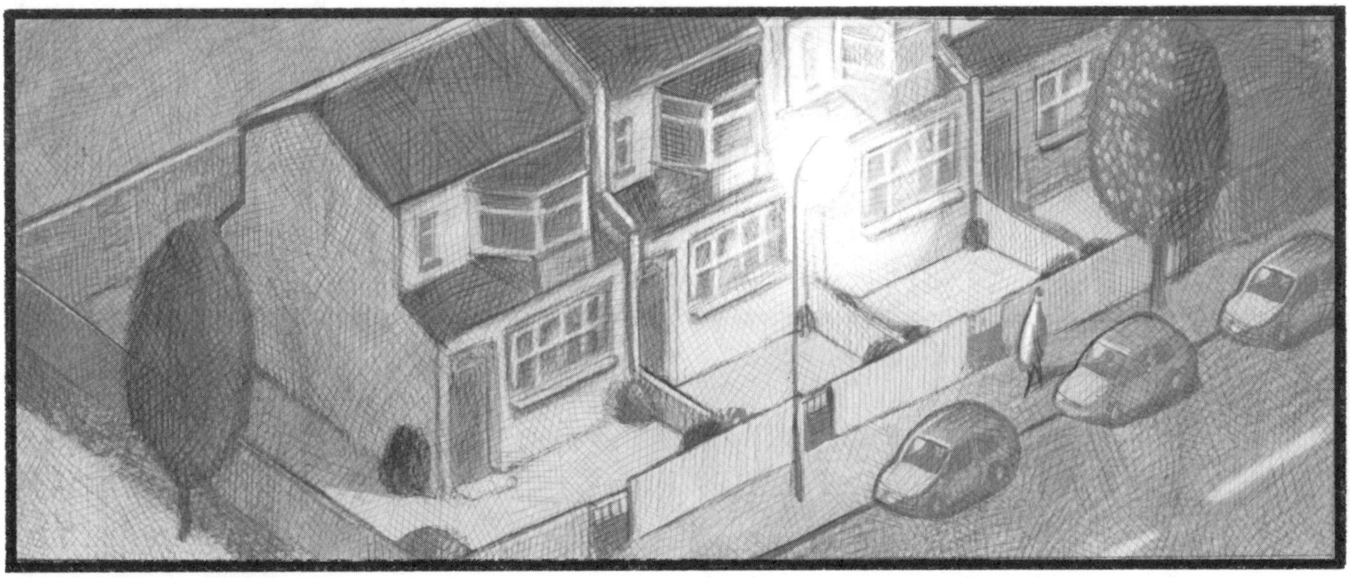

of everything

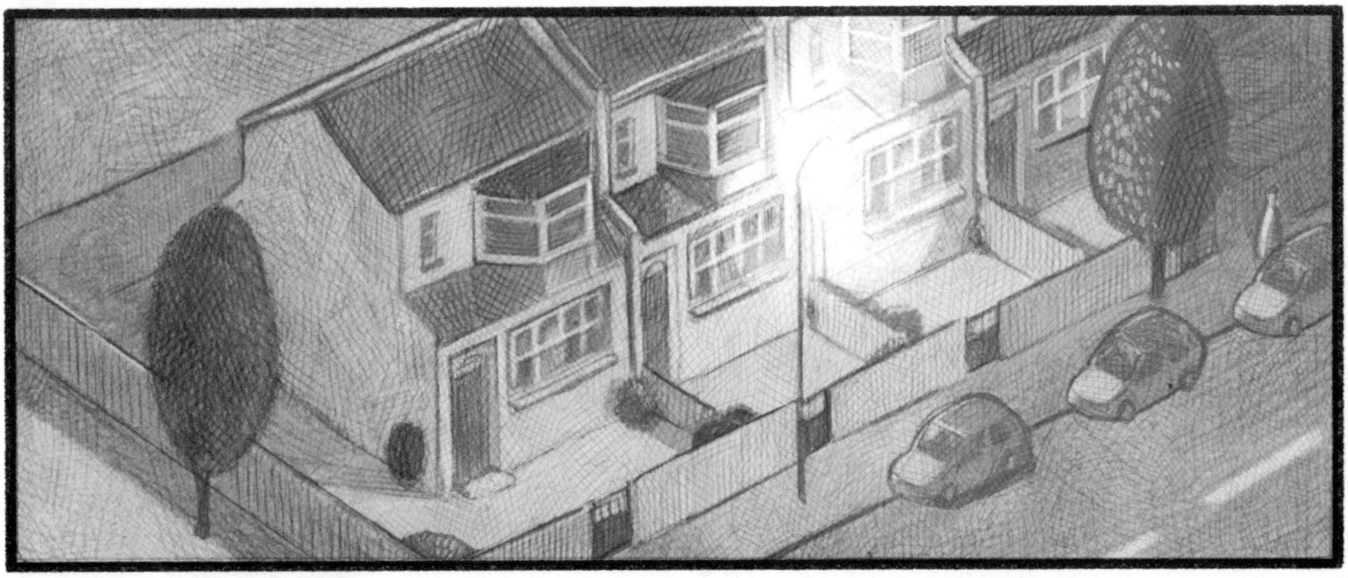

is something nobody can know.

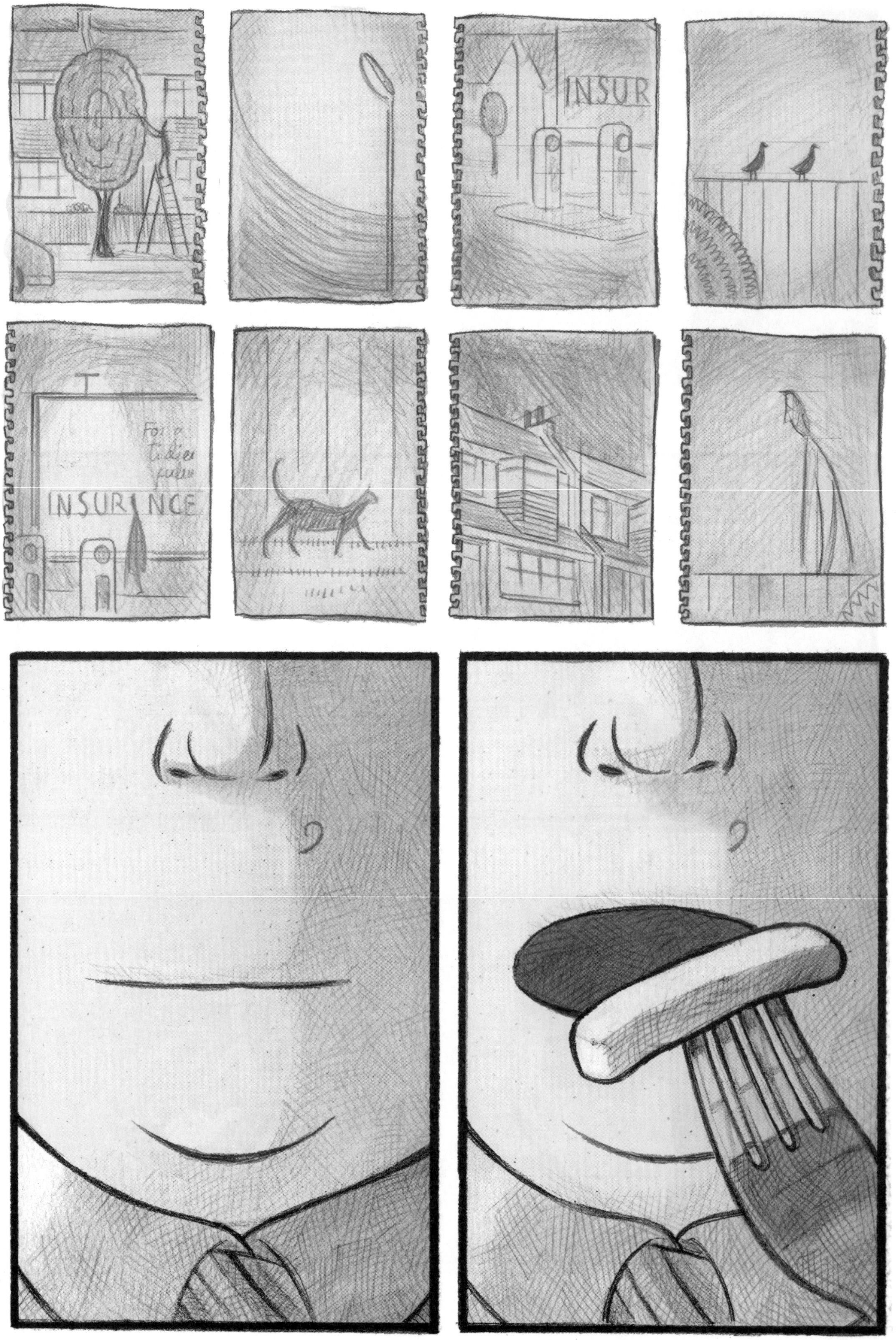
INSUR
INSUR NCE

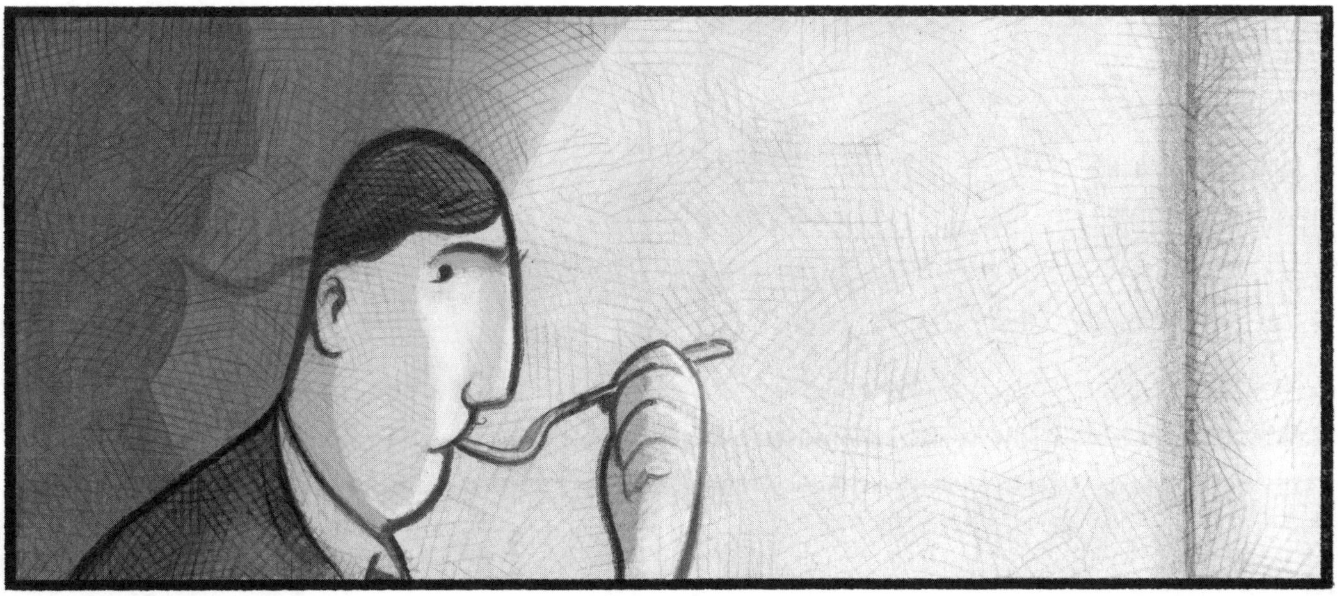

The job of the skin

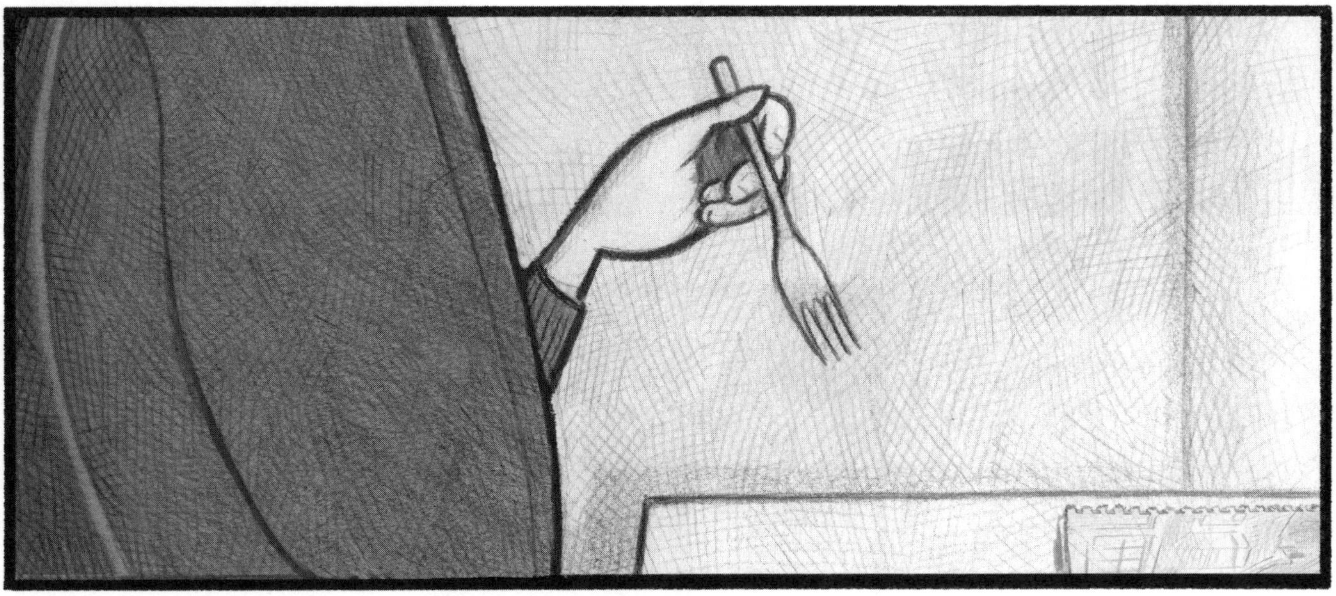

is to keep it all in

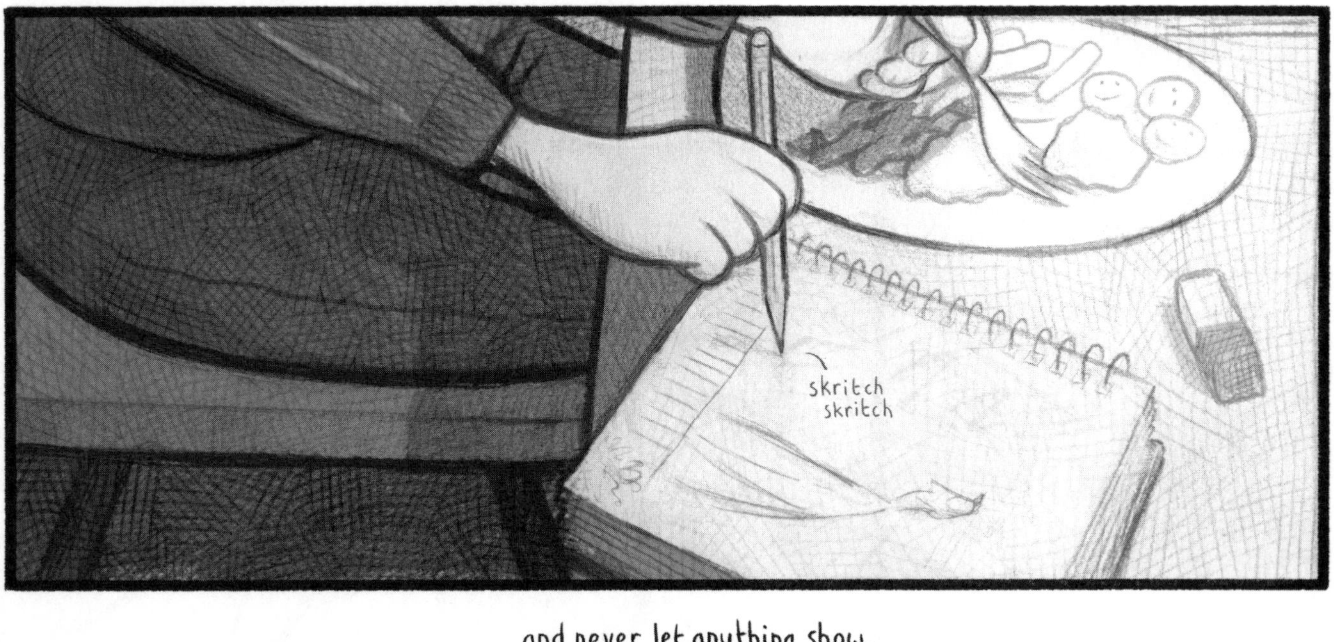
skritch
skritch

and never let anything show.

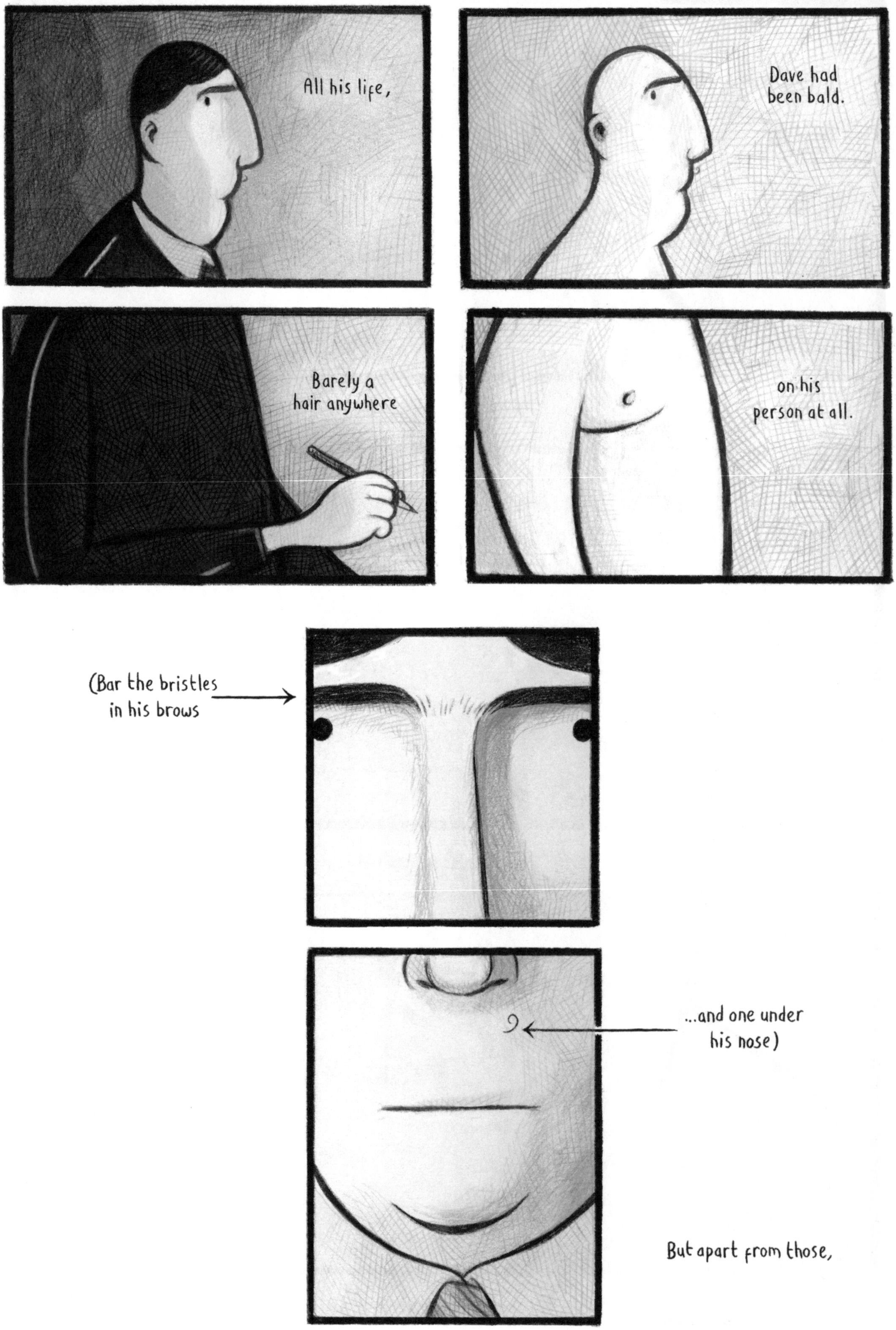
All his life,
Dave had been bald.
Barely a hair anywhere
on his person at all.
(Bar the bristles in his brows
...and one under his nose)
But apart from those,

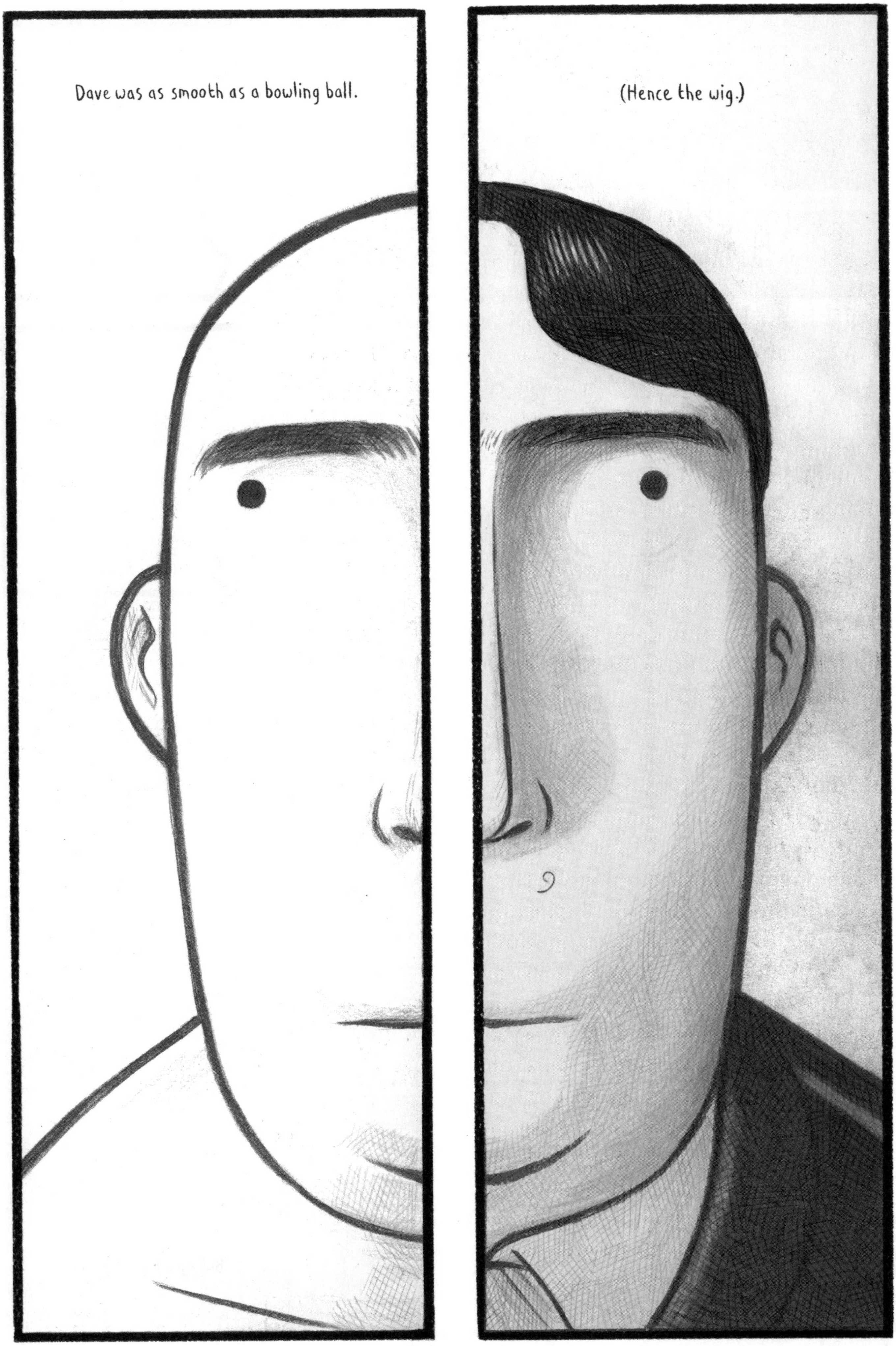
Dave was as smooth as a bowling ball.
(Hence the wig.)

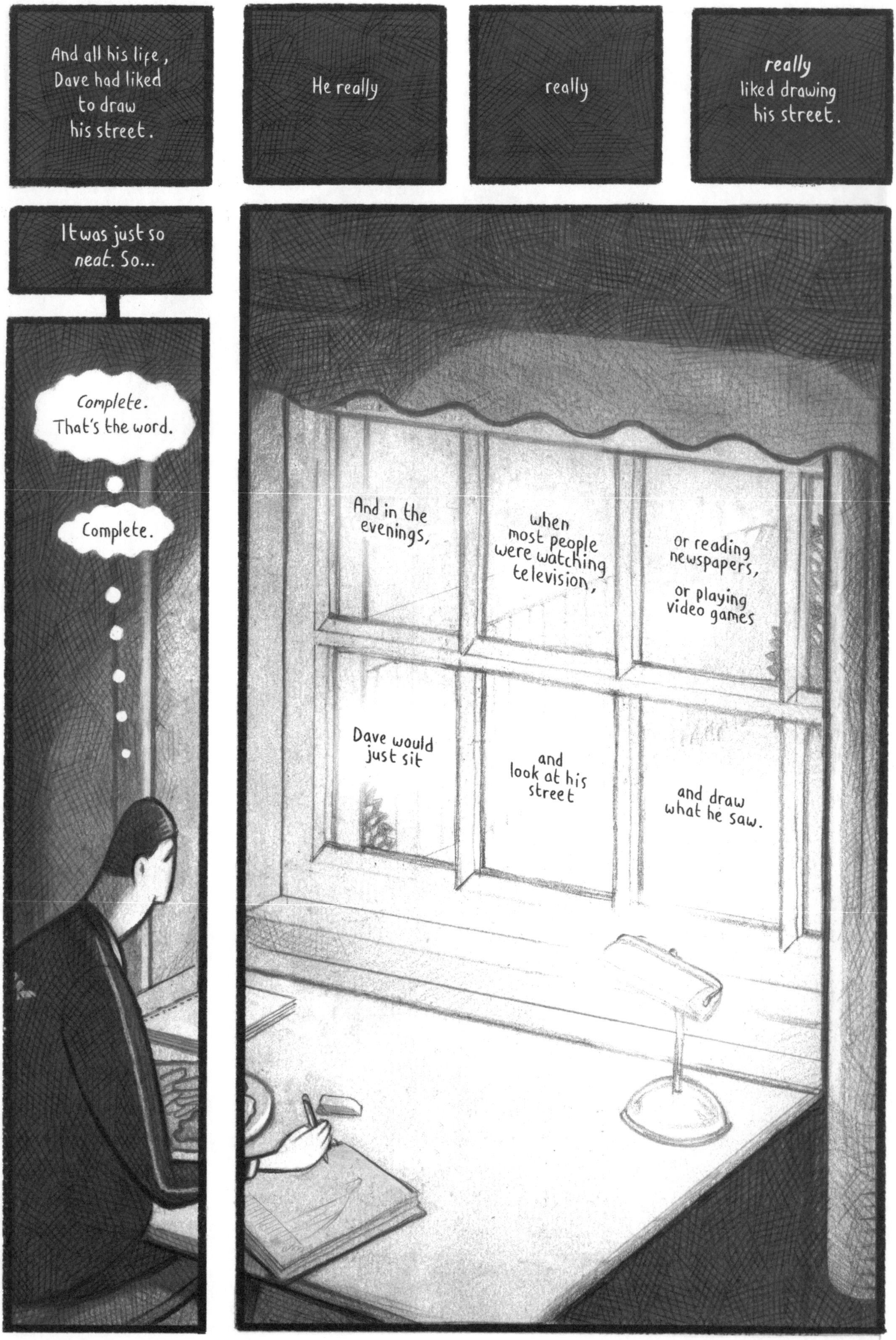
And all his life, Dave had liked to draw his street.
He really
really
really liked drawing his street.
It was just so *neat*. So...
Complete. That's the word.
Complete.
And in the evenings,
when most people were watching television,
or reading newspapers,
or playing video games
Dave would just sit
and look at his street
and draw what he saw.

He thought it was beautiful.

He found a certain comfort
in its tidiness.

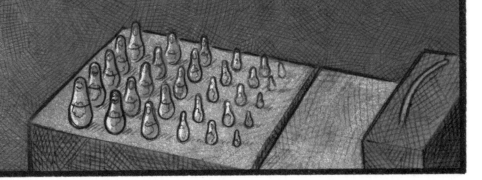

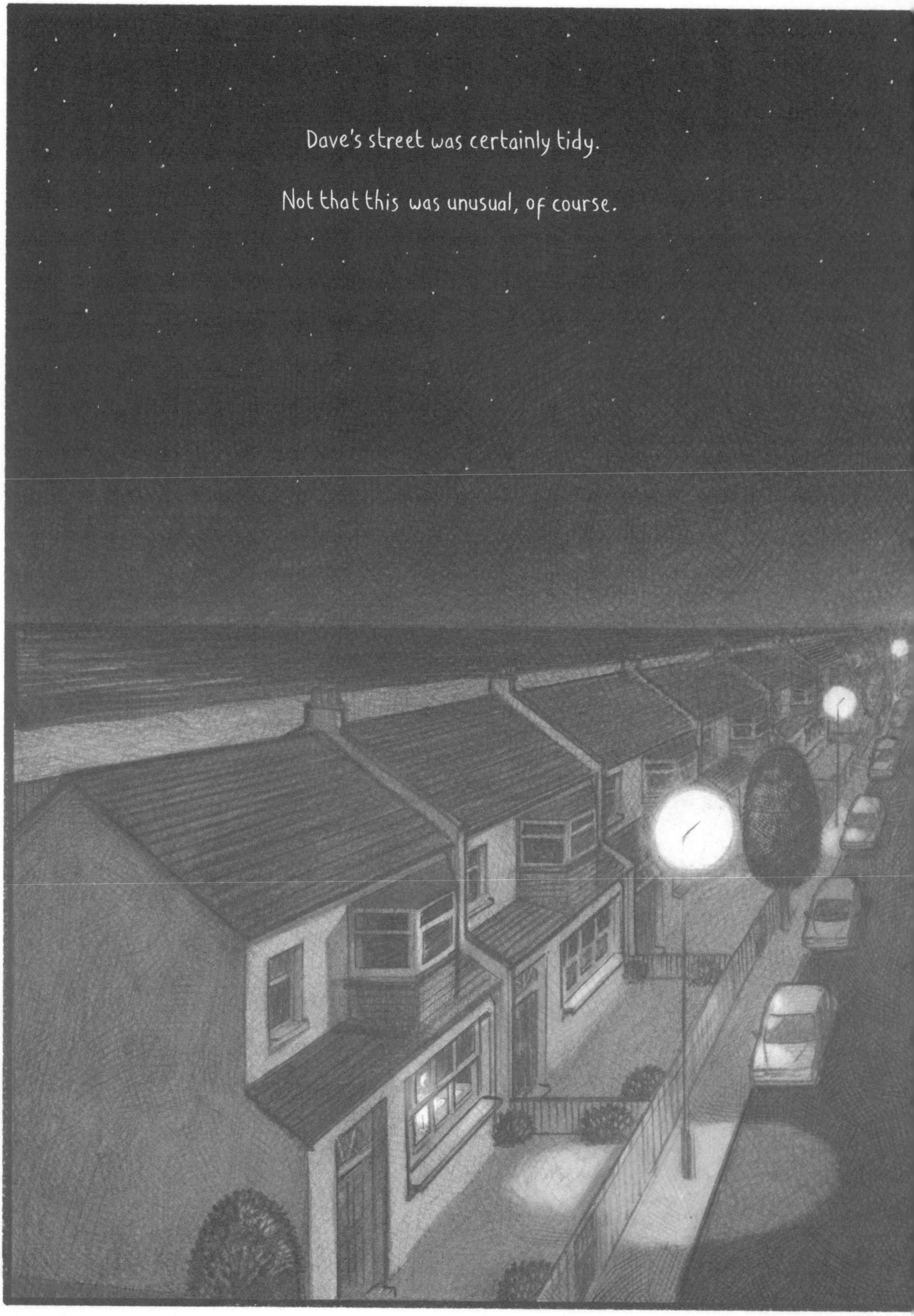
Dave's street was certainly tidy.
Not that this was unusual, of course.

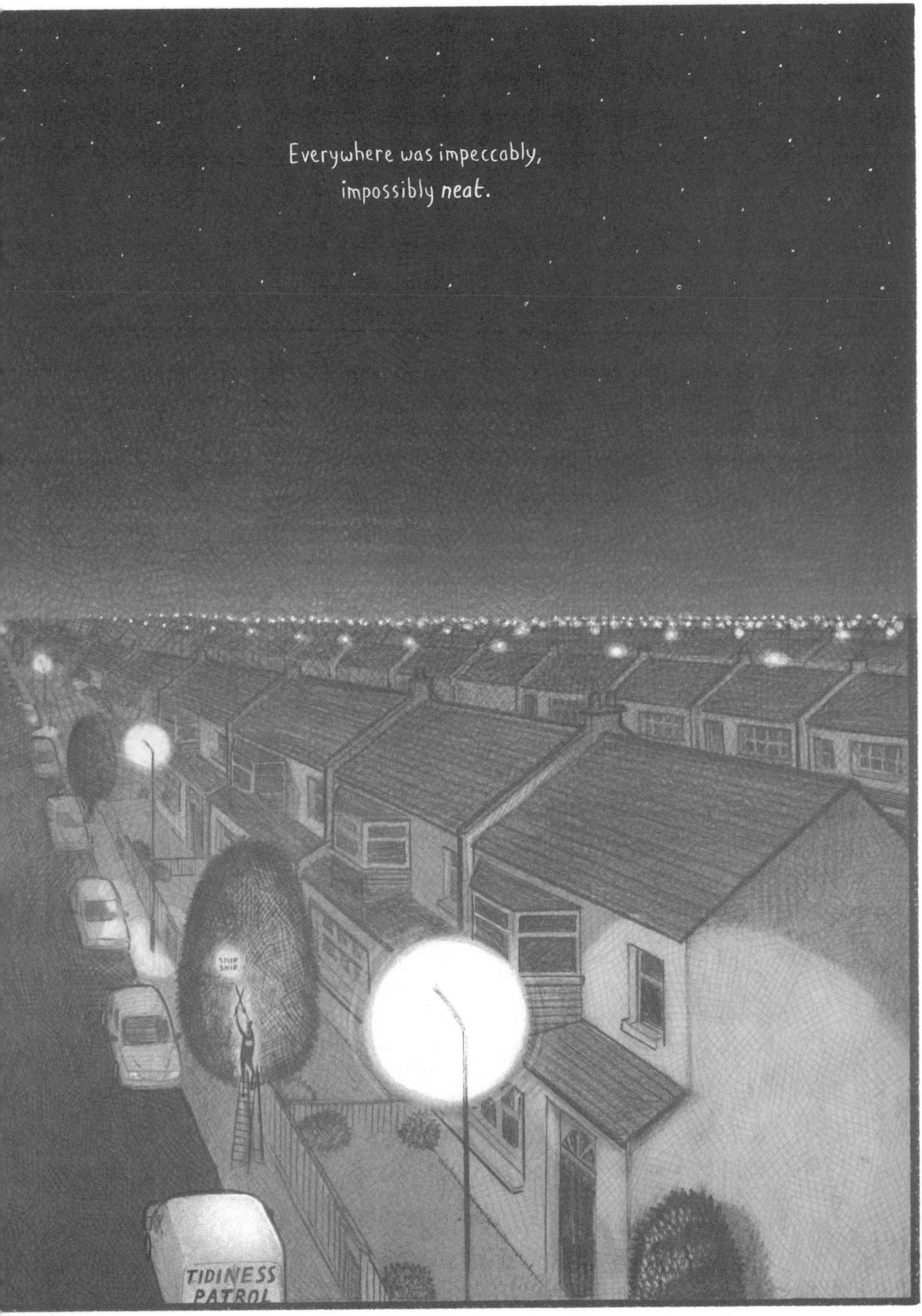
Everywhere was impeccably, impossibly *neat*.
SNIP SNIP
TIDINESS PATROL

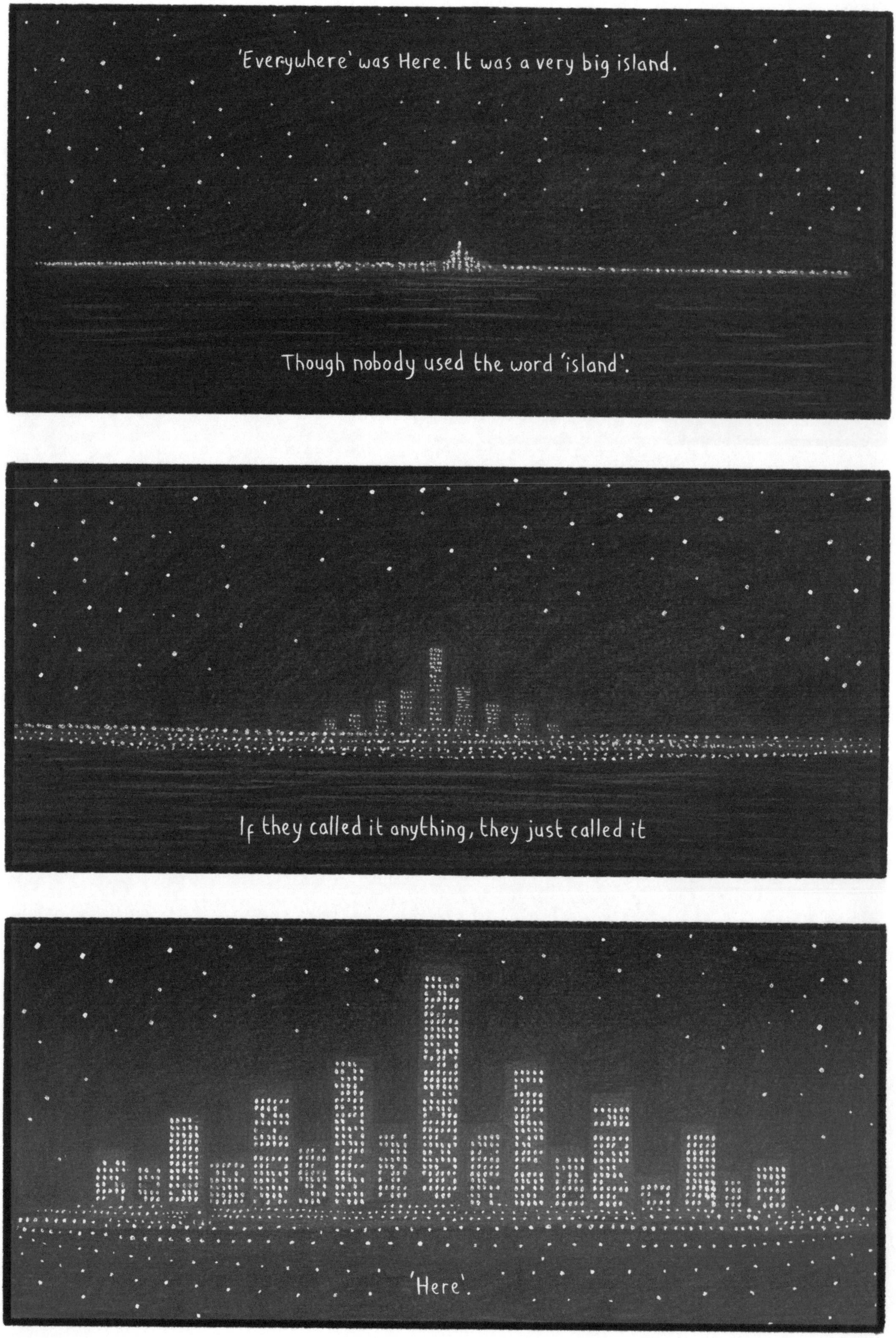
'Everywhere' was Here. It was a very big island.
Though nobody used the word 'island'.
If they called it anything, they just called it
'Here'.

Here, every tree was perfect.

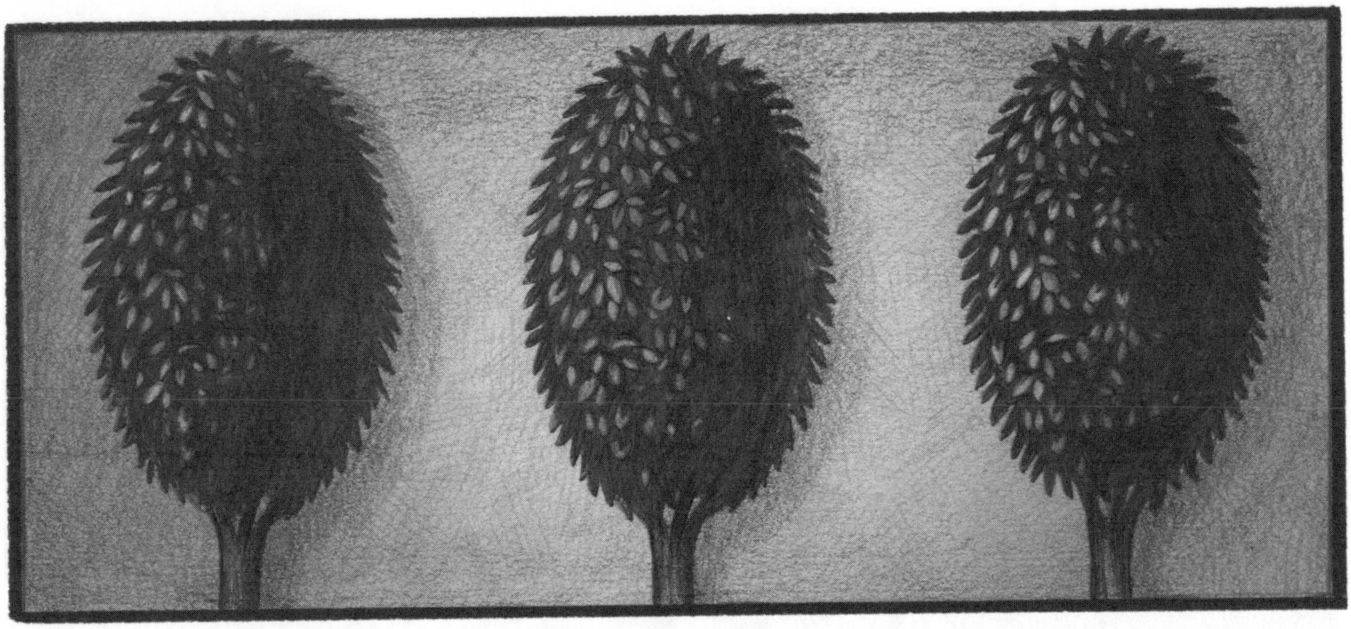

Every street was perfect.

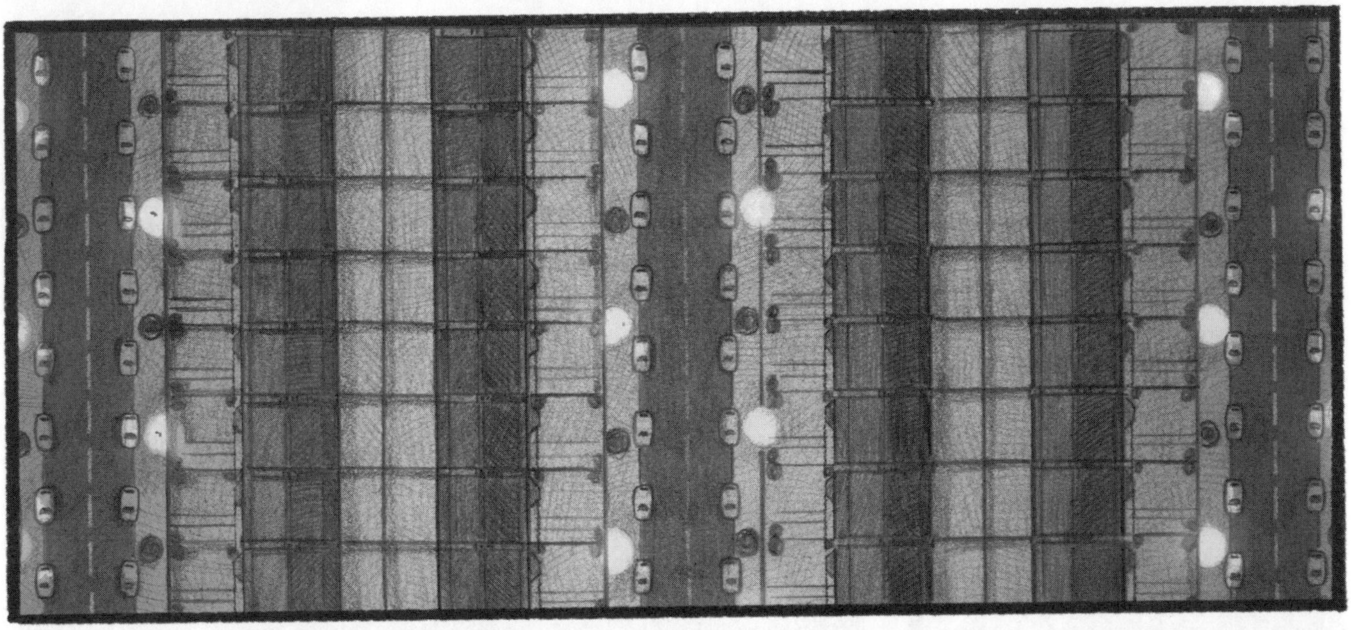

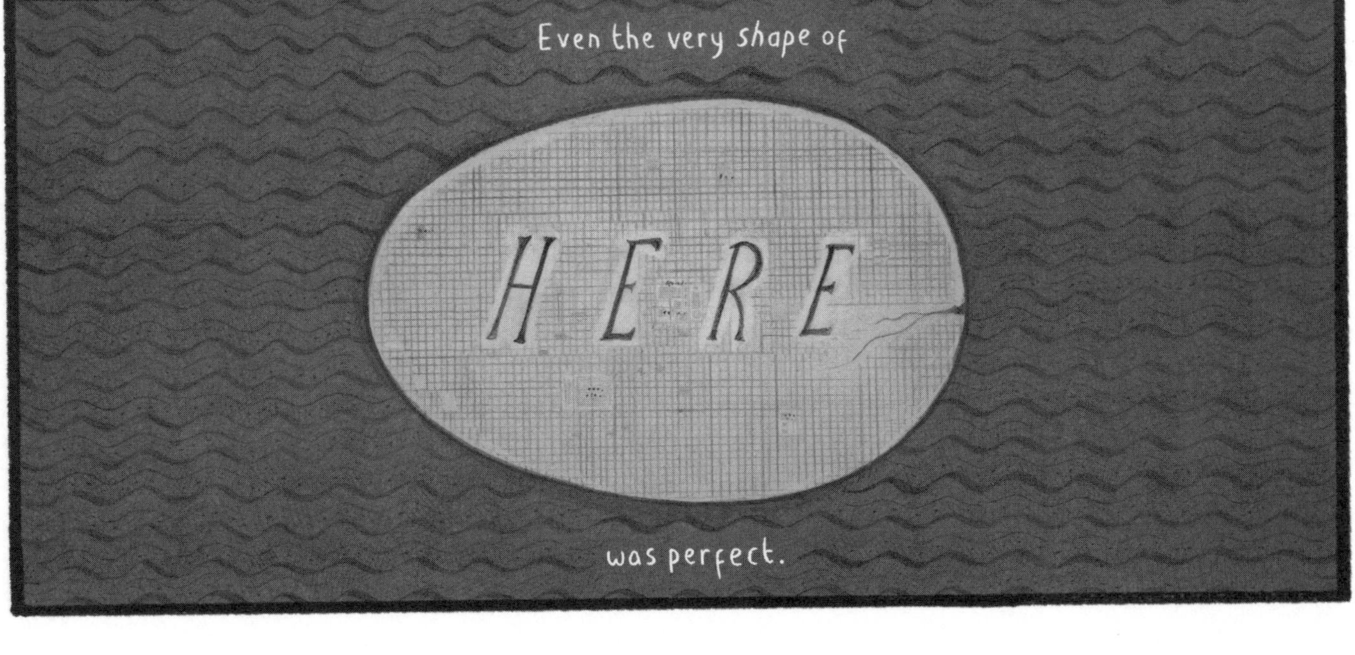
Even the very shape of
HERE
was perfect.

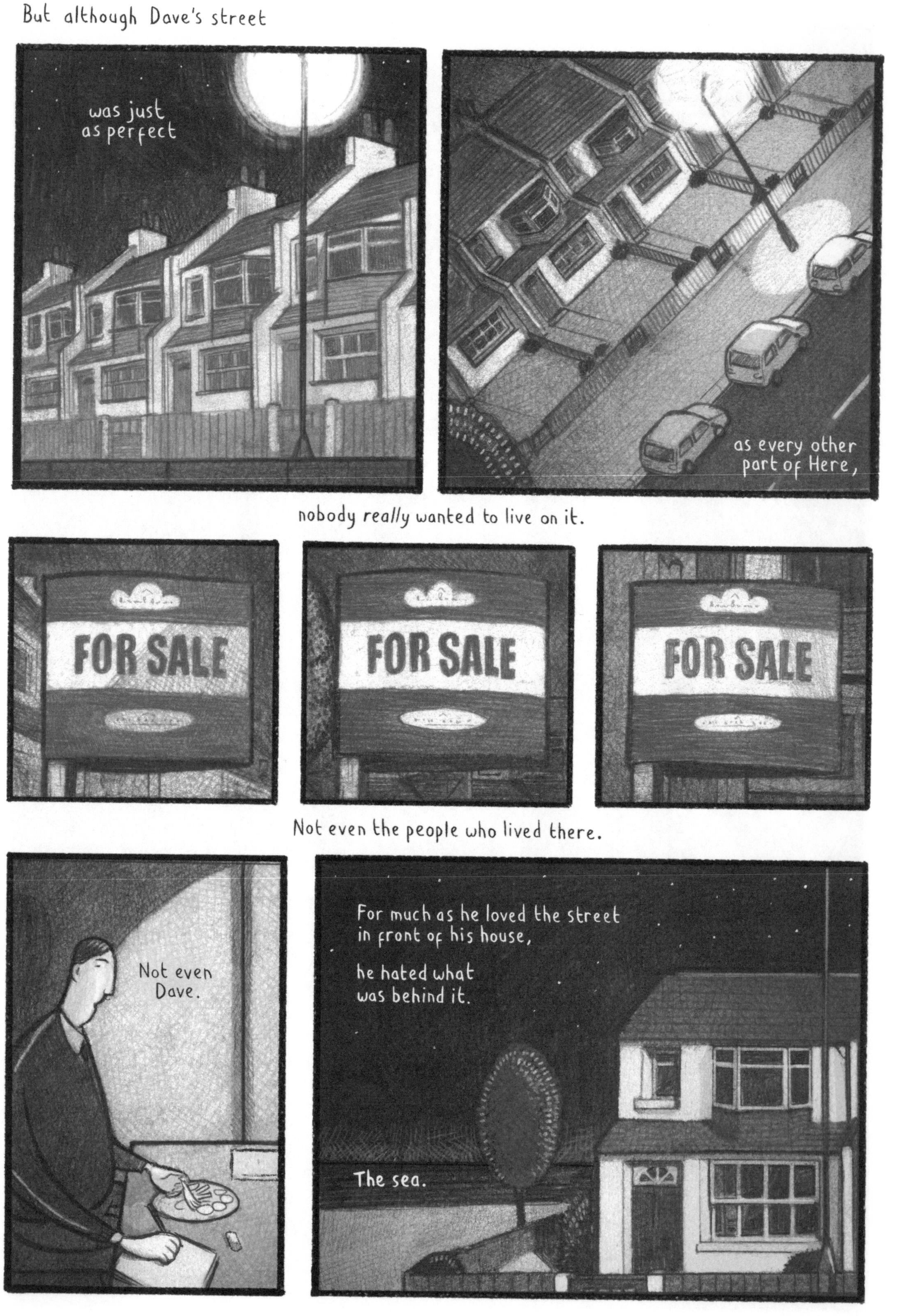
But although Dave's street
was just as perfect
as every other part of Here,
nobody *really* wanted to live on it.
FOR SALE
FOR SALE
FOR SALE
Not even the people who lived there.
Not even Dave.
For much as he loved the street in front of his house,
he hated what was behind it.
The sea.

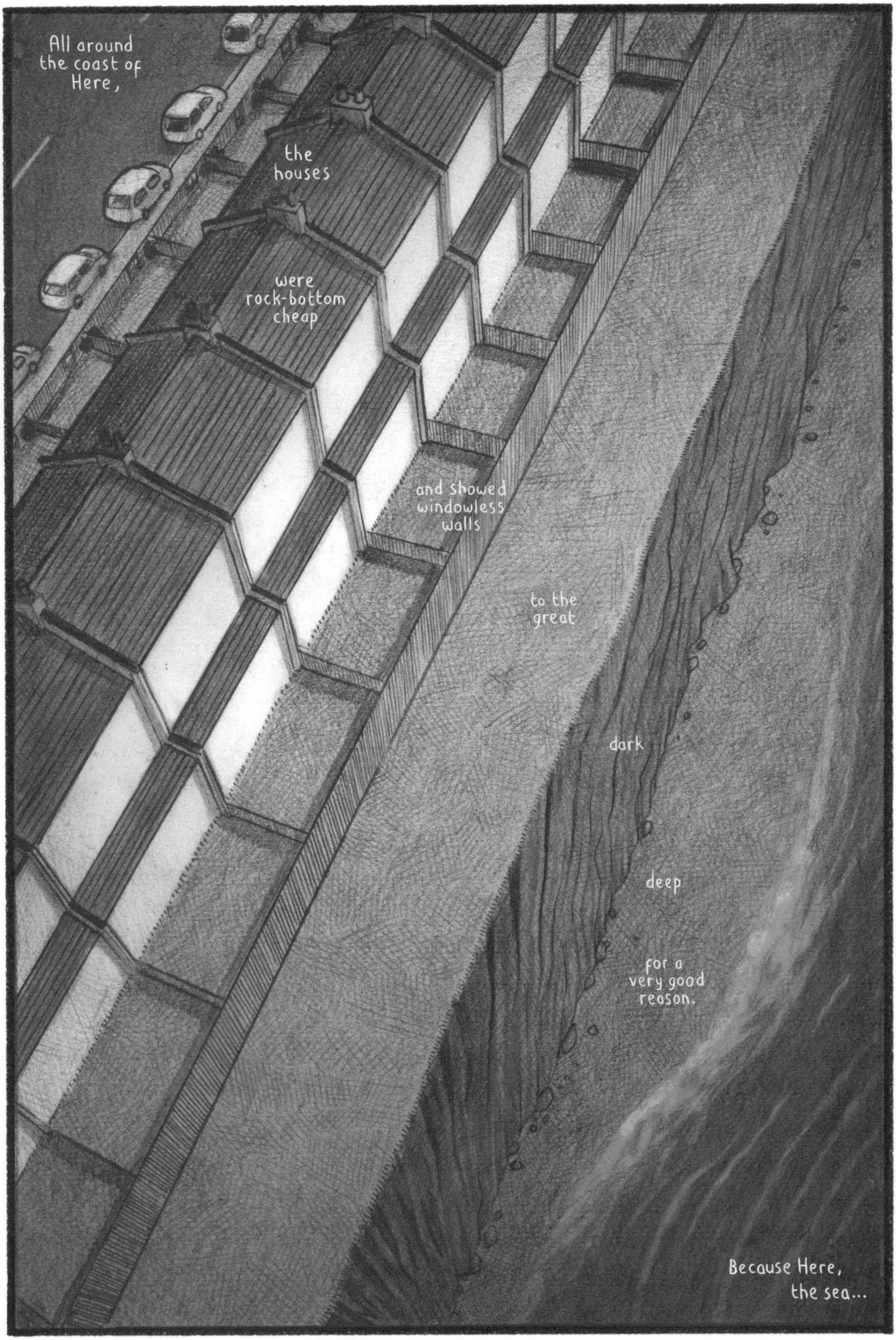
All around the coast of Here,
the houses
were rock-bottom cheap
and showed windowless walls
to the great
dark
deep
for a very good reason.
Because Here, the sea...

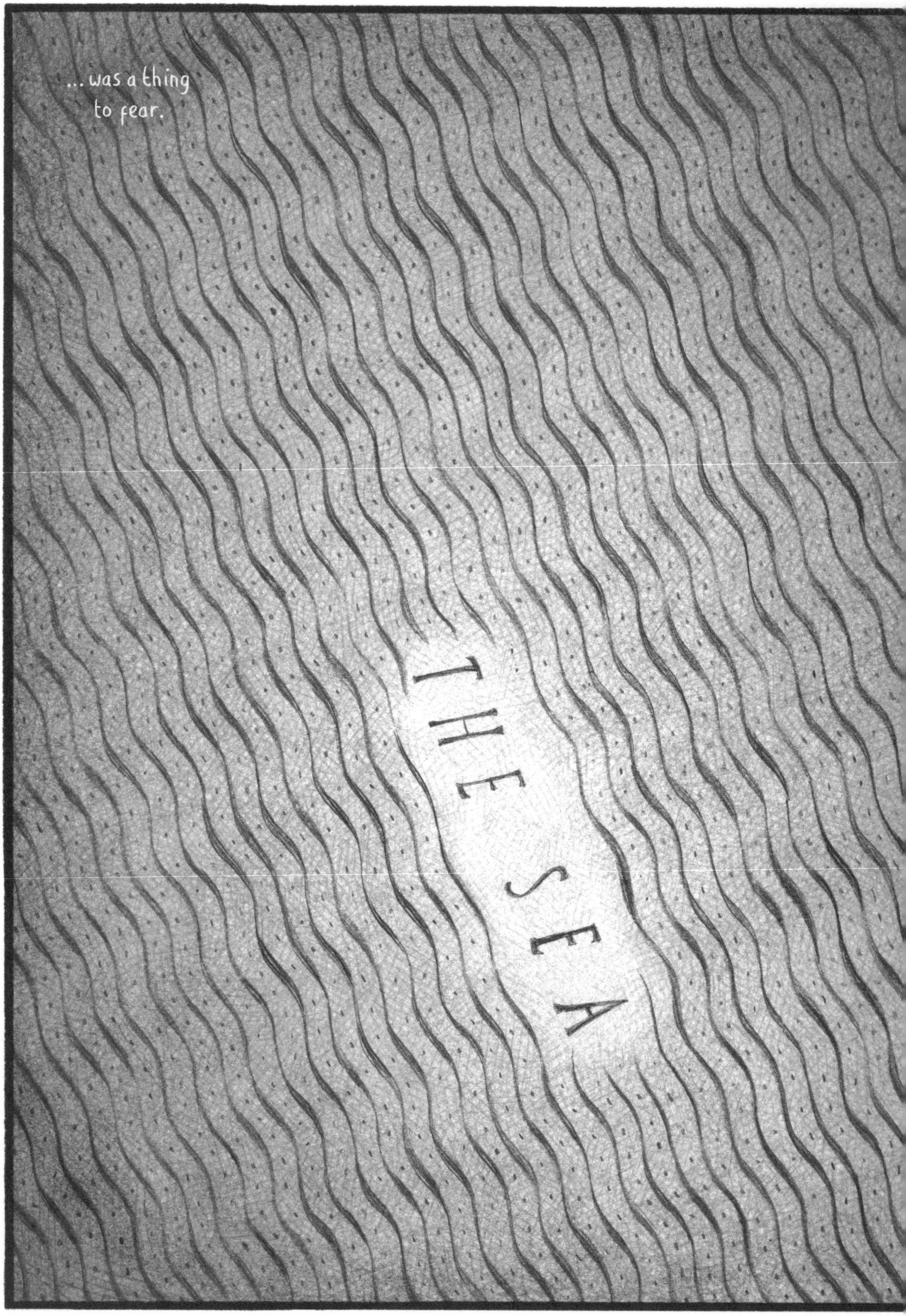
... was a thing
to fear.
THE SEA

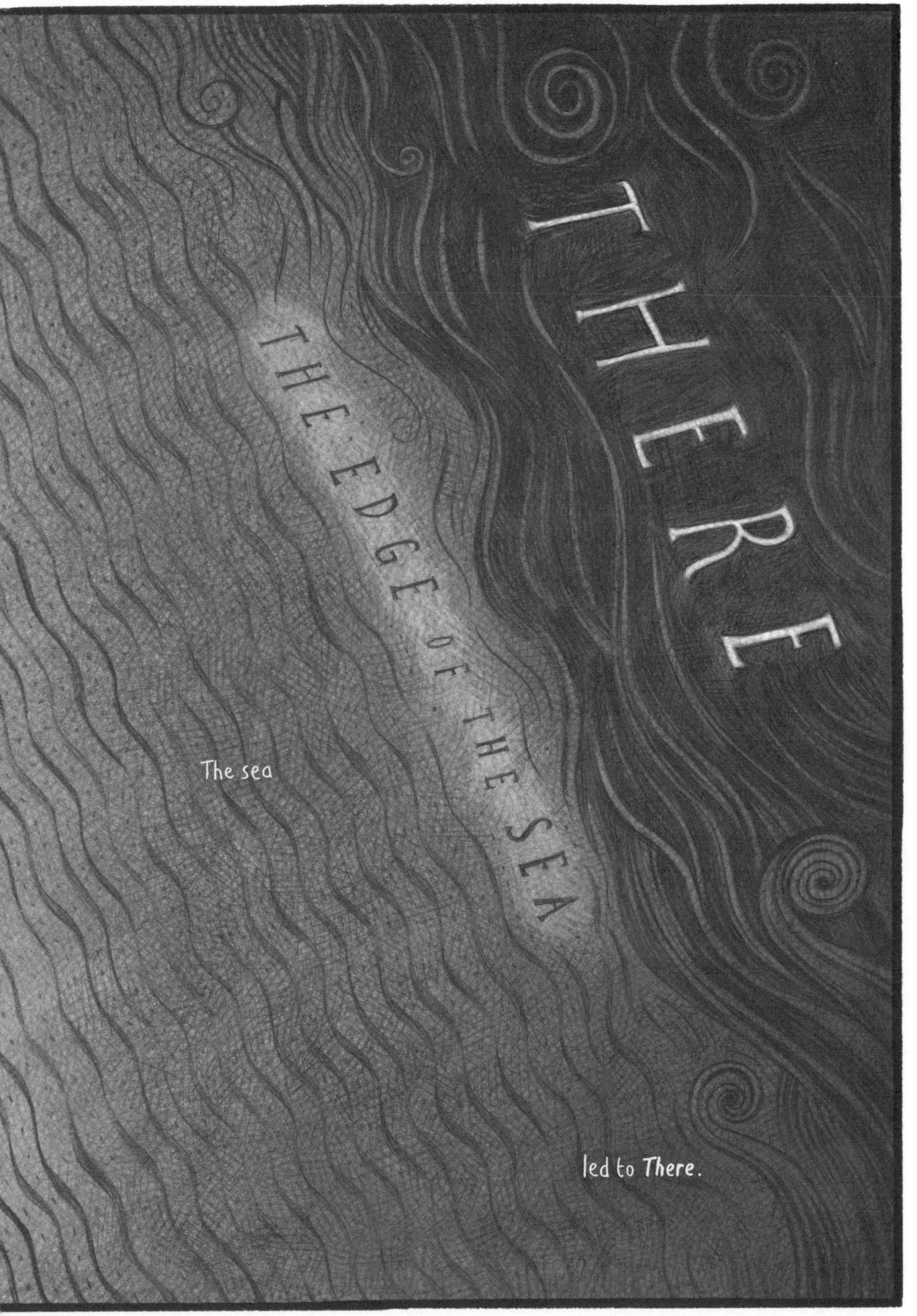
THERE
THE EDGE OF THE SEA
The sea
led to *There*.

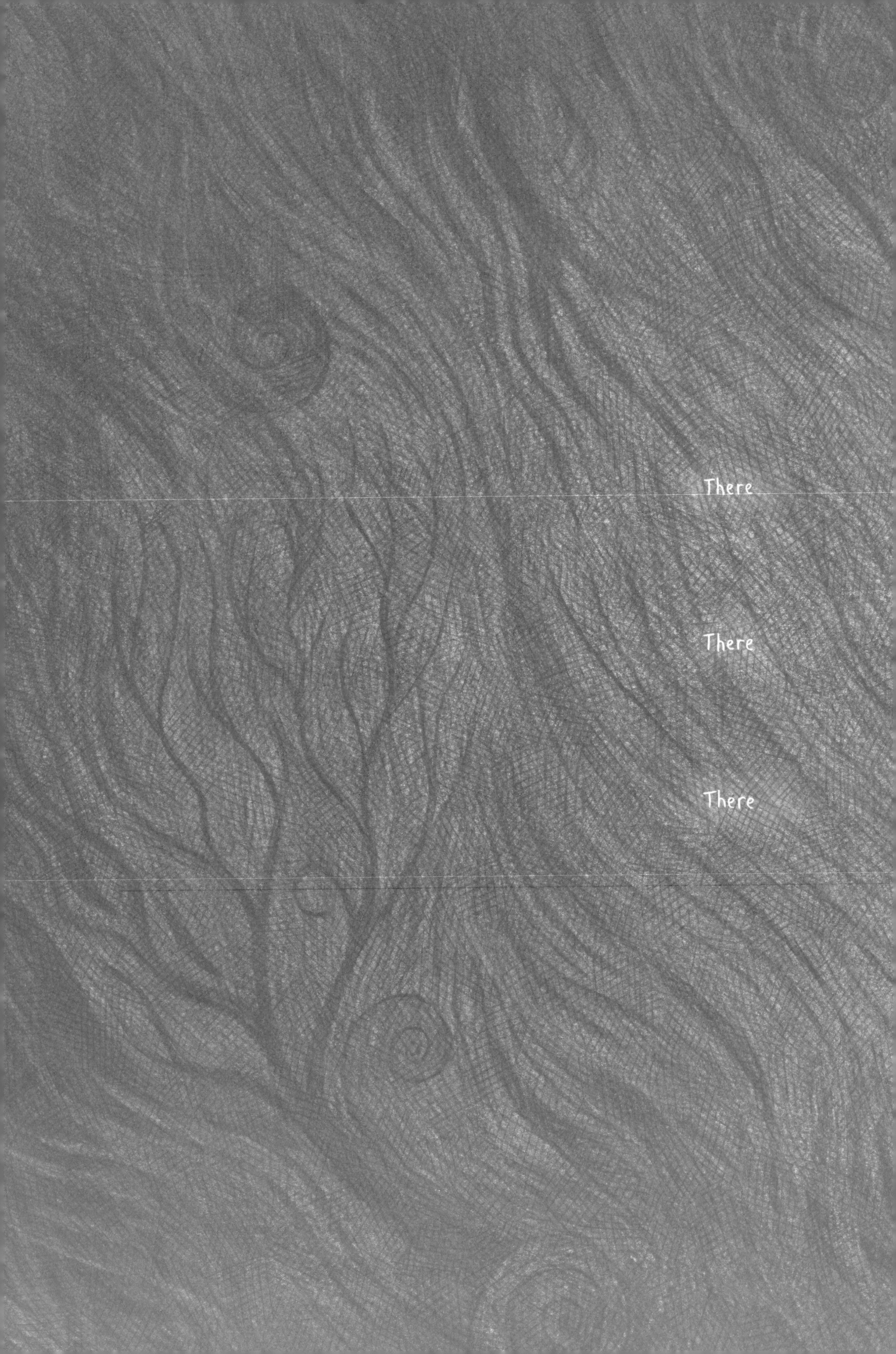
There
There
There

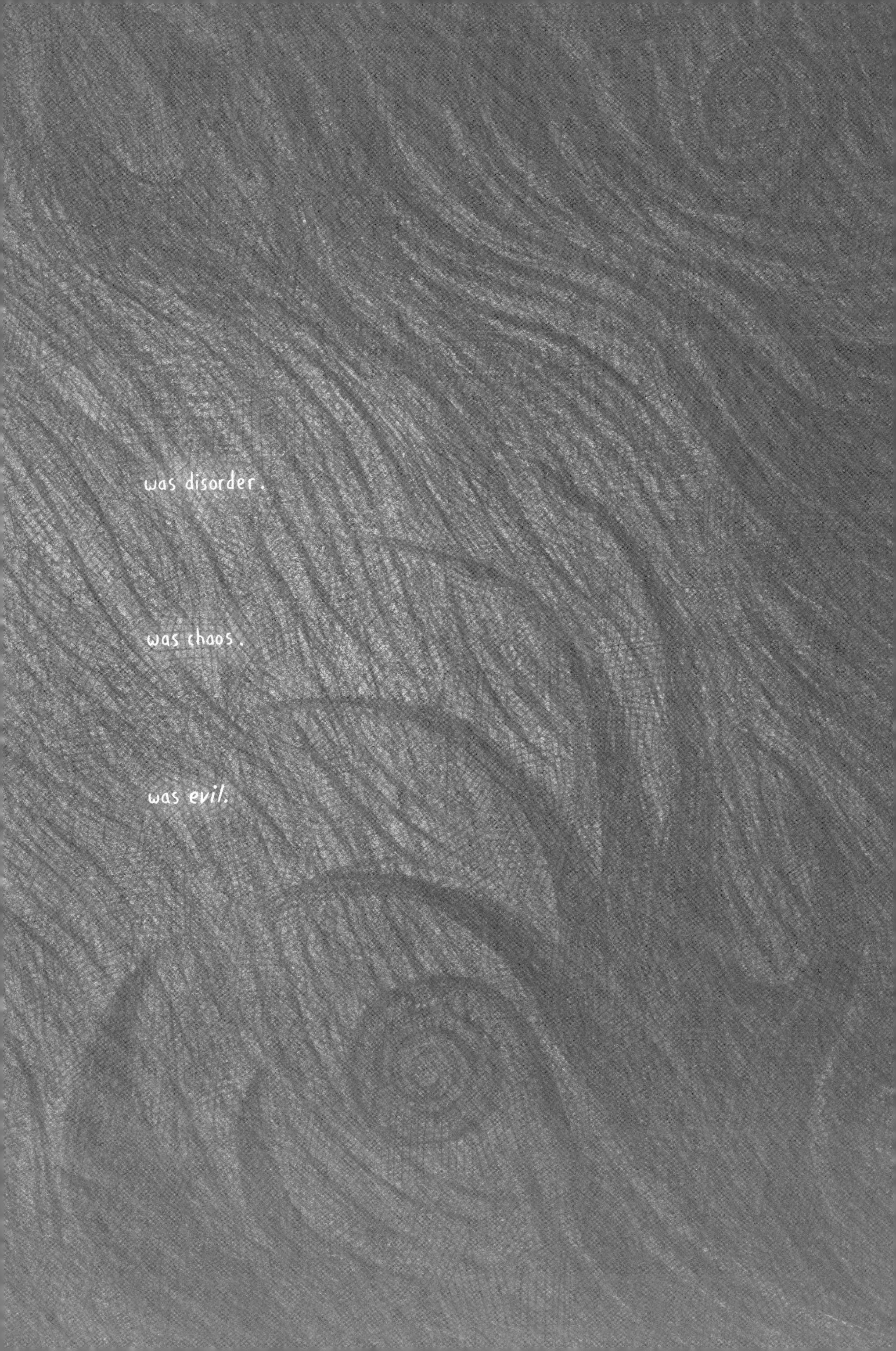
was disorder.
was chaos.
was *evil*.

In fact, There was a place to which nobody had ever even *been*. No one alive, anyway. The stories were enough for most people, including Dave.

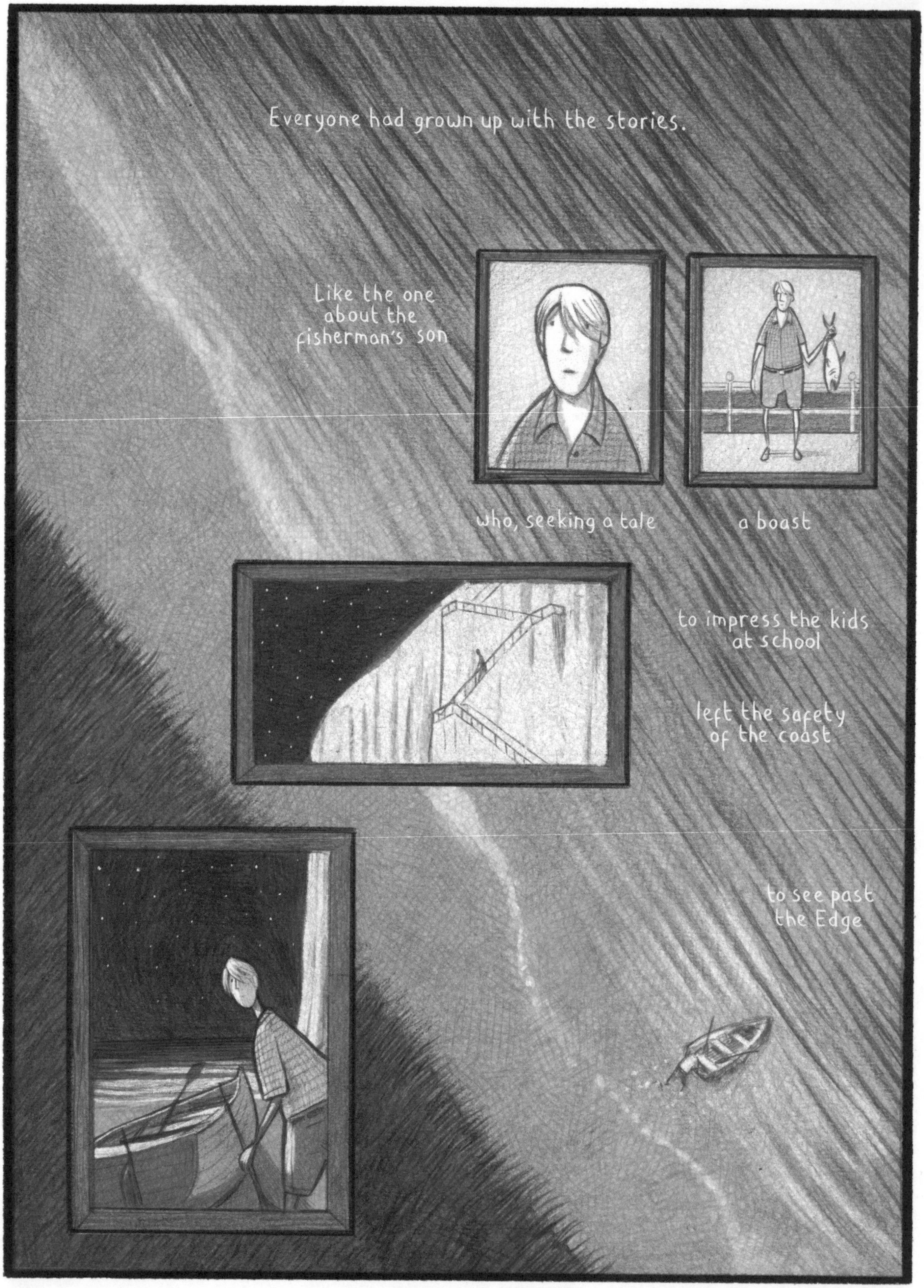
Everyone had grown up with the stories.
Like the one about the fisherman's son
who, seeking a tale
a boast
to impress the kids at school
left the safety of the coast
to see past the Edge

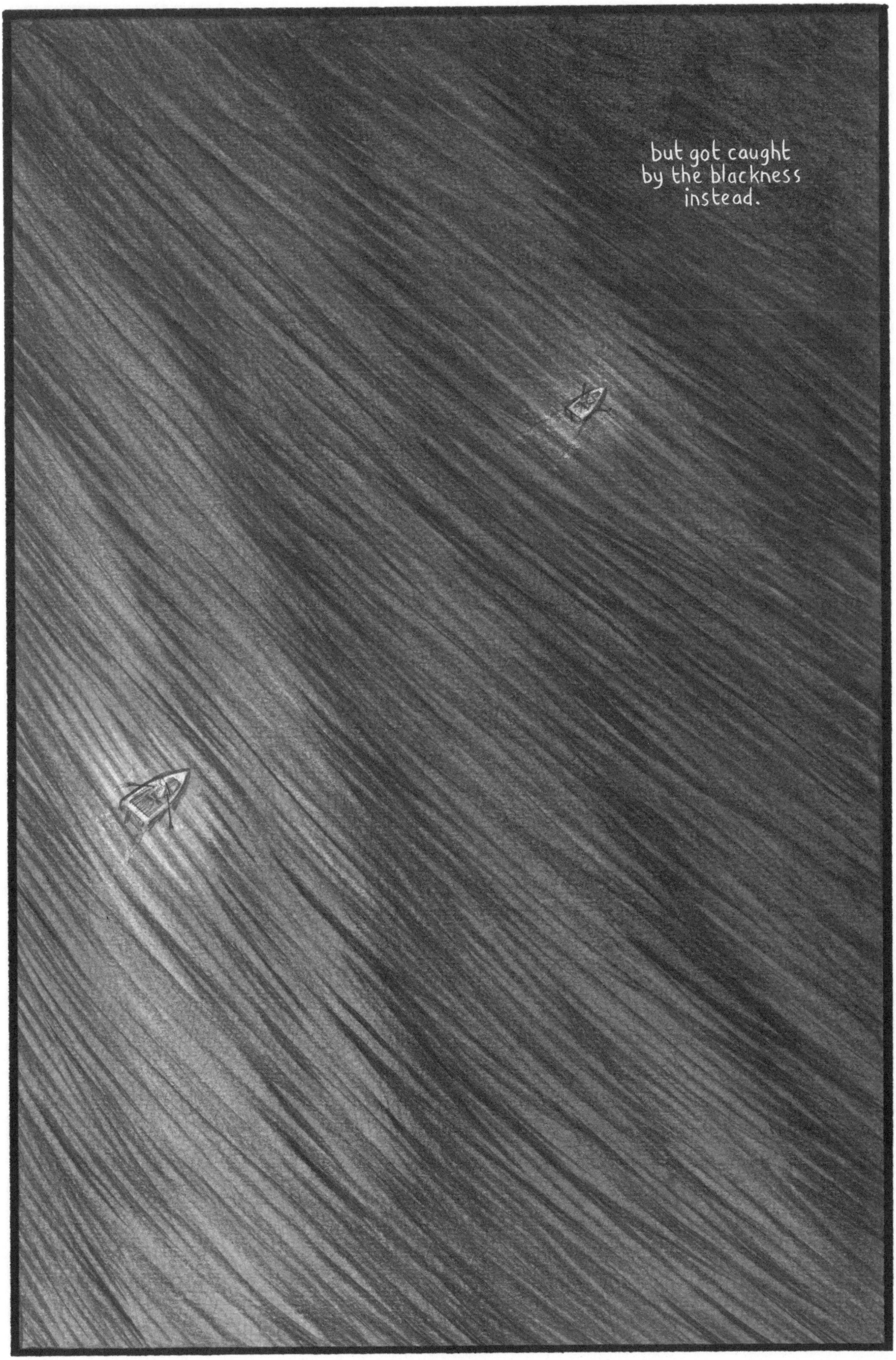
but got caught
by the blackness
instead.

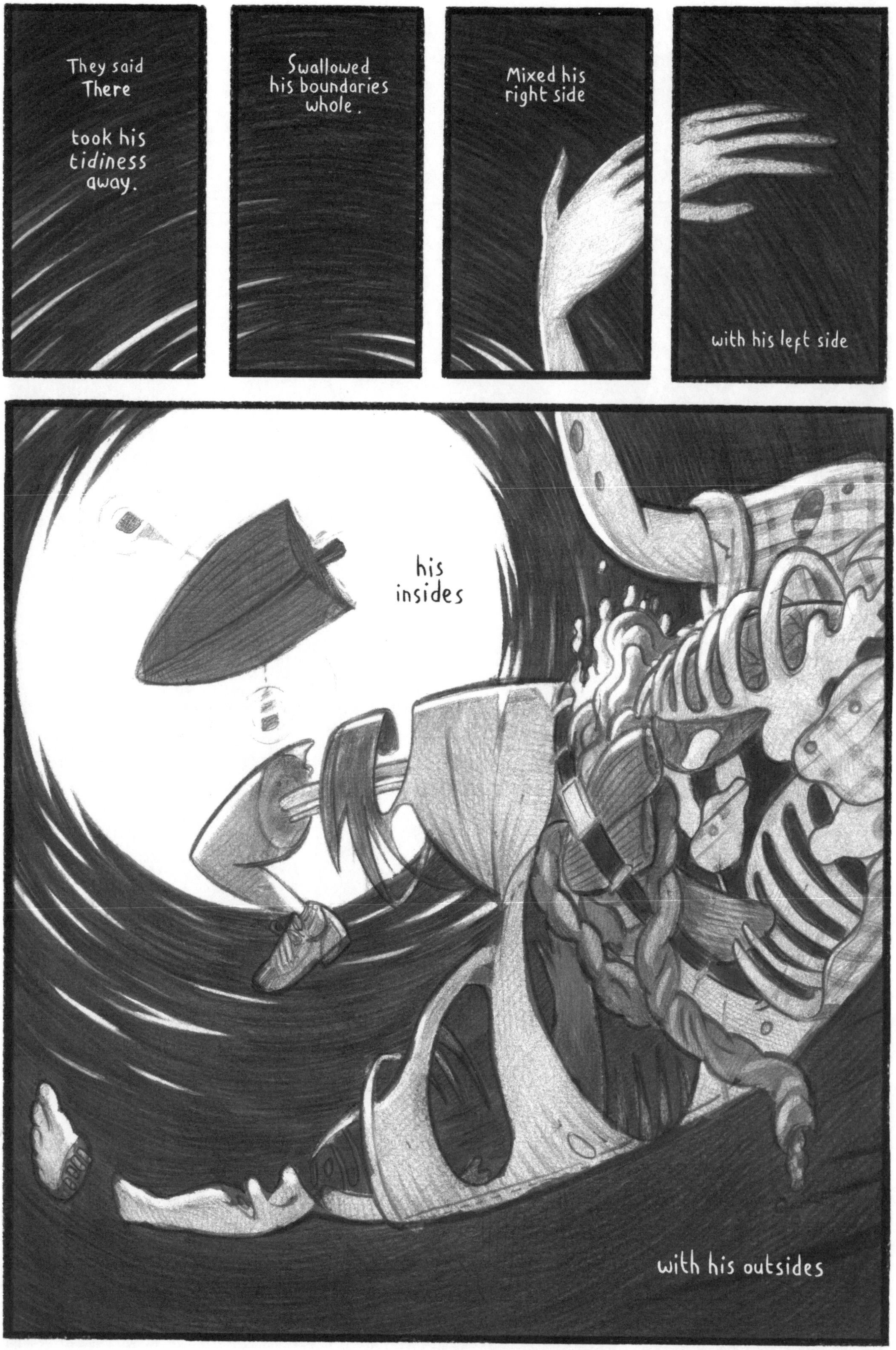
They said There
took his tidiness away.
Swallowed his boundaries whole.
Mixed his right side
with his left side
his insides
with his outsides

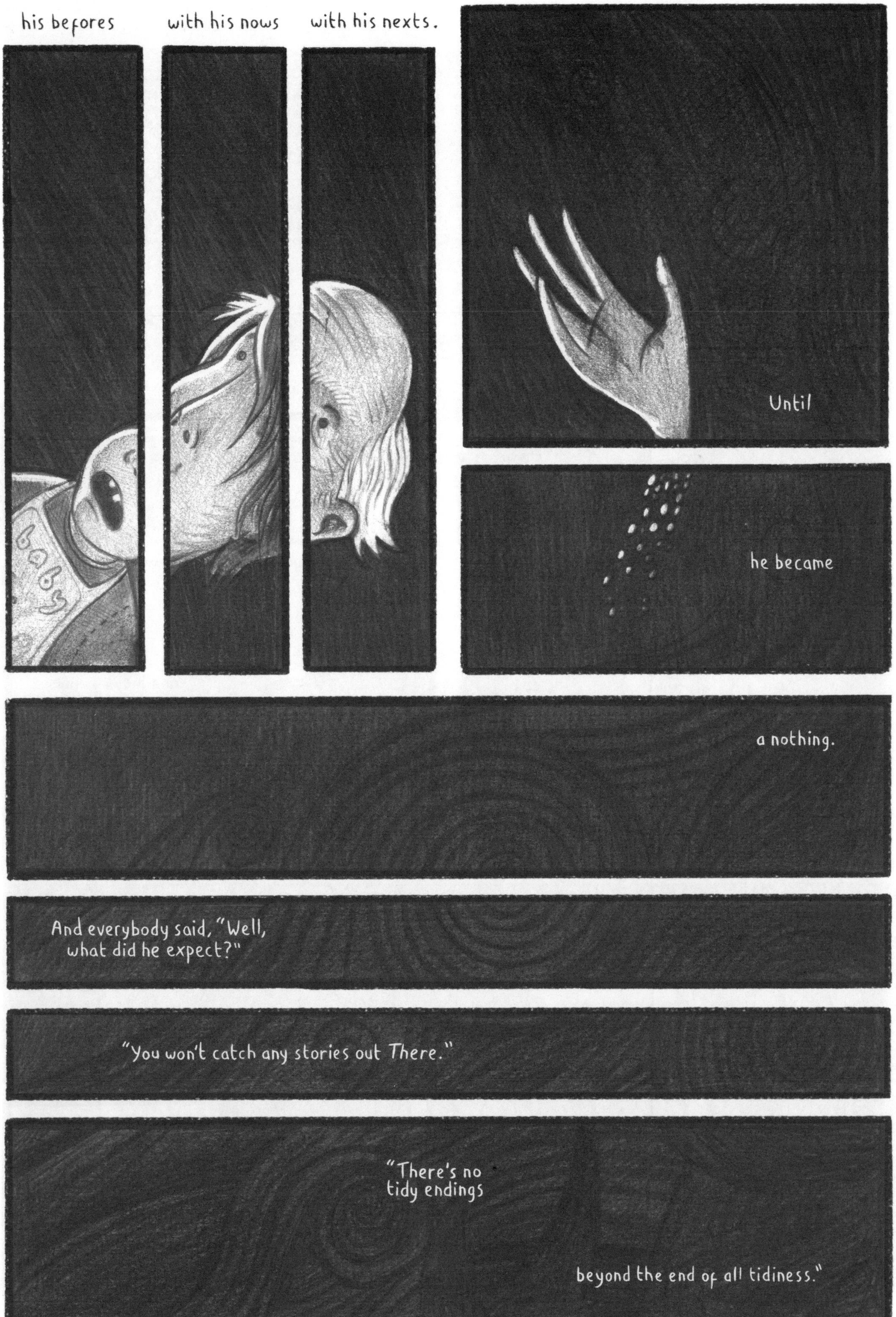
his befores
with his nows
with his nexts.
Until
he became
a nothing.
And everybody said, "Well, what did he expect?"
"You won't catch any stories out There."
"There's no tidy endings
beyond the end of all tidiness."

So you can see,
it was not strange for Dave

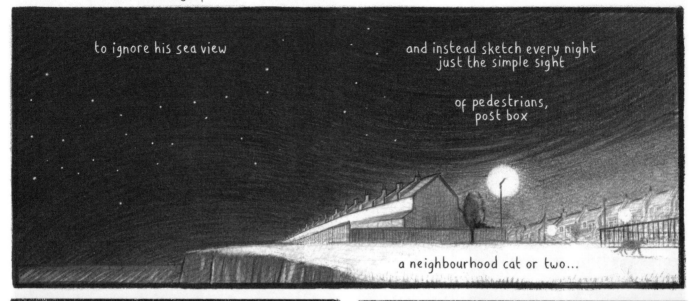

to ignore his sea view
and instead sketch every night
just the simple sight
of pedestrians,
post box
a neighbourhood cat or two...
It was, he felt
a way of keeping
a sense of order.
Of control.
Just his pencils,
his dinner,
and his drawings
of the street,
(and 'Eternal Flame' by The Bangles
on constant
constant
Eternal Flame
The Bangles
REPEAT
constant
ngles
REPEAT).

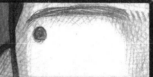

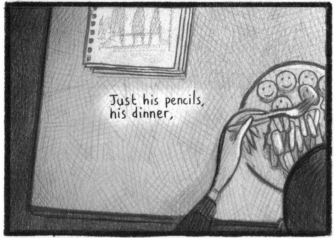

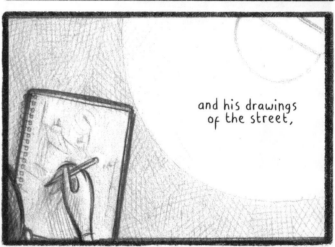

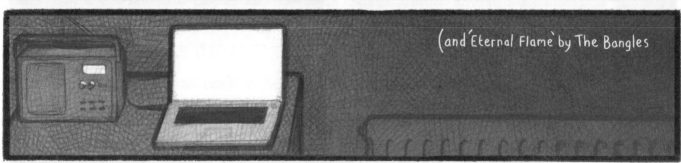

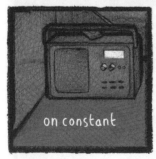

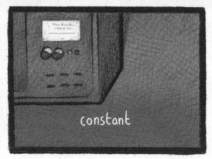

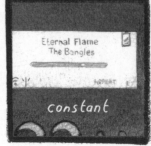

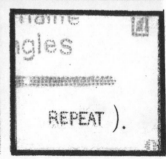

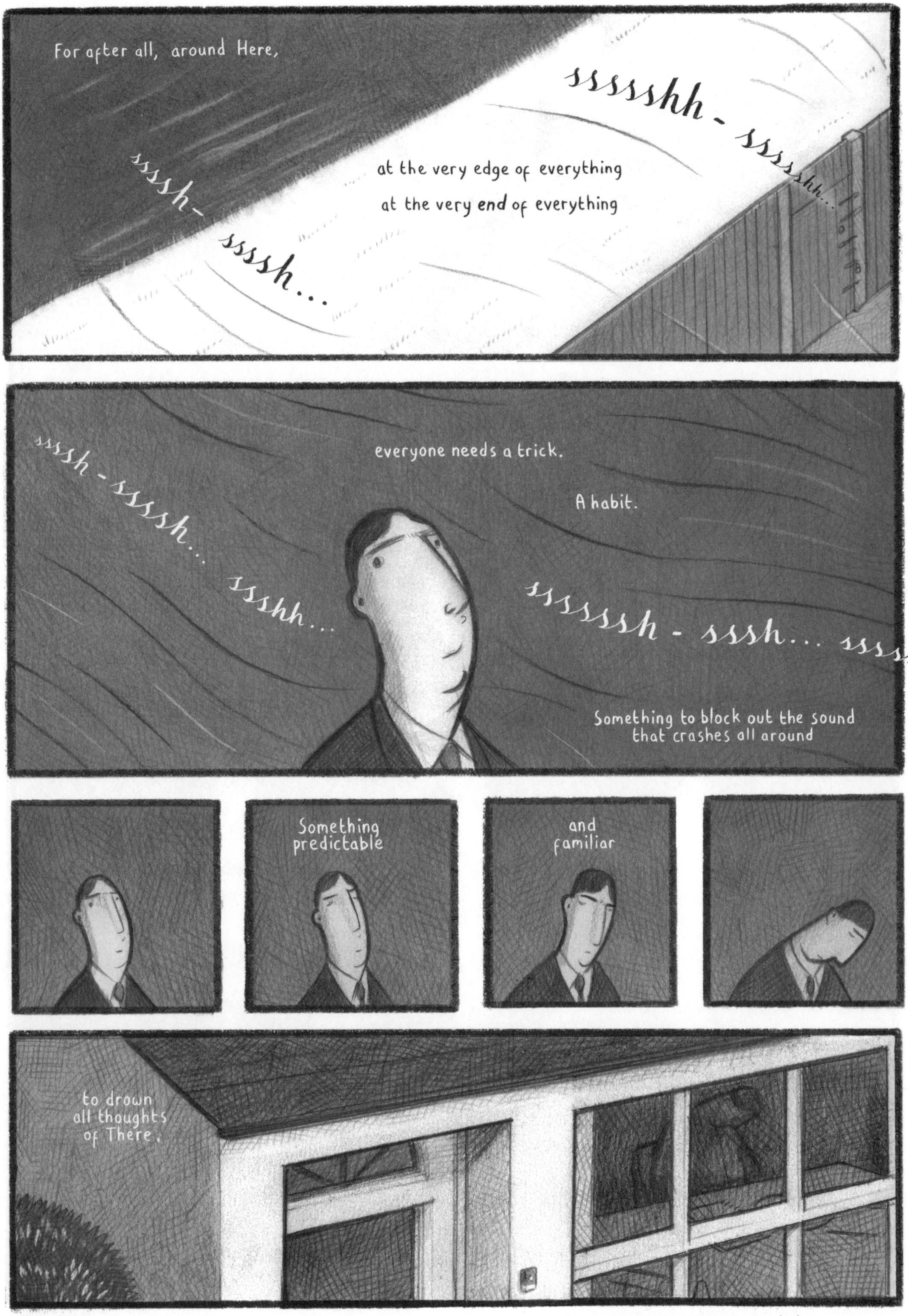
For after all, around Here,
sssssshh - sssssshh...
ssssh-
sssssh...
at the very edge of everything
at the very end of everything
sssssh - sssssh...
everyone needs a trick.
A habit.
ssshh...
sssssssh - sssh... ssssssh...
Something to block out the sound that crashes all around
Something predictable
and familiar
to drown all thoughts of There.
Something, please God, to help ward off...

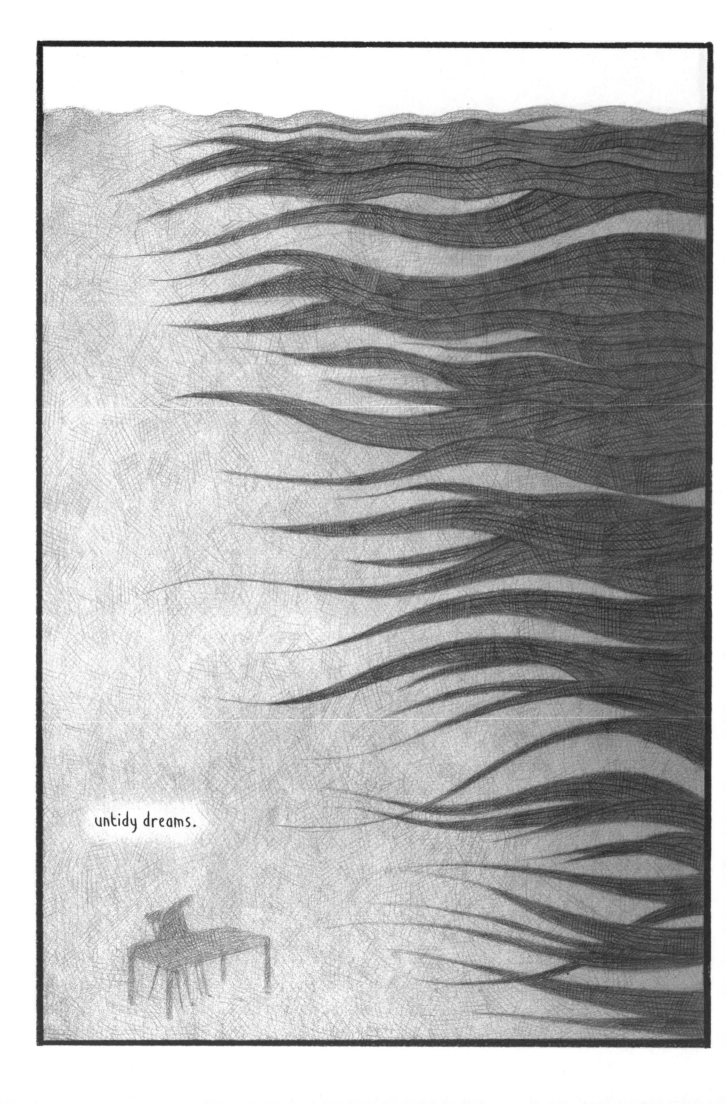

untidy dreams.

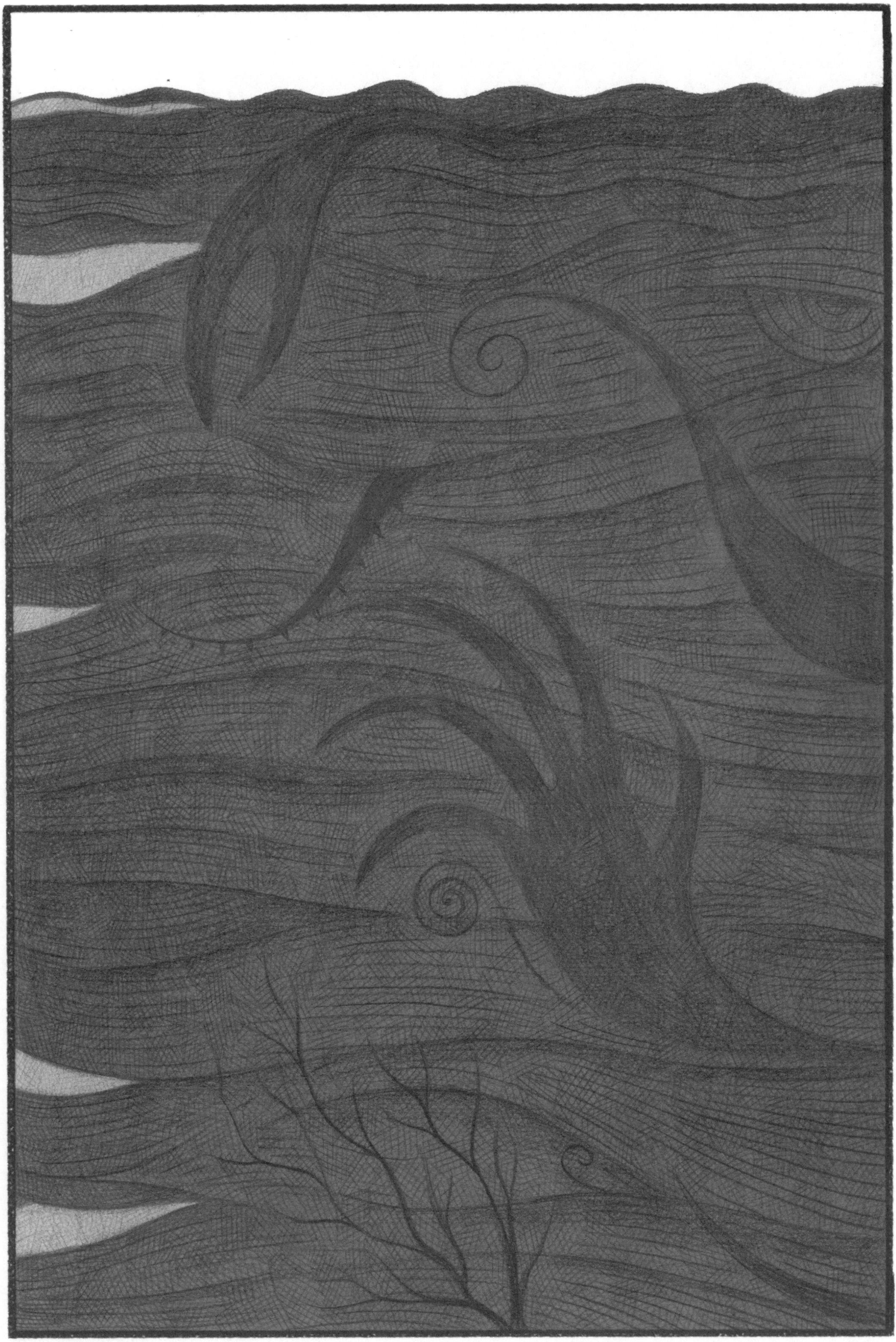

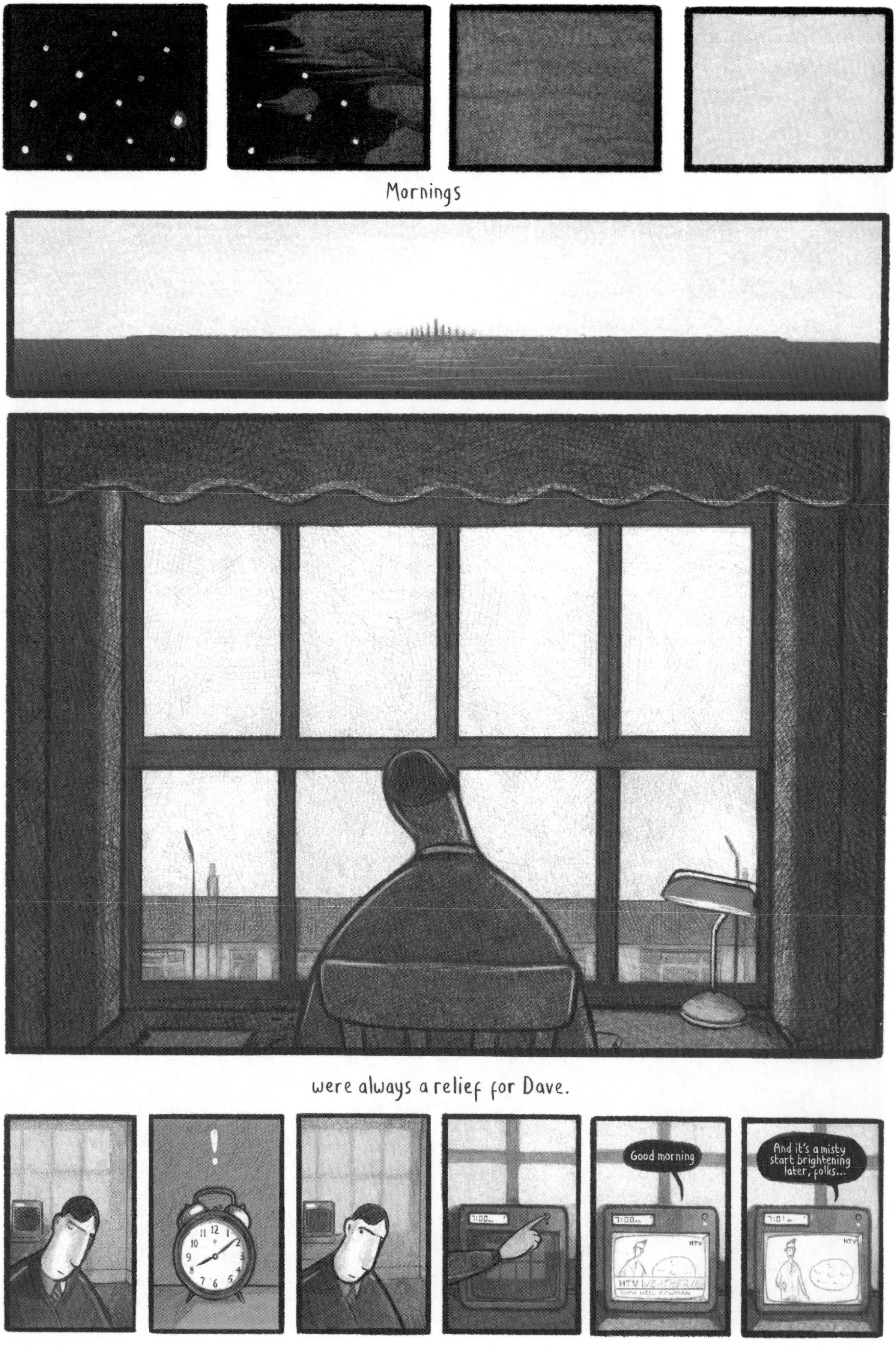
Mornings
were always a relief for Dave.
!
7:00
Good morning
7:00
HTV
HTV WEATHER
WITH NEIL BOWMAN
And it's a misty start brightening later, folks...
7:01
HTV

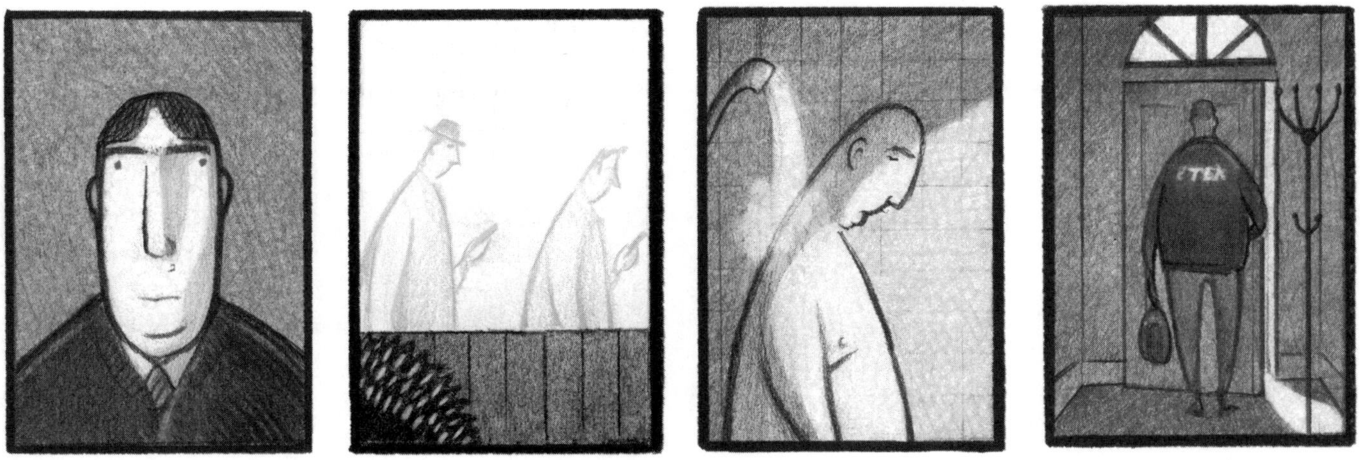

He *relished* the mornings.

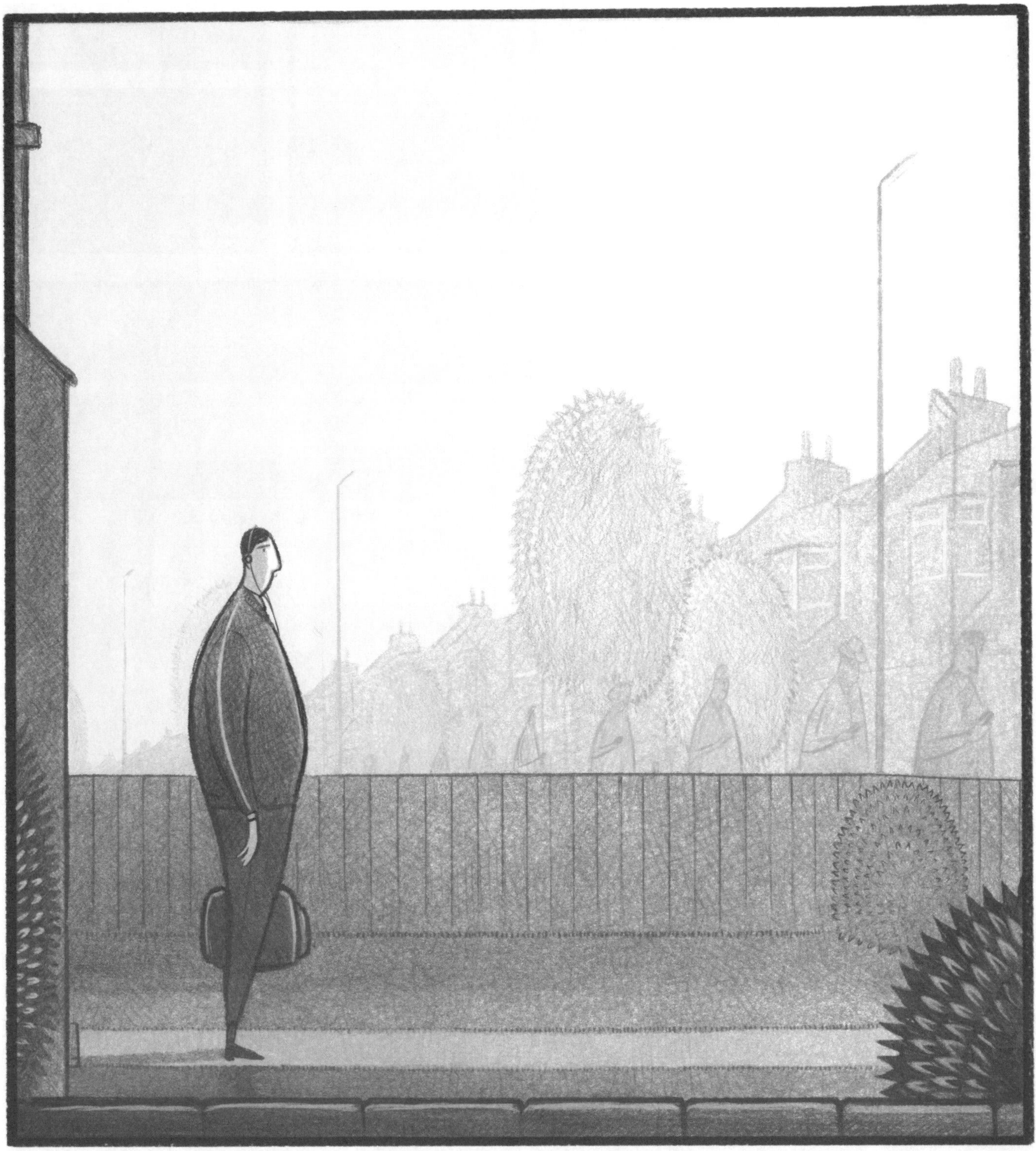

Because mornings meant work

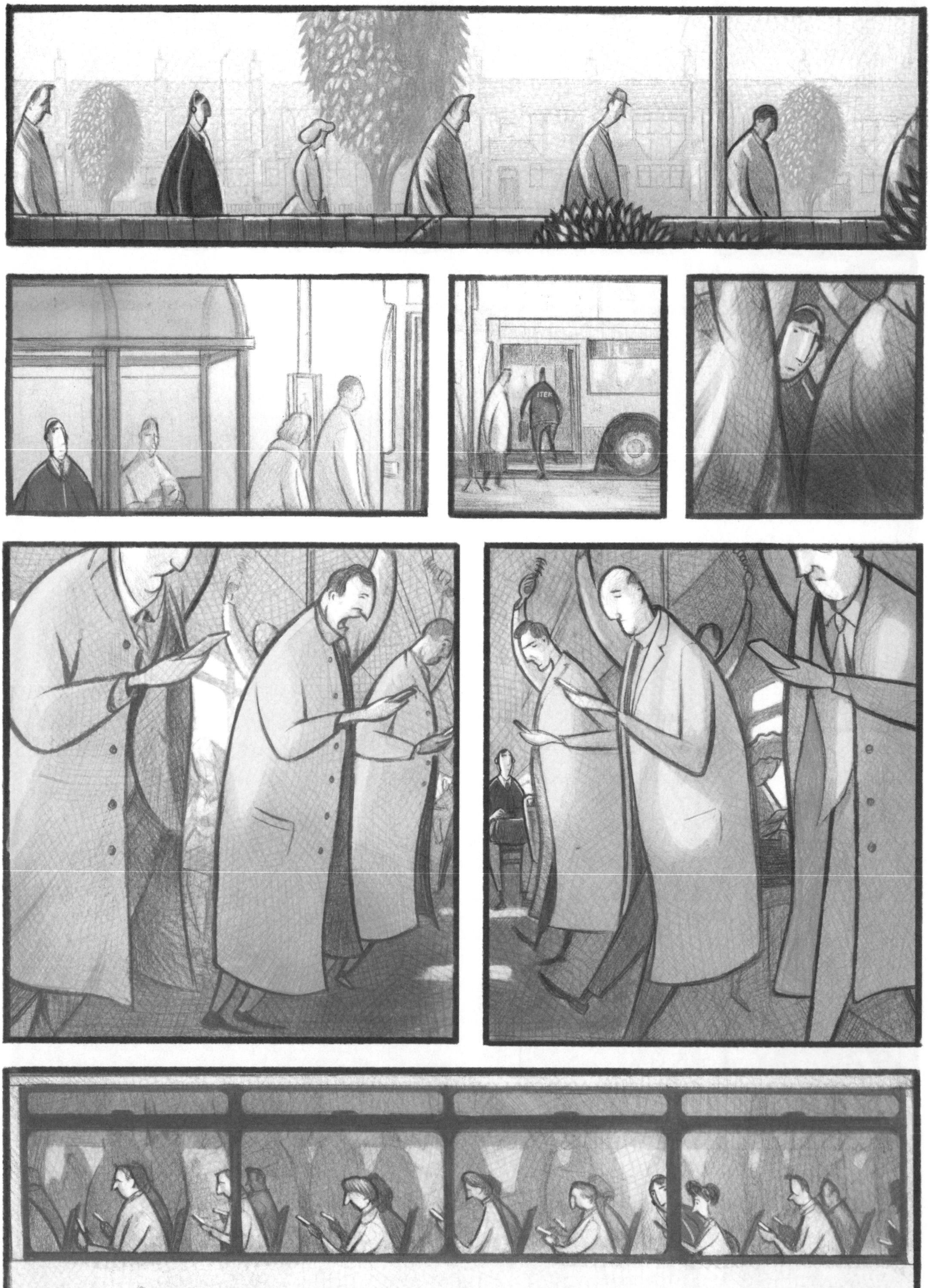

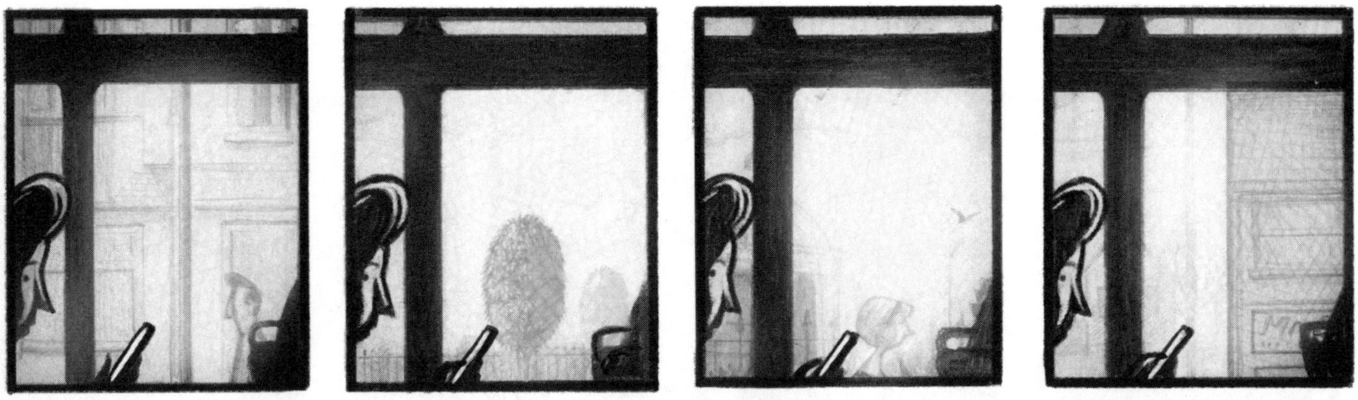

and work was as far away from There

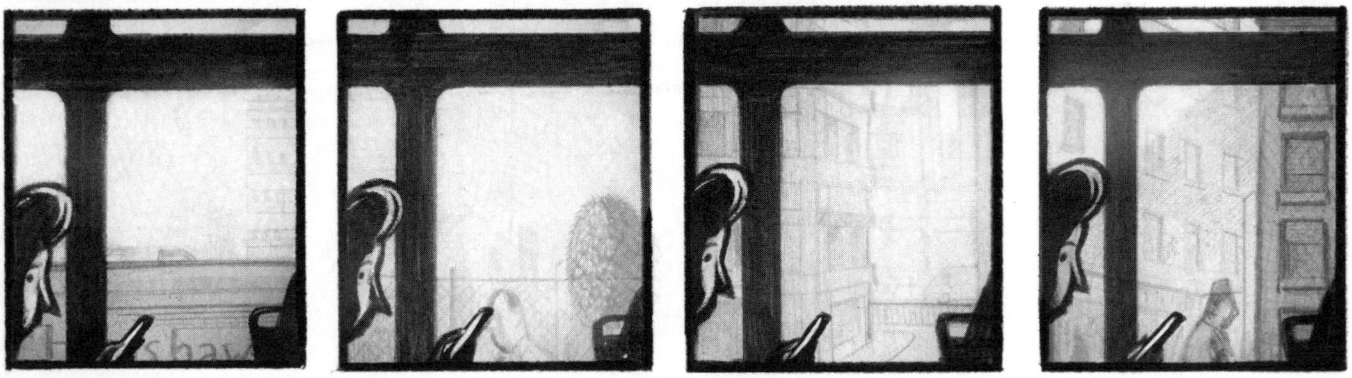

as it was possible to be.

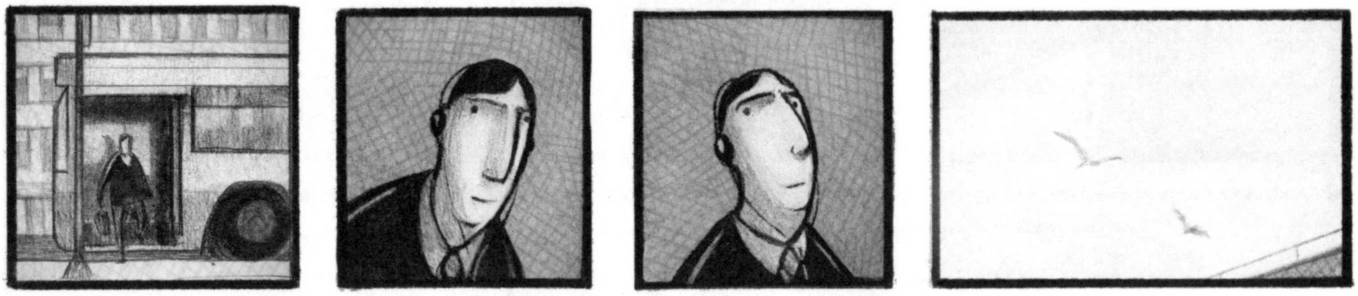

Right in the very centre of Here.

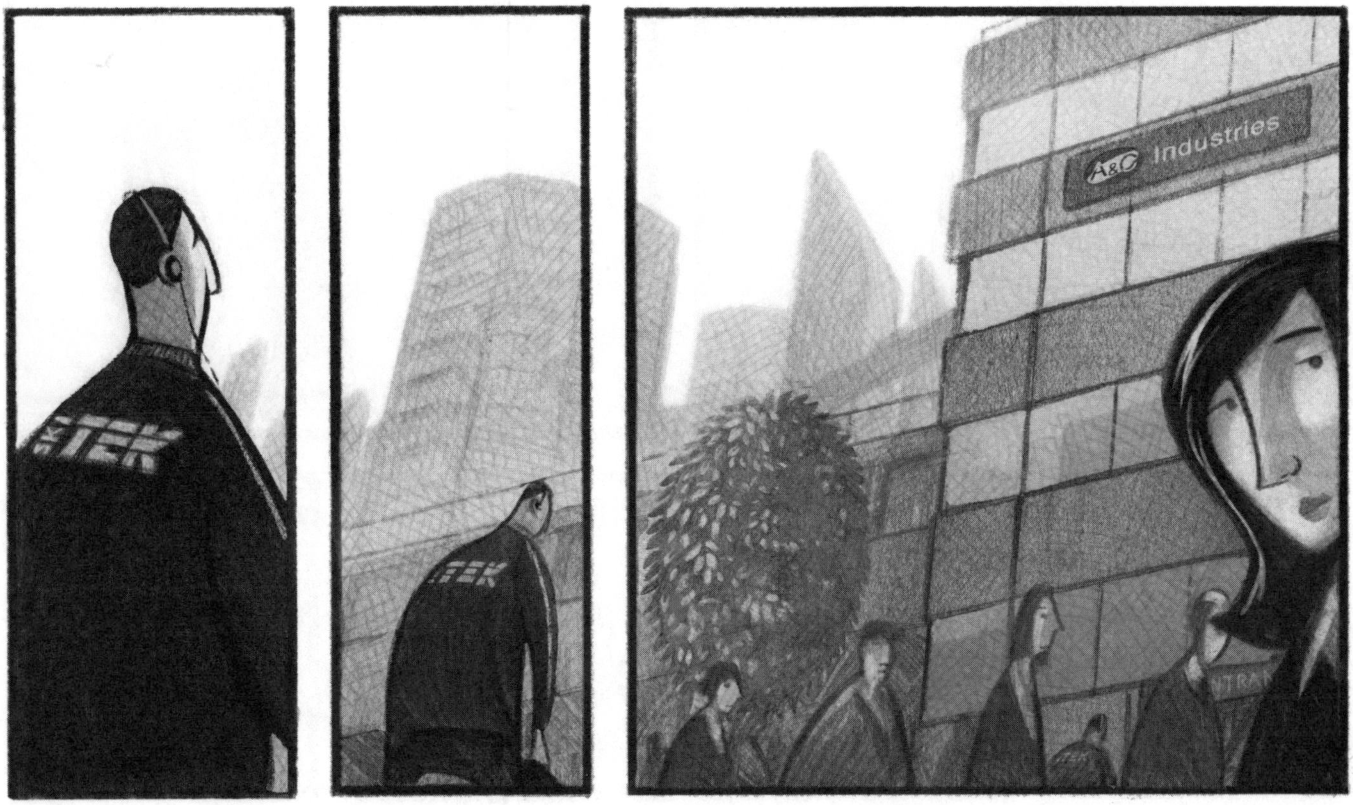
A&C Industries

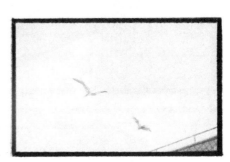

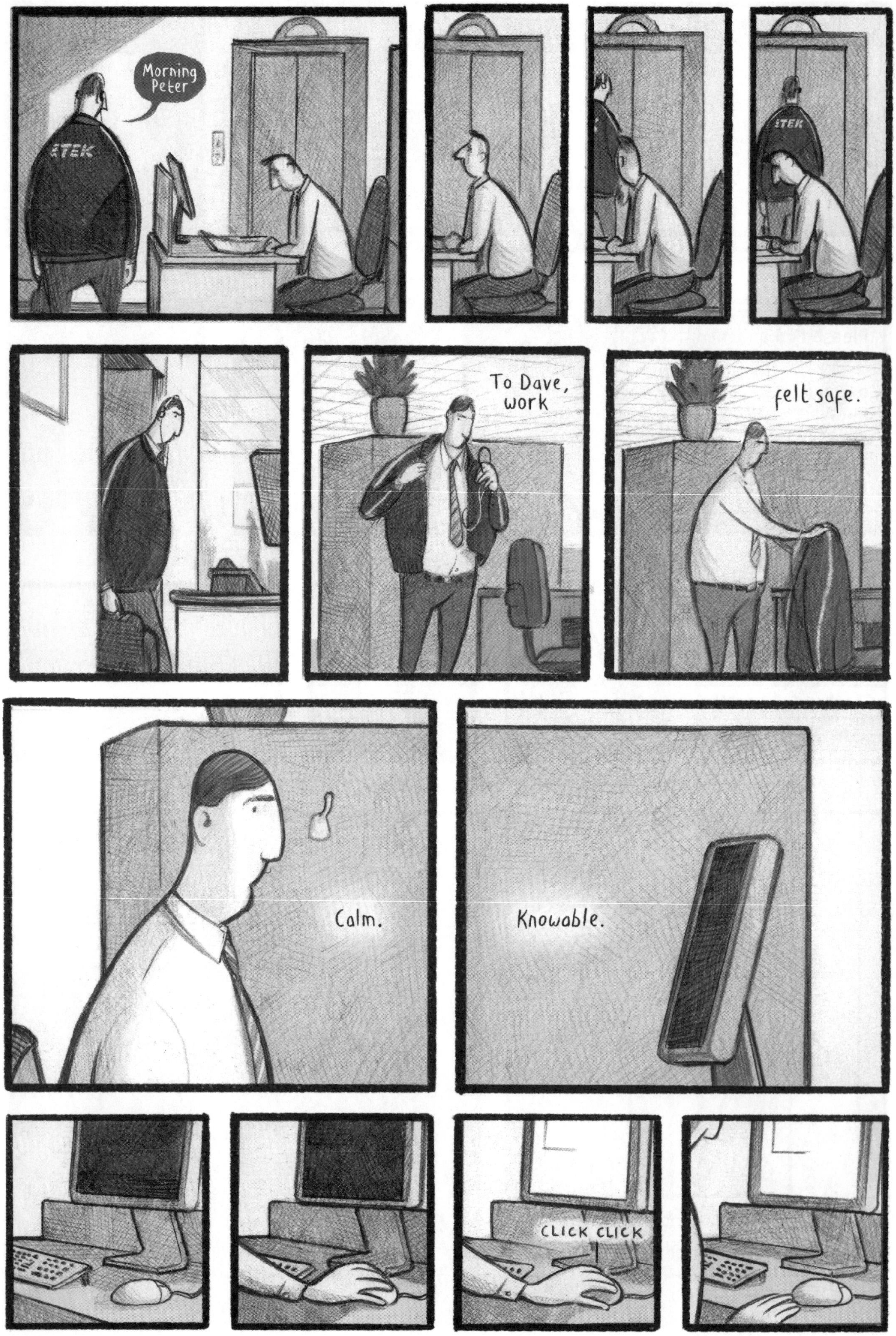
Morning Peter
TEK
TEK
To Dave, work
felt safe.
Calm.
Knowable.
CLICK CLICK

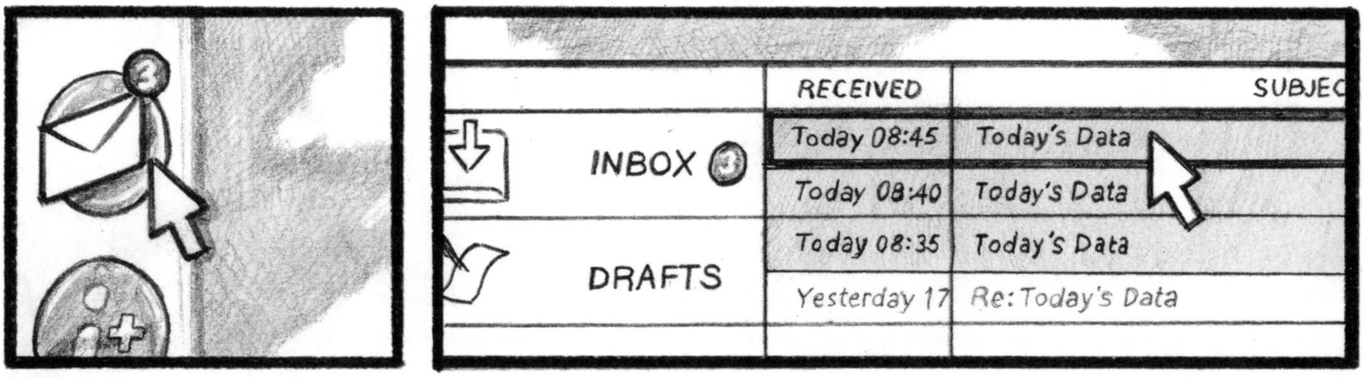
RECEIVED
INBOX
DRAFTS
Today 08:45 Today's Data
Today 08:40 Today's Data
Today 08:35 Today's Data
Yesterday 17 Re: Today's Data

He liked the tidiness of numbers and charts

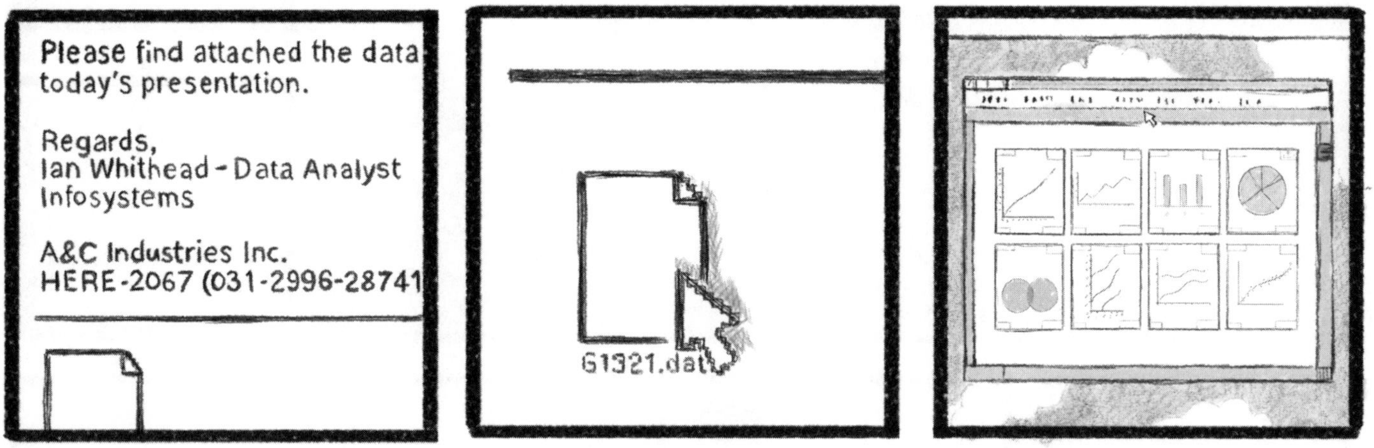
Please find attached the data
today's presentation.
Regards,
Ian Whithead - Data Analyst
Infosystems
A&C Industries Inc.
HERE-2067 (031-2996-28741
61321.dat

and the patterns of his day

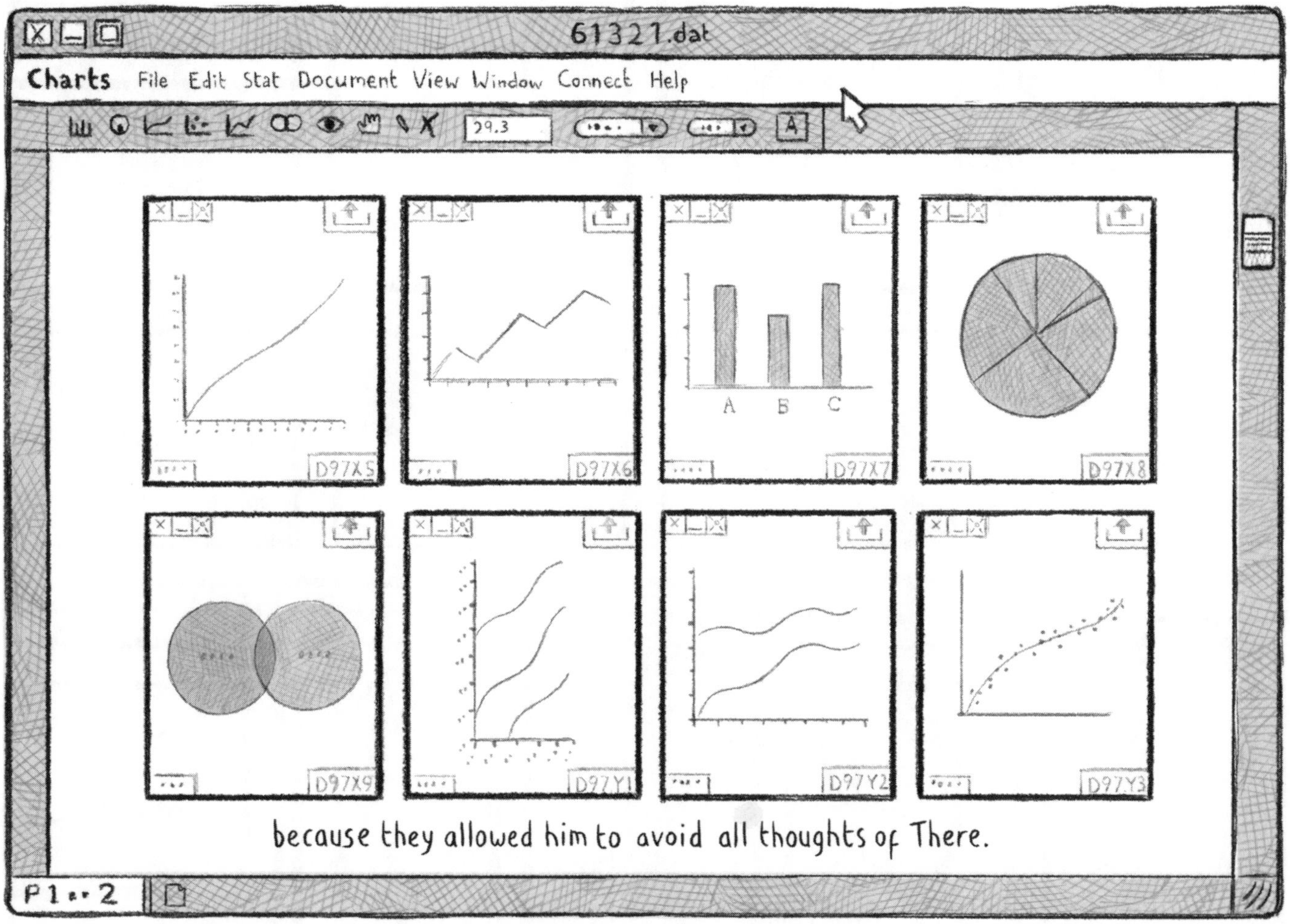
61321.dat
Charts File Edit Stat Document View Window Connect Help
29.3
D97X5
D97X6
A B C
D97X7
D97X8
D97X9
D97Y1
D97Y2
D97Y3
because they allowed him to avoid all thoughts of There.
P1 .. 2

(At least, for most of the time.)

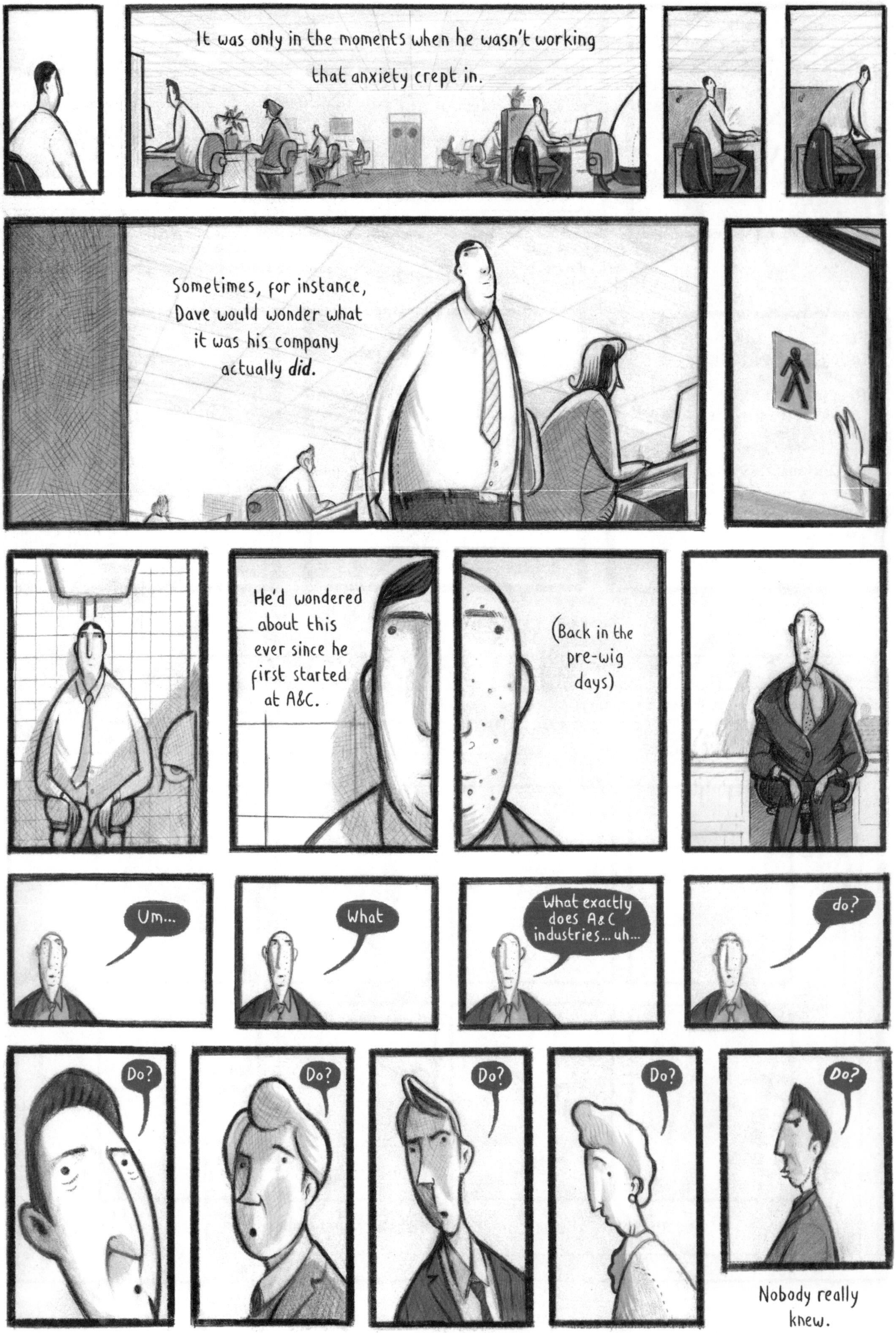
It was only in the moments when he wasn't working
that anxiety crept in.
Sometimes, for instance, Dave would wonder what it was his company actually *did*.
He'd wondered about this ever since he first started at A&C.
(Back in the pre-wig days)
Um...
What
What exactly does A&C industries... uh...
do?
Do?
Do?
Do?
Do?
Do?
Nobody really knew.

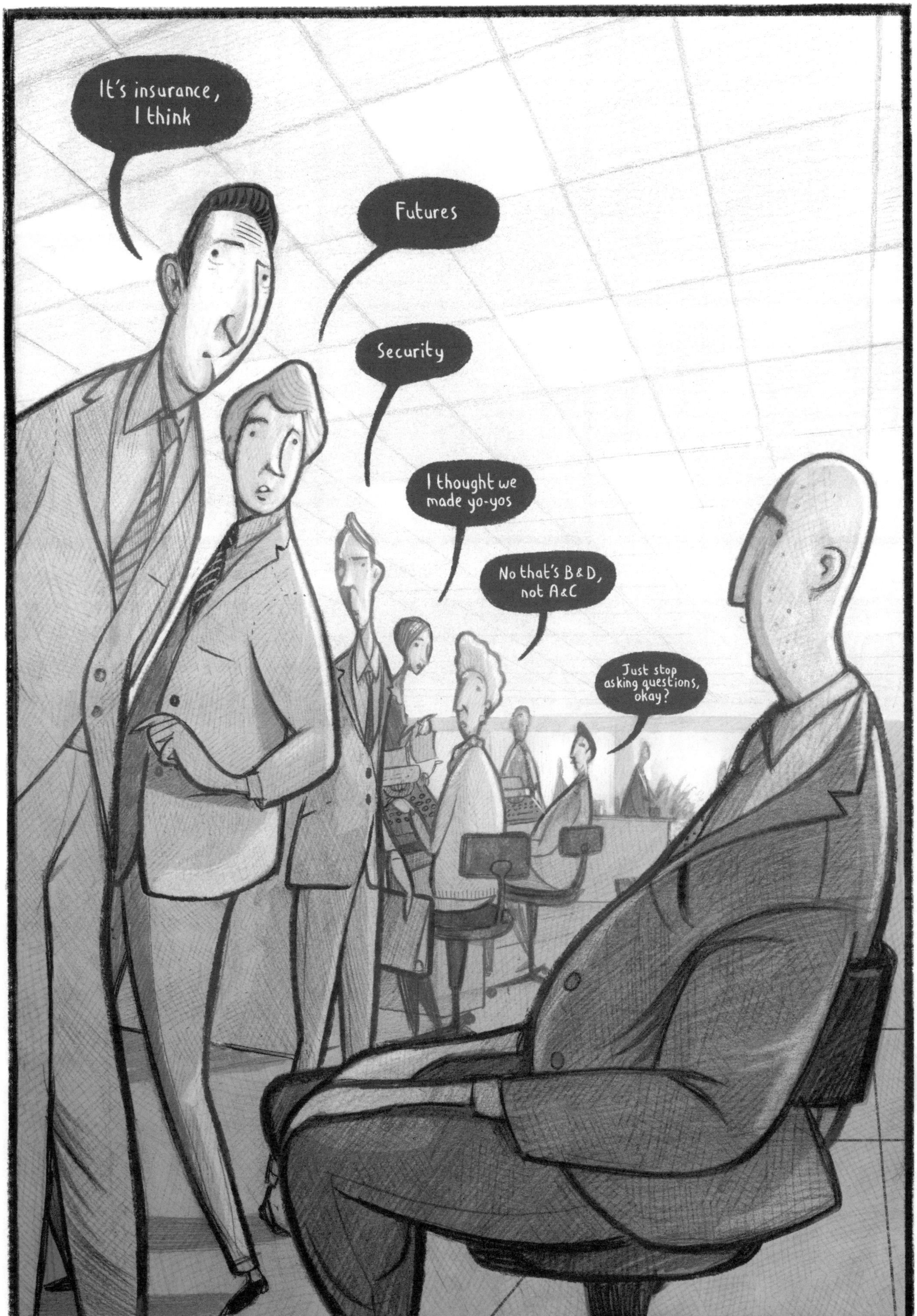
It's insurance, I think
Futures
Security
I thought we made yo-yos
No that's B&D, not A&C
Just stop asking questions, okay?

So Dave didn't ask again.

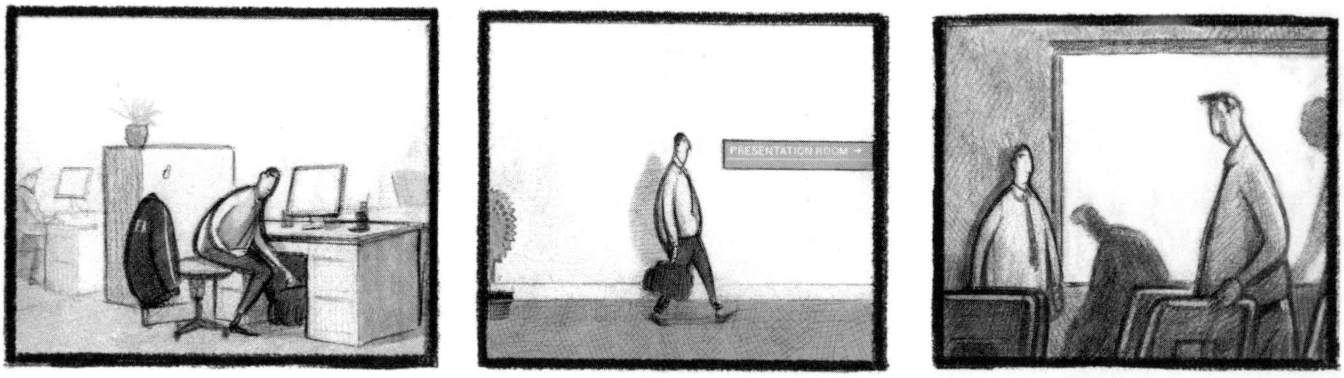
PRESENTATION ROOM →

And every lunchtime, once he'd conveyed

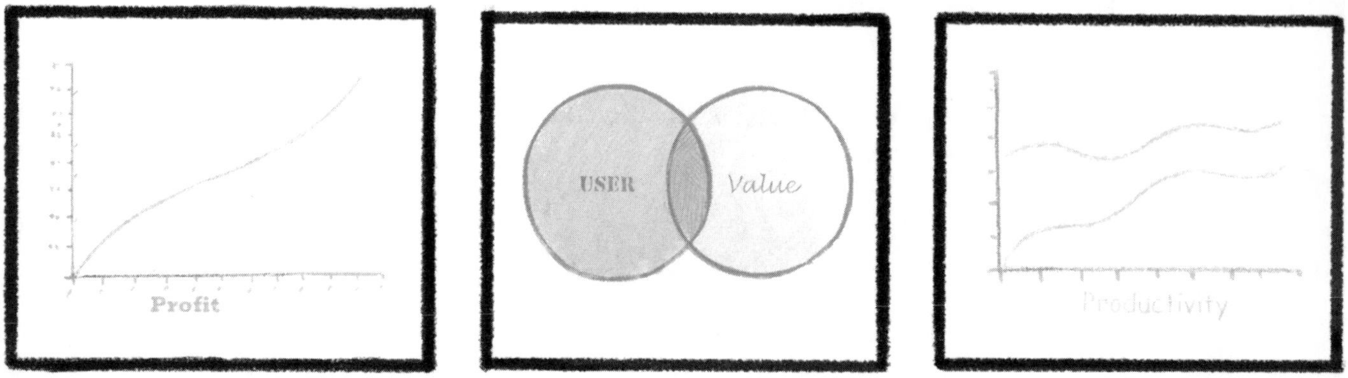
Profit
USER
Value
Productivity

all of the latest information

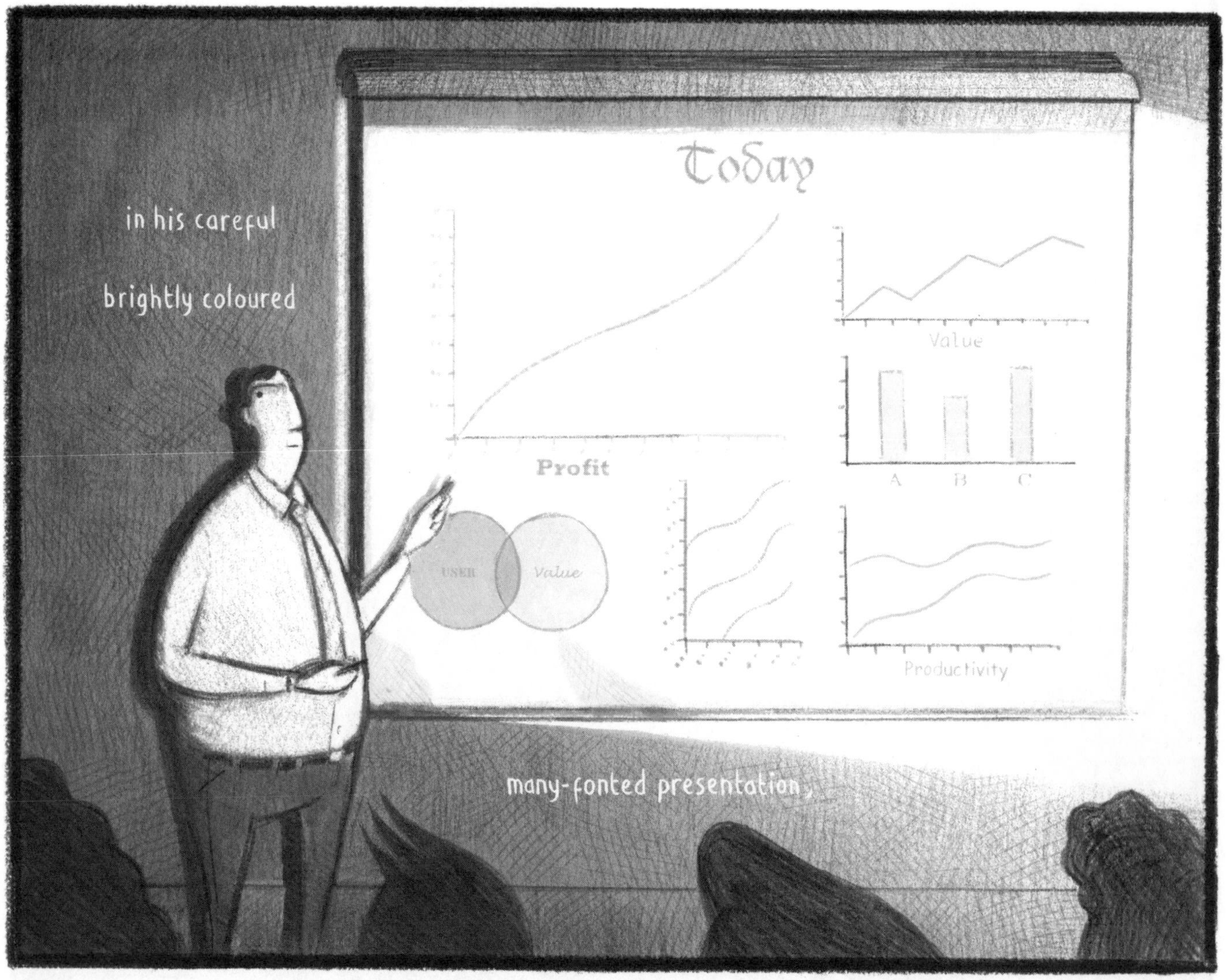
in his careful
brightly coloured
Today
Profit
Value
A
B
C
USER
Value
Productivity
many-fonted presentation,

Dave was always left with a nagging question at the end:

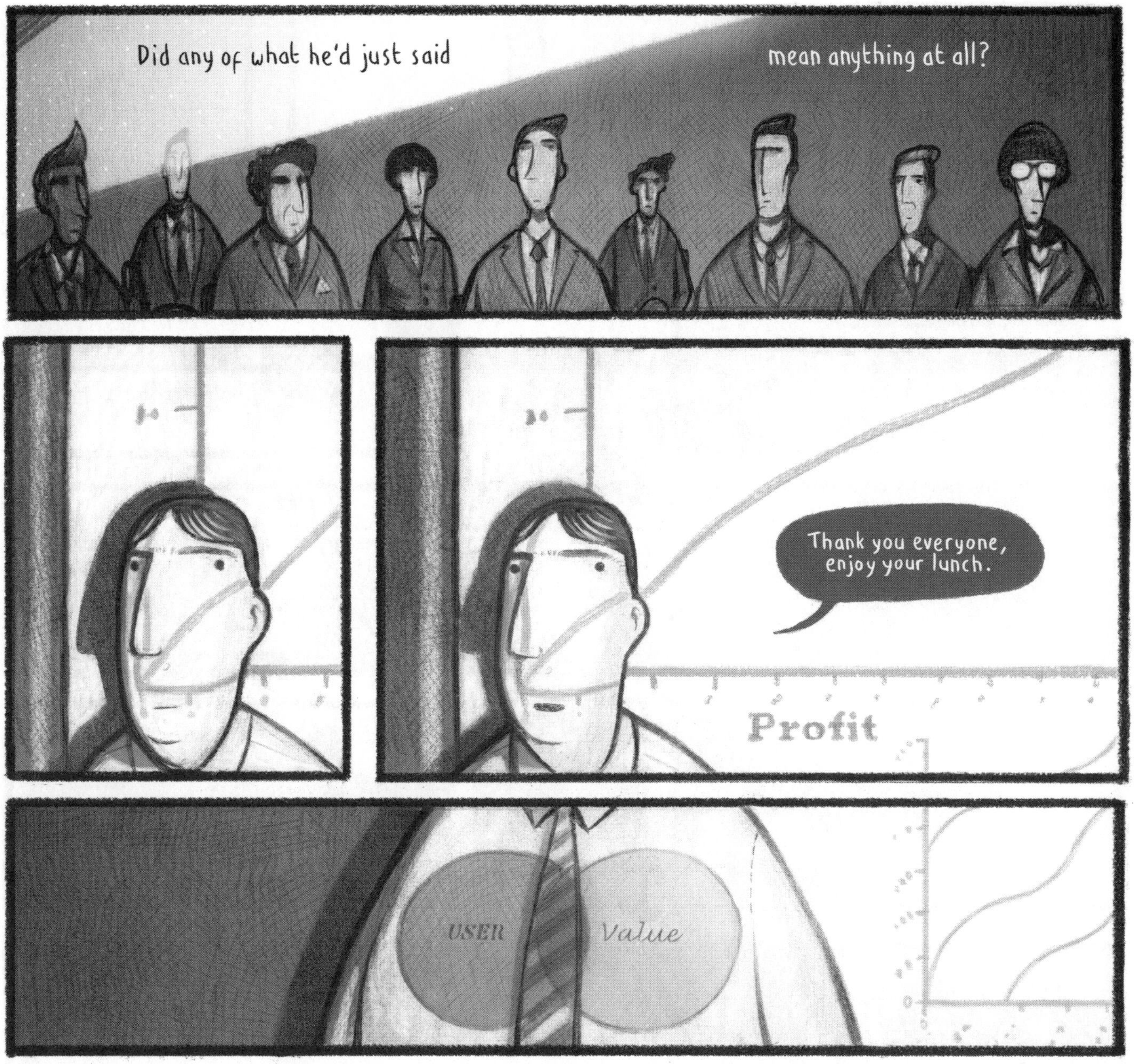
Did any of what he'd just said
mean anything at all?
Thank you everyone, enjoy your lunch.
Profit
USER
Value

And following this question, the familiar, disturbing suspicion

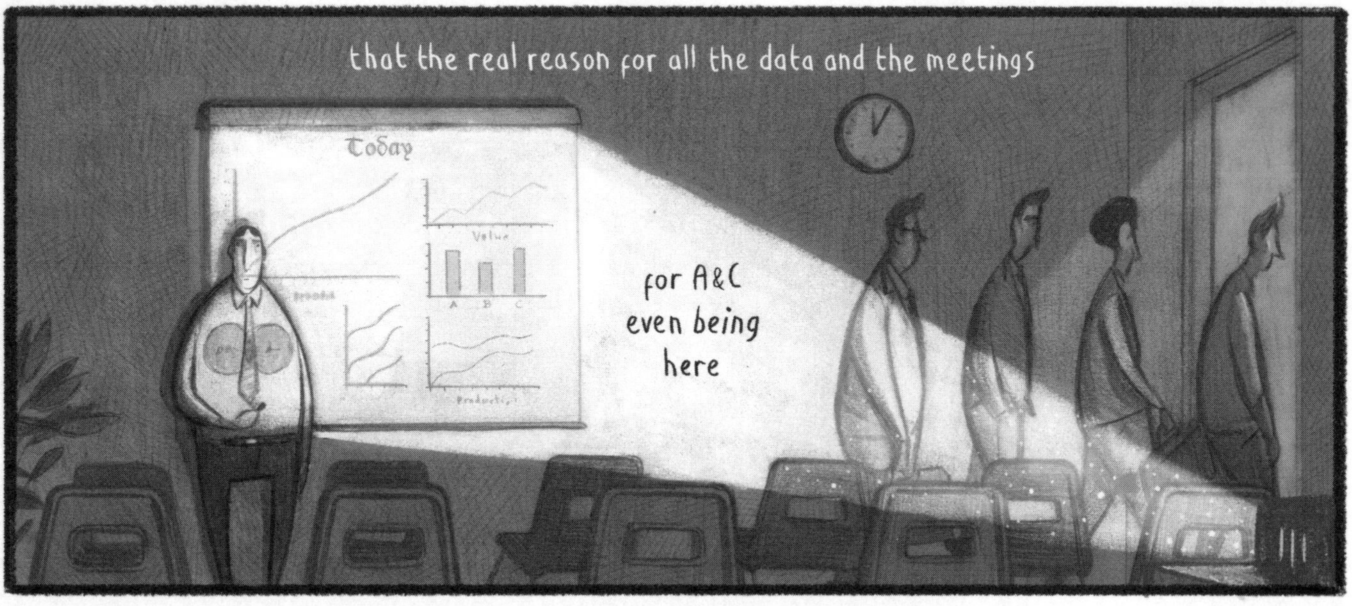
that the real reason for all the data and the meetings
Today
Value
for A&C even being here

was fear.

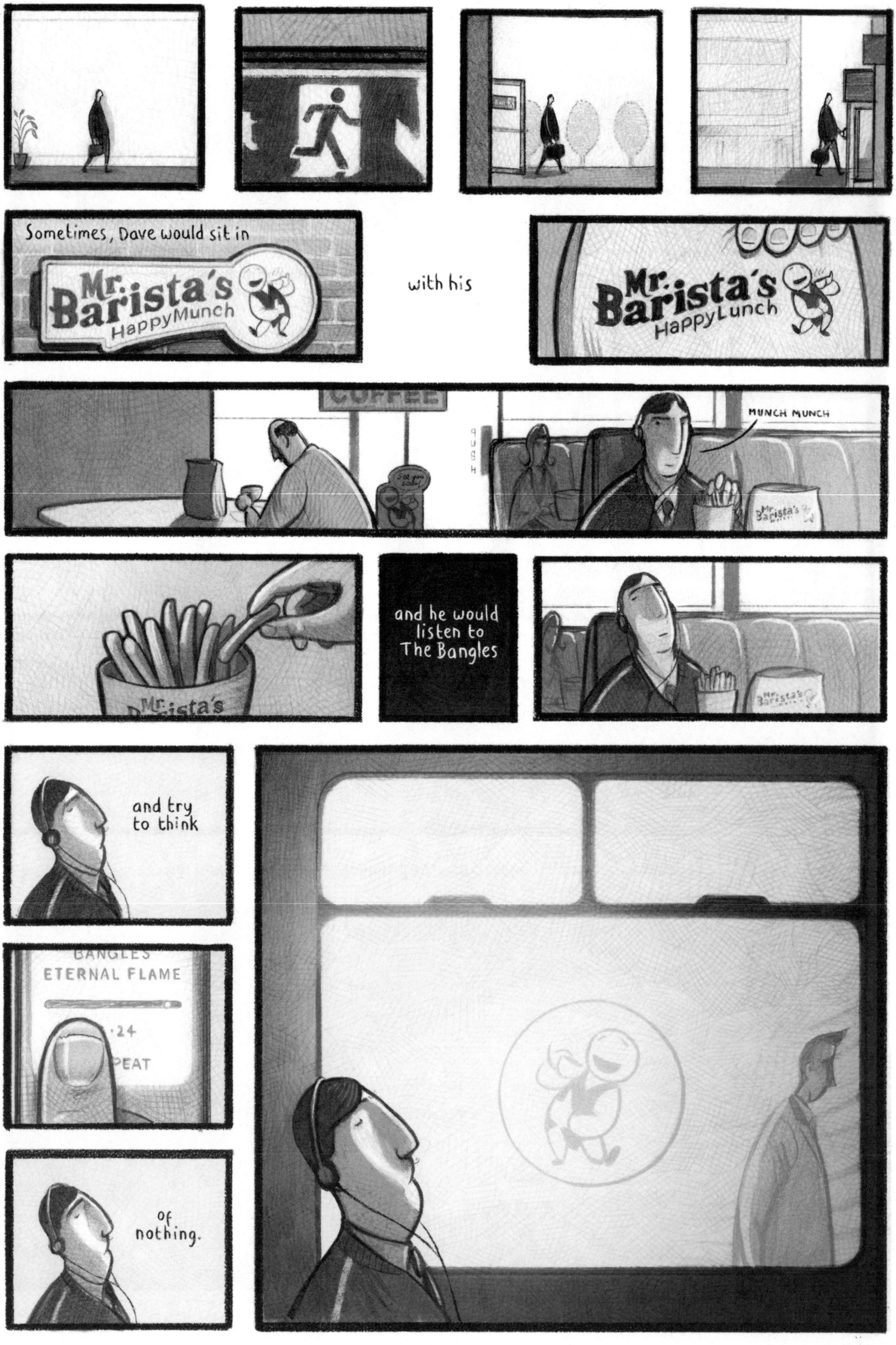
Sometimes, Dave would sit in
Mr. Barista's HappyMunch
with his
Mr. Barista's HappyLunch
MUNCH MUNCH
Mr. Barista's
and he would listen to The Bangles
and try to think
ETERNAL FLAME
of nothing.

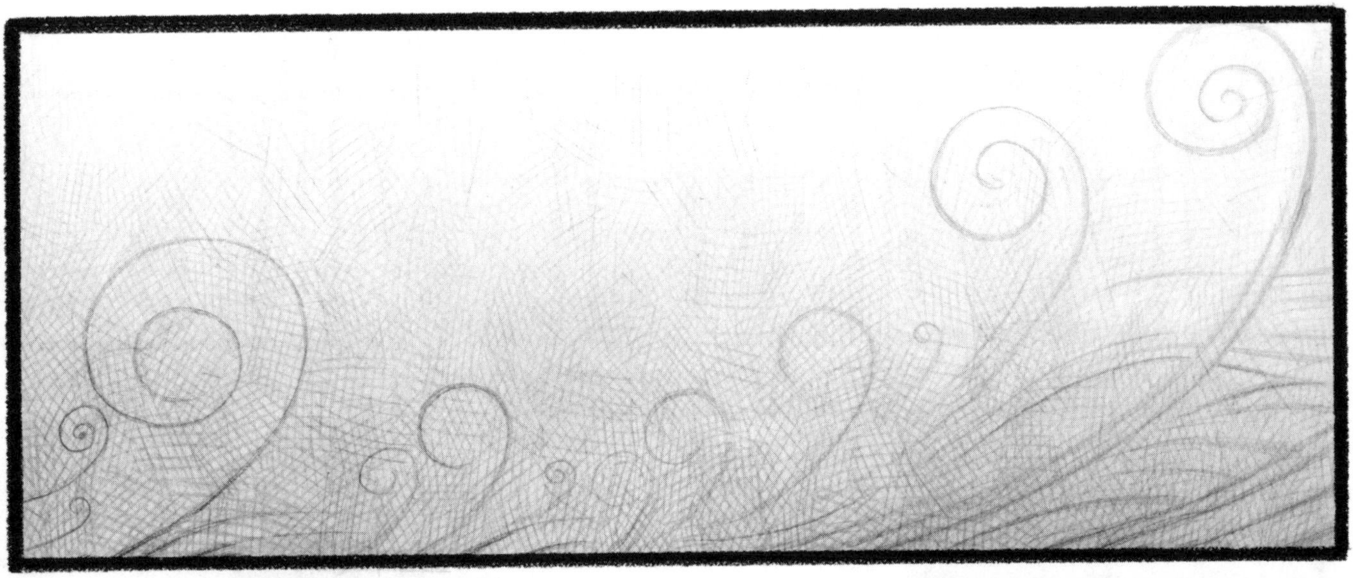

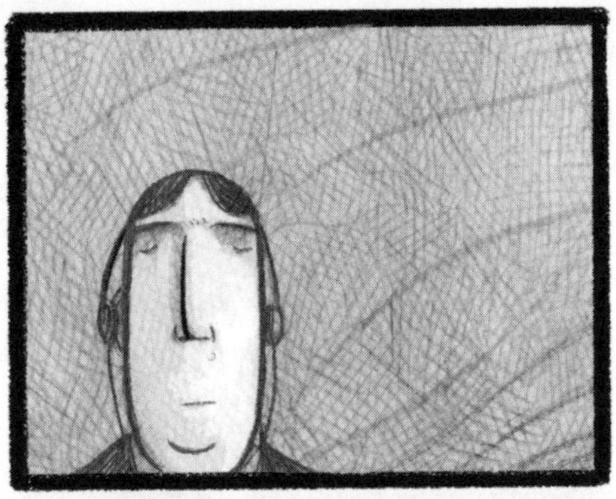

But it didn't
always work.

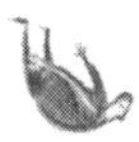

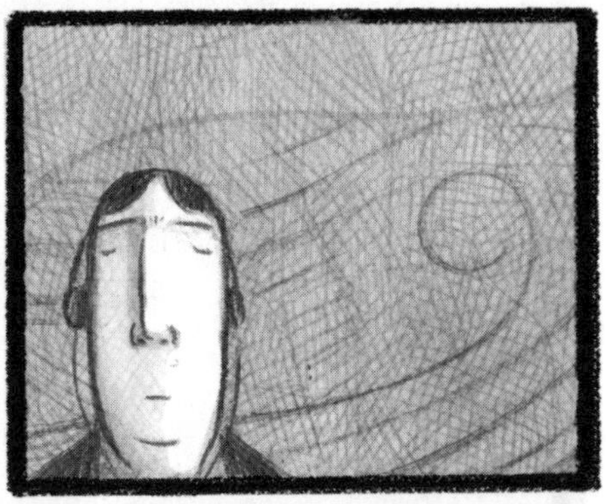

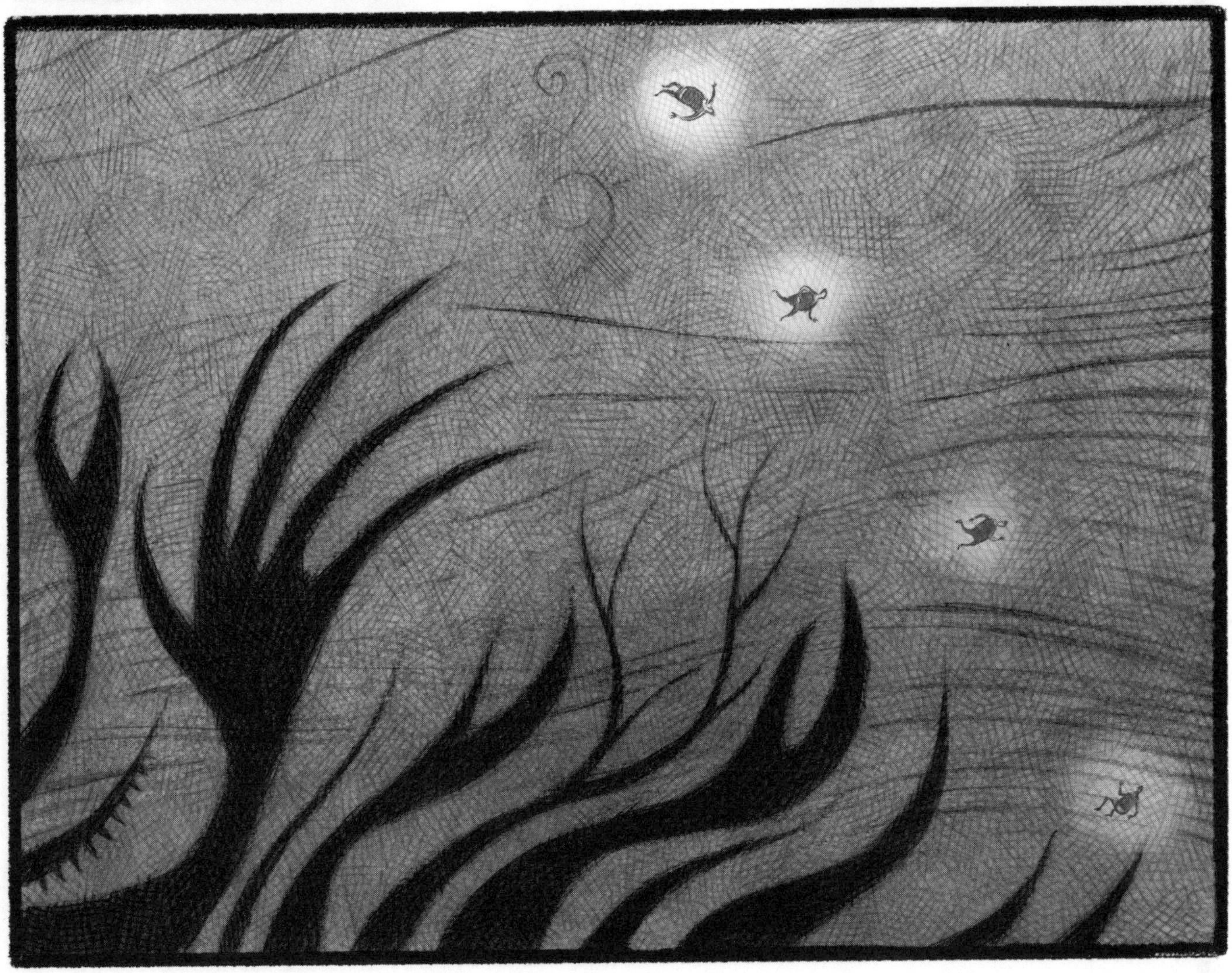

For Dave, as for most people on Here,

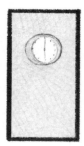    

there was never really any getting away from it.

The idea of There was always just

there.

Sitting, silently...

somewhere

Like...

... a weed... that crawls up between the cracks...

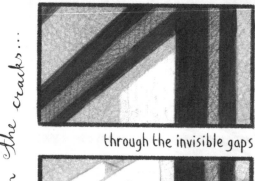

through the invisible gaps

which connect

one moment

to the next.

just to the left of vision.

Lacking form or precision.

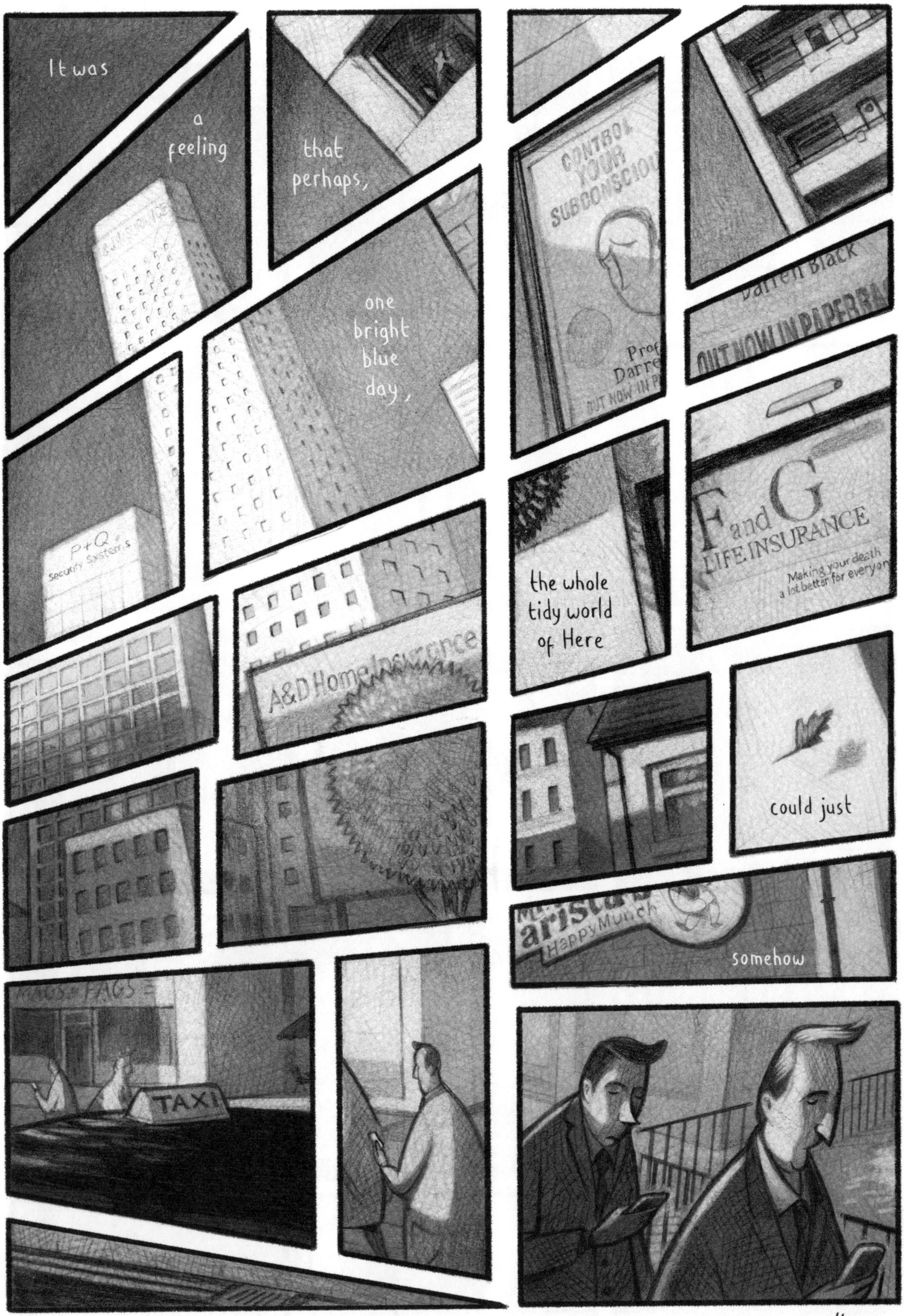
It was
a feeling
that perhaps,
P+Q Security Systems
one bright blue day,
A&D Home Insurance
CONTROL YOUR SUBCONSCIOU
Darren Black
OUT NOW IN PAPERBA
F and G LIFE INSURANCE
Making your death a lot better for everyon
the whole tidy world of Here
could just
HappyMunch
somehow
TAXI
collapse.

It was beneath the skin of things.

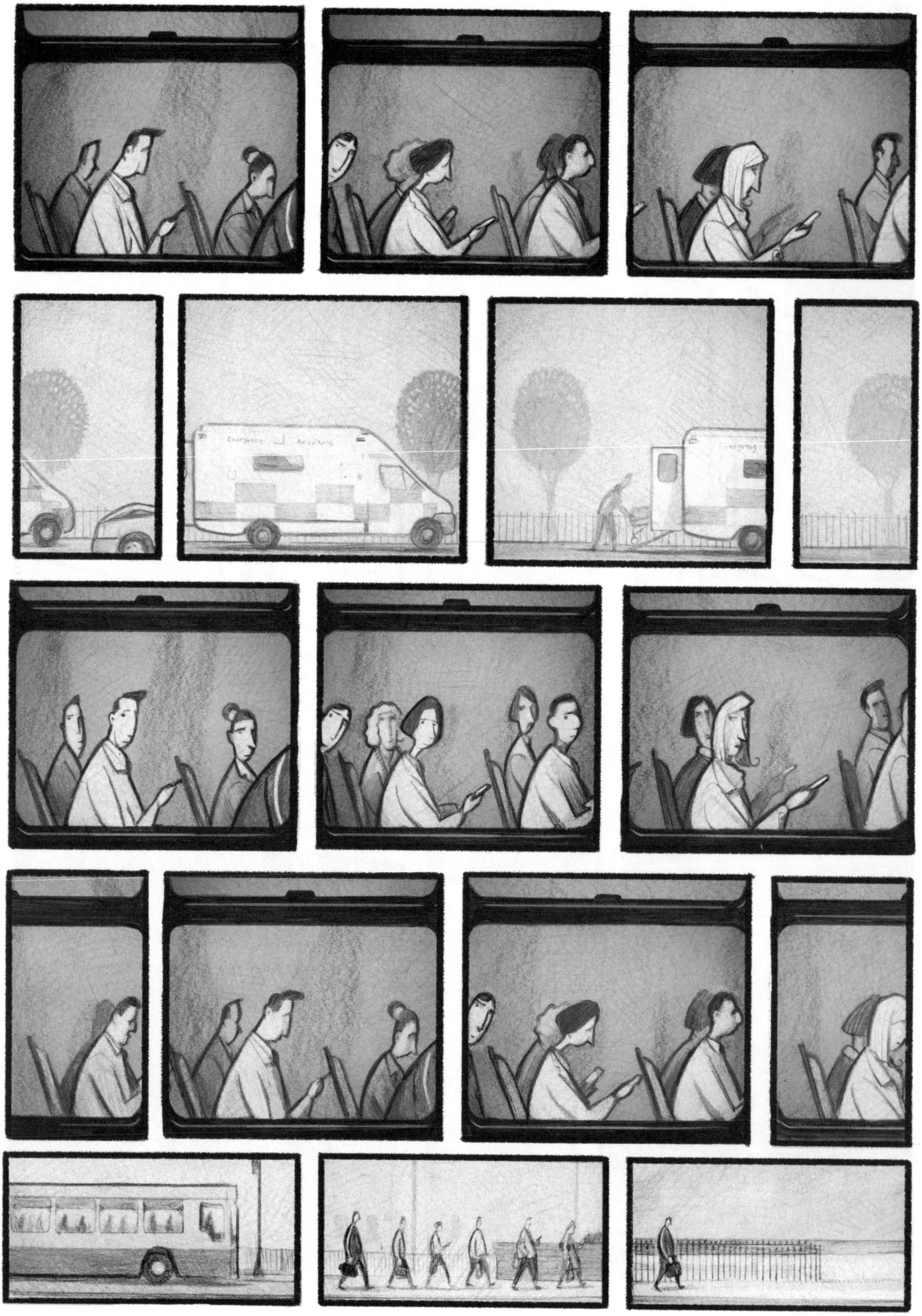

Behind the pattern of things.

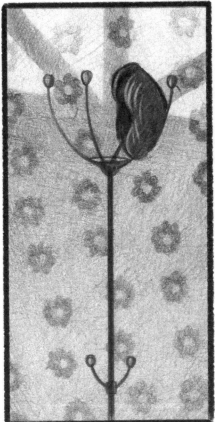

THE BANGLES
ETERNAL FLAME
42,7096,483 plays

You might like:
R KELLY
IGNITION REMIX

X CLOSE WINDOW

HE KNEW W...

NIC MONDAY

ERNAL FLAME

ALK LIKE AN...

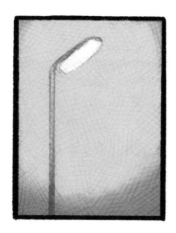

It was under the streetlamp half-light

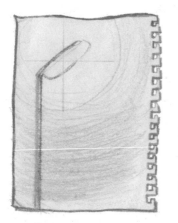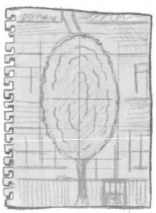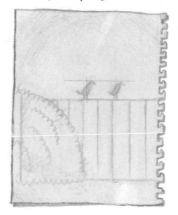

that the night-time brings.

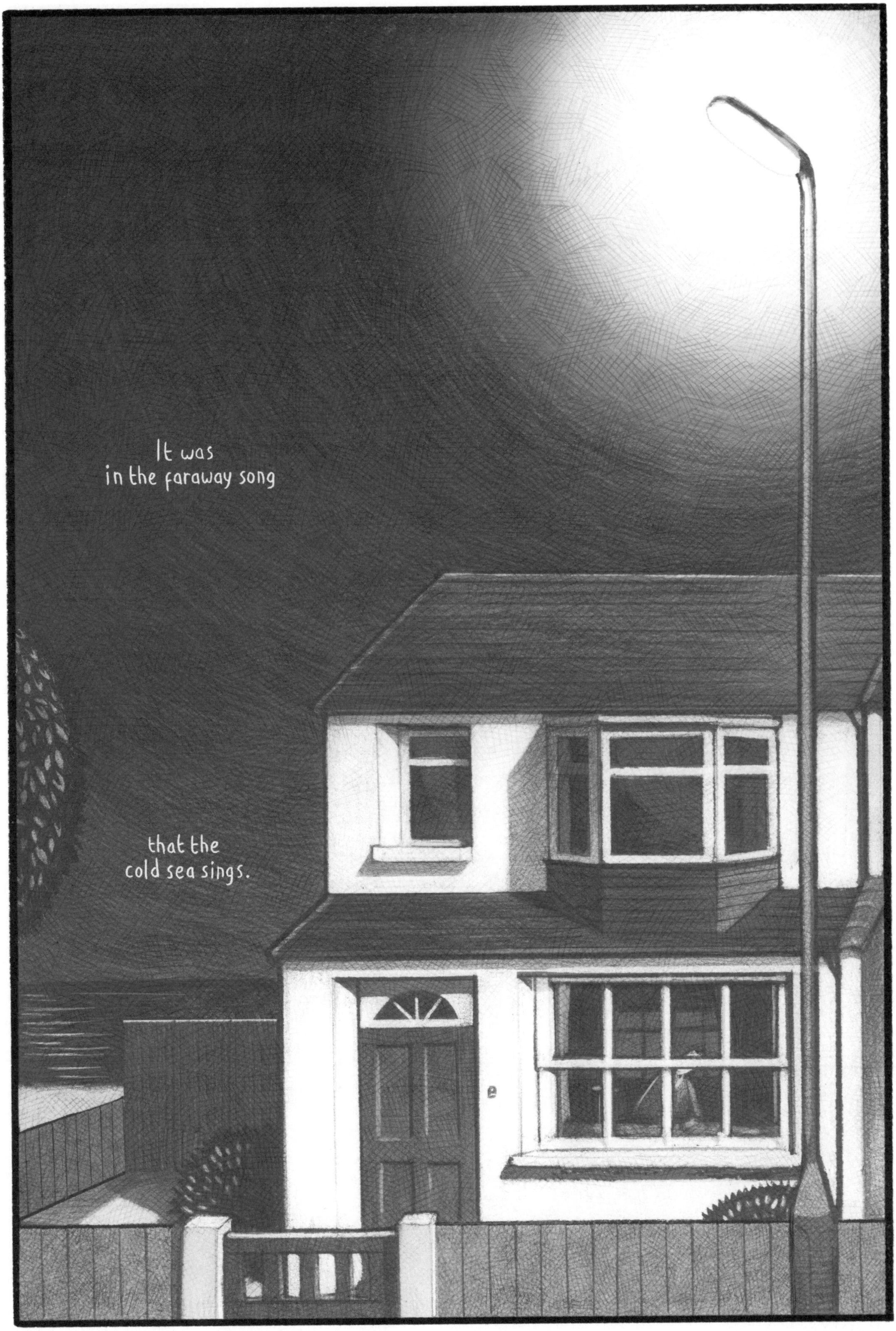
It was
in the faraway song
that the
cold sea sings.

2.

THE HAIR

The hair

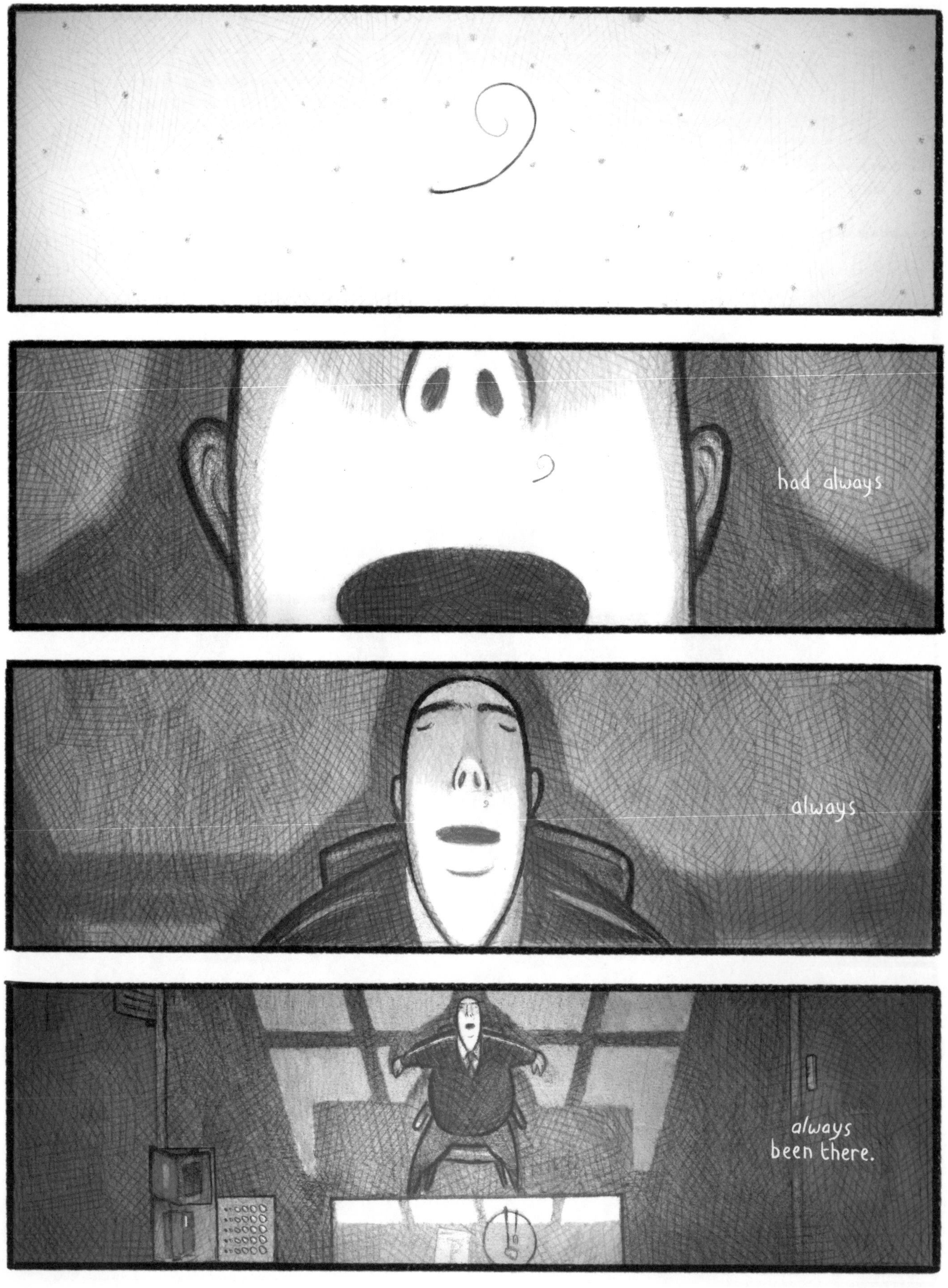
had always
always
always
been there.

!
And it's a misty start brightening later today folks...
UTV
UTV WEATHER
It must have been the strangest, strongest hair in the world.
For whether it was shorn
plucked
snipped
ripped
OW
or waxed,
within half an hour
it would always grow back.
Exactly the same as it was before.

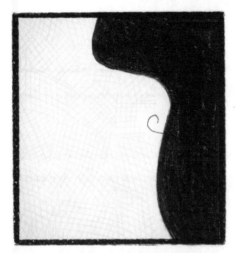

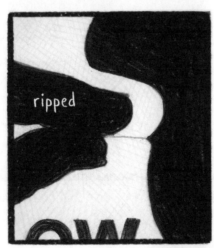

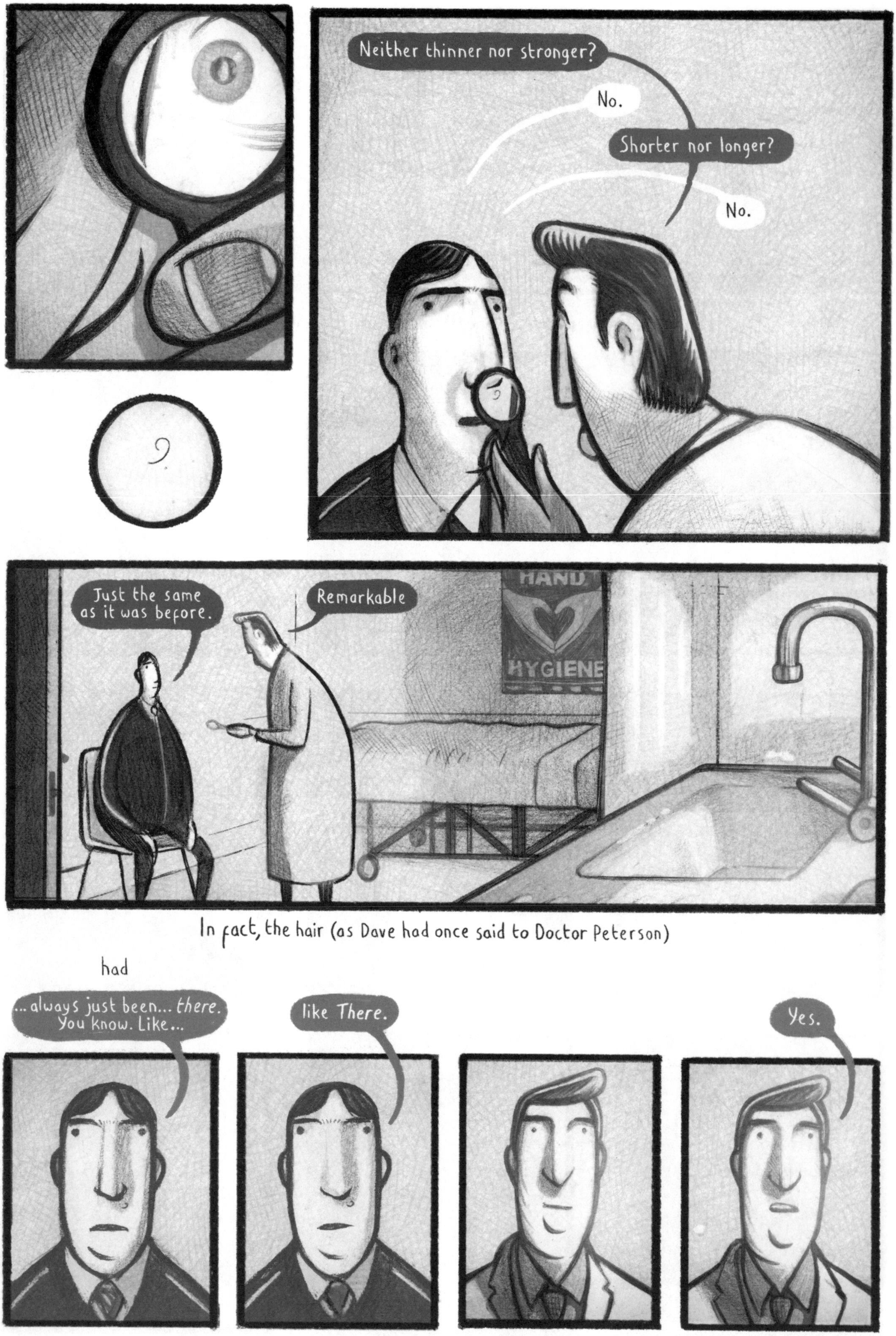
9
Neither thinner nor stronger?
No.
Shorter nor longer?
No.
Just the same as it was before.
Remarkable
HAND
HYGIENE
In fact, the hair (as Dave had once said to Doctor Peterson)
had
...always just been... *there*. You know. Like...
like There.
Yes.

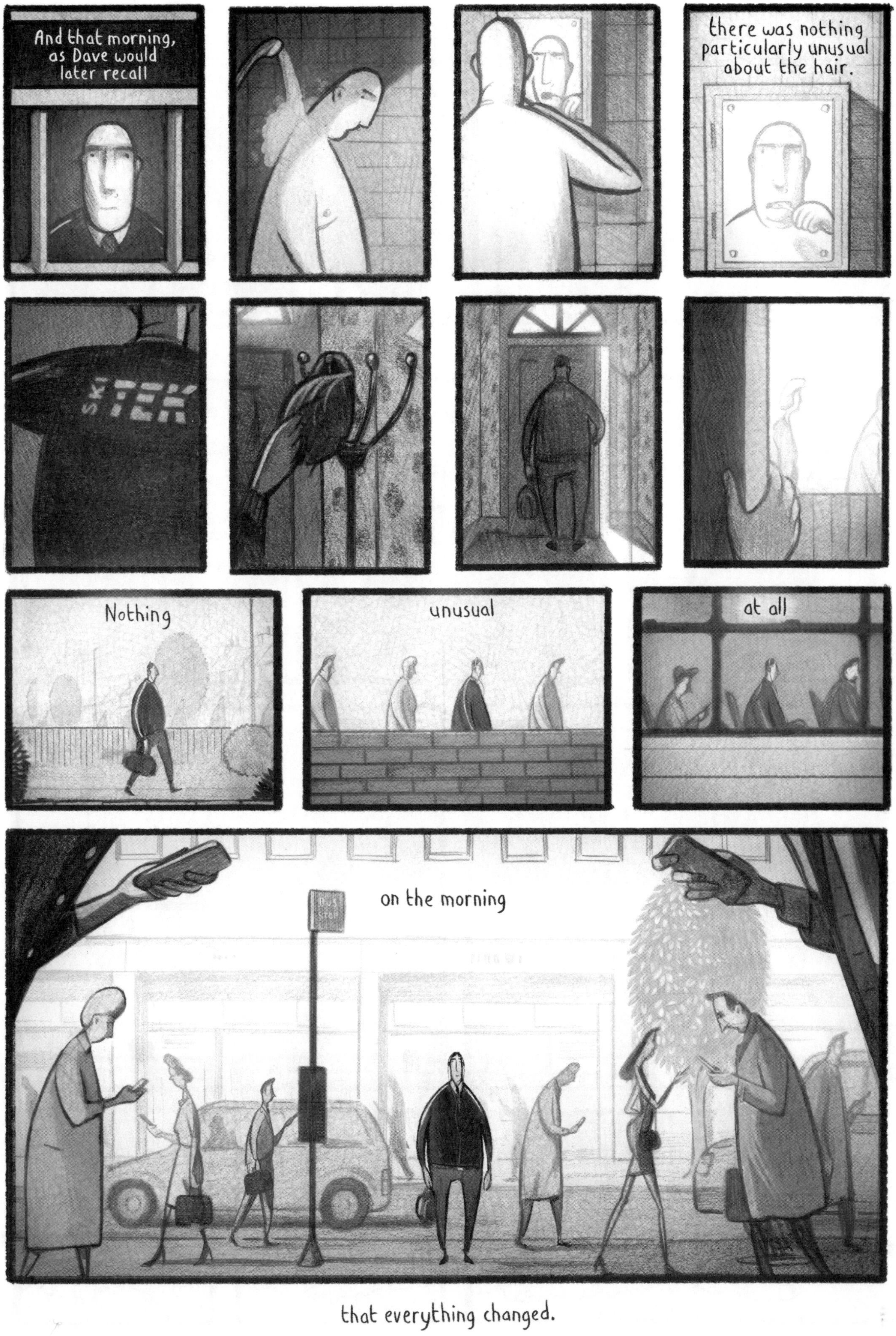
And that morning, as Dave would later recall
there was nothing particularly unusual about the hair.
Nothing
unusual
at all
BUS STOP
on the morning

that everything changed.

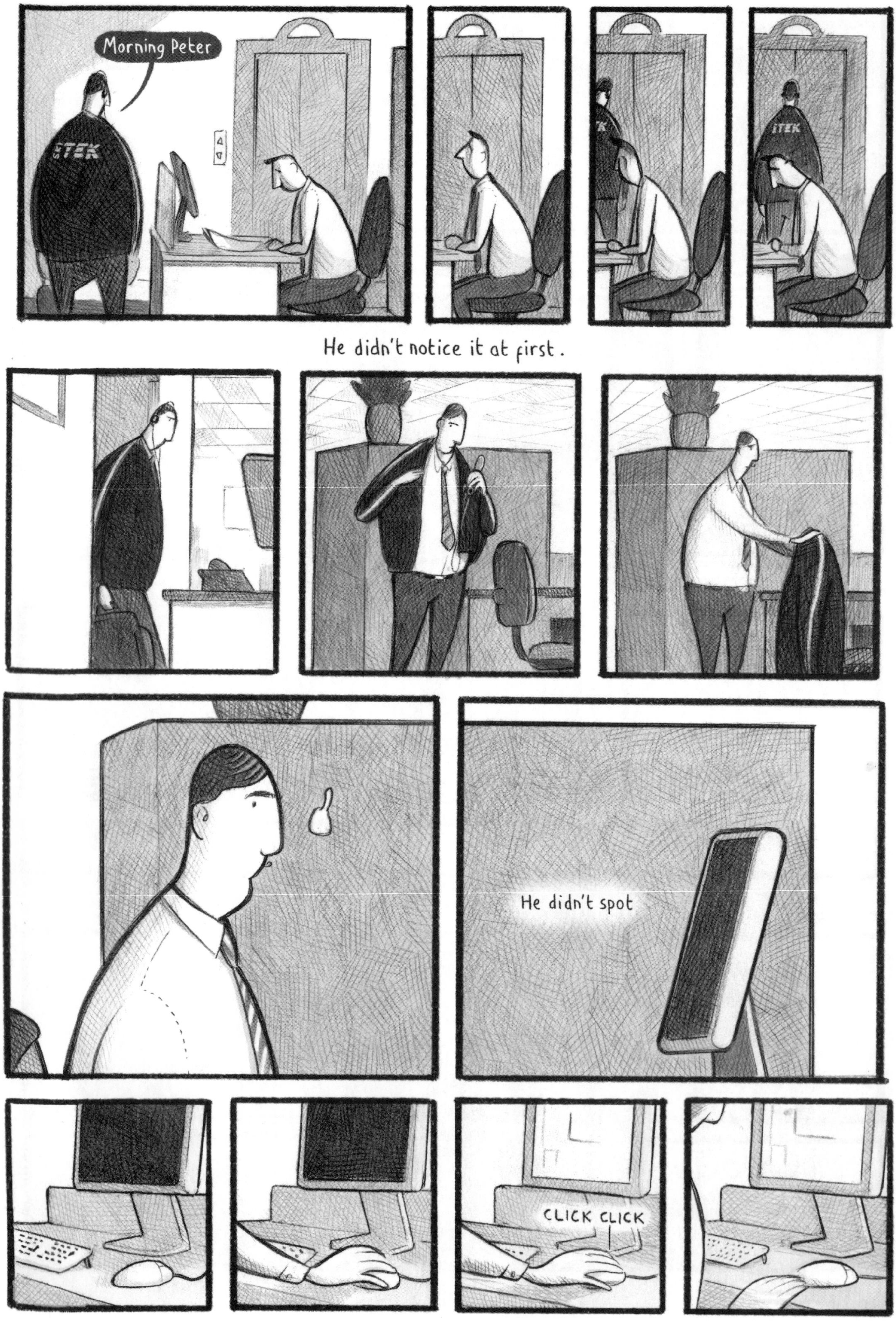
Morning Peter
He didn't notice it at first.
He didn't spot
CLICK CLICK

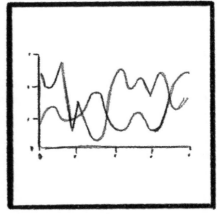

RECEIVED
SUBJEC
INBOX 3
DRAFTS
Today 08:45 Today's Data
Today 08:40 Today's Data
Today 08:35 Today's Data
Yesterday 17 Re: Today's Data
that the data which greeted him that day seemed unusually random.
Value
The scatter charts in particular were more chaotic than normal.
A little too scattered.
For Dave, as ever
if the data was there,
that was all
that mattered.

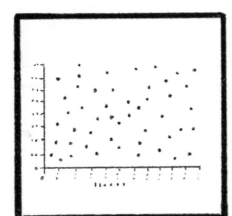

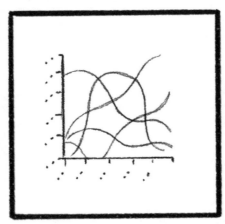

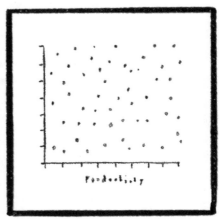

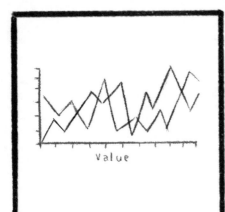

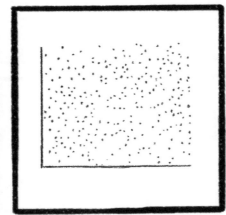

It was his boss who saw it first.

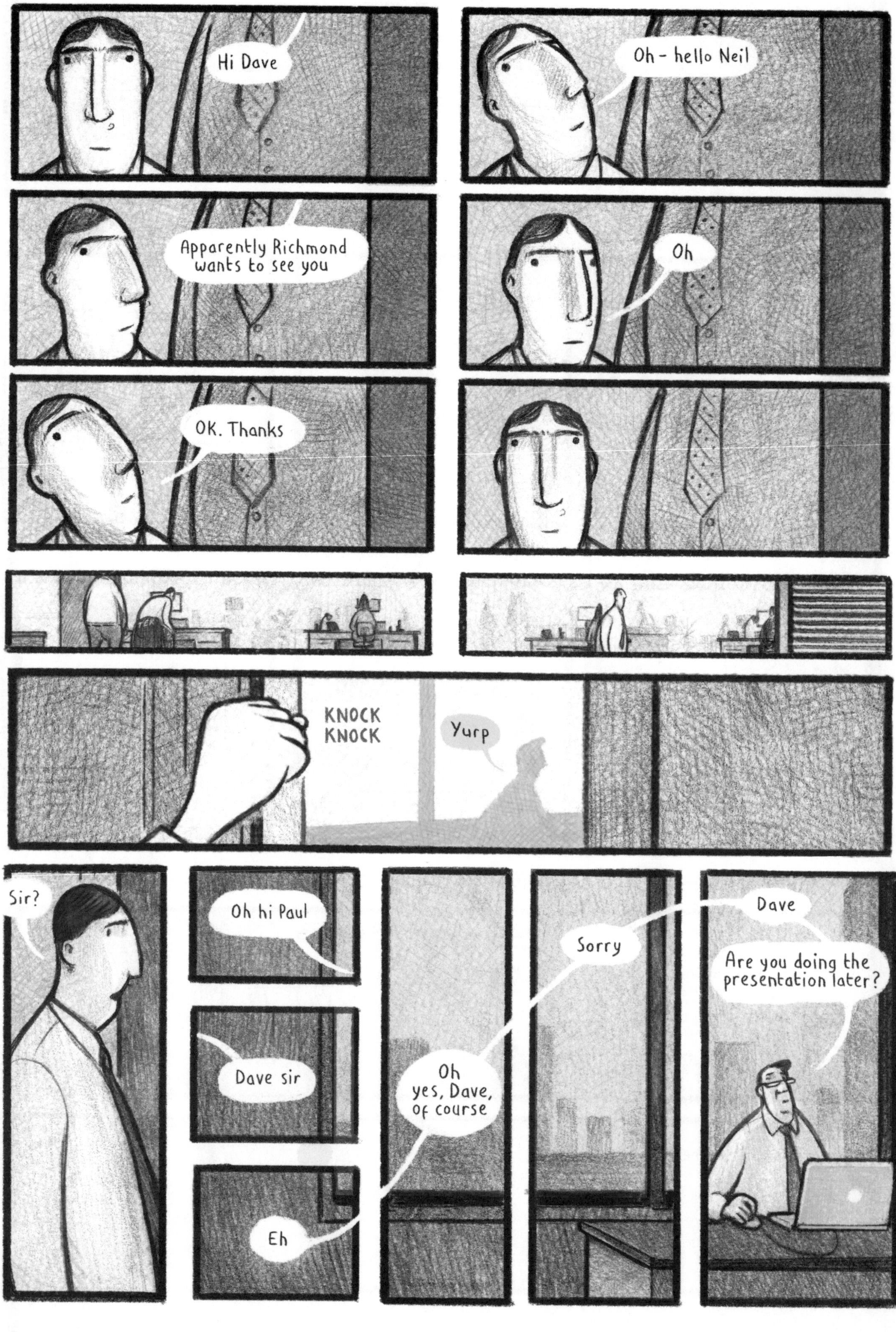
Hi Dave
Oh - hello Neil
Apparently Richmond wants to see you
Oh
OK. Thanks
KNOCK KNOCK
Yurp
Sir?
Oh hi Paul
Dave sir
Eh
Oh yes, Dave, of course
Sorry
Dave
Are you doing the presentation later?

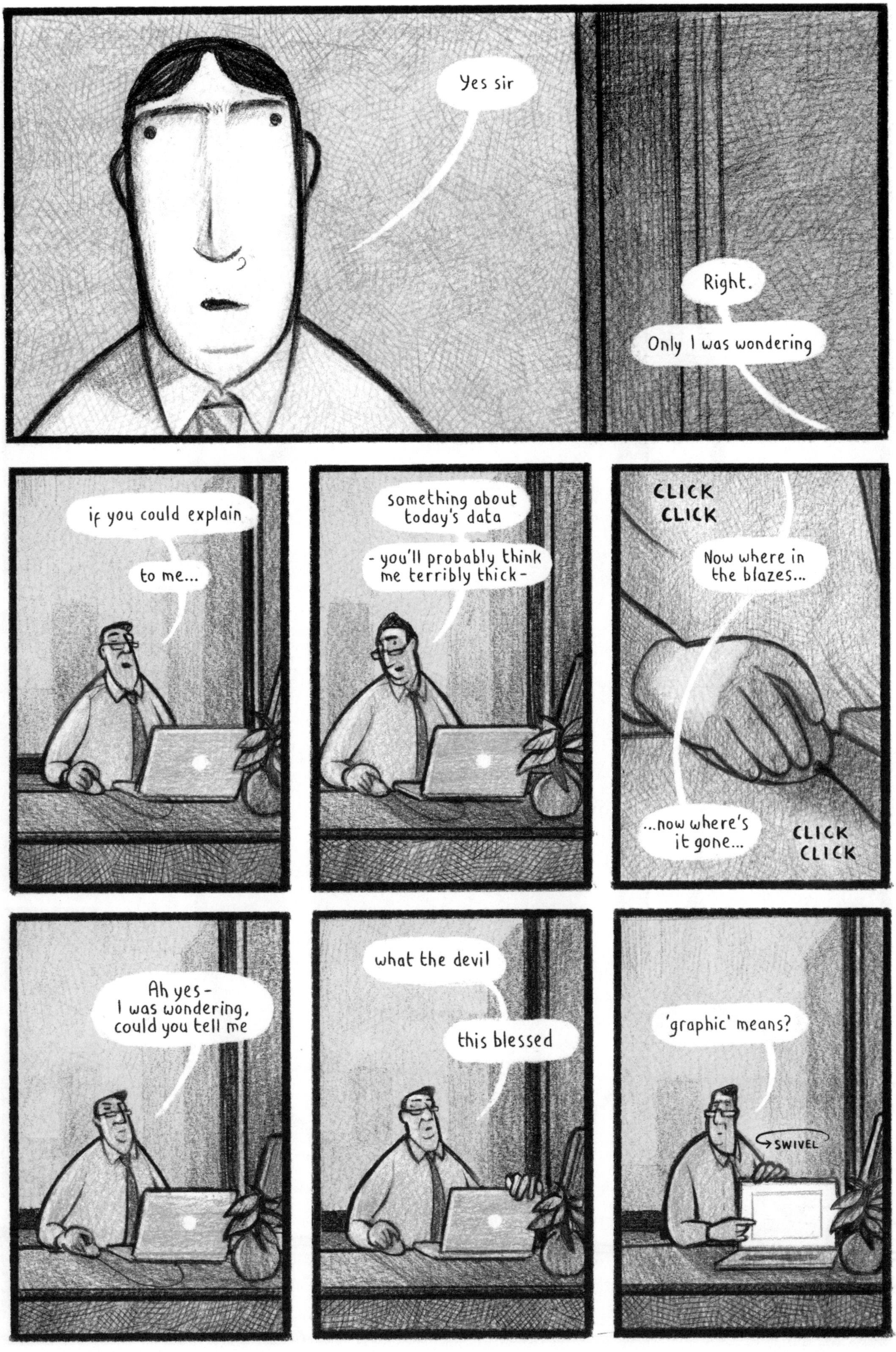
Yes sir
Right.
Only I was wondering
if you could explain
to me...
something about today's data
- you'll probably think me terribly thick -
CLICK CLICK
Now where in the blazes...
...now where's it gone...
CLICK CLICK
Ah yes - I was wondering, could you tell me
what the devil
this blessed
'graphic' means?
SWIVEL

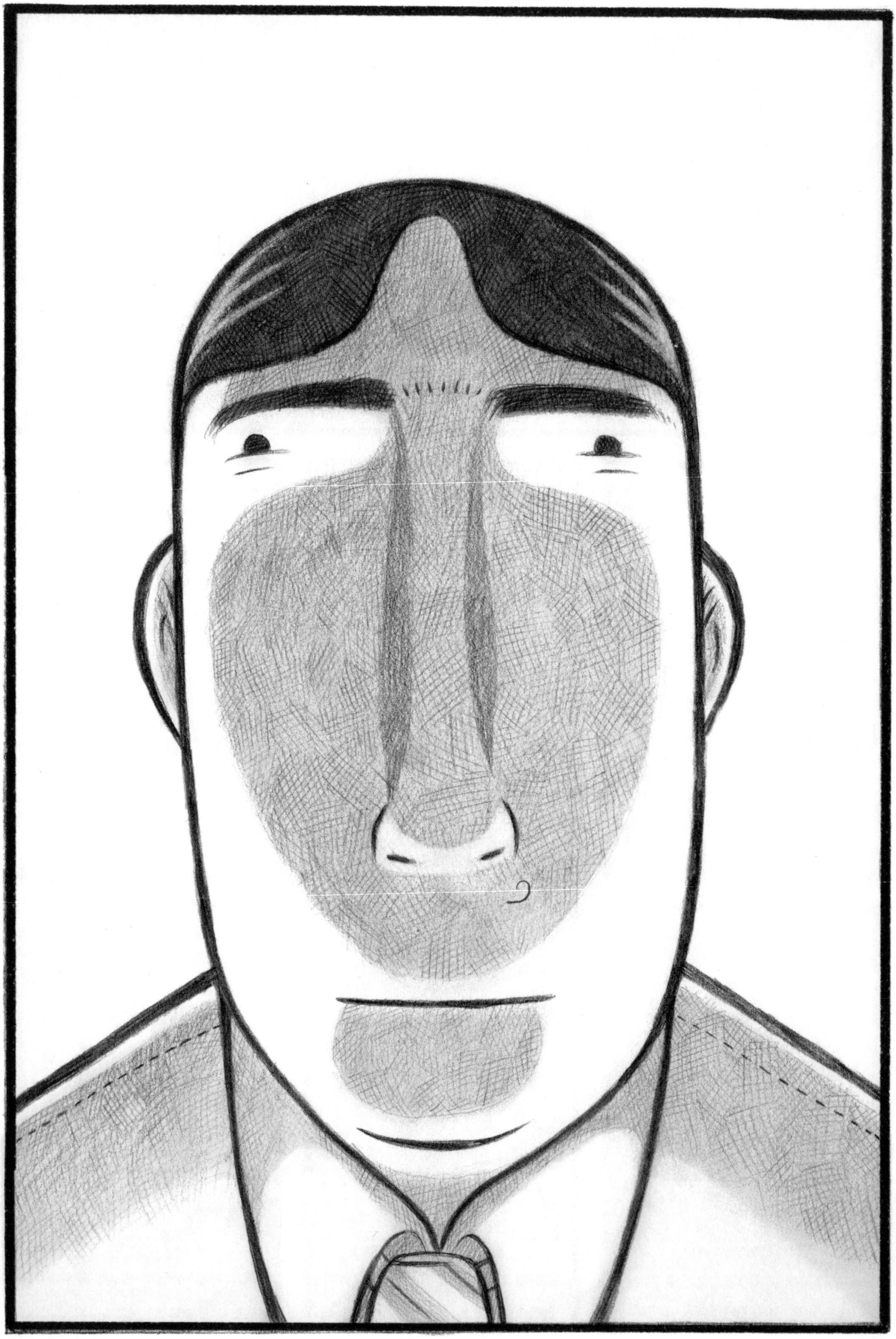

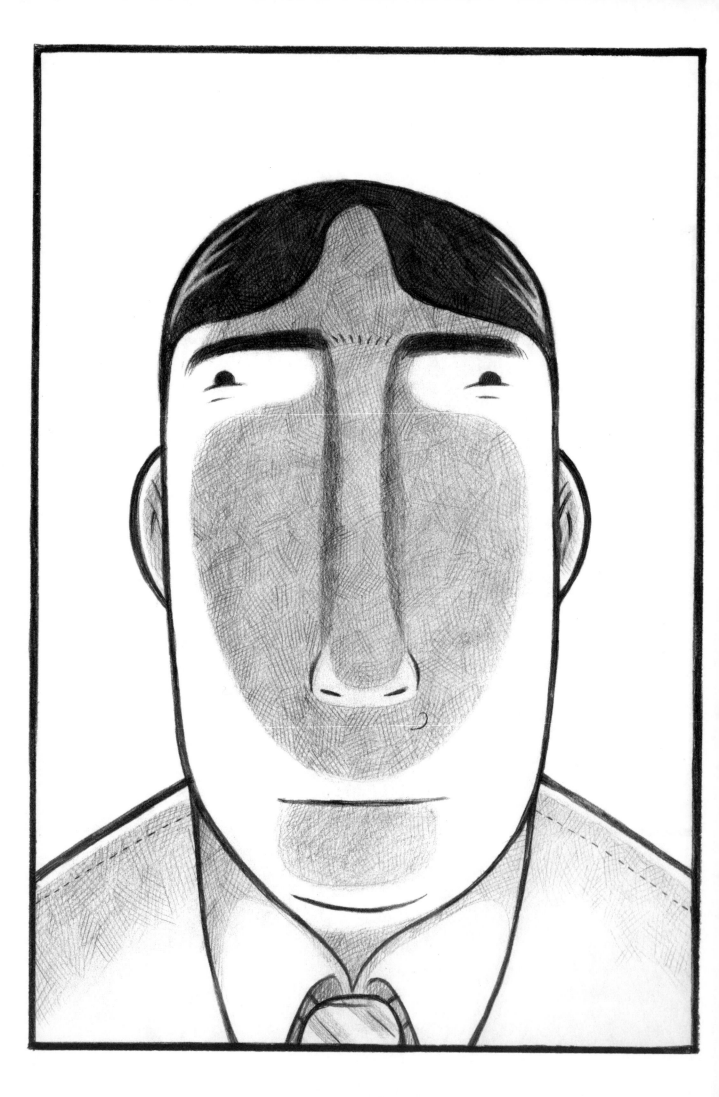

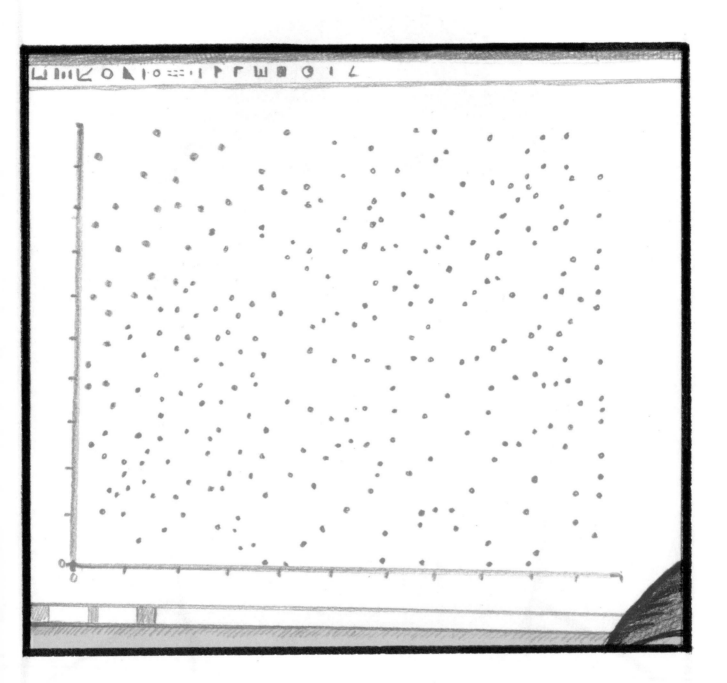

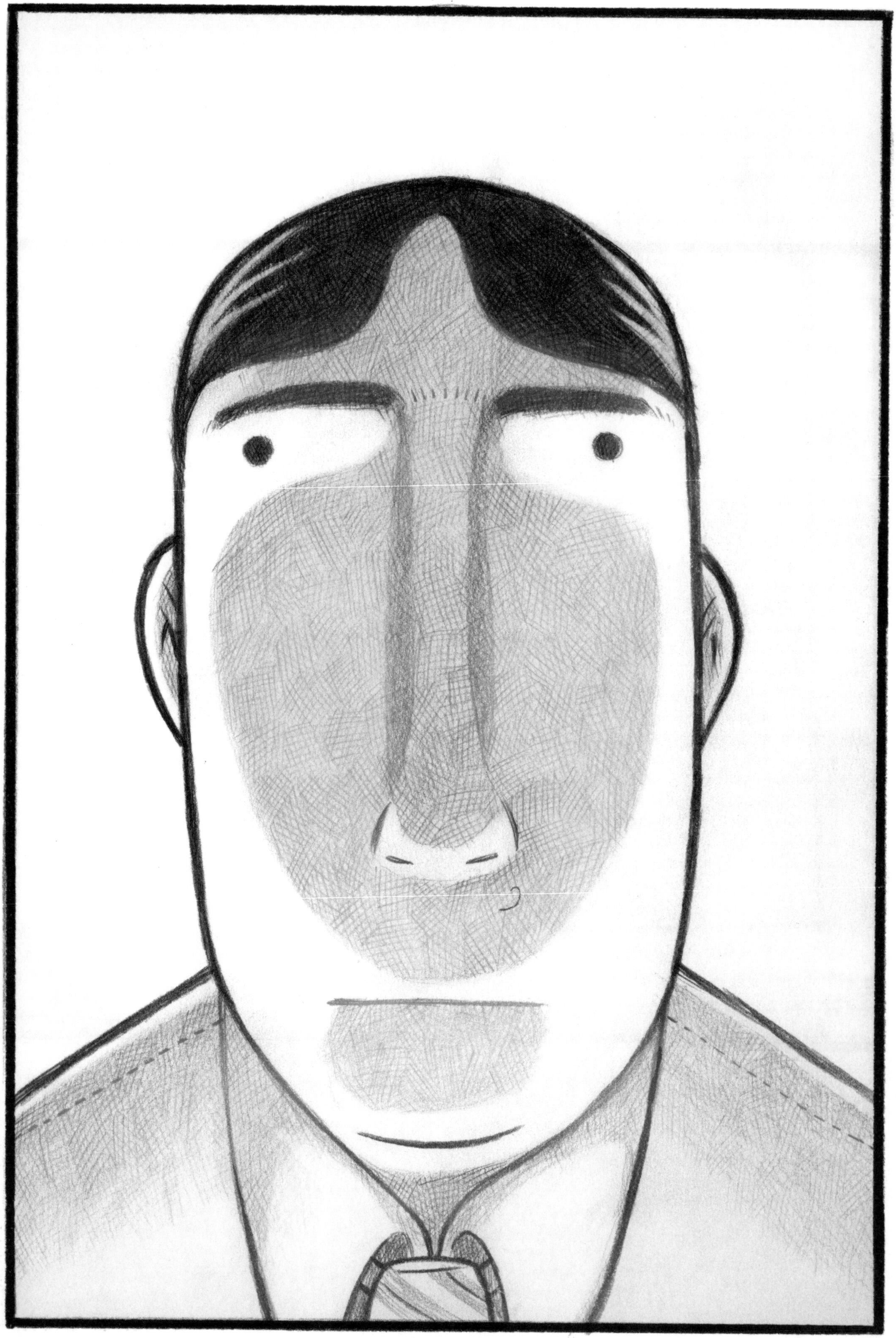

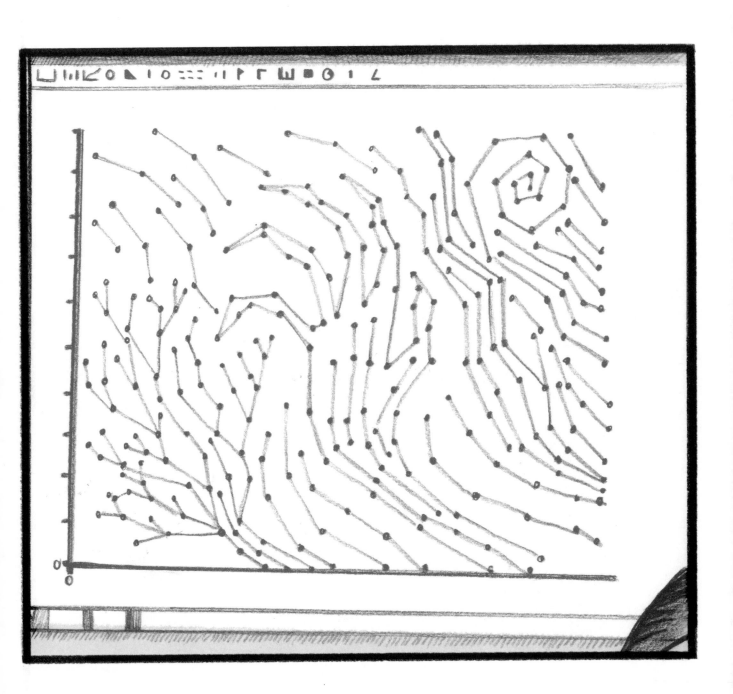

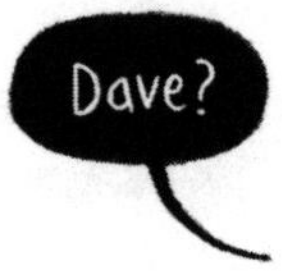
Dave?

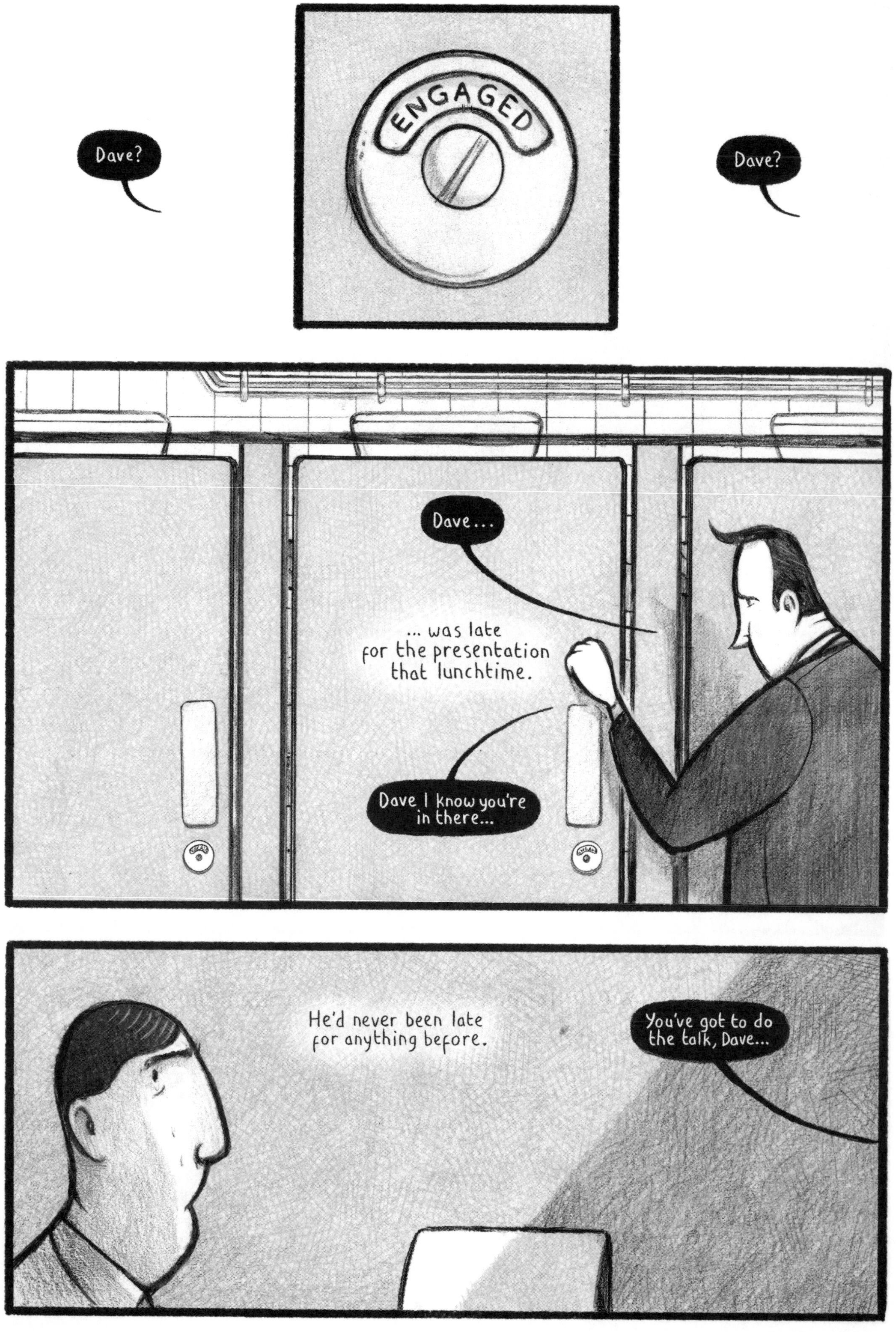

Dave?
ENGAGED
Dave?
Dave...
... was late for the presentation that lunchtime.
Dave I know you're in there...
He'd never been late for anything before.
You've got to do the talk, Dave...

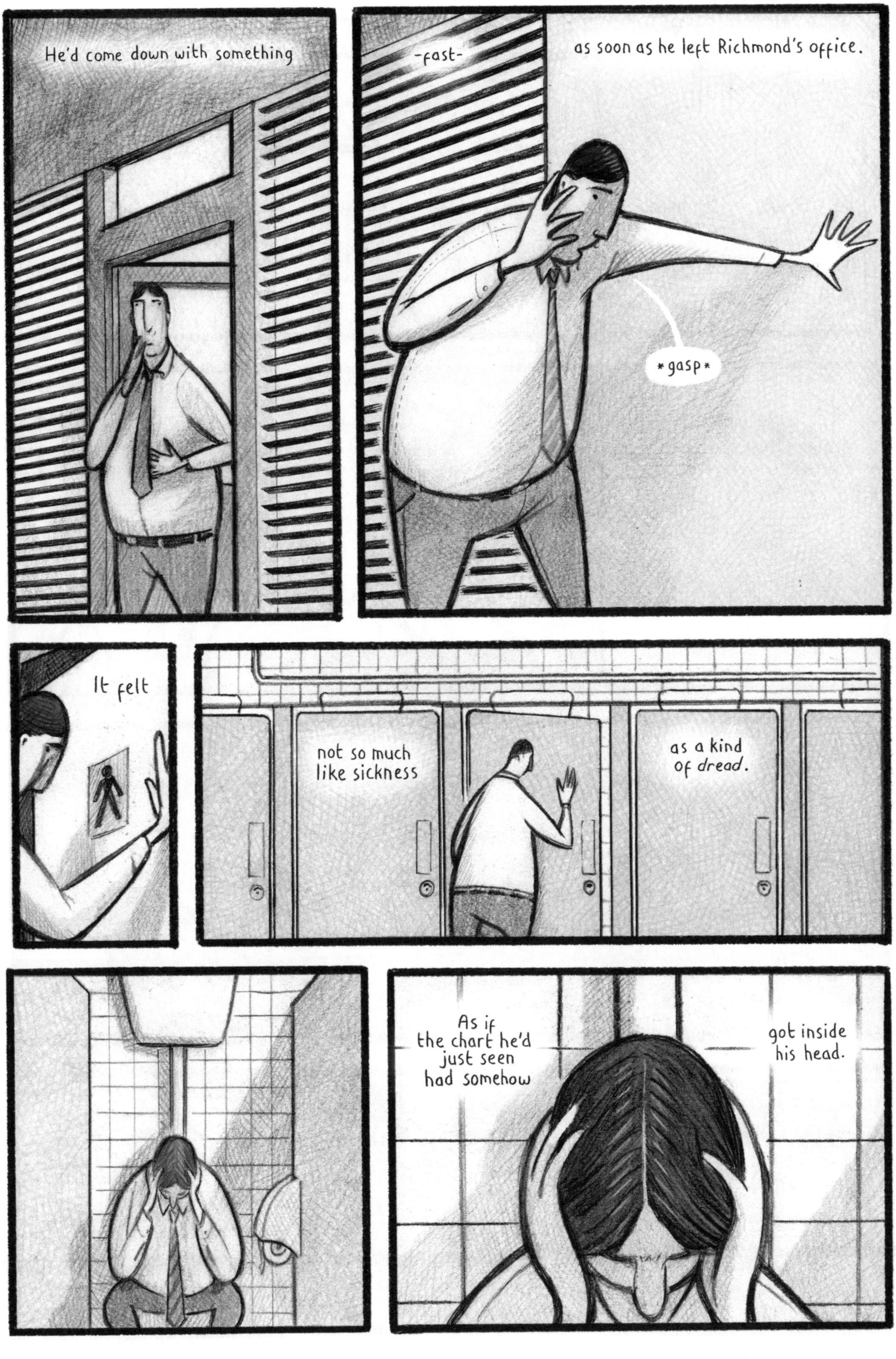
He'd come down with something
-fast-
as soon as he left Richmond's office.
gasp
It felt
not so much like sickness
as a kind of *dread*.
As if the chart he'd just seen had somehow
got inside his head.

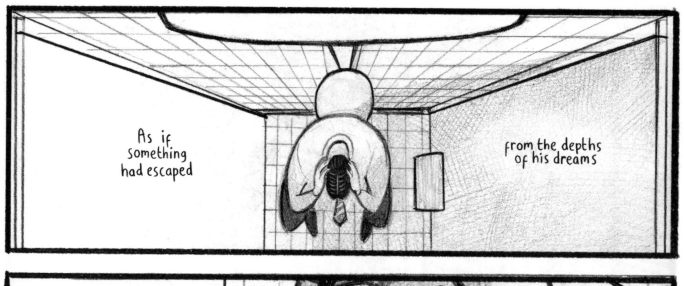

As if
something
had escaped

from the depths
of his dreams

to crawl up

into the day.

To bleed through
the seams.

Dave,
come **on!**

Outwardly, nothing seemed amiss.

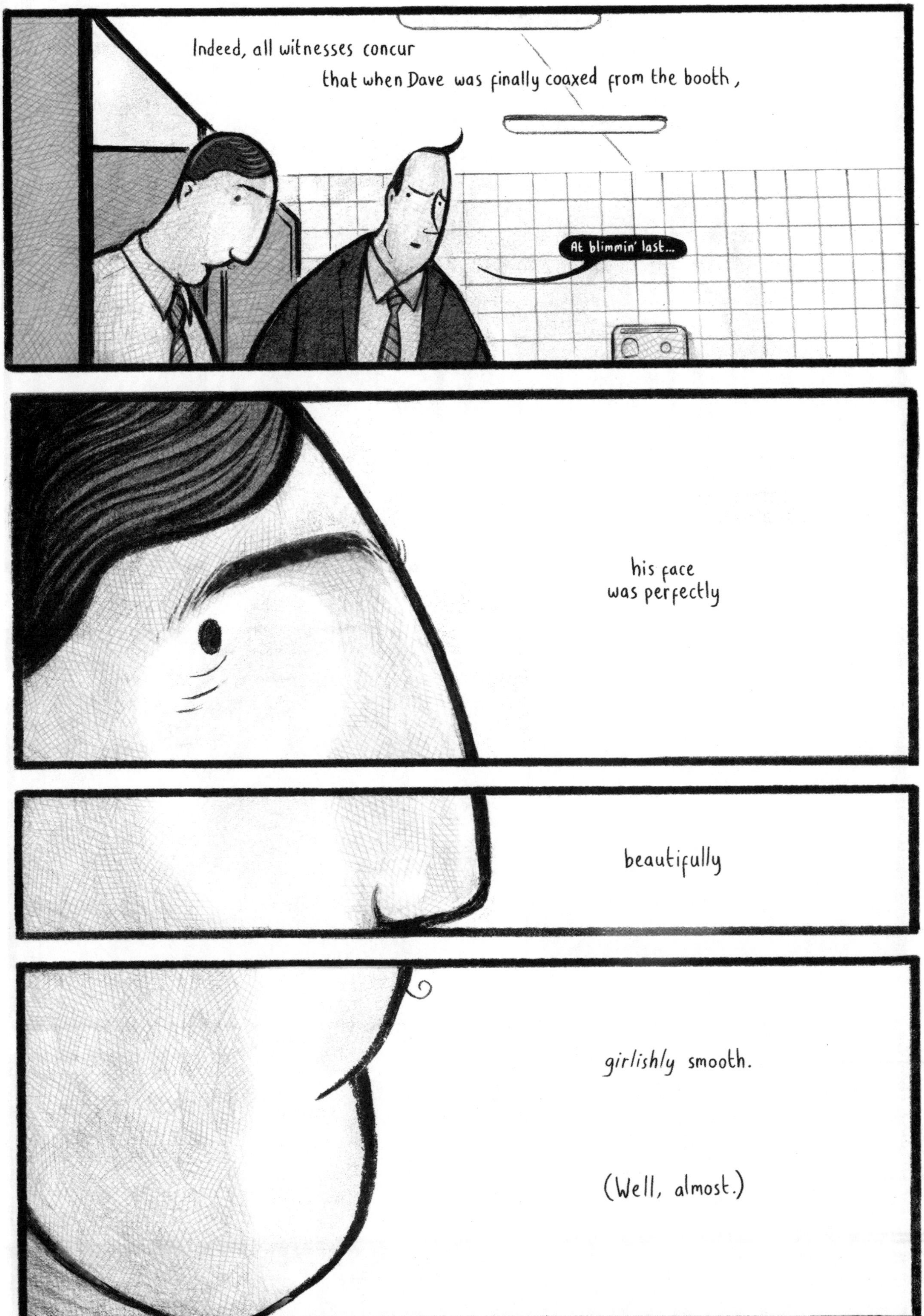
Indeed, all witnesses concur
that when Dave was finally coaxed from the booth,
At blimmin' last...
his face
was perfectly
beautifully
girlishly smooth.
(Well, almost.)

And if what happened during Dave's presentation that afternoon

was the sort of thing

that *stories* are made of...

Hello Ladies,

gentle-men...

If it were possible

to connect

this to that

that to this

and somehow show

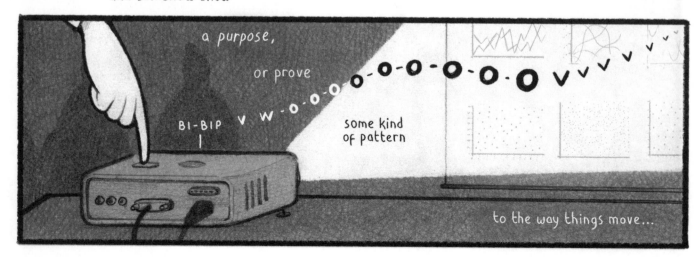
a *purpose,*

or prove

some kind of pattern

BI-BIP

to the way things move...

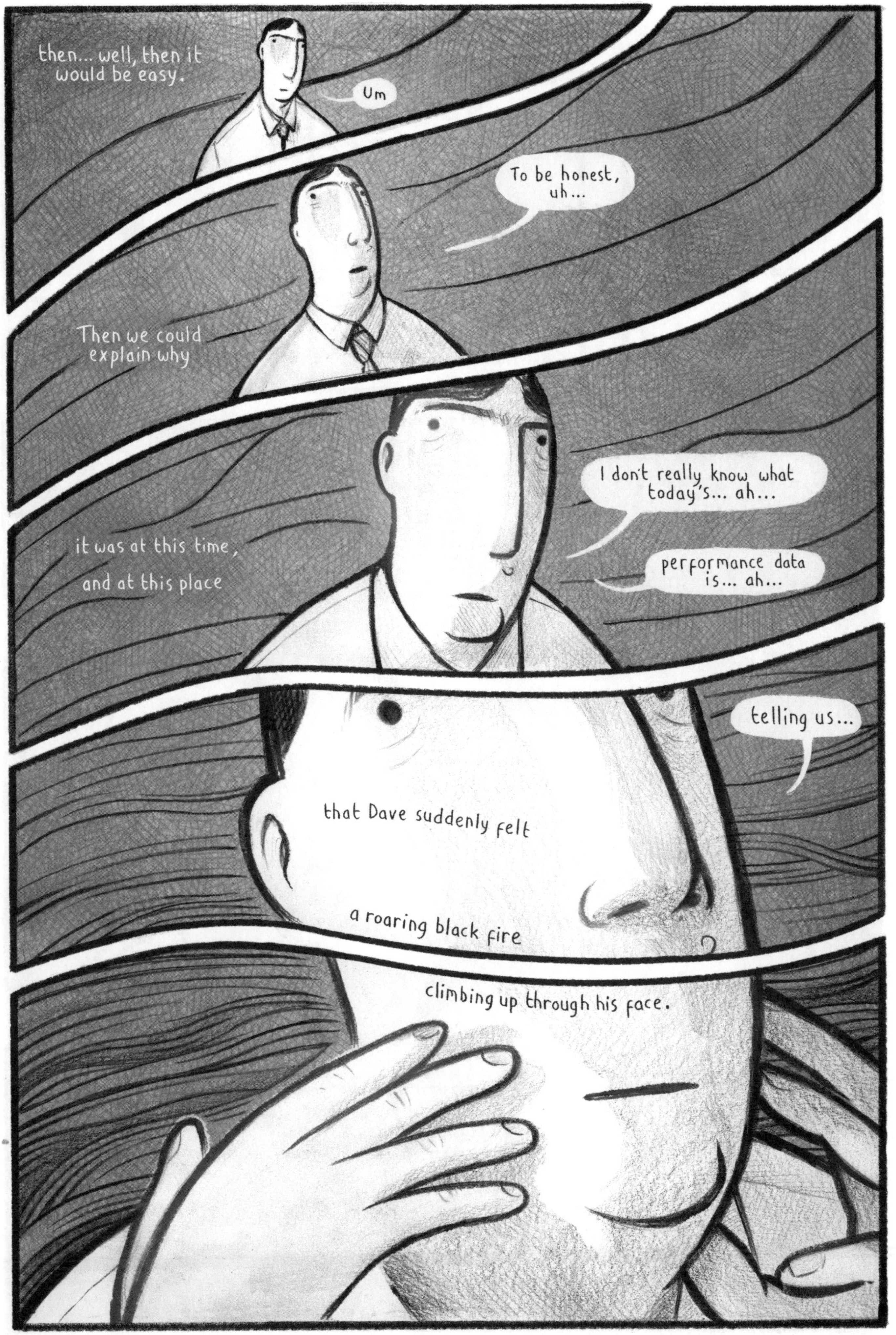
then... well, then it would be easy.
Um
To be honest, uh...
Then we could explain why
I don't really know what today's... ah...
it was at this time,
and at this place
performance data is... ah...
telling us...
that Dave suddenly felt
a roaring black fire
climbing up through his face.

But the problem is,

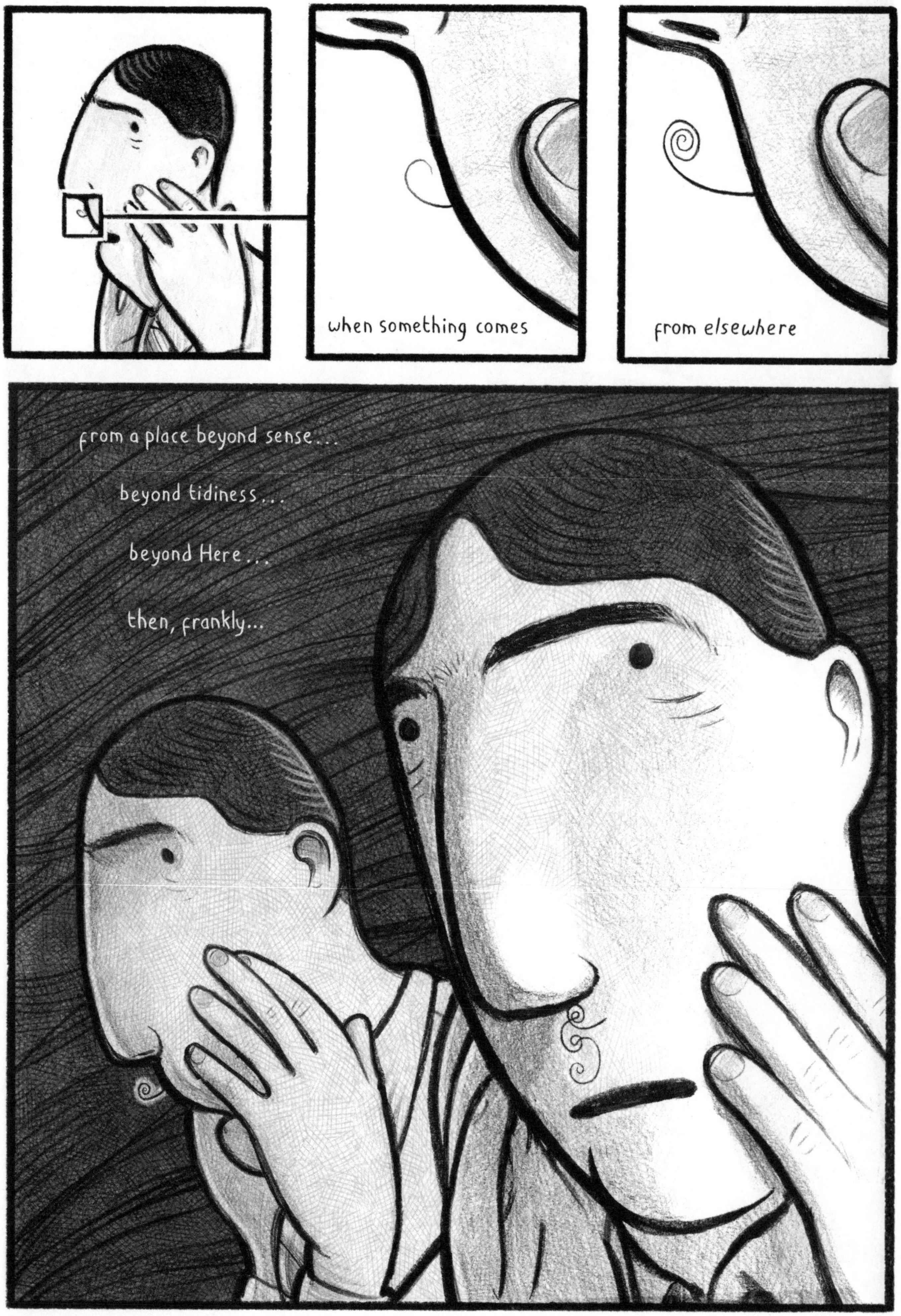
when something comes
from elsewhere
from a place beyond sense...
beyond tidiness...
beyond Here...
then, frankly...

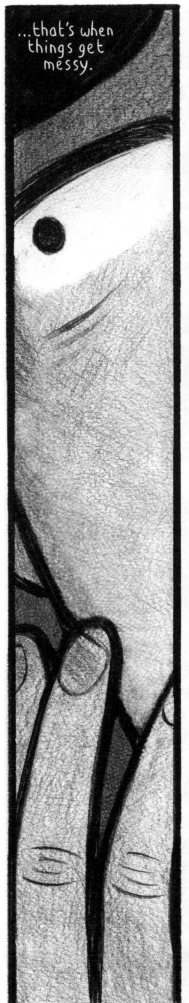

...that's when things get messy.

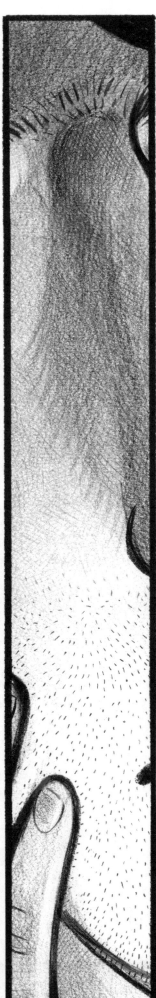

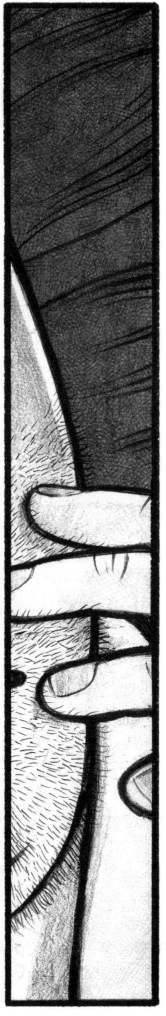

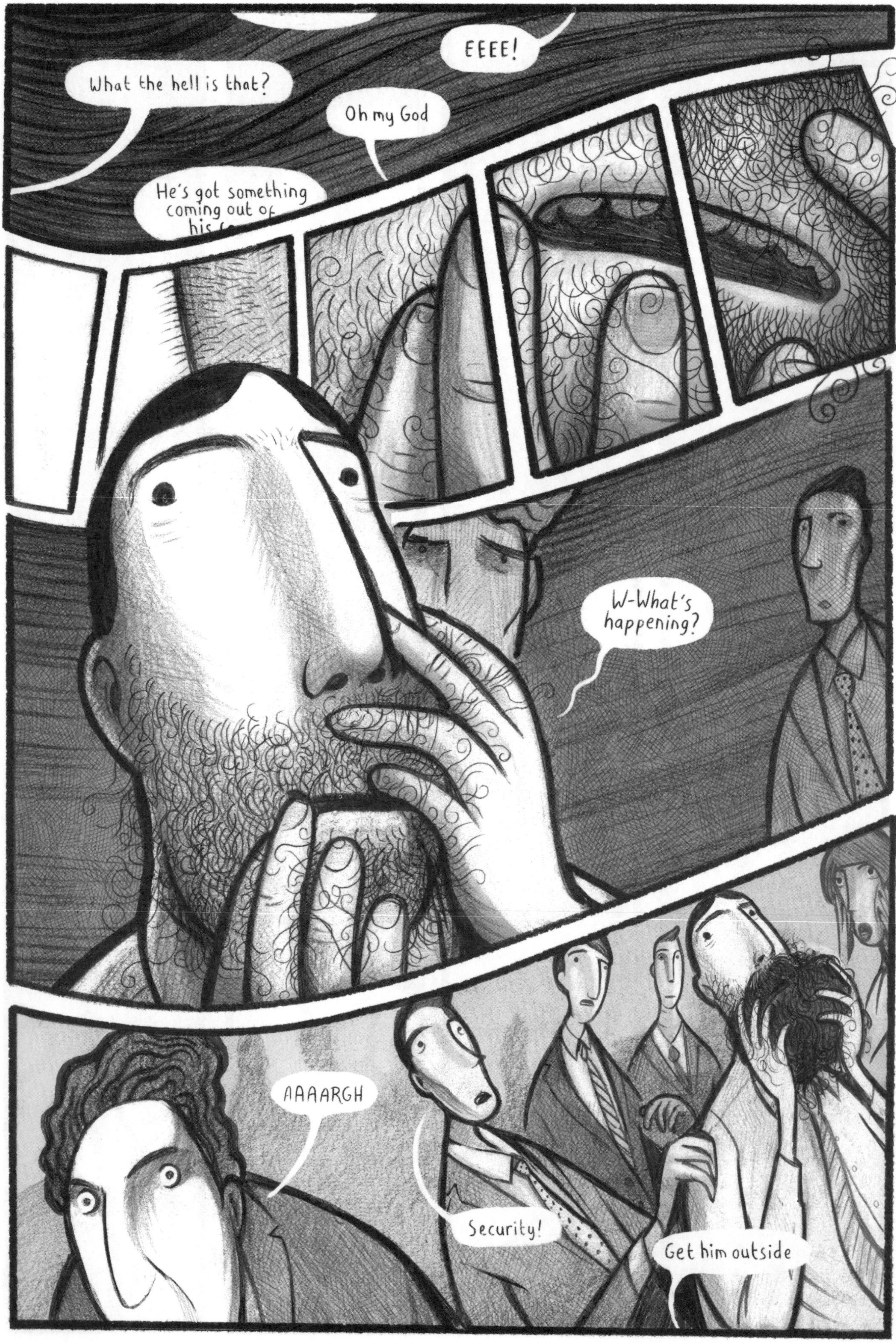
EEEE!
What the hell is that?
Oh my God
He's got something coming out of his
W-What's happening?
AAAARGH
Security!
Get him outside

And it would have been nice, looking back, to have carried on thinking

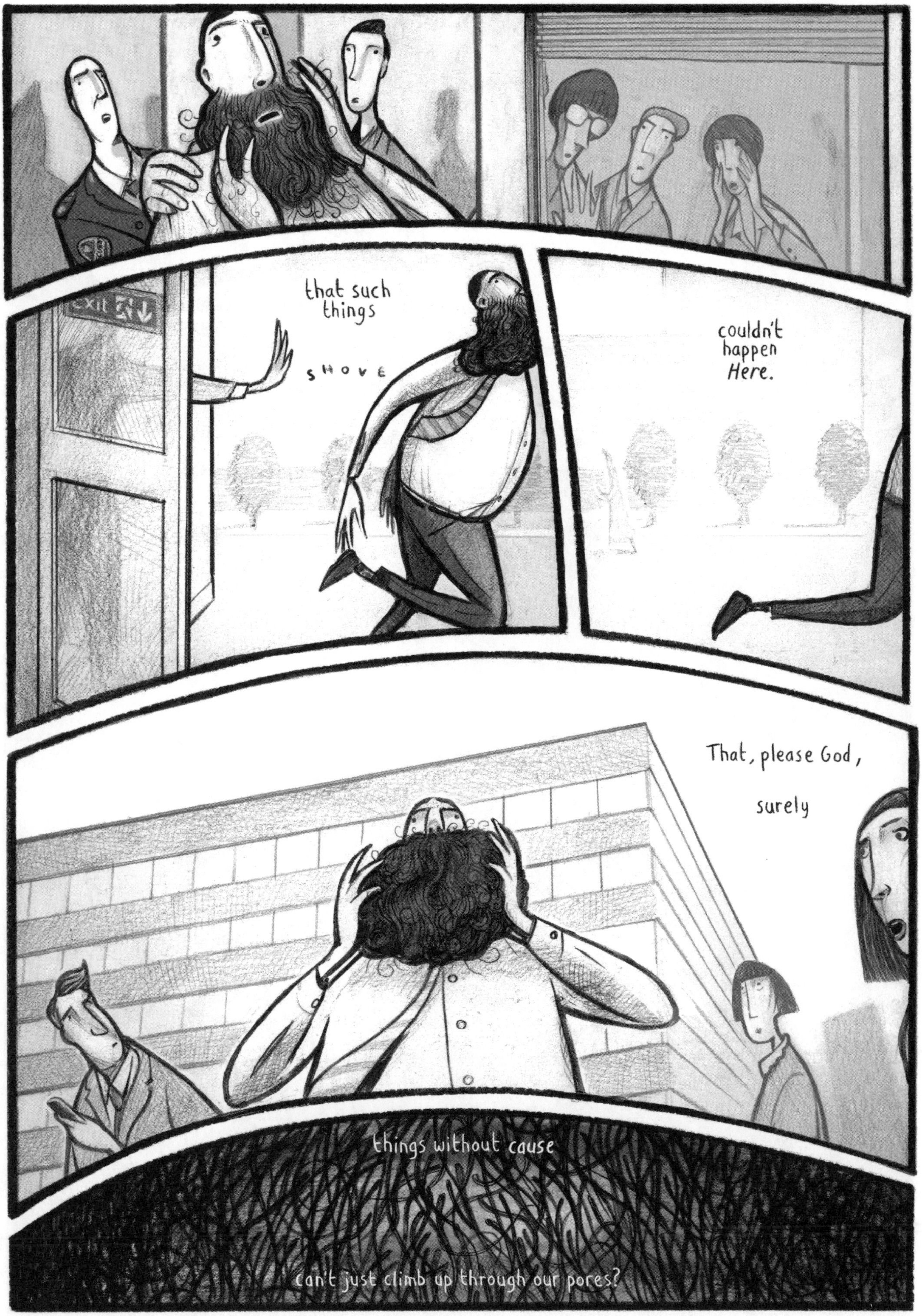
exit
that such things
SHOVE
couldn't happen Here.
That, please God,
surely
things without cause
can't just climb up through our pores?

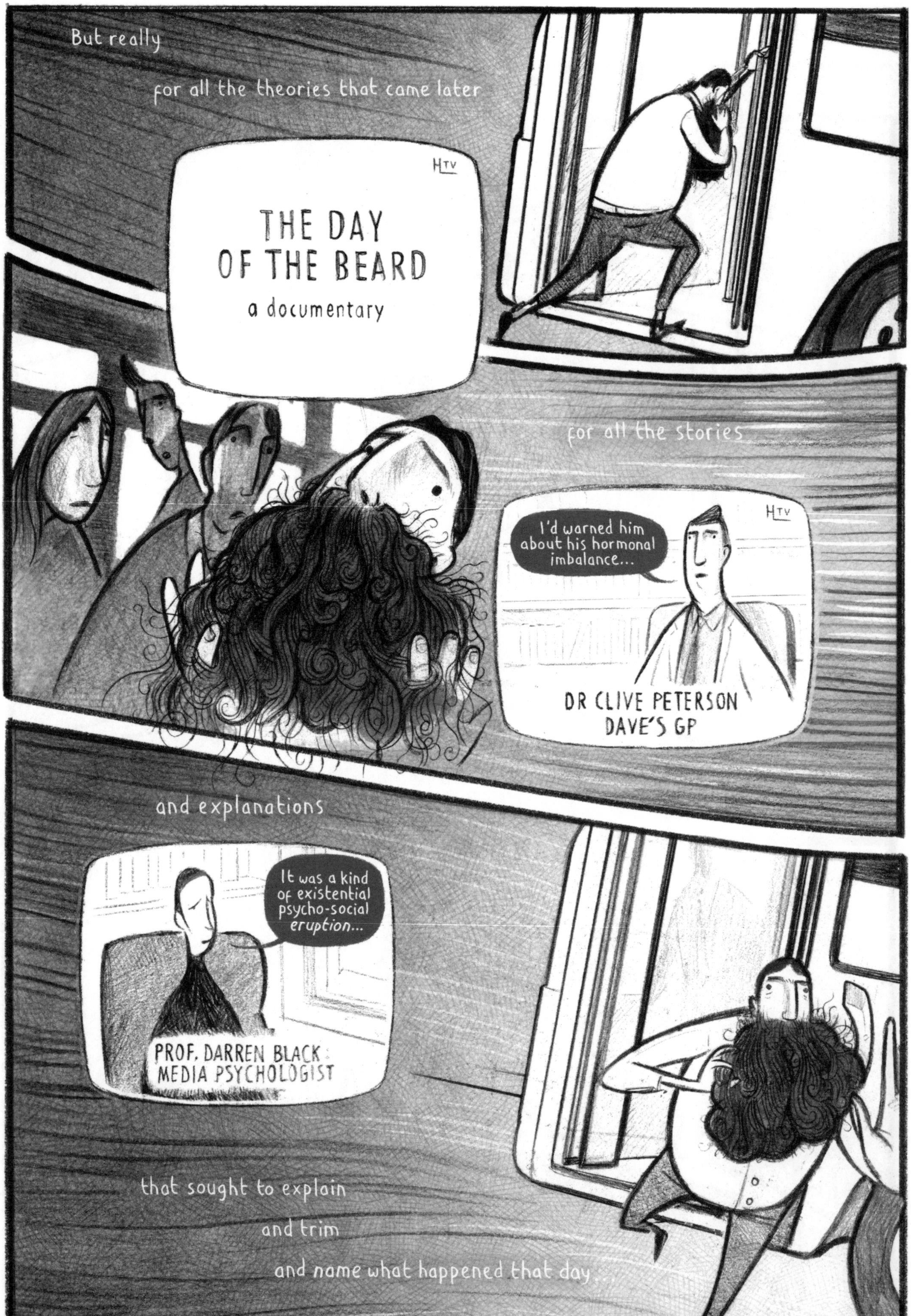

But really
for all the theories that came later
HTV
THE DAY OF THE BEARD
a documentary
for all the stories
HTV
I'd warned him about his hormonal imbalance...
DR CLIVE PETERSON
DAVE'S GP
and explanations
It was a kind of existential psycho-social eruption...
PROF. DARREN BLACK:
MEDIA PSYCHOLOGIST
that sought to explain
and trim
and name what happened that day...

there really is, in the end,
only one thing that can truthfully be said:

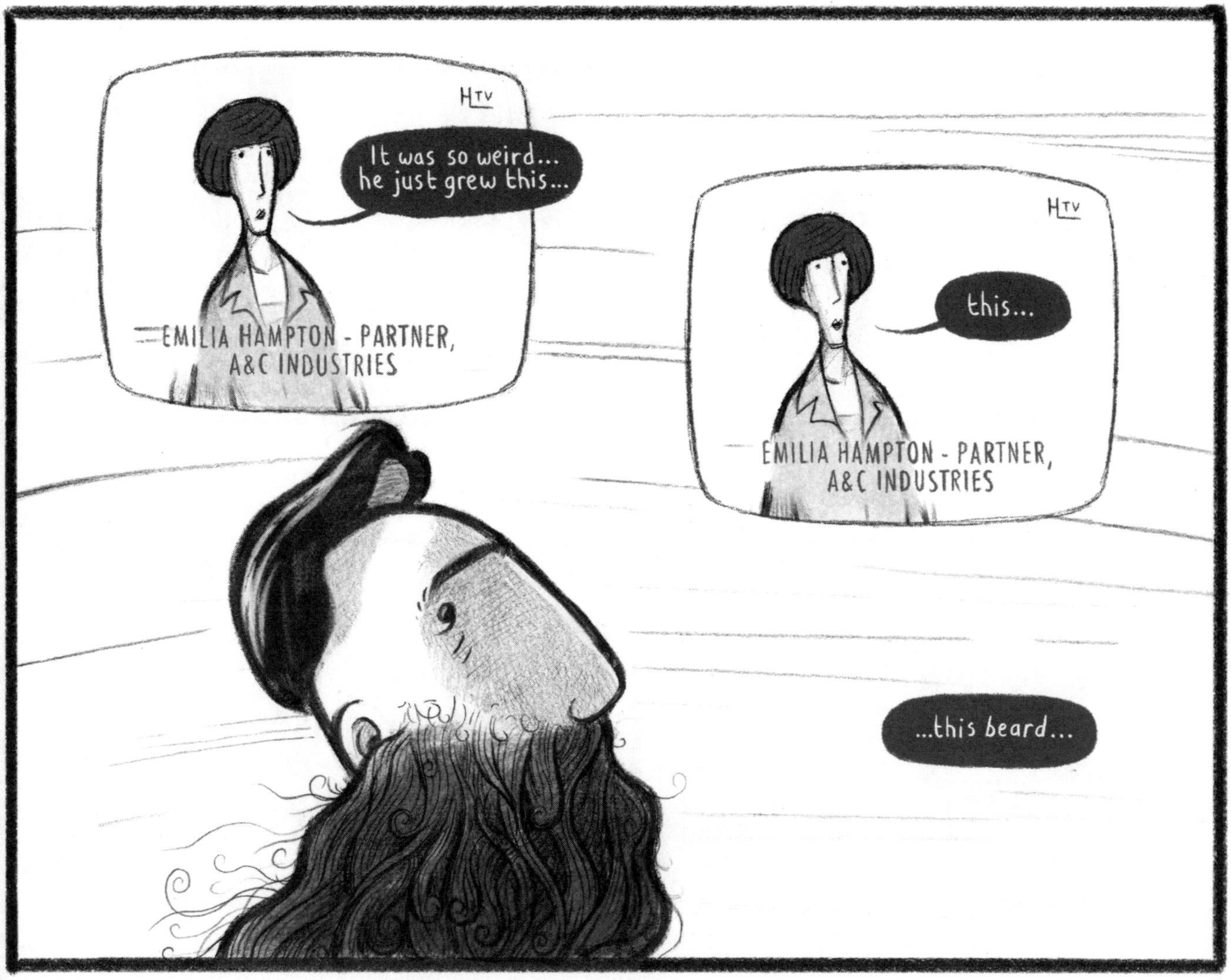
HTV
It was so weird... he just grew this...
EMILIA HAMPTON - PARTNER, A&C INDUSTRIES
HTV
this...
EMILIA HAMPTON - PARTNER, A&C INDUSTRIES
...this beard...

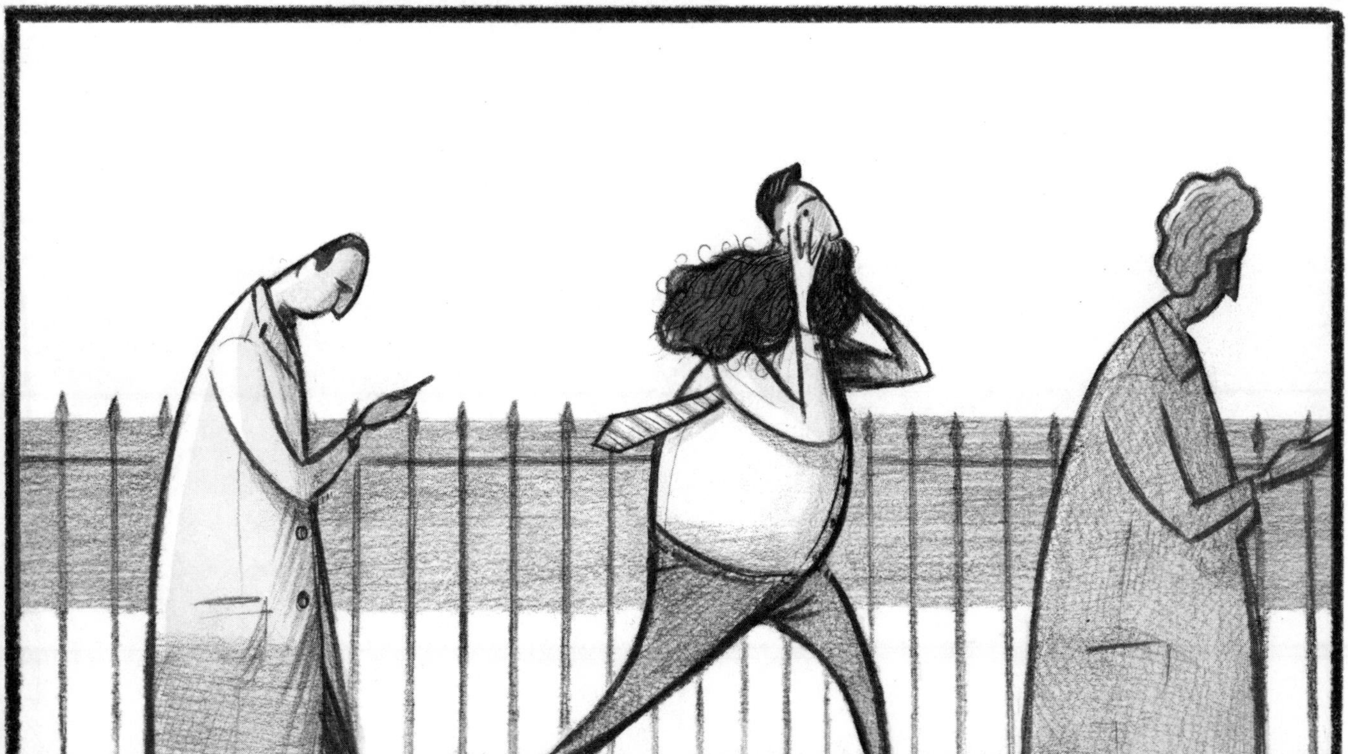

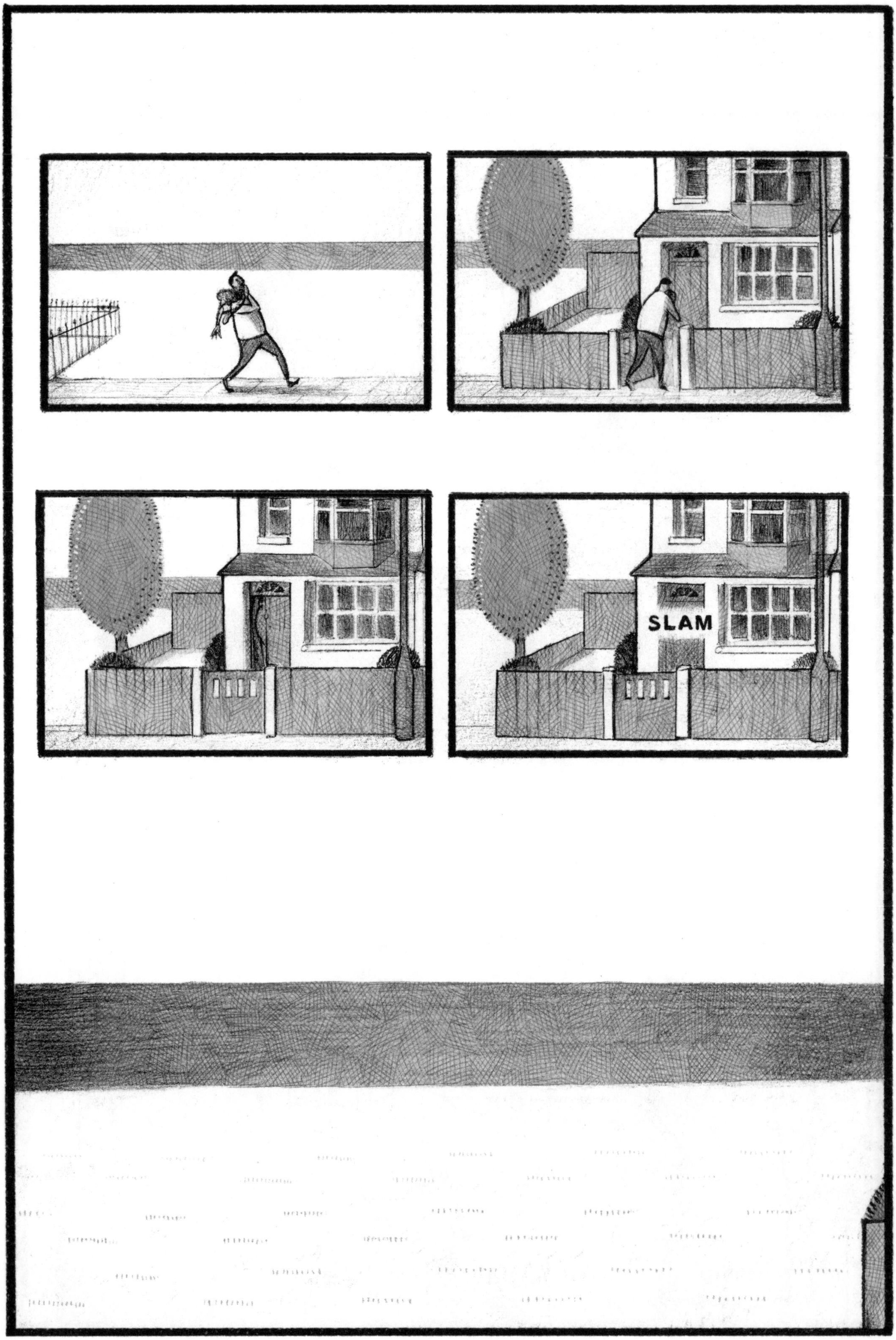
SLAM

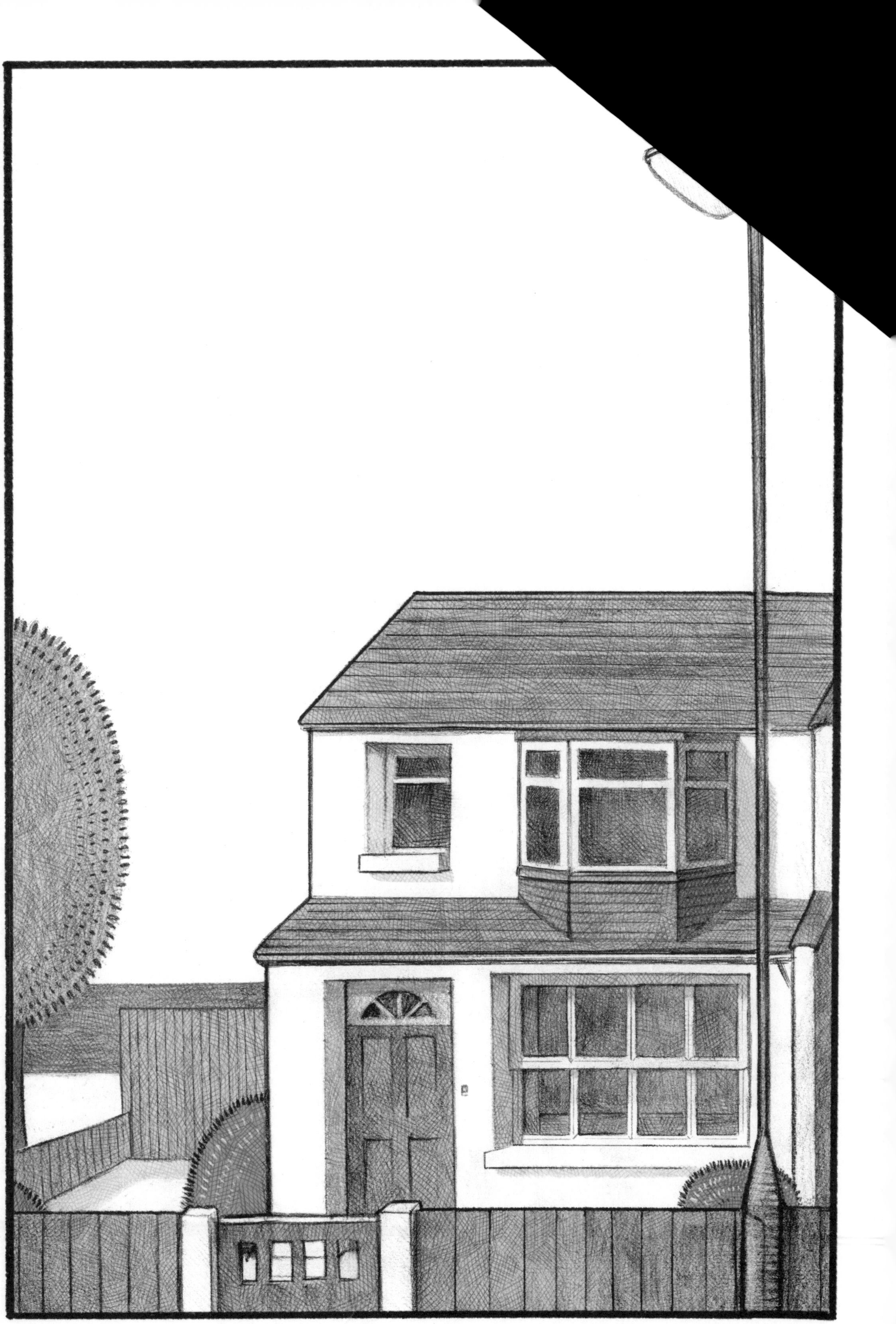

3.

THE BEARD

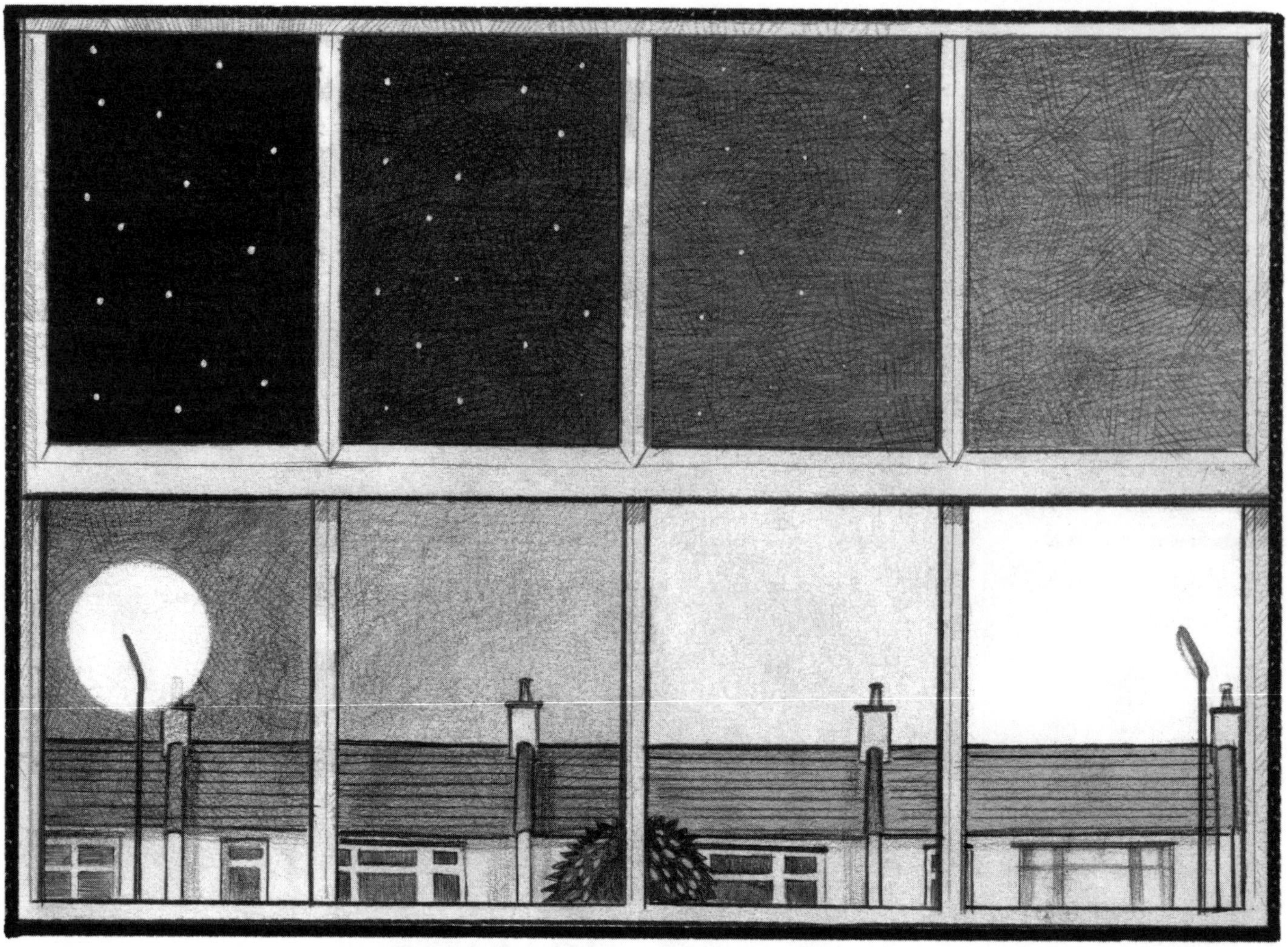

All night
long, Dave

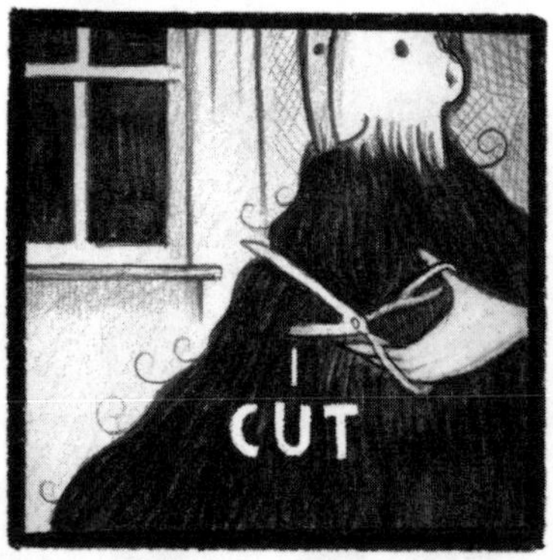
CUT

and

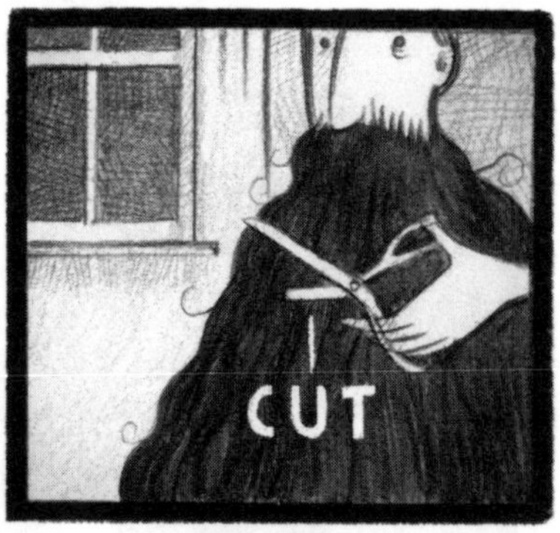
CUT

and

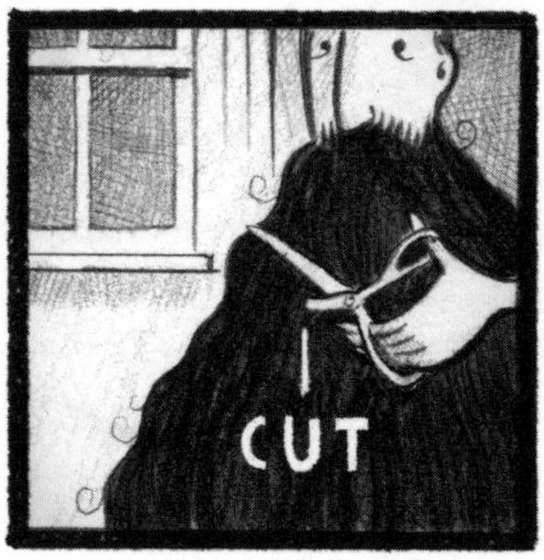
CUT

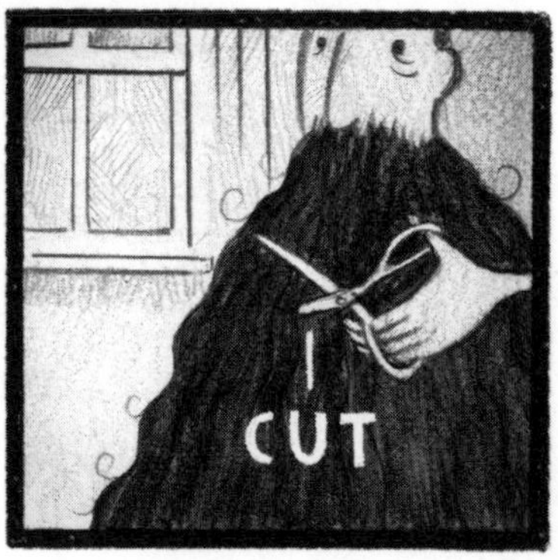
CUT

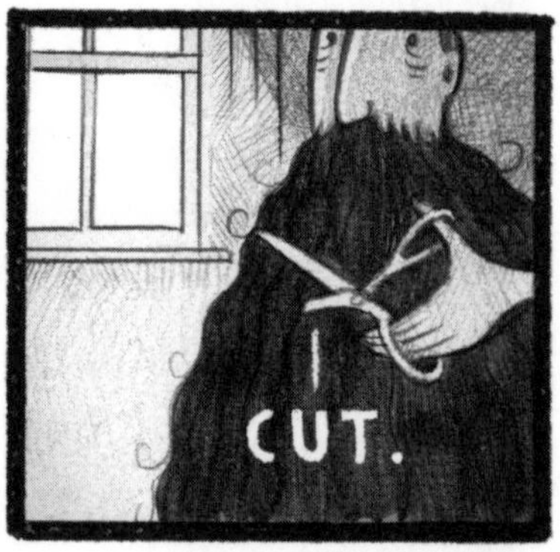
CUT.

Until, in the morning,

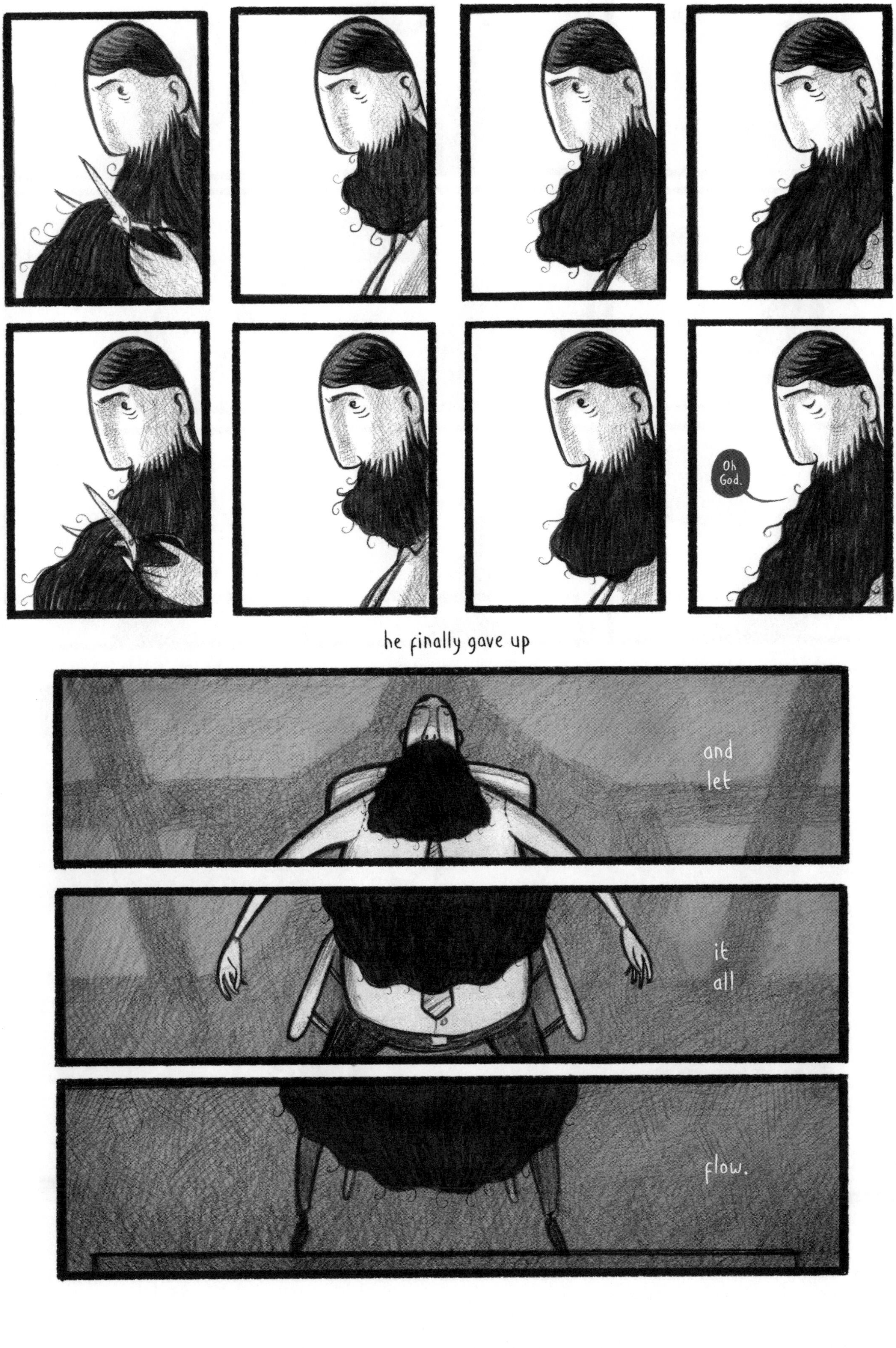
Oh God.
he finally gave up
and let
it all
flow.

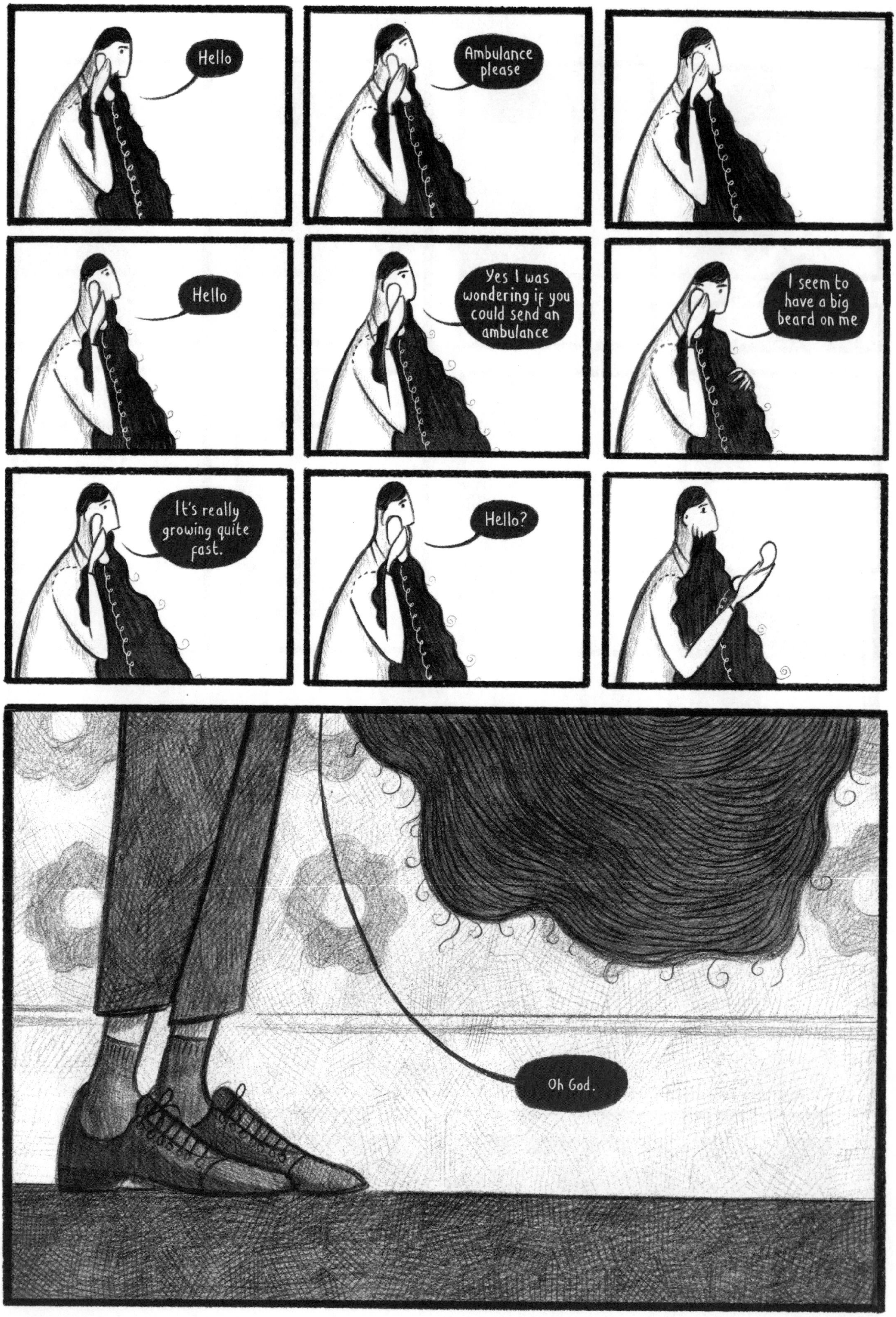
Hello
Ambulance please
Hello
Yes I was wondering if you could send an ambulance
I seem to have a big beard on me
It's really growing quite fast.
Hello?
Oh God.

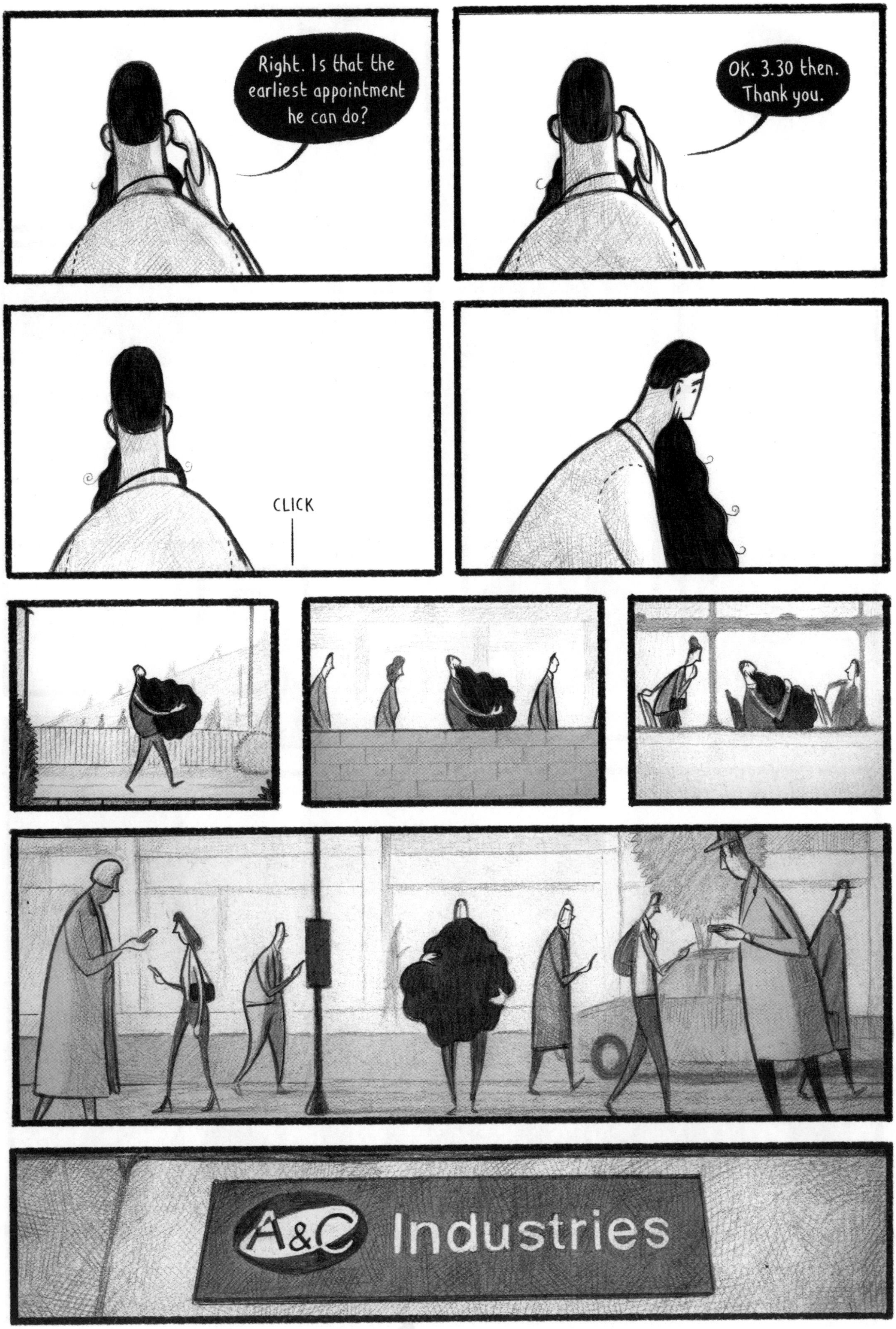
Right. Is that the earliest appointment he can do?
OK. 3.30 then. Thank you.
CLICK
A&C Industries

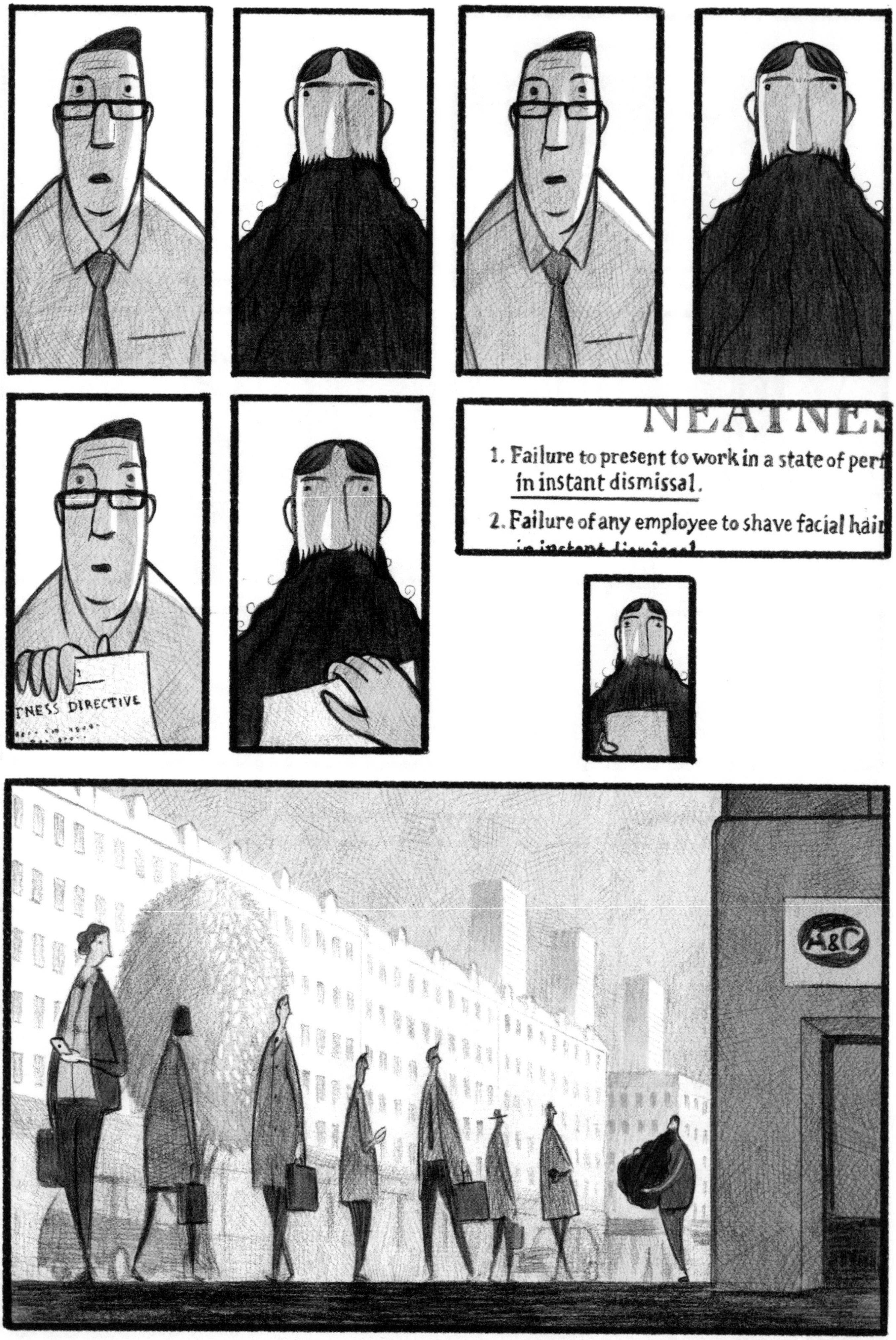
NEATNES
1. Failure to present to work in a state of perf
in instant dismissal.
2. Failure of any employee to shave facial hai
TNESS DIRECTIVE
A&C

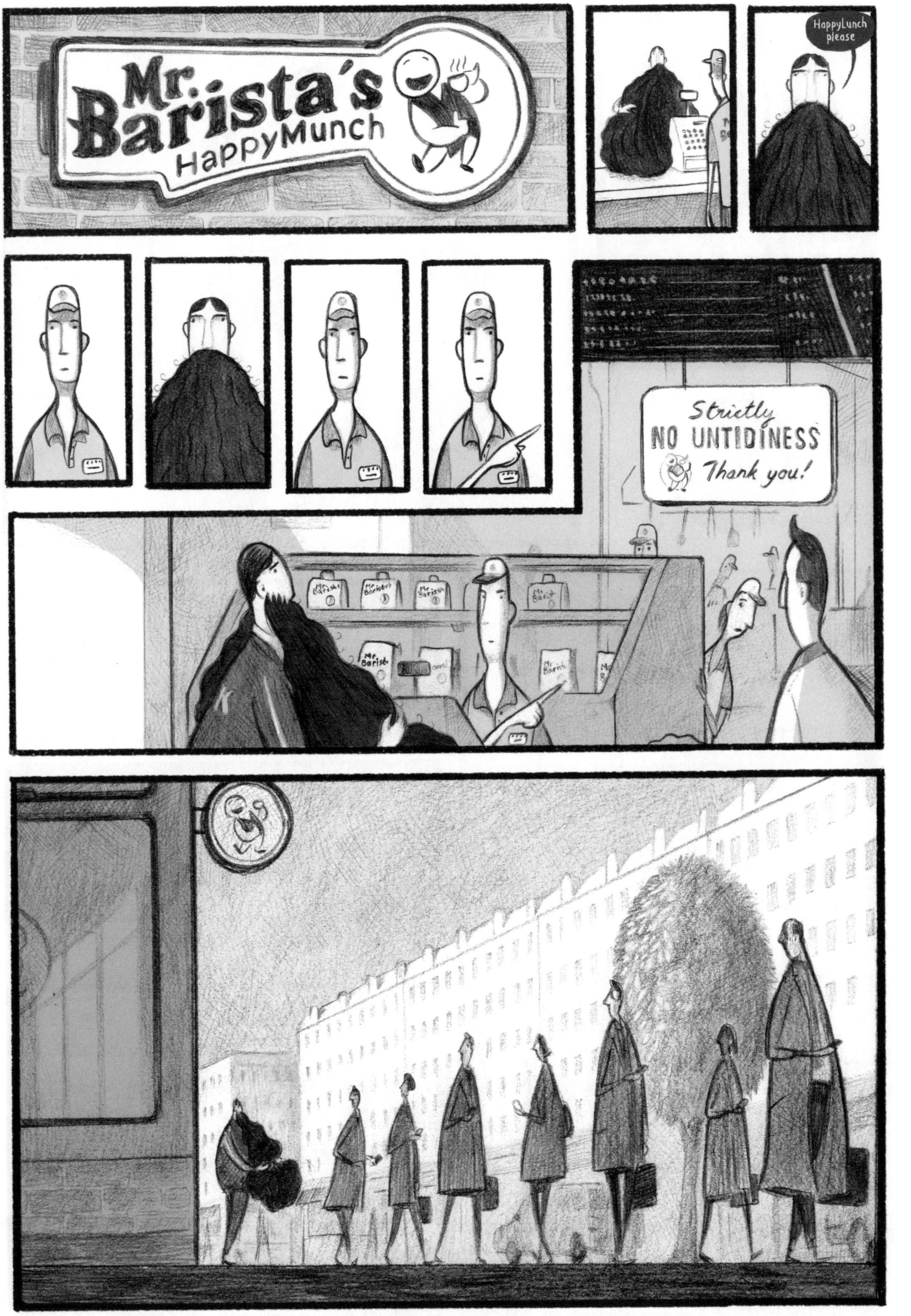
Mr. Barista's
HappyMunch
HappyLunch please
Strictly
NO UNTIDINESS
Thank you!

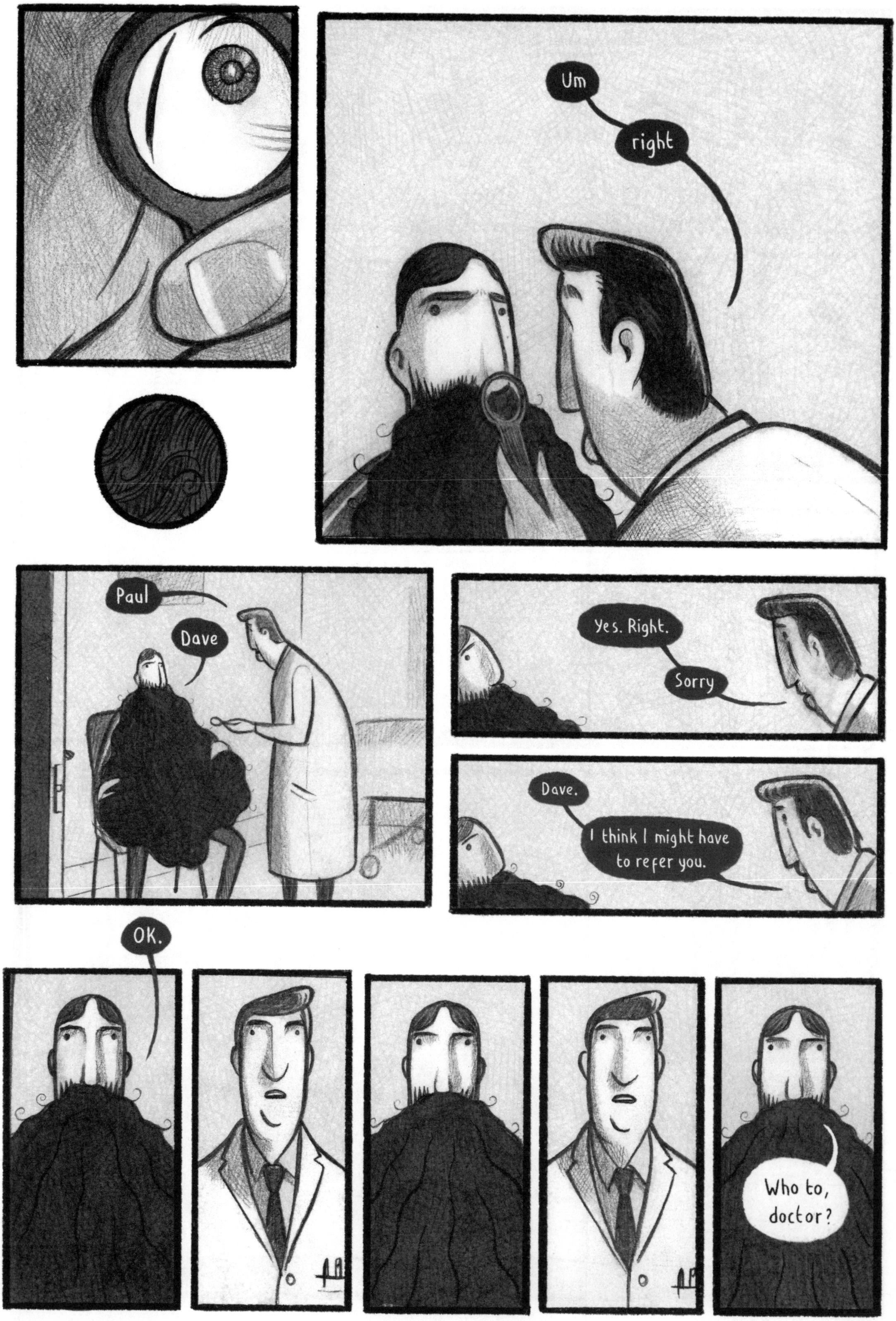
Um
right
Paul
Dave
Yes. Right.
Sorry
Dave.
I think I might have to refer you.
OK.
Who to, doctor?

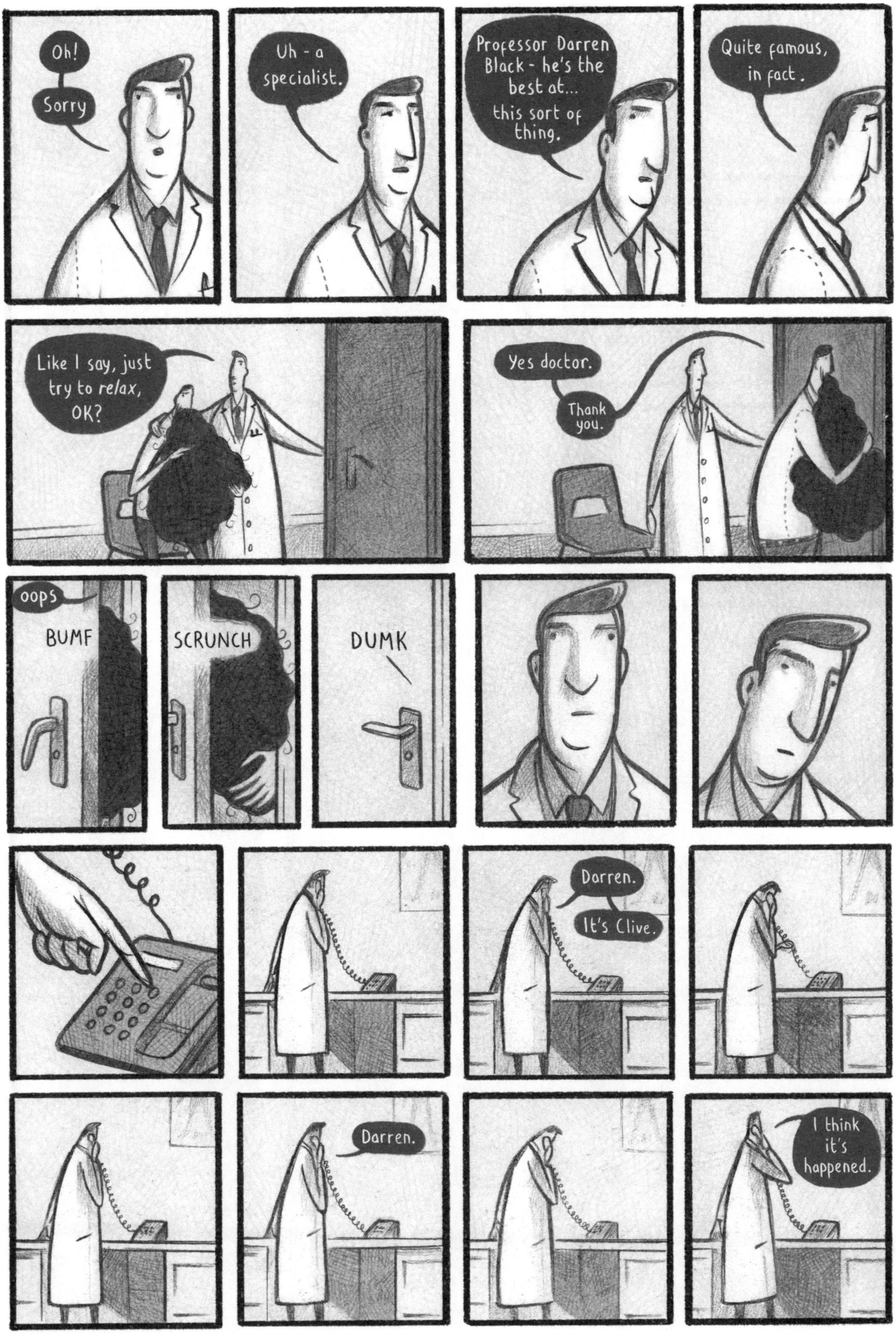
Oh!
Sorry
Uh - a specialist.
Professor Darren Black - he's the best at... this sort of thing.
Quite famous, in fact.
Like I say, just try to relax, OK?
Yes doctor.
Thank you.
oops
BUMF
SCRUNCH
DUMK
Darren.
It's Clive.
Darren.
I think it's happened.

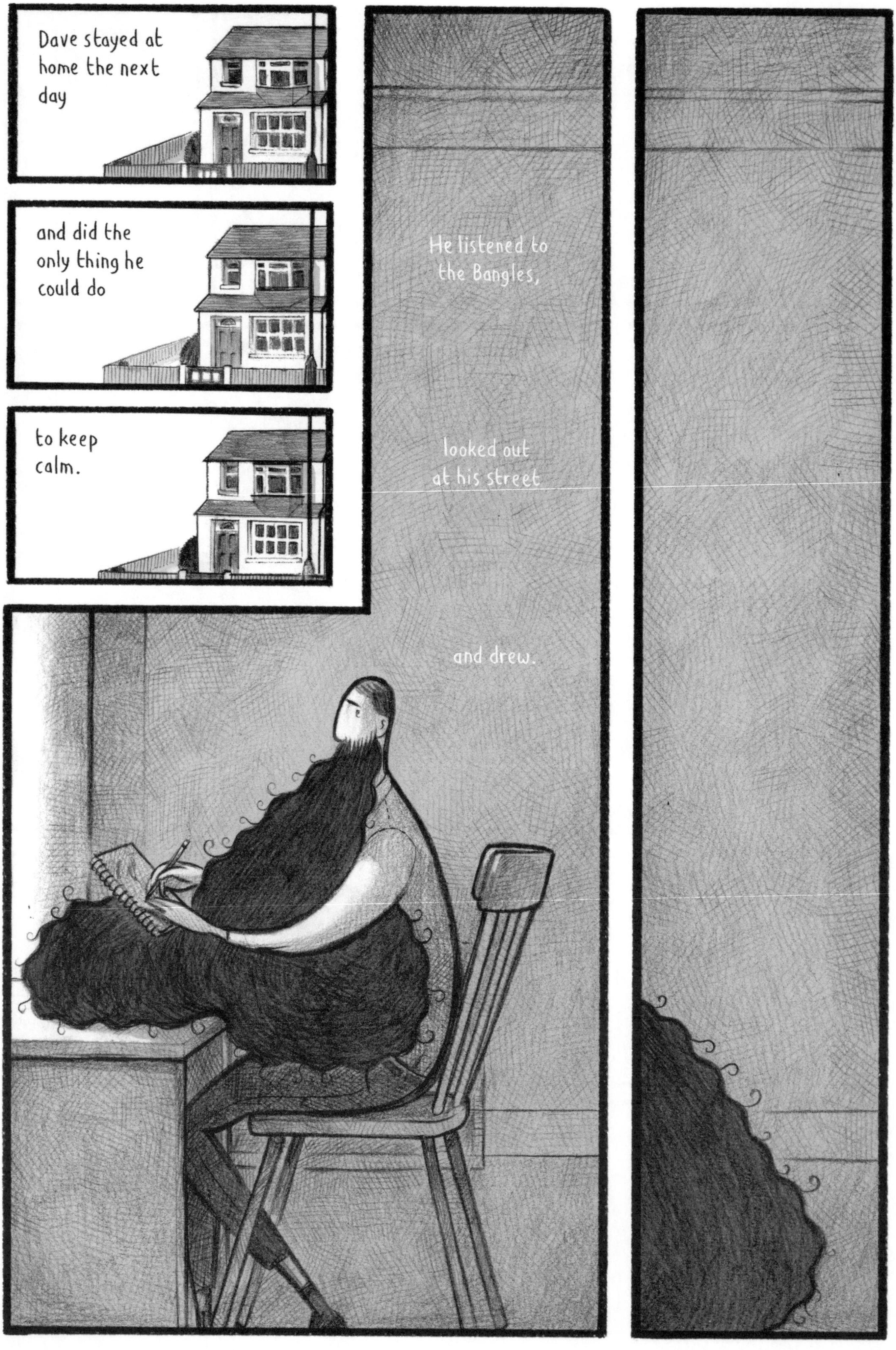
Dave stayed at home the next day
and did the only thing he could do
to keep calm.
He listened to the Bangles,
looked out at his street
and drew.

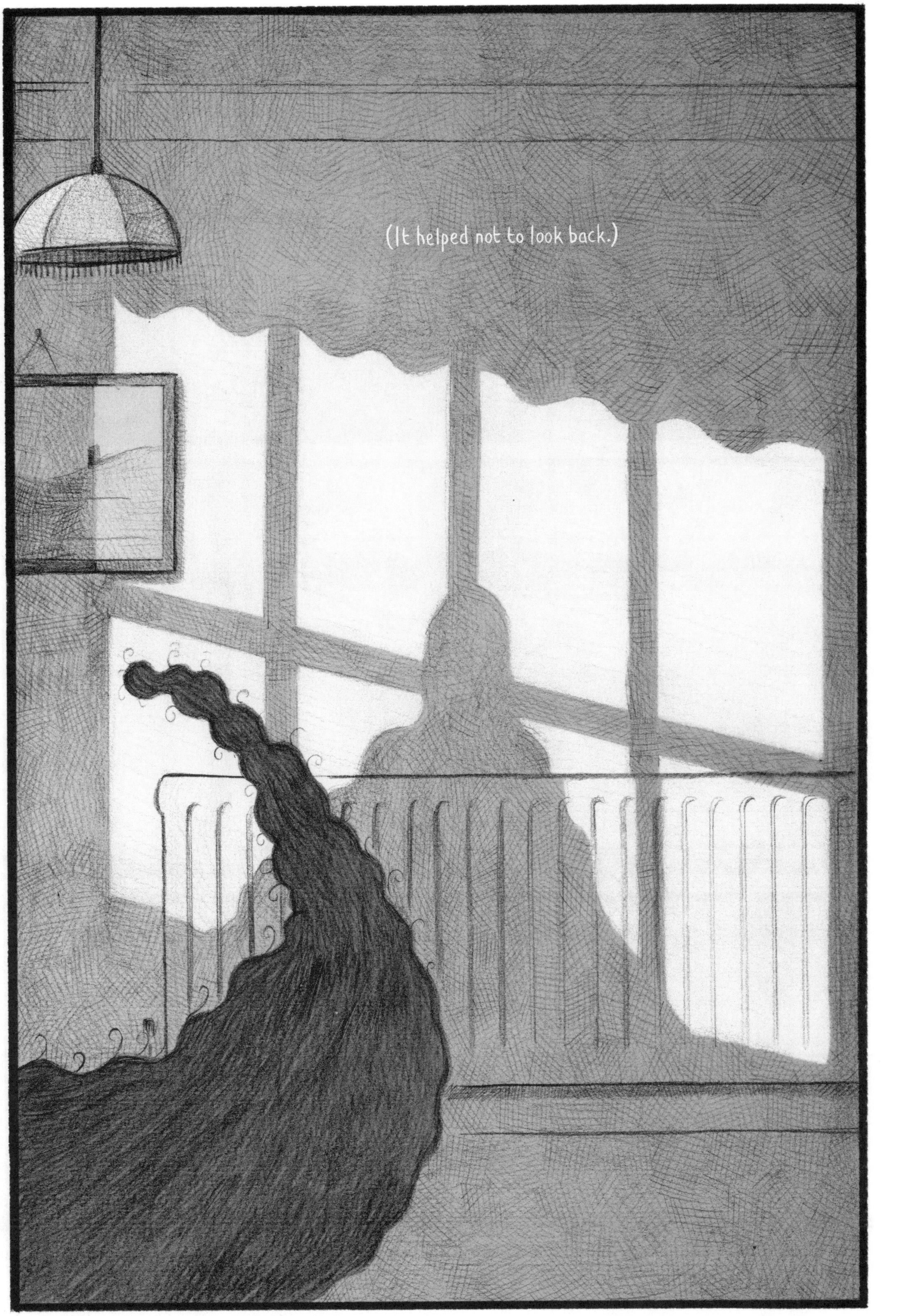
(It helped not to look back.)

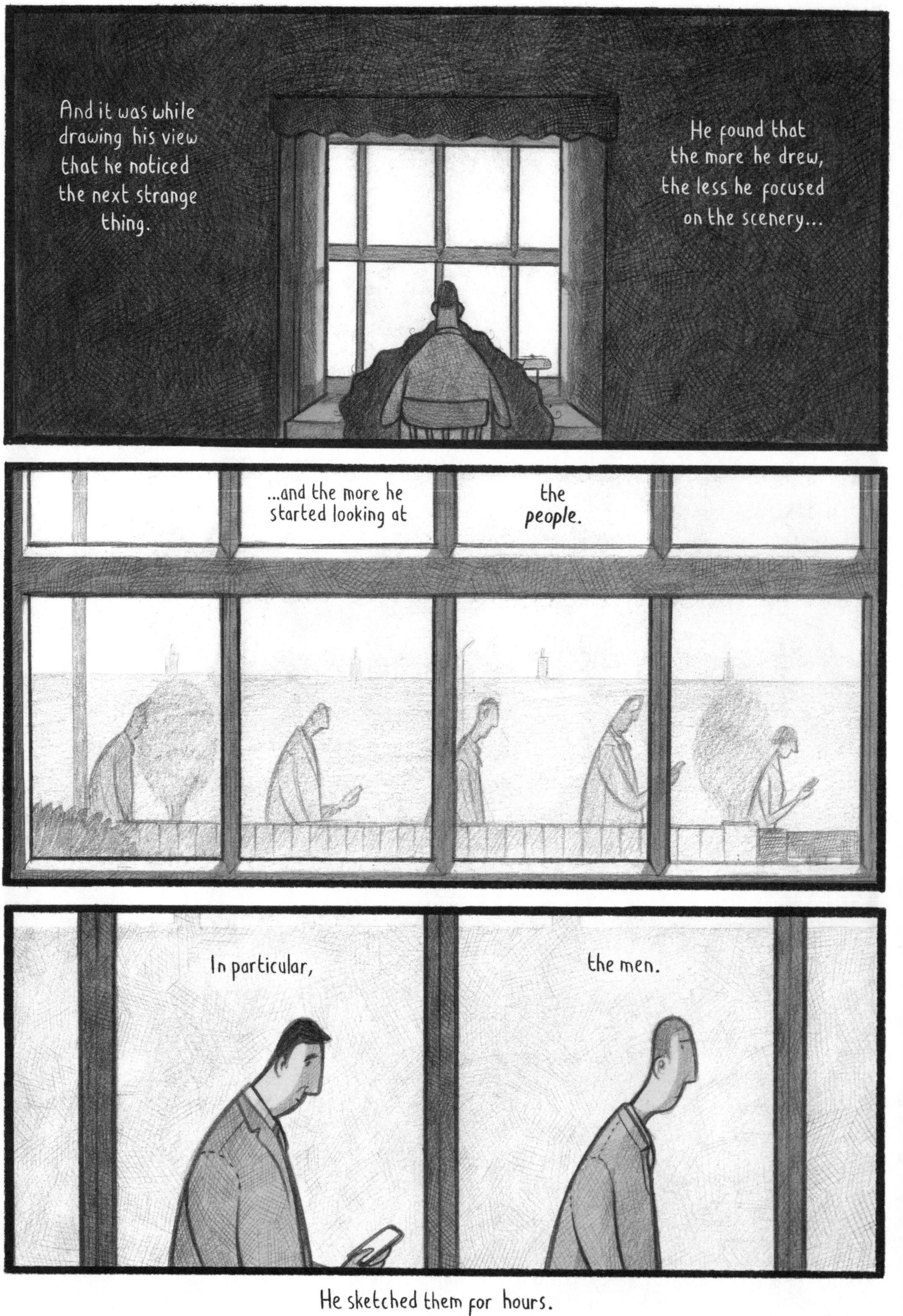
And it was while drawing his view that he noticed the next strange thing.
He found that the more he drew, the less he focused on the scenery...
...and the more he started looking at
the *people*.
In particular,
the men.

He sketched them for hours.

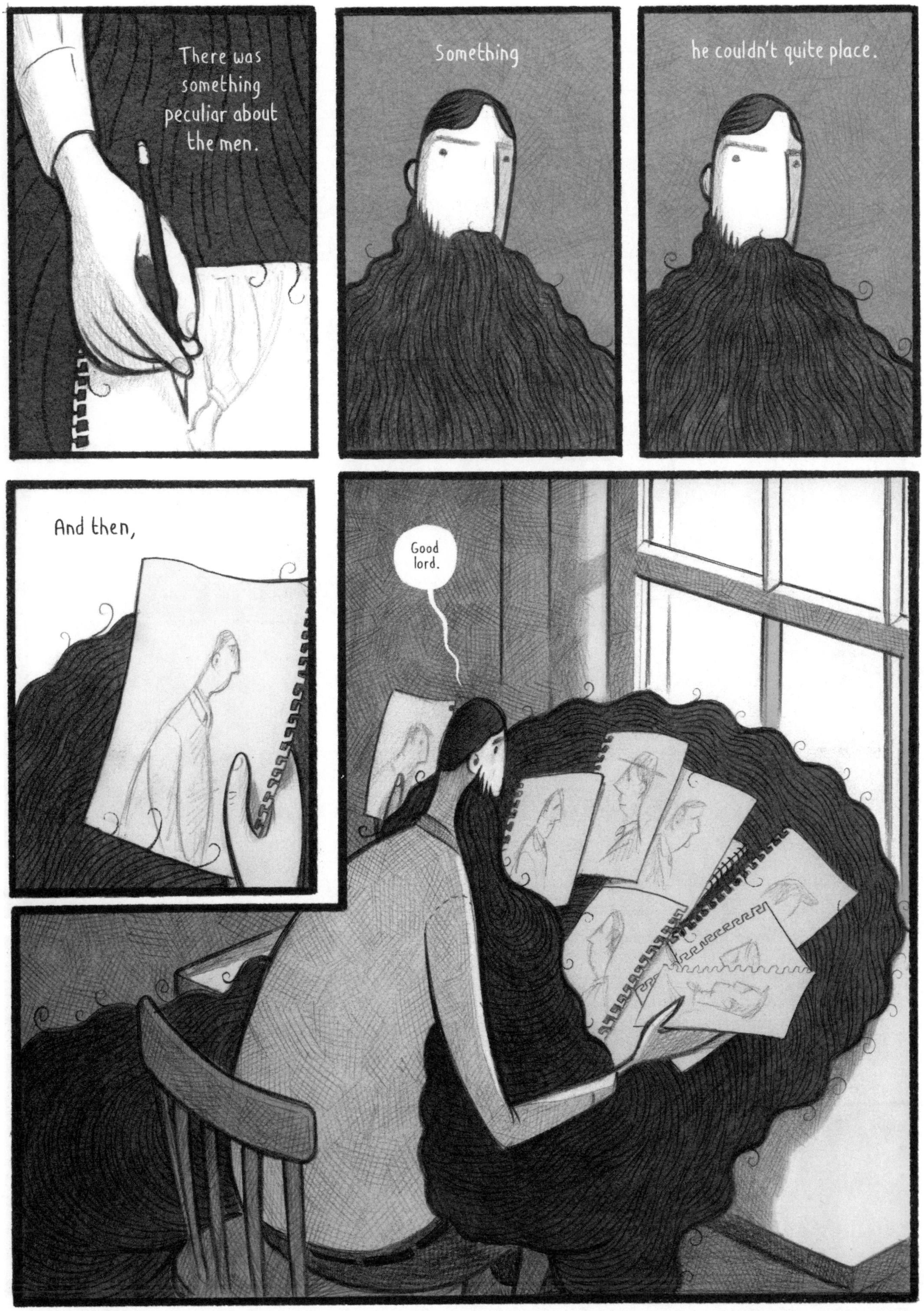
There was something peculiar about the men.
Something
he couldn't quite place.
And then,
Good lord.
he saw what it was.

He saw

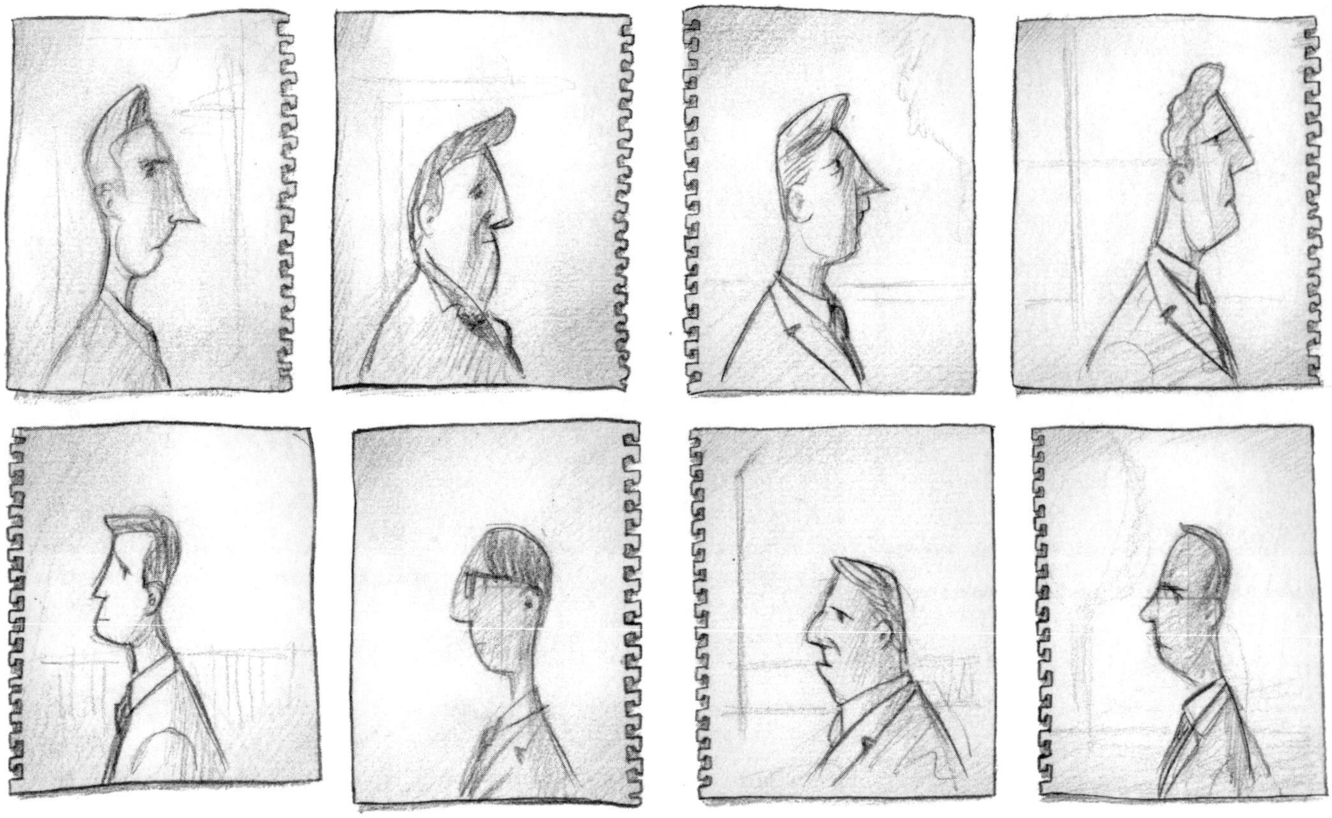

what had been under his nose all along.

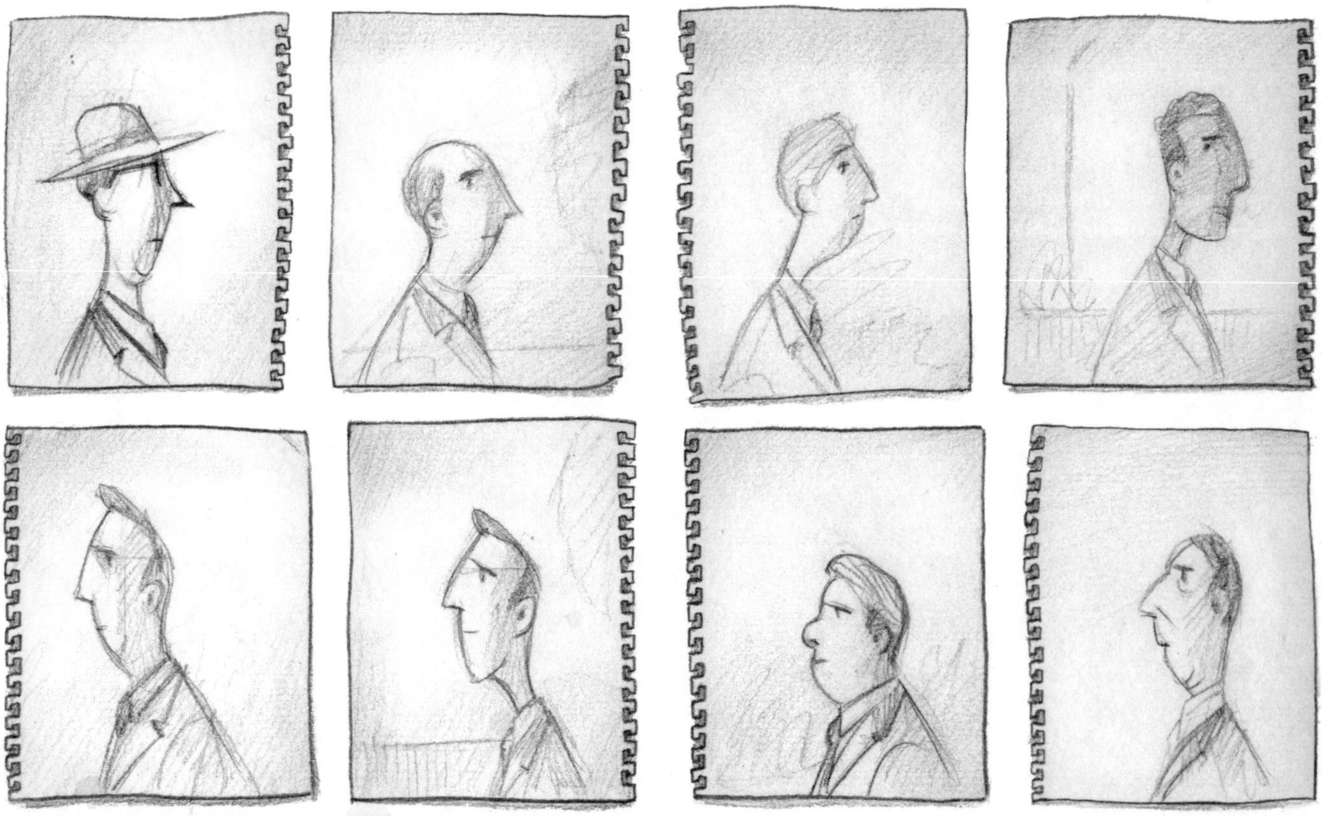

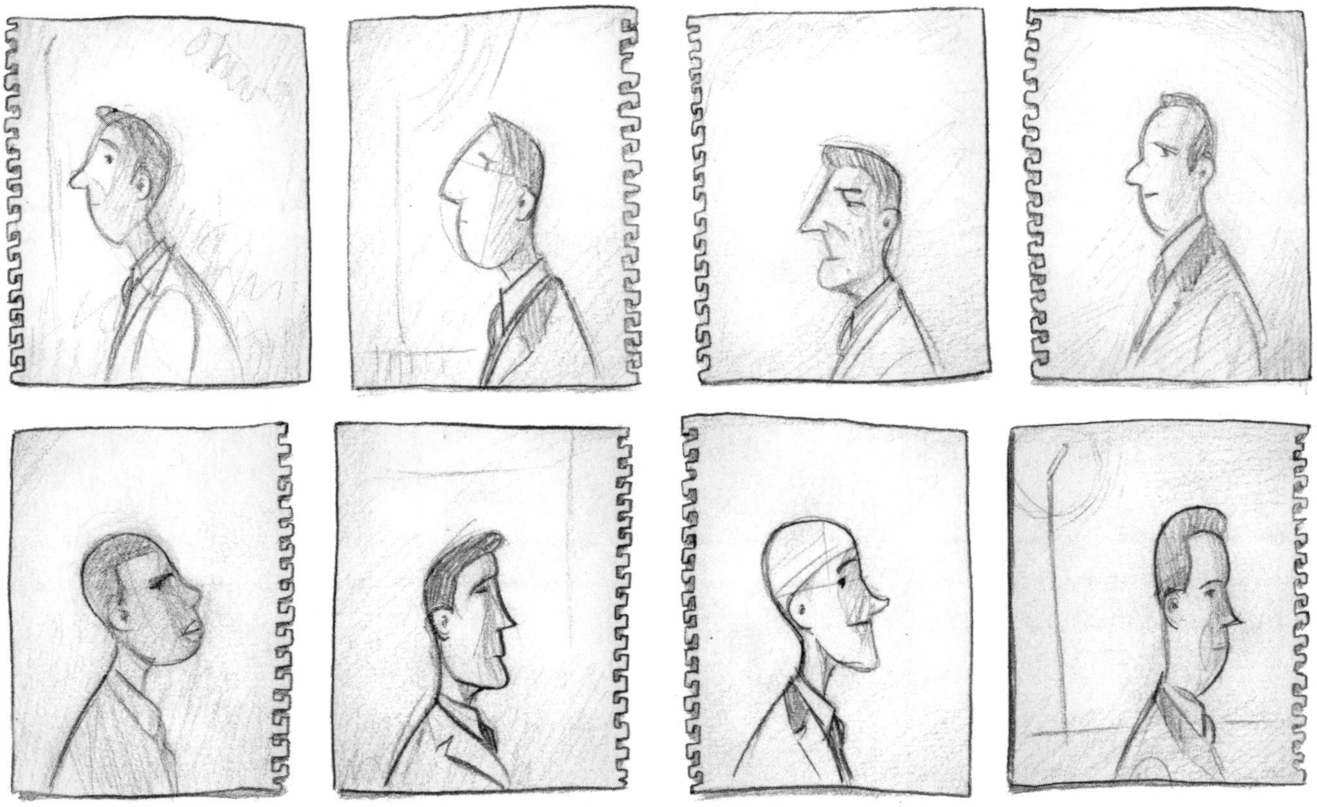

(Or, indeed, what hadn't.)

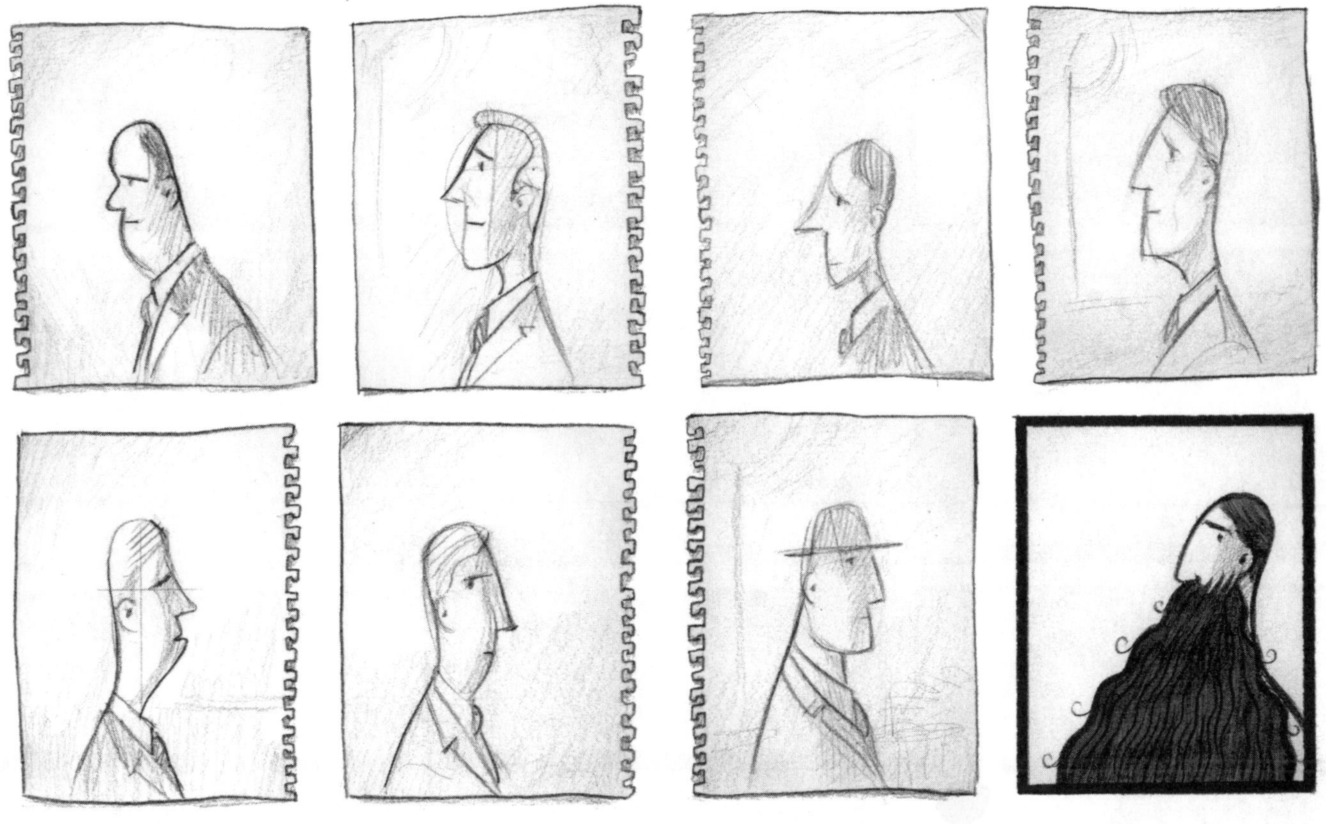

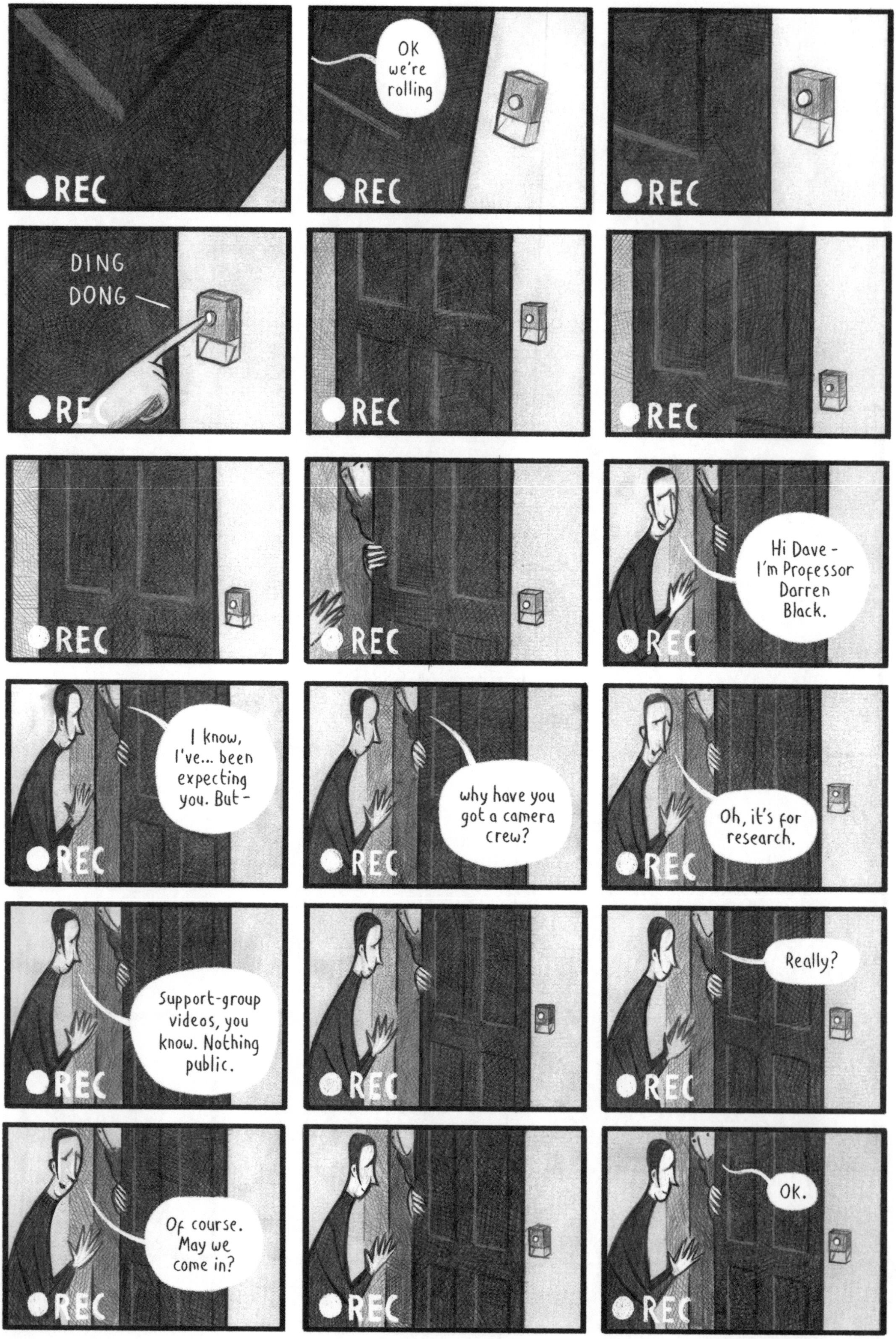
REC
OK we're rolling
REC
REC
DING DONG
REC
REC
REC
REC
REC
Hi Dave - I'm Professor Darren Black.
REC
I know, I've... been expecting you. But -
REC
why have you got a camera crew?
REC
Oh, it's for research.
REC
Support-group videos, you know. Nothing public.
REC
REC
Really?
REC
Of course. May we come in?
REC
REC
OK.
REC

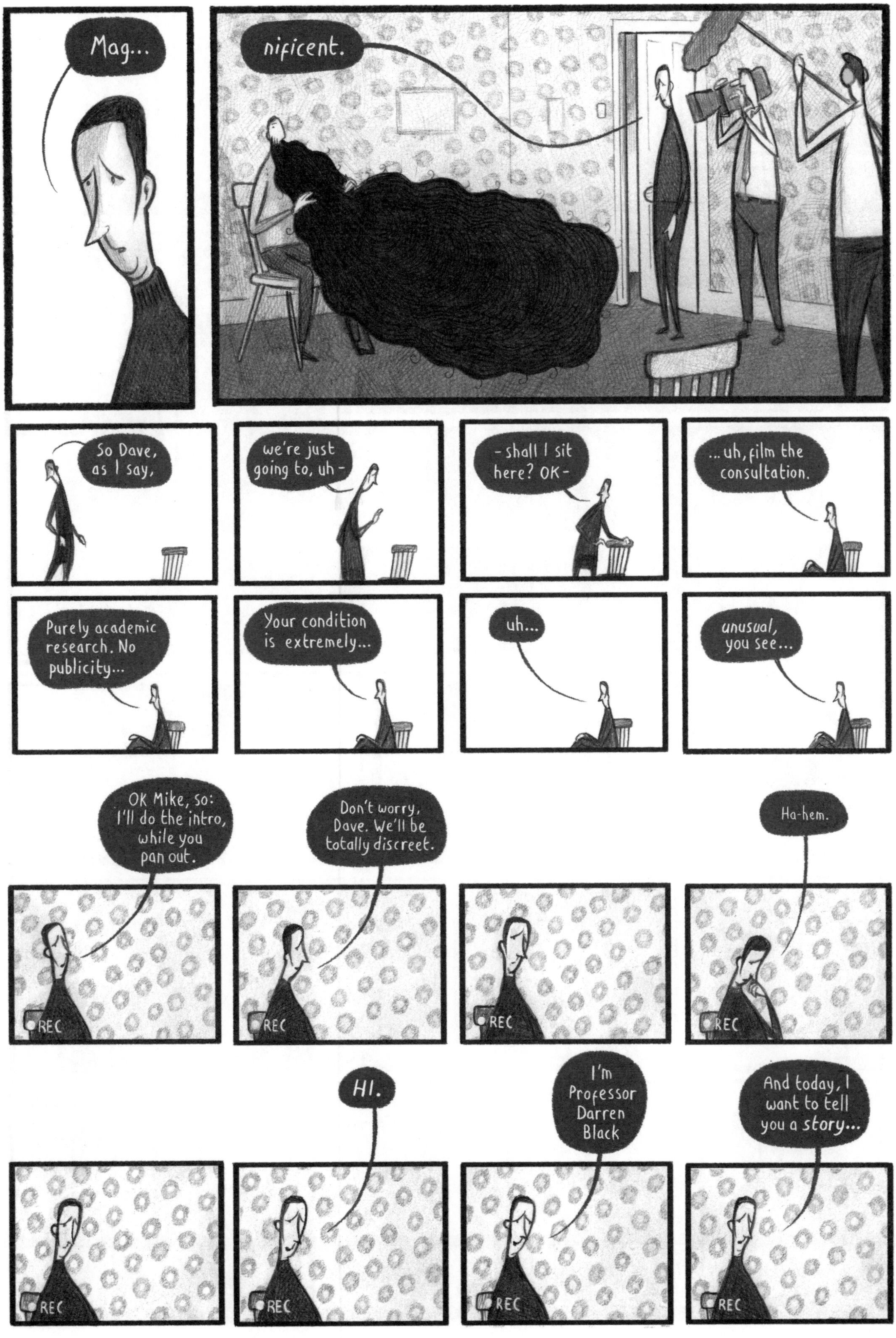
Mag...
nificent.
So Dave, as I say,
we're just going to, uh -
- shall I sit here? OK -
... uh, film the consultation.
Purely academic research. No publicity...
Your condition is extremely...
uh...
unusual, you see...
OK Mike, so: I'll do the intro, while you pan out.
REC
Don't worry, Dave. We'll be totally discreet.
REC
REC
Ha-hem.
REC
REC
HI.
REC
I'm Professor Darren Black
REC
And today, I want to tell you a *story*...
REC

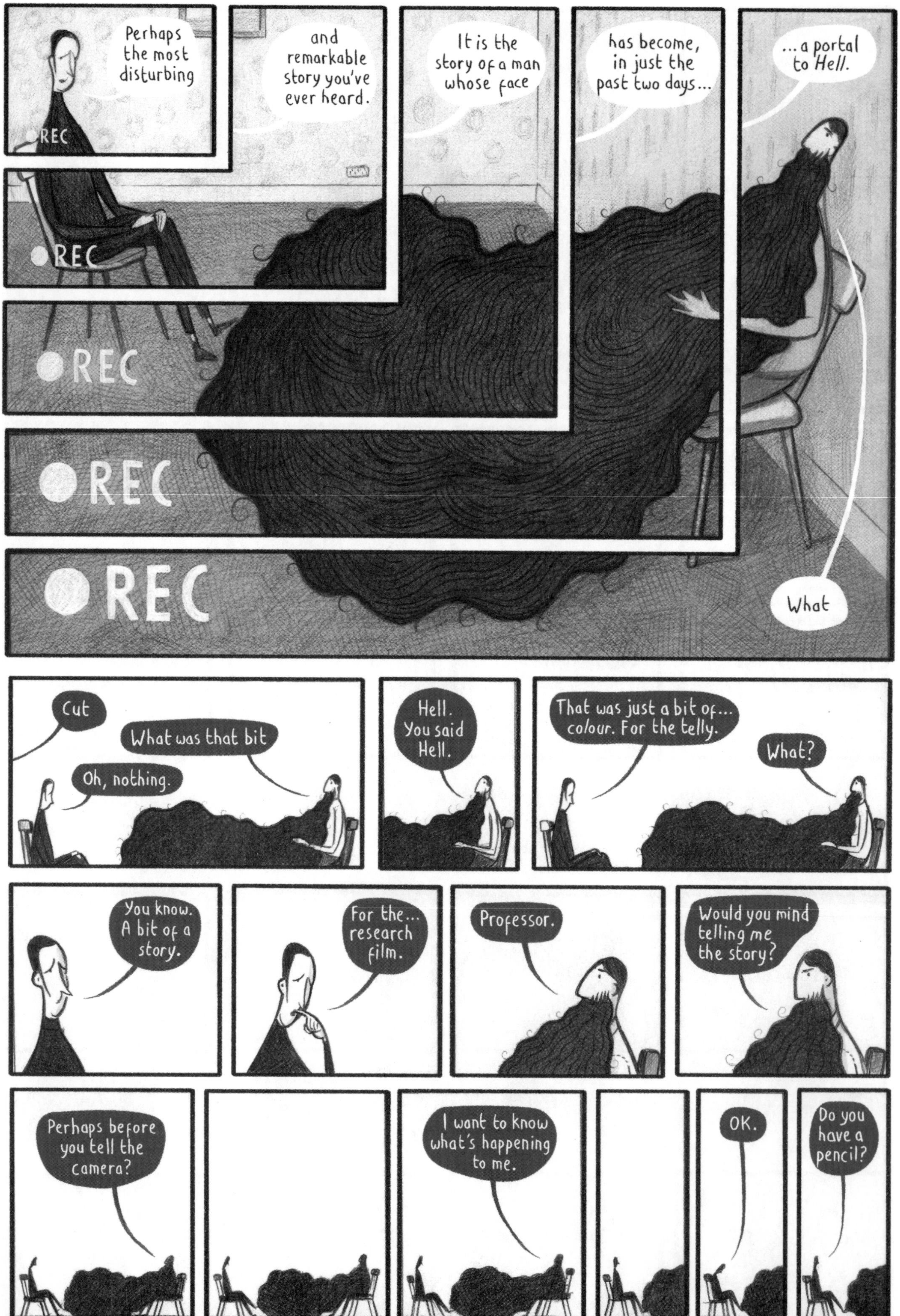
Perhaps the most disturbing
REC
and remarkable story you've ever heard.
REC
It is the story of a man whose face
REC
has become, in just the past two days...
REC
...a portal to *Hell*.
REC
What
Cut
What was that bit
Oh, nothing.
Hell. You said Hell.
That was just a bit of... colour. For the telly.
What?
You know. A bit of a story.
For the... research film.
Professor.
Would you mind telling me the story?
Perhaps before you tell the camera?
I want to know what's happening to me.
OK.
Do you have a pencil?

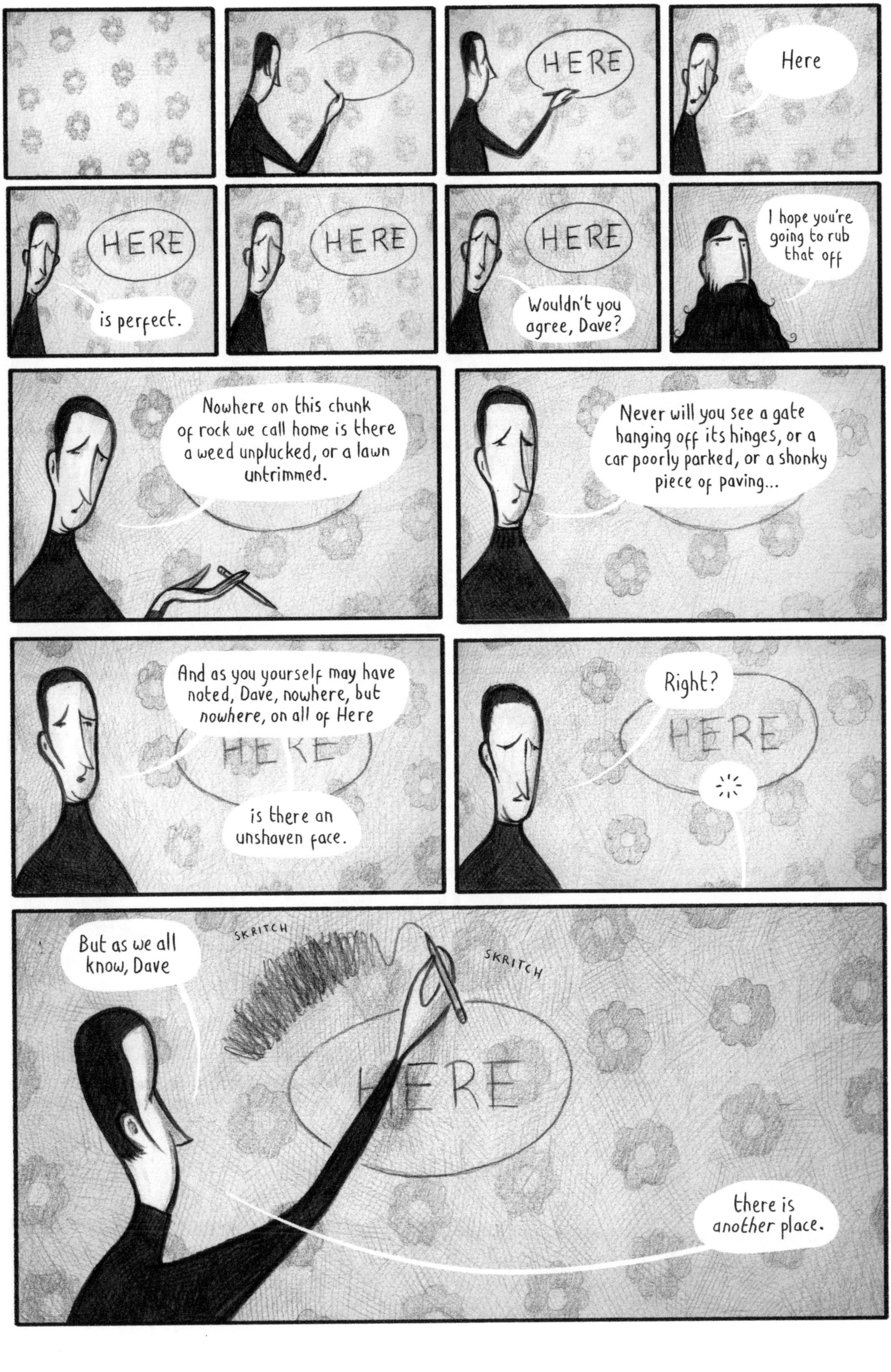
HERE
Here
HERE
is perfect.
HERE
HERE
Wouldn't you agree, Dave?
I hope you're going to rub that off
Nowhere on this chunk of rock we call home is there a weed unplucked, or a lawn untrimmed.
Never will you see a gate hanging off its hinges, or a car poorly parked, or a shonky piece of paving...
And as you yourself may have noted, Dave, nowhere, but *nowhere*, on all of Here
HERE
is there an unshaven face.
Right?
HERE
But as we all know, Dave
SKRITCH
SKRITCH
HERE
there is *another* place.

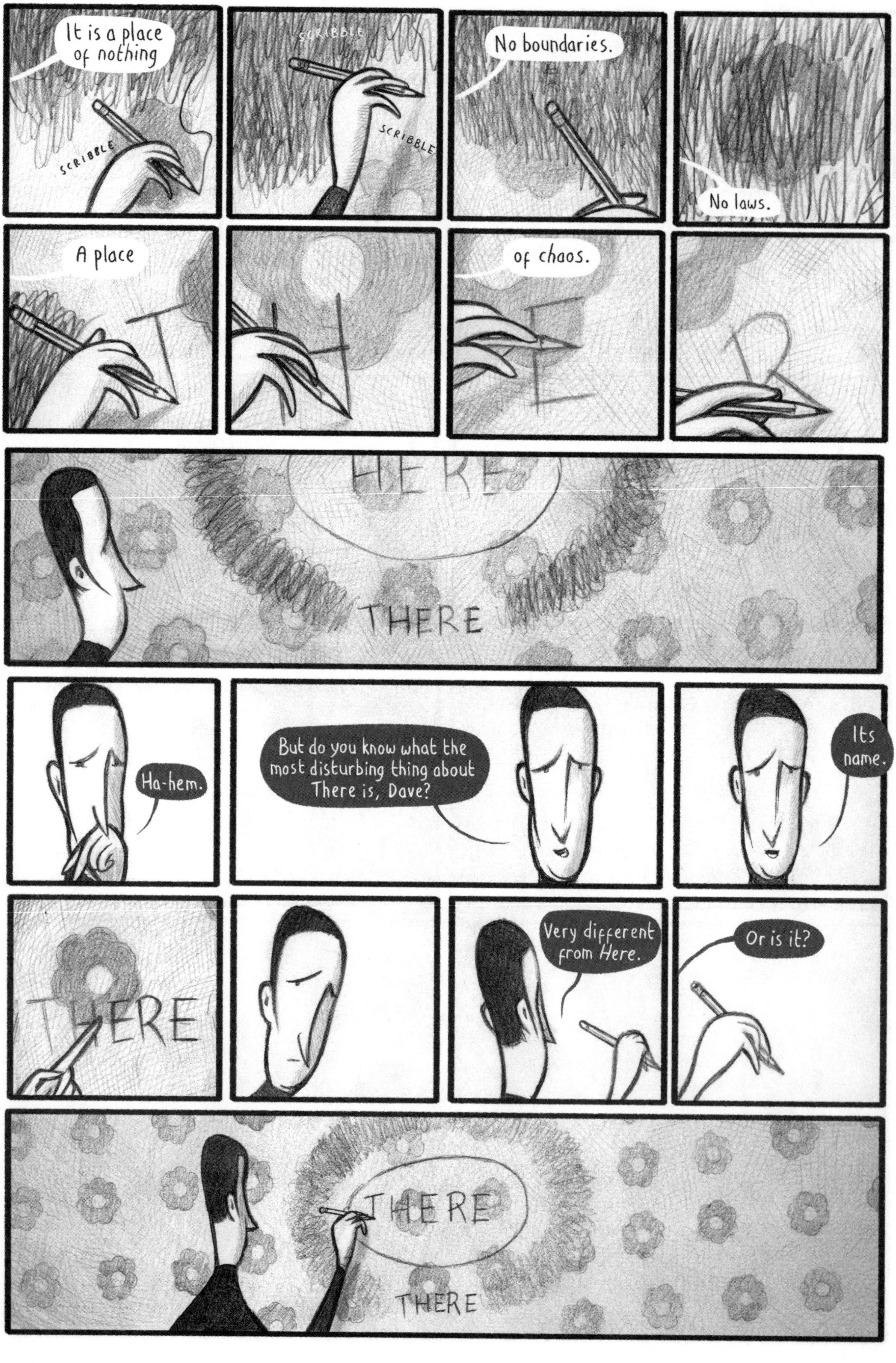
It is a place of nothing
SCRIBBLE
SCRIBBLE
SCRIBBLE
No boundaries.
No laws.
A place
of chaos.
HERE
THERE
Ha-hem.
But do you know what the most disturbing thing about There is, Dave?
Its name.
THERE
Very different from Here.
Or is it?
THERE
THERE

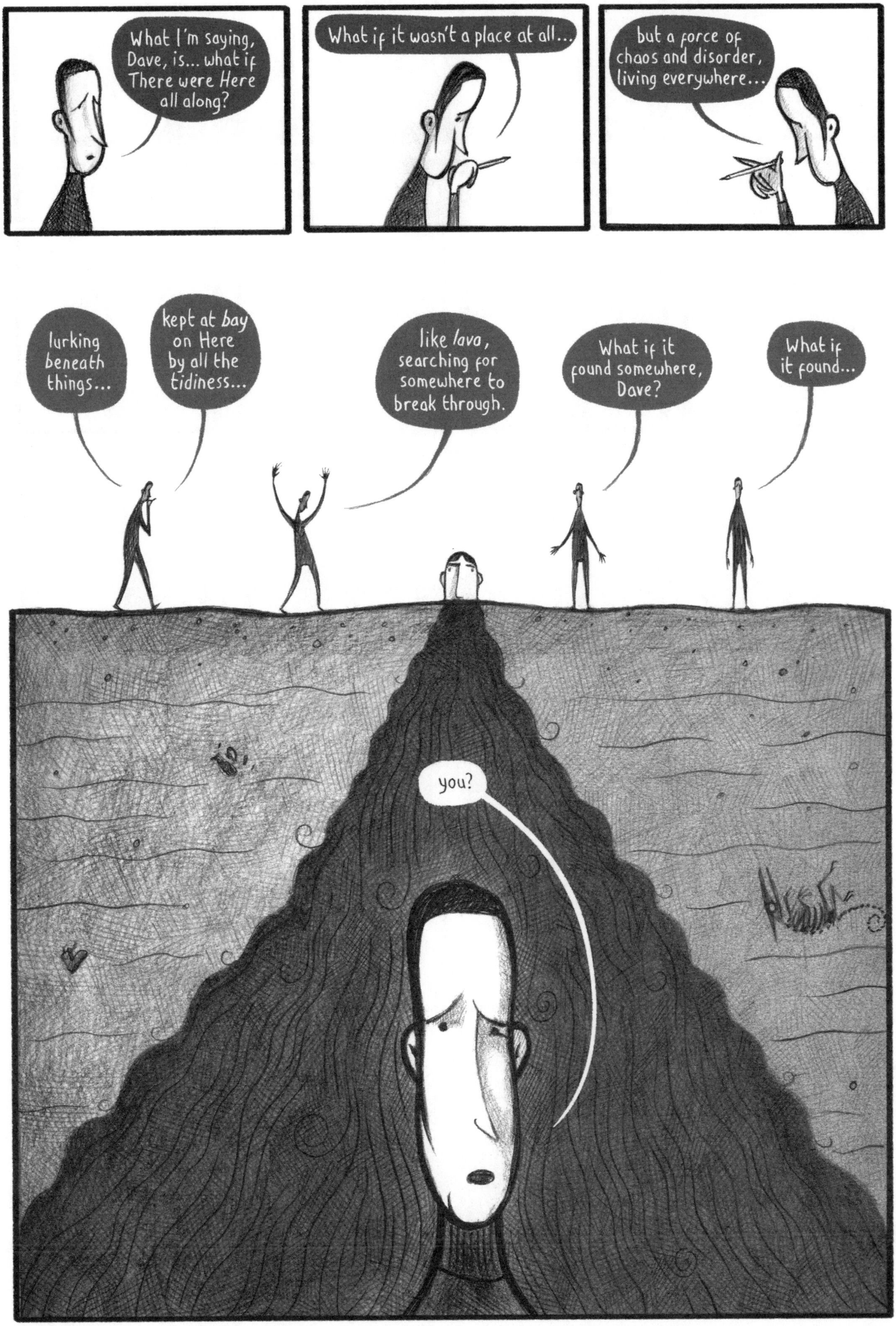
What I'm saying, Dave, is... what if There were Here all along?
What if it wasn't a place at all...
but a *force* of chaos and disorder, living everywhere...
lurking beneath things...
kept at *bay* on Here by all the tidiness...
like *lava*, searching for somewhere to break through.
What if it found somewhere, Dave?
What if it found...
you?

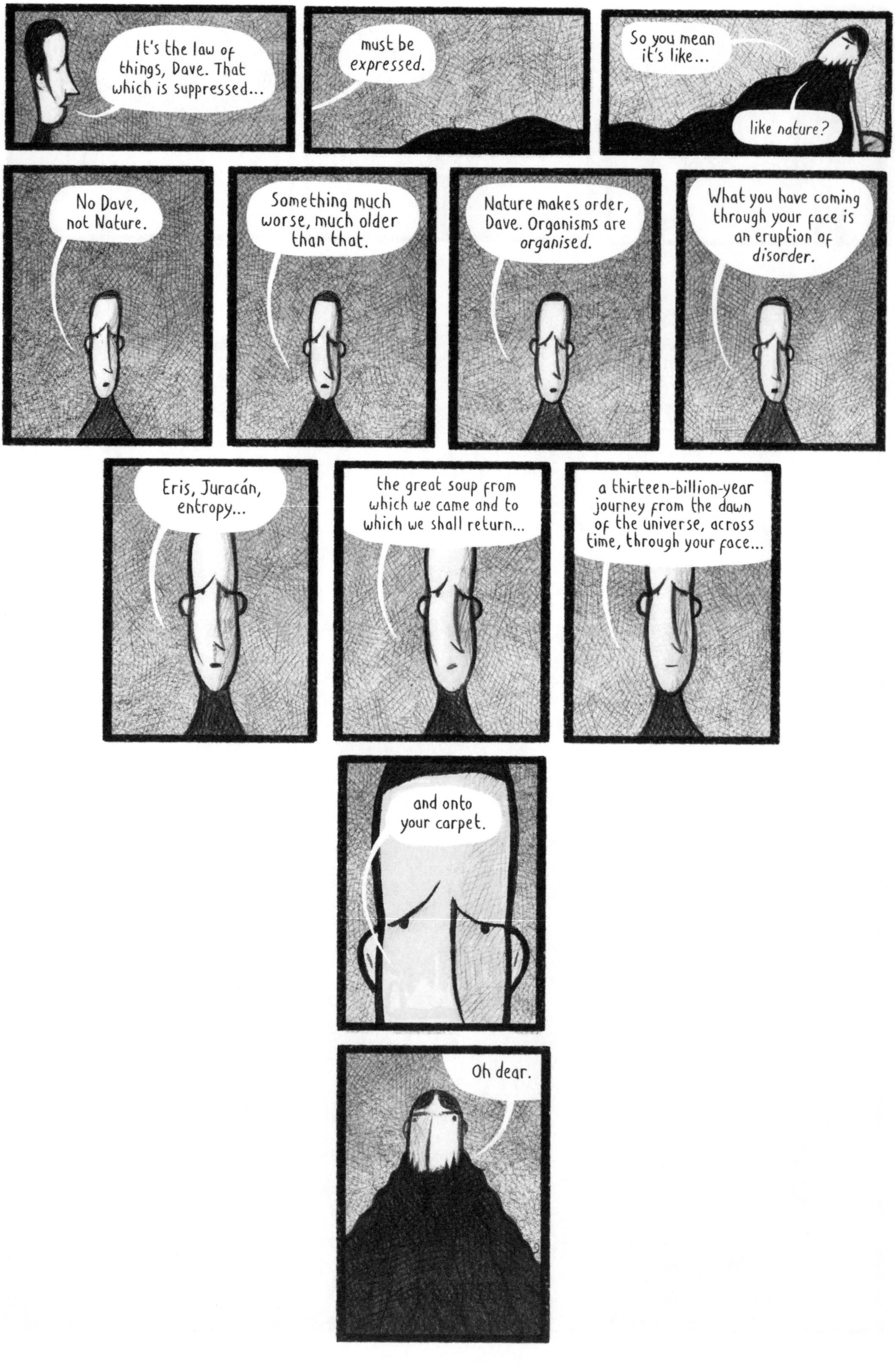
It's the law of things, Dave. That which is suppressed...
must be expressed.
So you mean it's like...
like nature?
No Dave, not Nature.
Something much worse, much older than that.
Nature makes order, Dave. Organisms are organised.
What you have coming through your face is an eruption of disorder.
Eris, Juracán, entropy...
the great soup from which we came and to which we shall return...
a thirteen-billion-year journey from the dawn of the universe, across time, through your face...
and onto your carpet.
Oh dear.

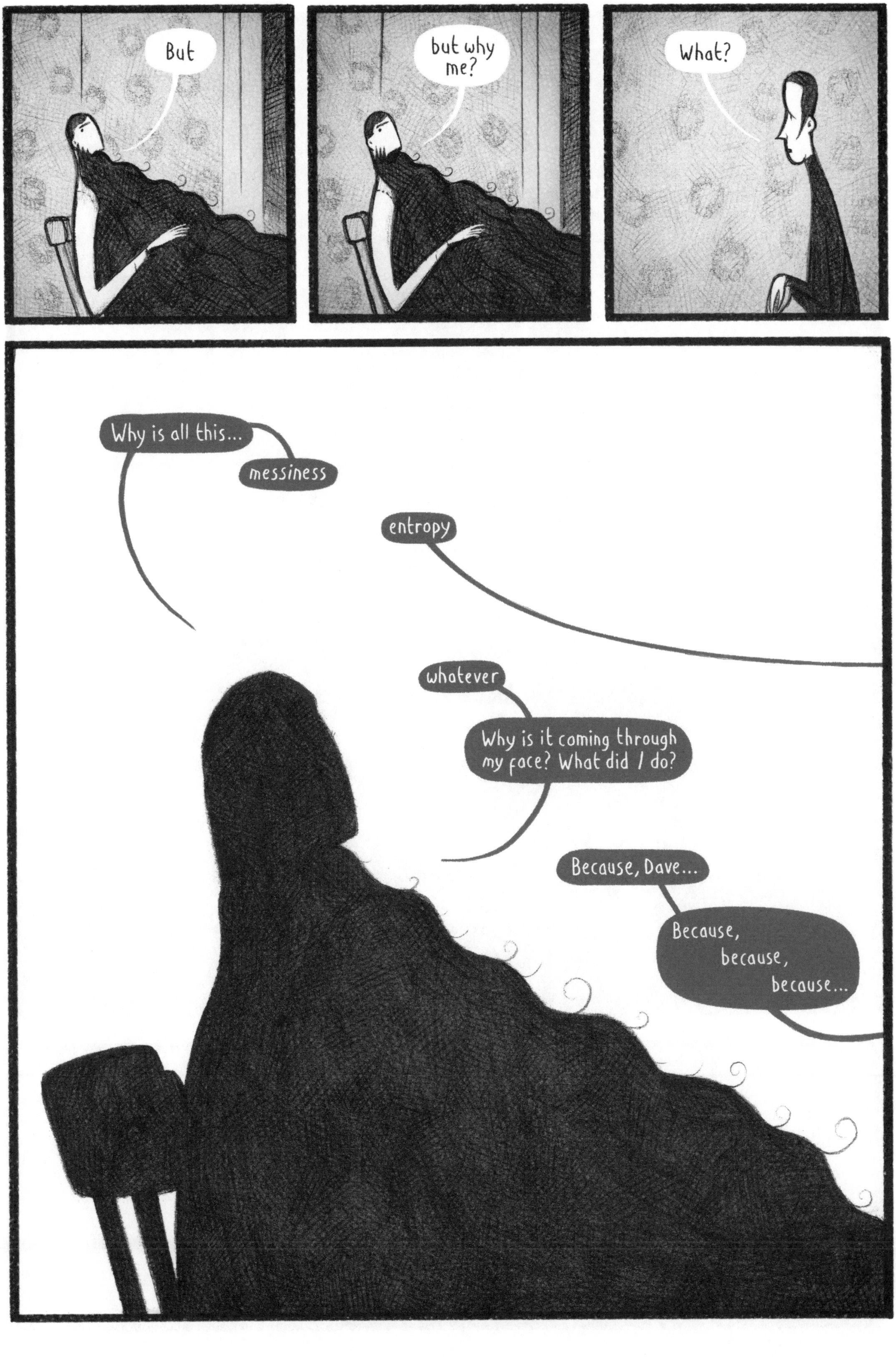
But
but why me?
What?
Why is all this...
messiness
entropy
whatever
Why is it coming through my face? What did I do?
Because, Dave...
Because, because, because...

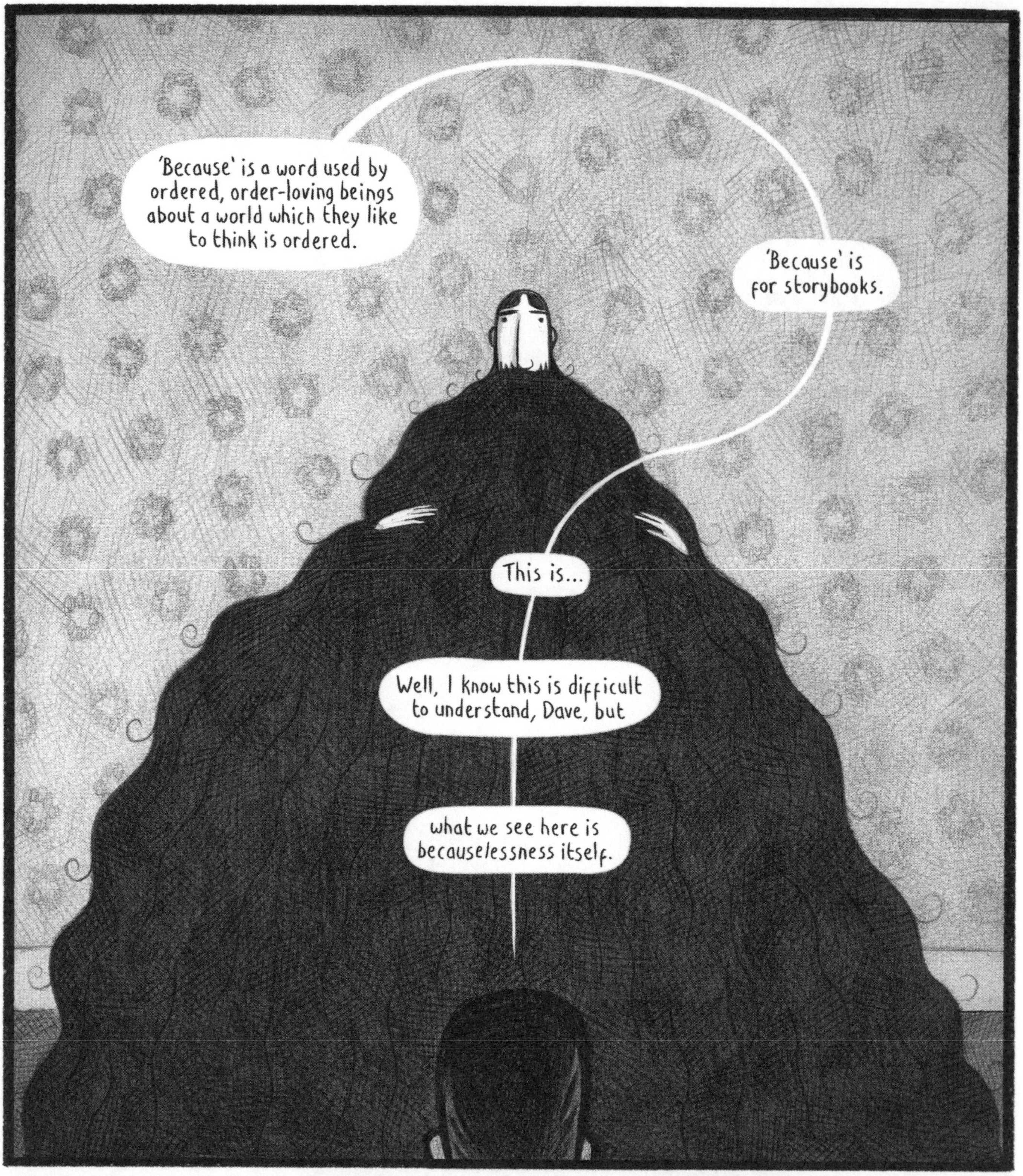
'Because' is a word used by ordered, order-loving beings about a world which they like to think is ordered.
'Because' is for storybooks.
This is...
Well, I know this is difficult to understand, Dave, but
what we see here is becauselessness itself.

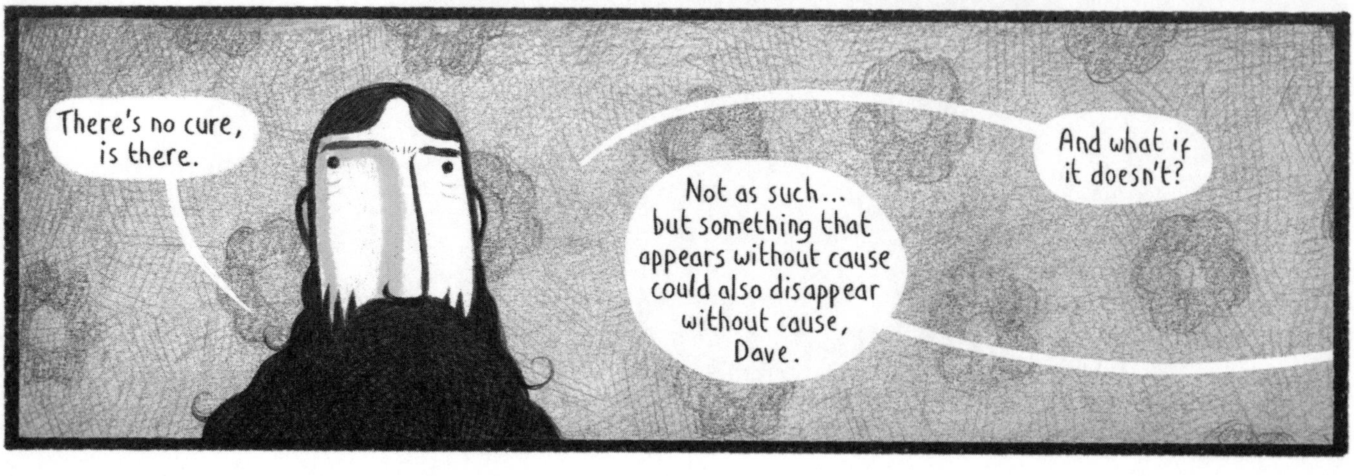
There's no cure, is there.
Not as such... but something that appears without cause could also disappear without cause, Dave.
And what if it doesn't?

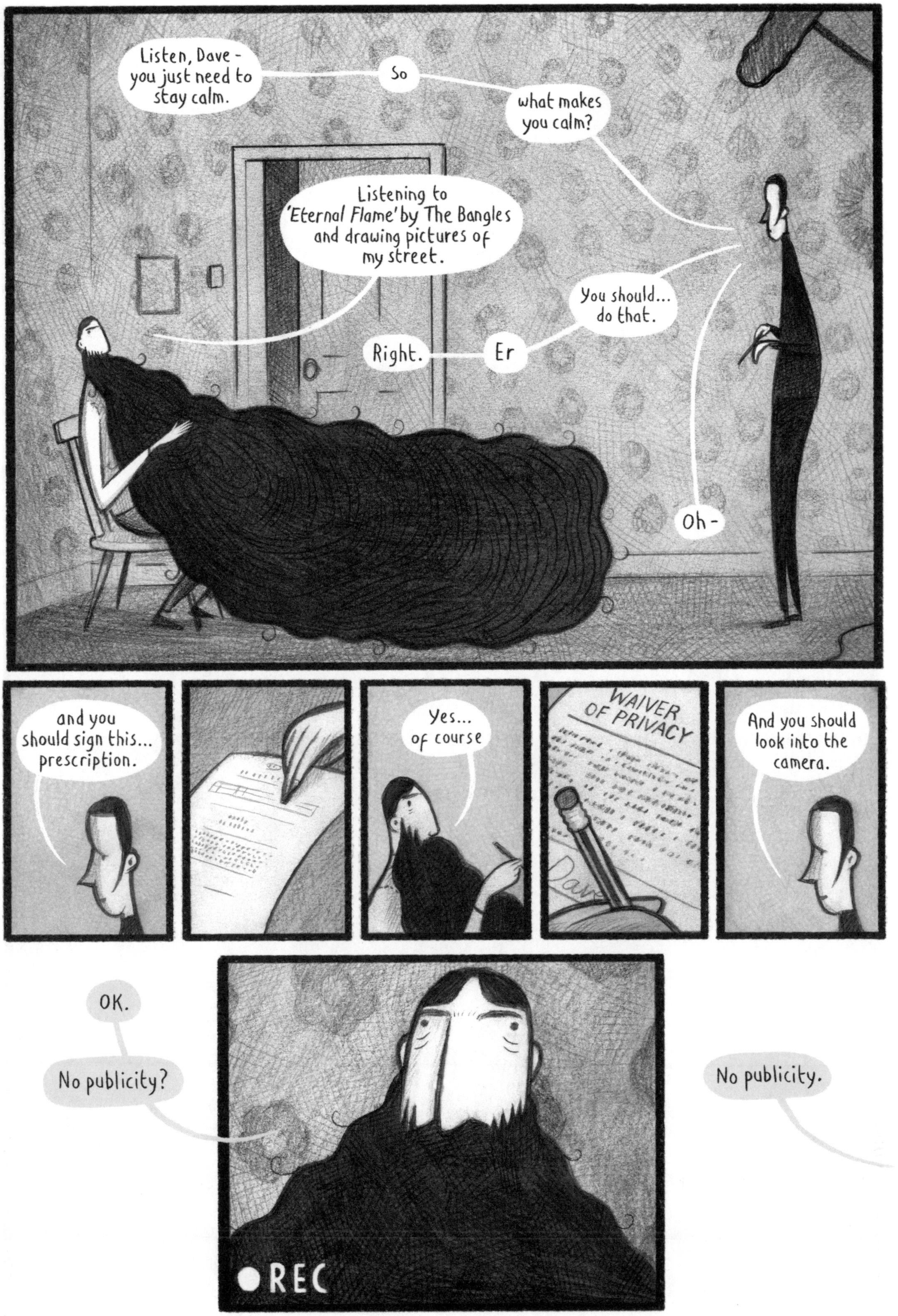

Listen, Dave - you just need to stay calm.
So
what makes you calm?
Listening to 'Eternal Flame' by The Bangles and drawing pictures of my street.
You should... do that.
Er
Right.
Oh-
and you should sign this... prescription.
Yes... of course
WAIVER OF PRIVACY
And you should look into the camera.
OK.
No publicity?
No publicity.
REC

REAKING NEWS
EARD FROM THERE' ERUPTS FROM MAN'S F
Publicitymax

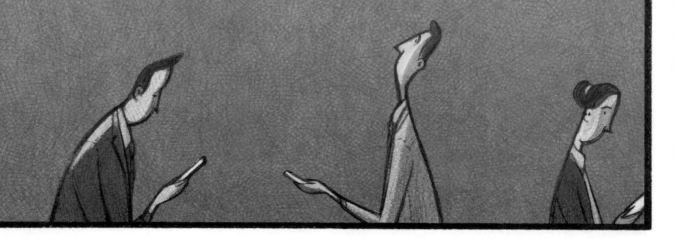

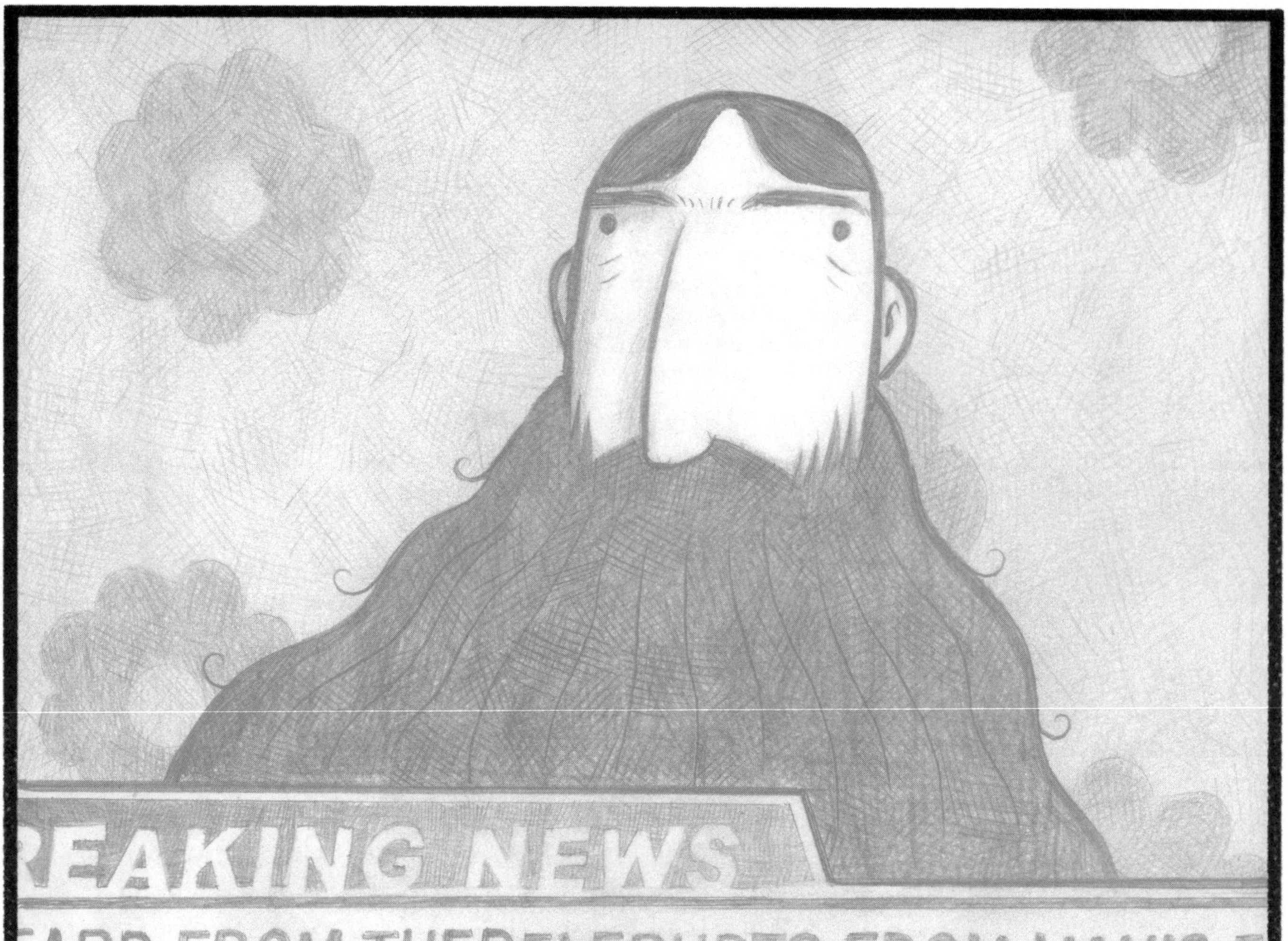

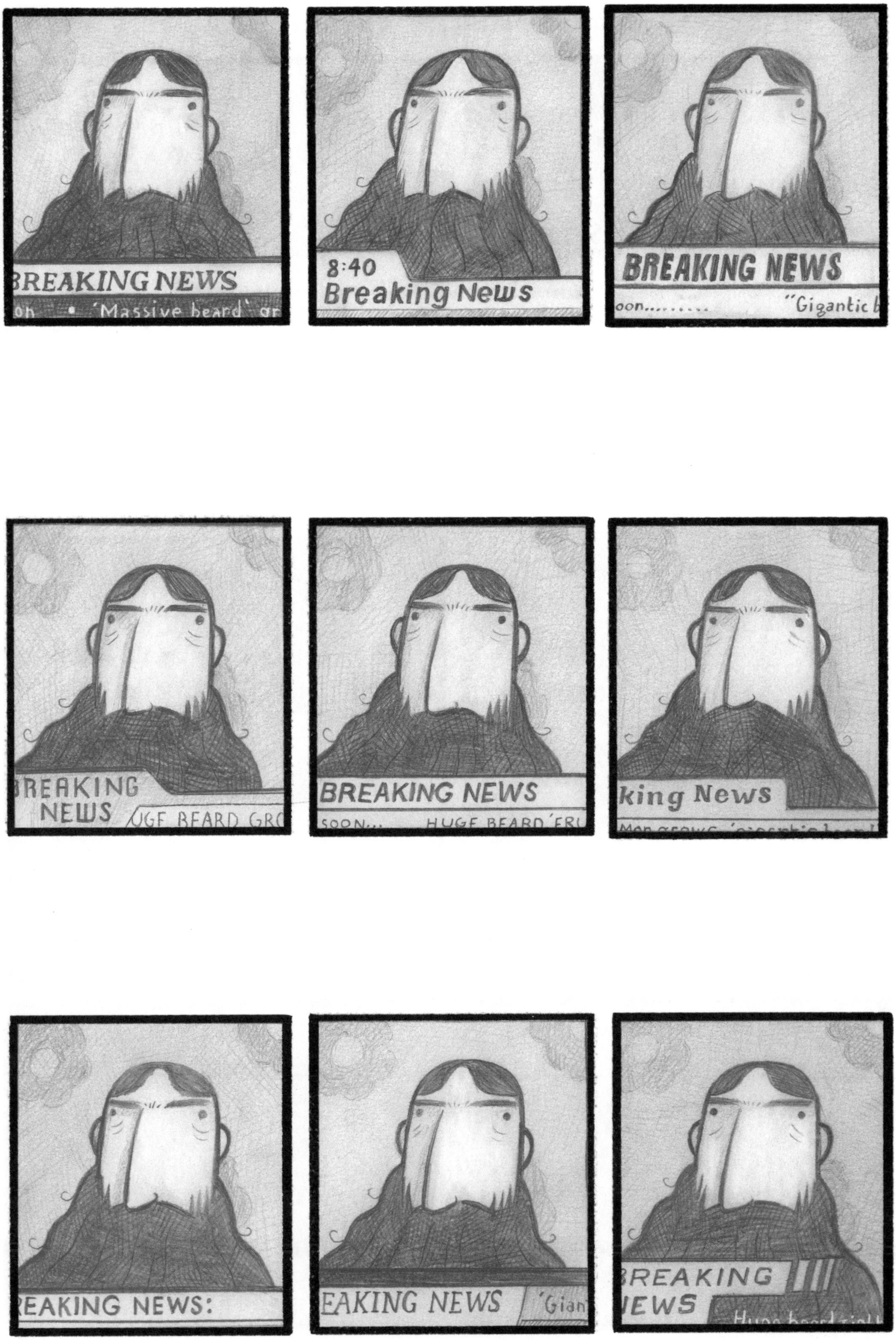

REAKING NEWS
on • 'Massive beard' gr
8:40
Breaking News
BREAKING NEWS
oon........ "Gigantic b
REAKING
NEWS
UGE BEARD GRO
BREAKING NEWS
SOON... HUGE BEARD 'ERU
king News
EAKING NEWS:
EAKING NEWS
'Gian
REAKING
EWS

Soon enough Dave, who had for so long lived on the edge of things, became...

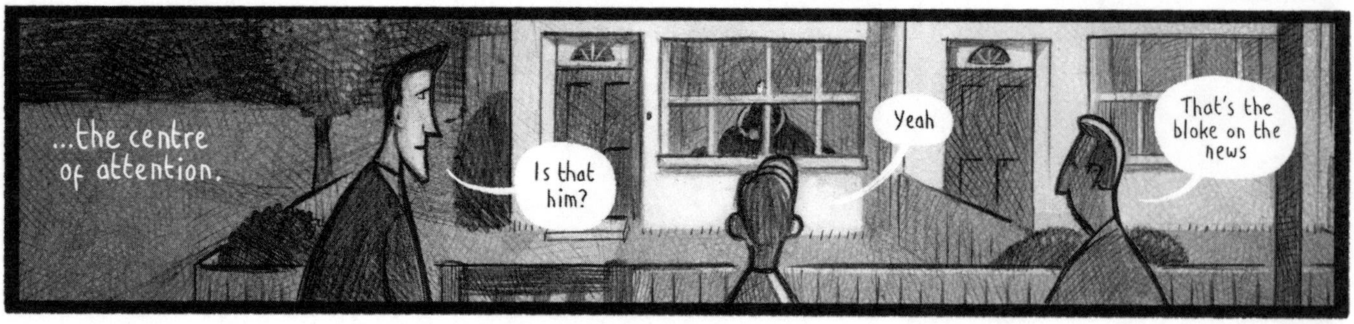
...the centre of attention.
Is that him?
Yeah
That's the bloke on the news

And as he tried to keep calm by sketching his view,

he found himself no longer drawing passers-by

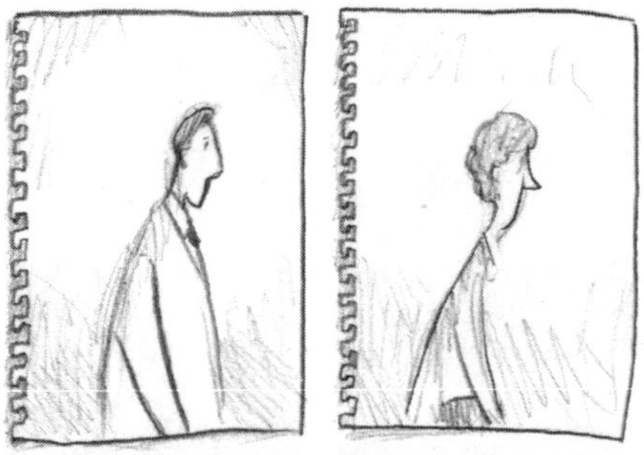

but spectators instead.

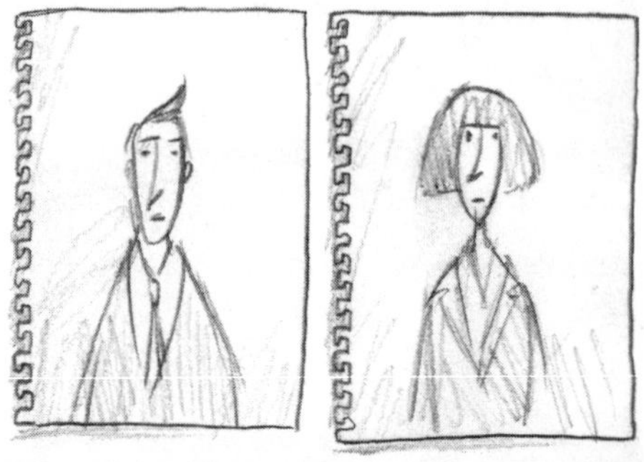

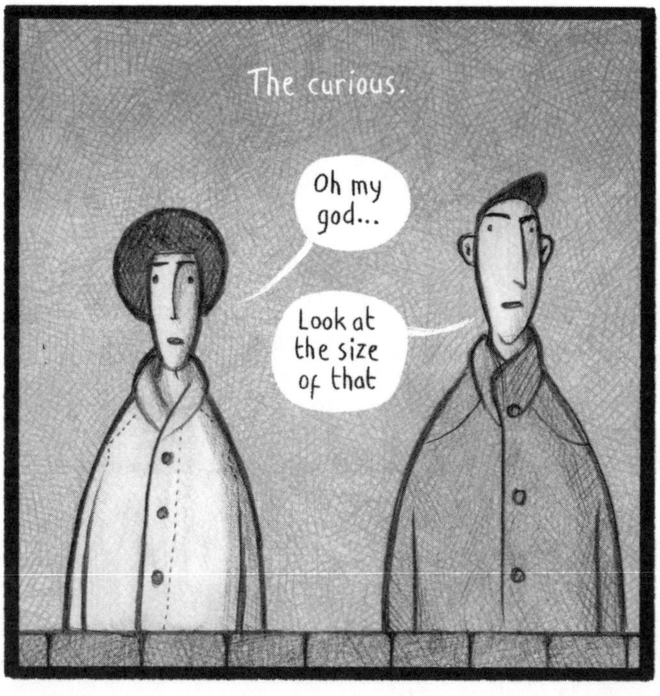
The curious.
Oh my god...
Look at the size of that

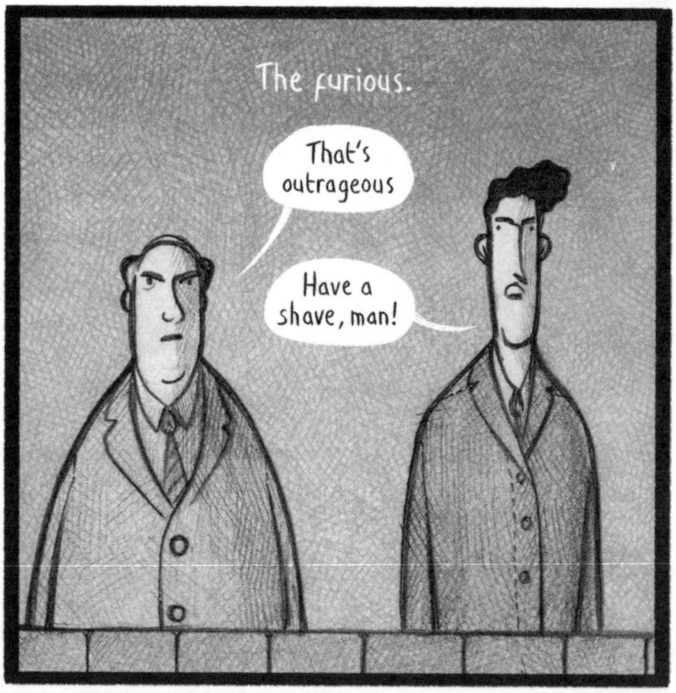
The furious.
That's outrageous
Have a shave, man!

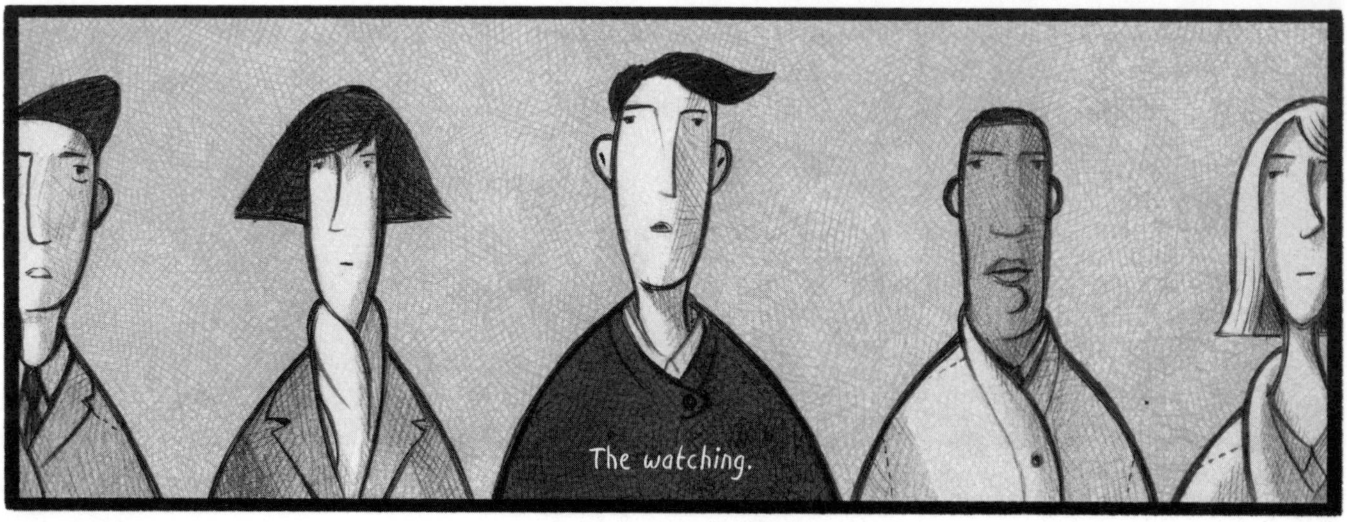
The watching.

And it would later be thought significant

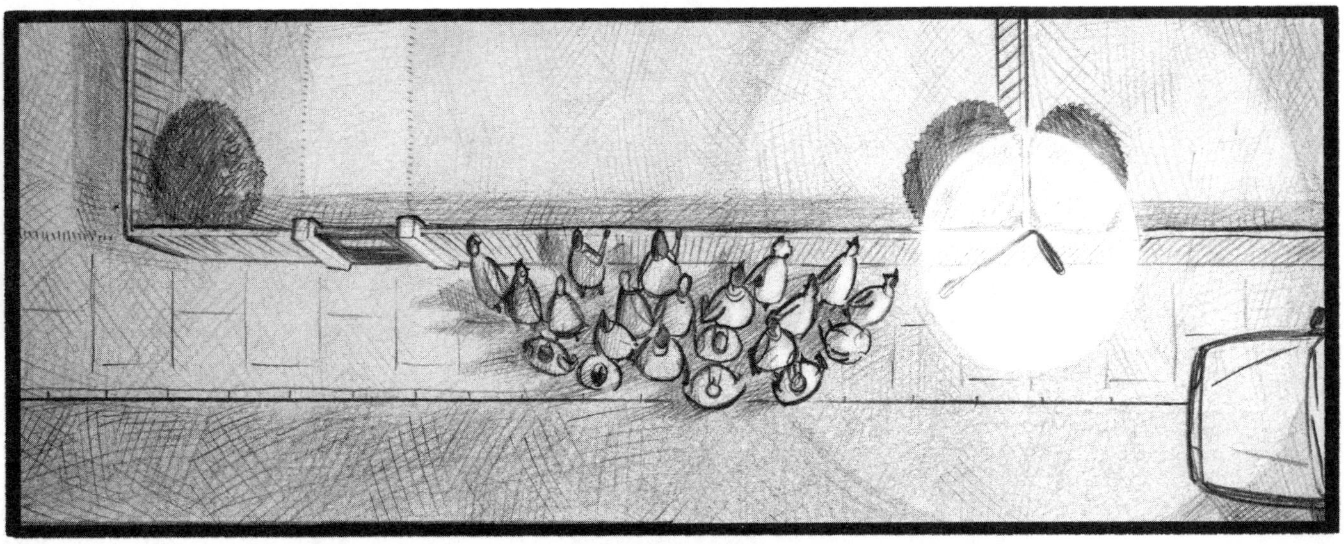

that as the number of visitors grew

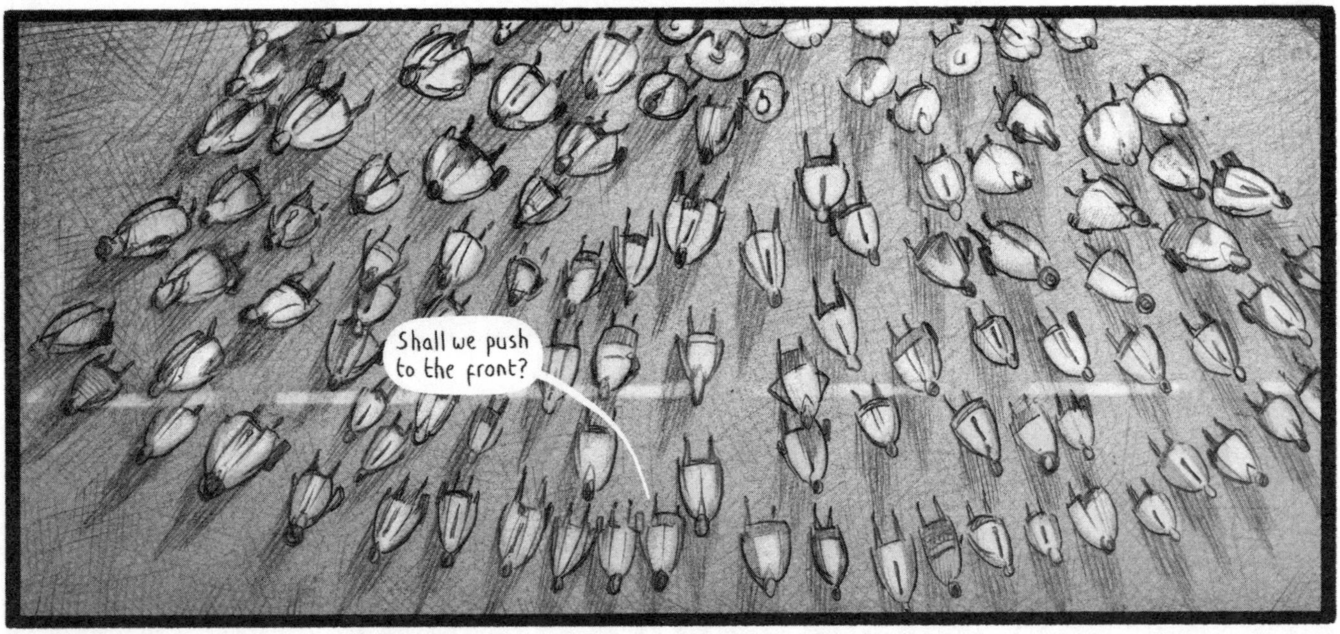
Shall we push to the front?

and grew,

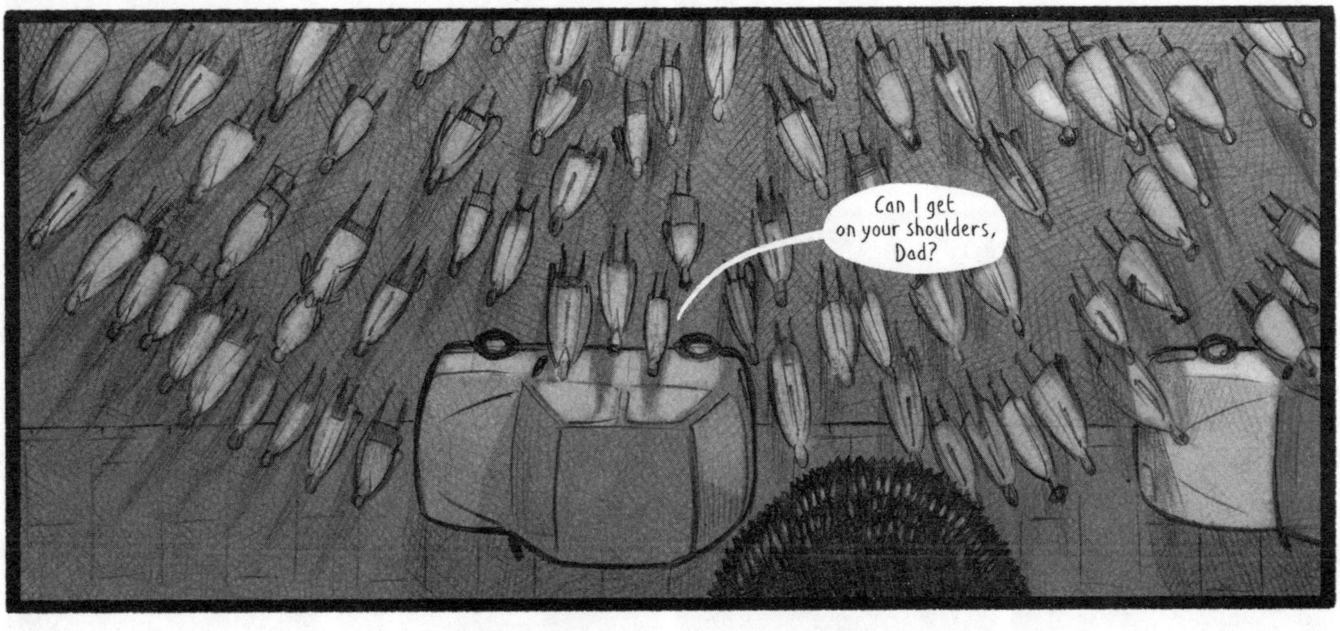
Can I get on your shoulders, Dad?

nobody even *thought* of forming an orderly queue.

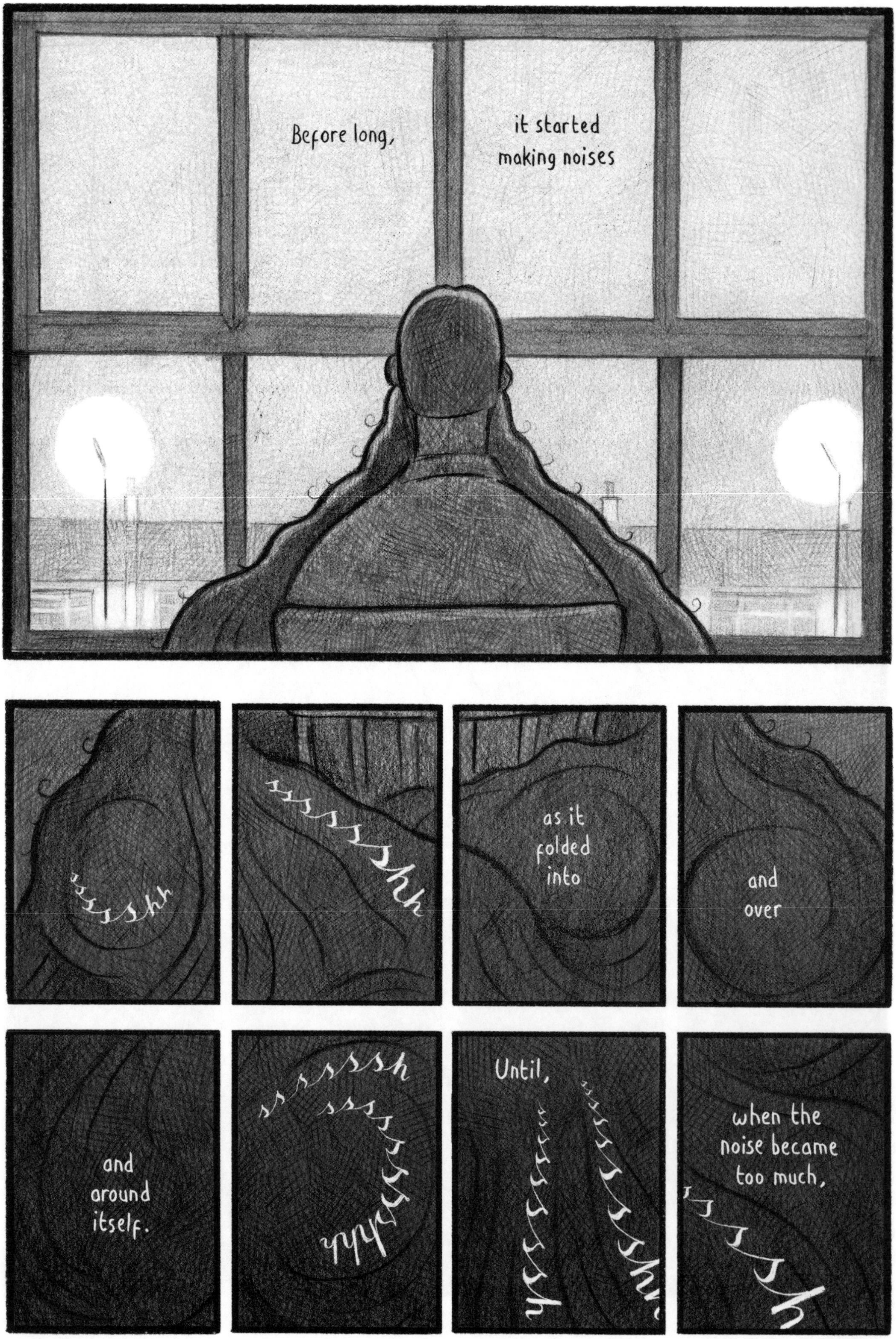
Before long,
it started making noises
ssssshh
sssssshh
as it folded into
and over
and around itself.
ssssssh
ssssssshhh
Until,
ssssssh
sssssshh
when the noise became too much,
ssssh

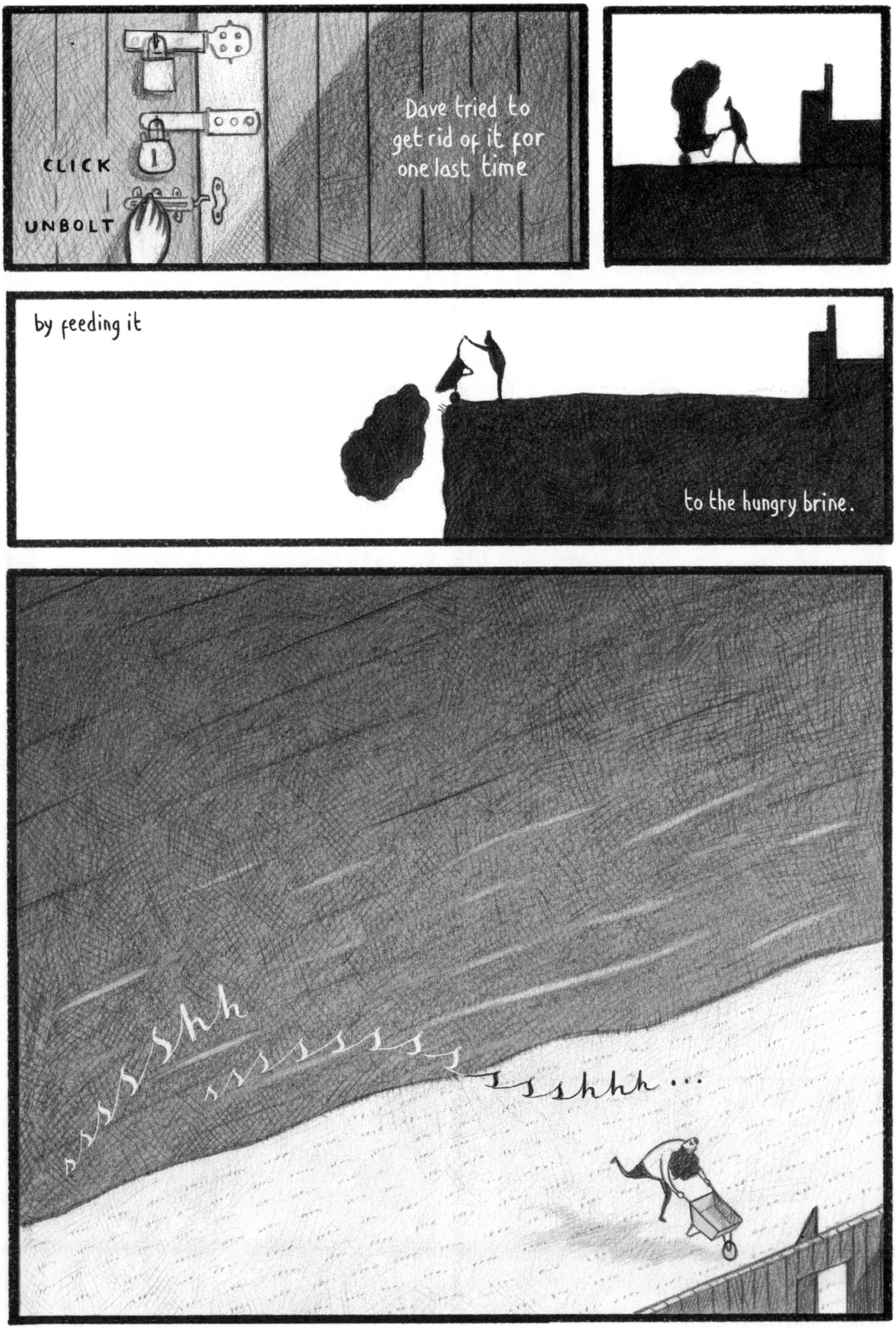
CLICK
UNBOLT
Dave tried to get rid of it for one last time
by feeding it
to the hungry brine.
ssssshh
ssssssssssshhh...

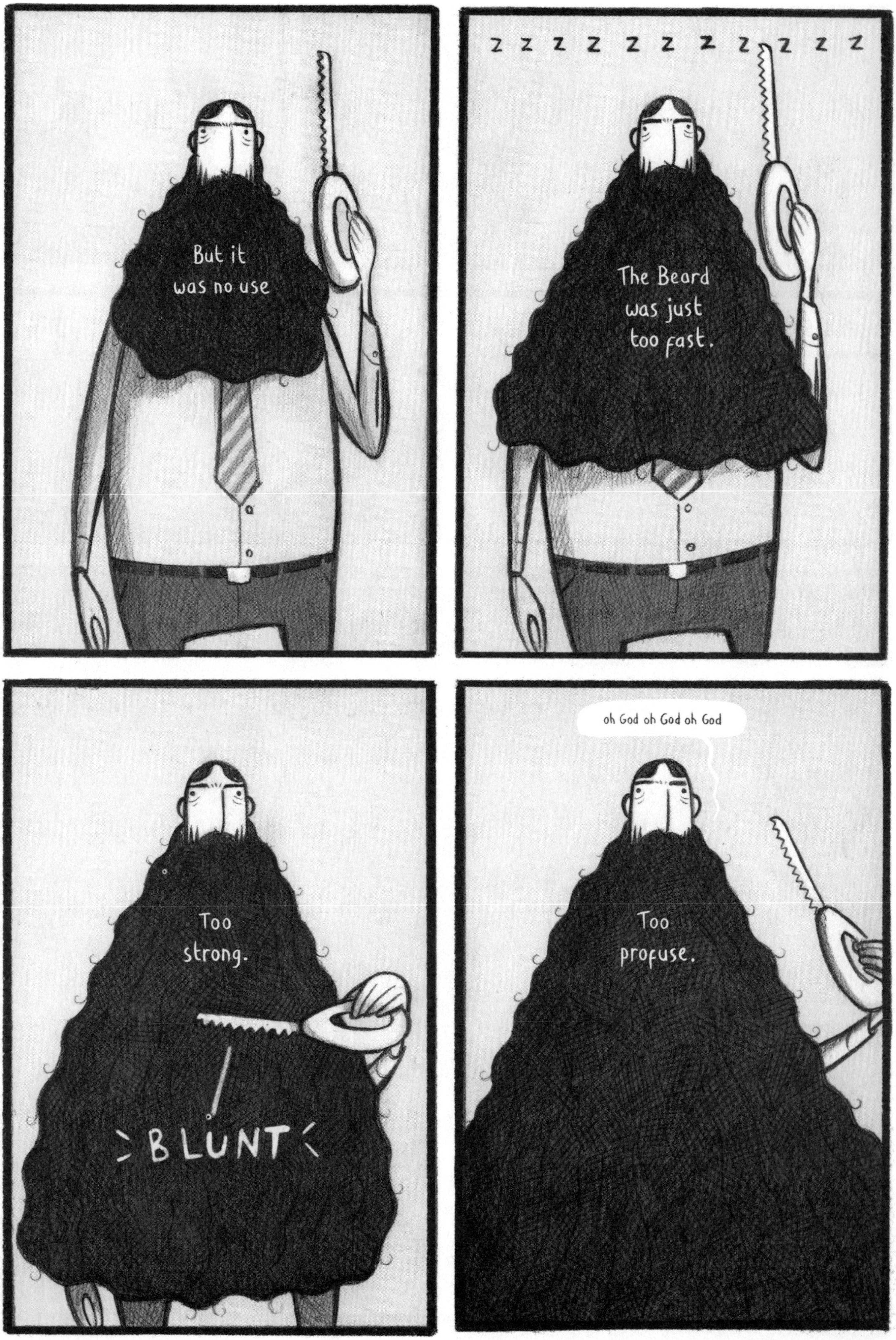
But it was no use
Z Z Z Z Z Z Z Z Z Z Z
The Beard was just too fast.
Too strong.
BLUNT
oh God oh God oh God
Too profuse.

It filled Dave's room.

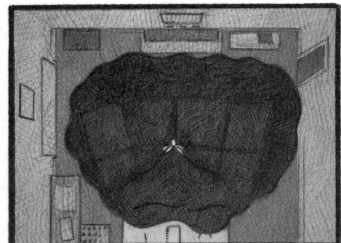

It untidied his things.

And all he could do

was watch as it grew

And listen to it sing.

Is this burning...

...an eternal

"ssssssh - sssshh...

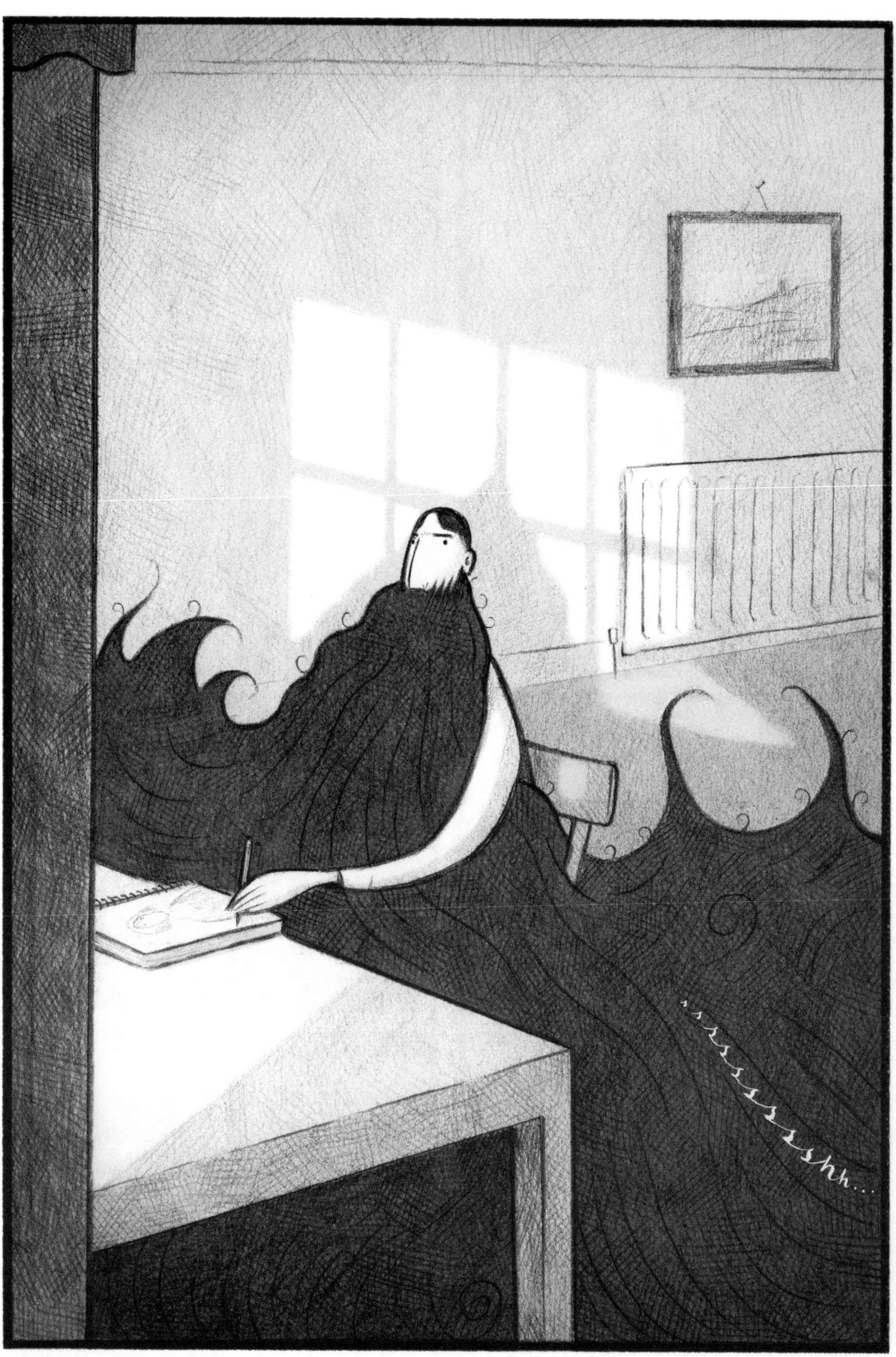

ssssssssshh...

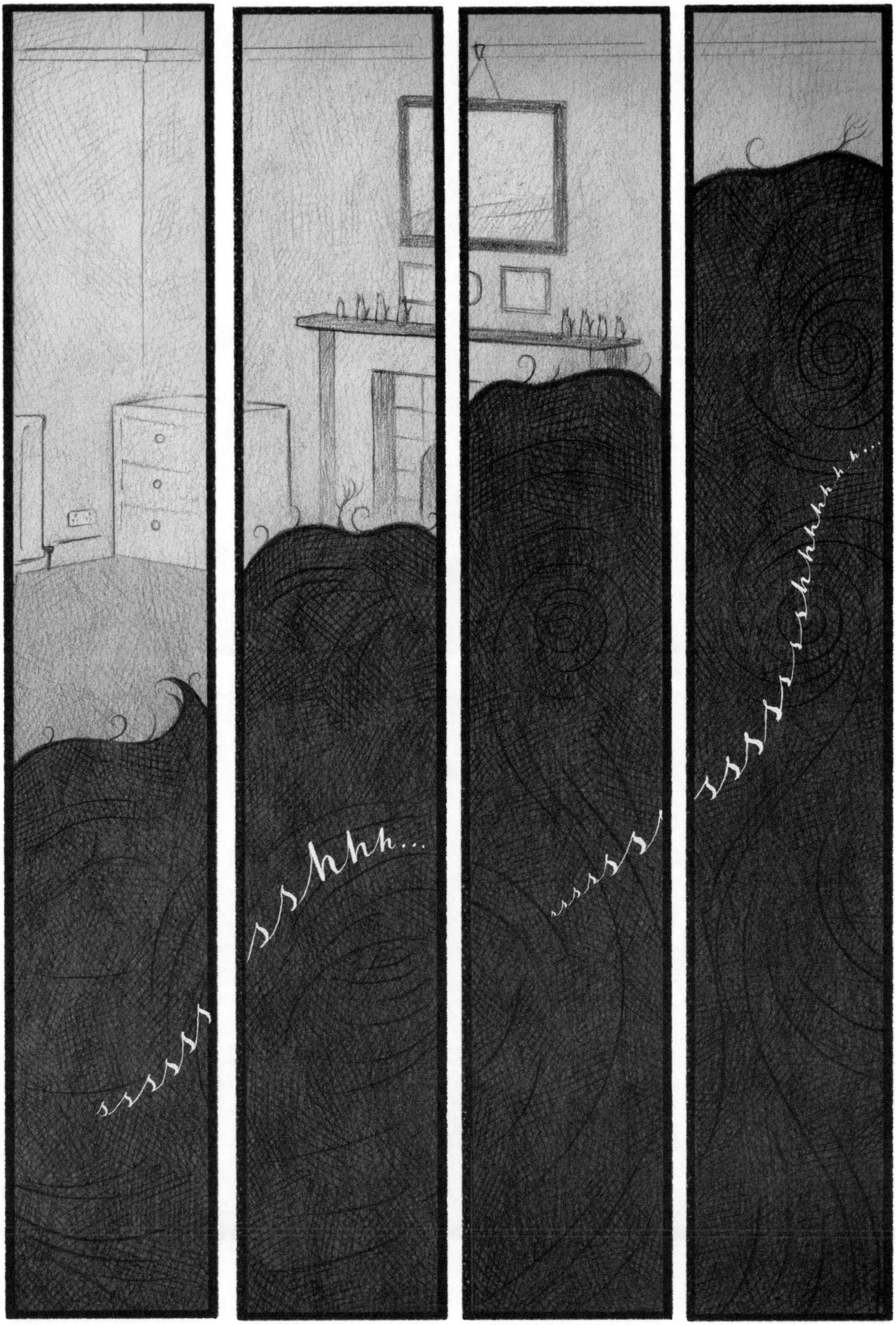
ssssss
sshhh...
ssssss
ssssshhhhhh...

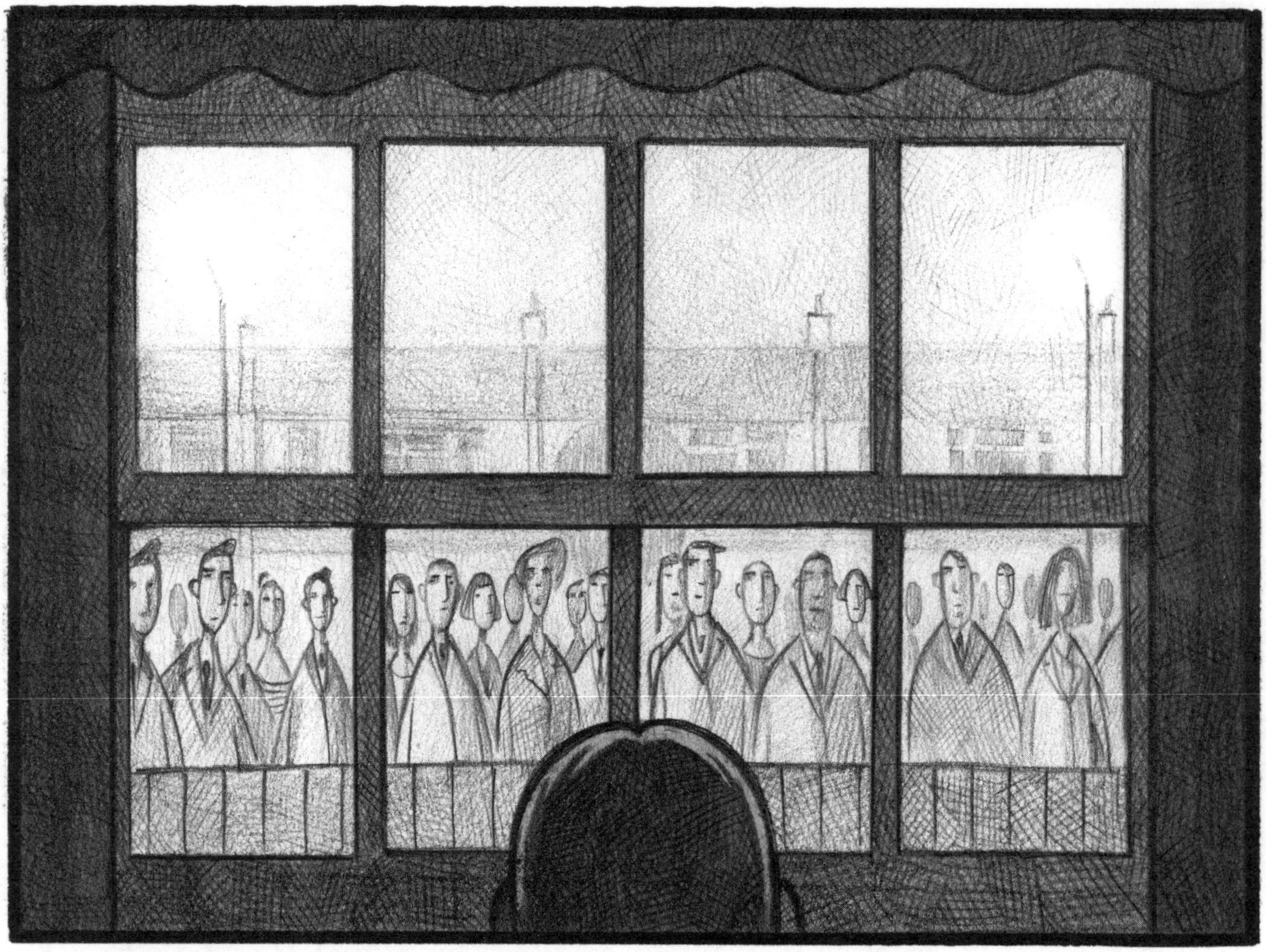

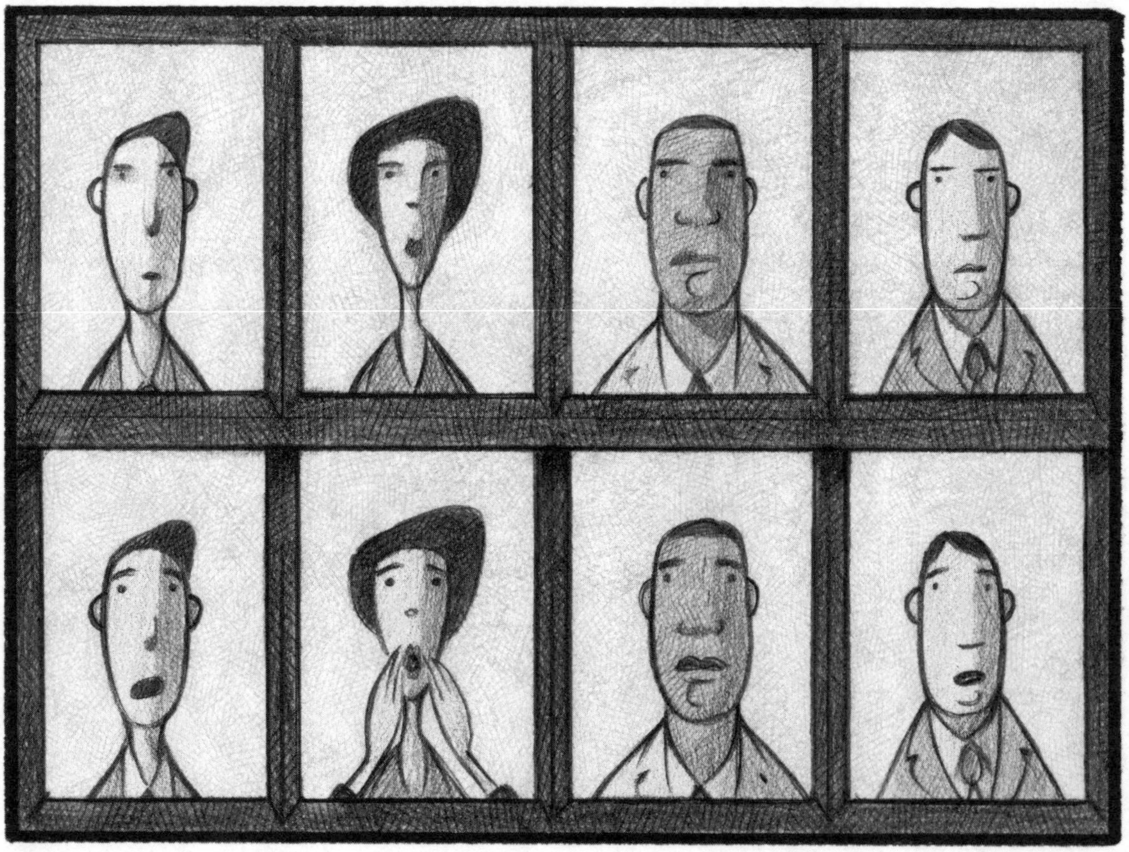

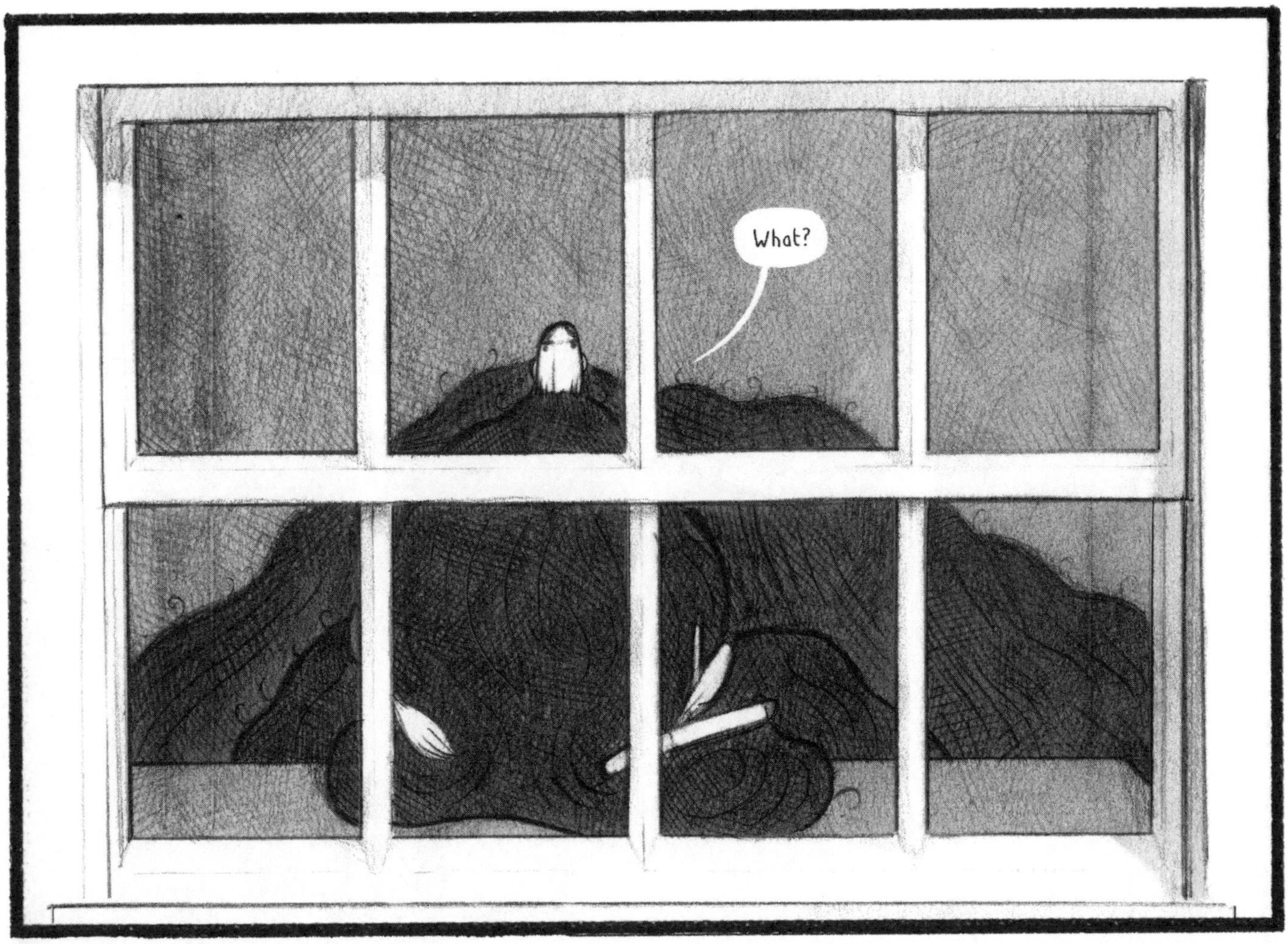
What?

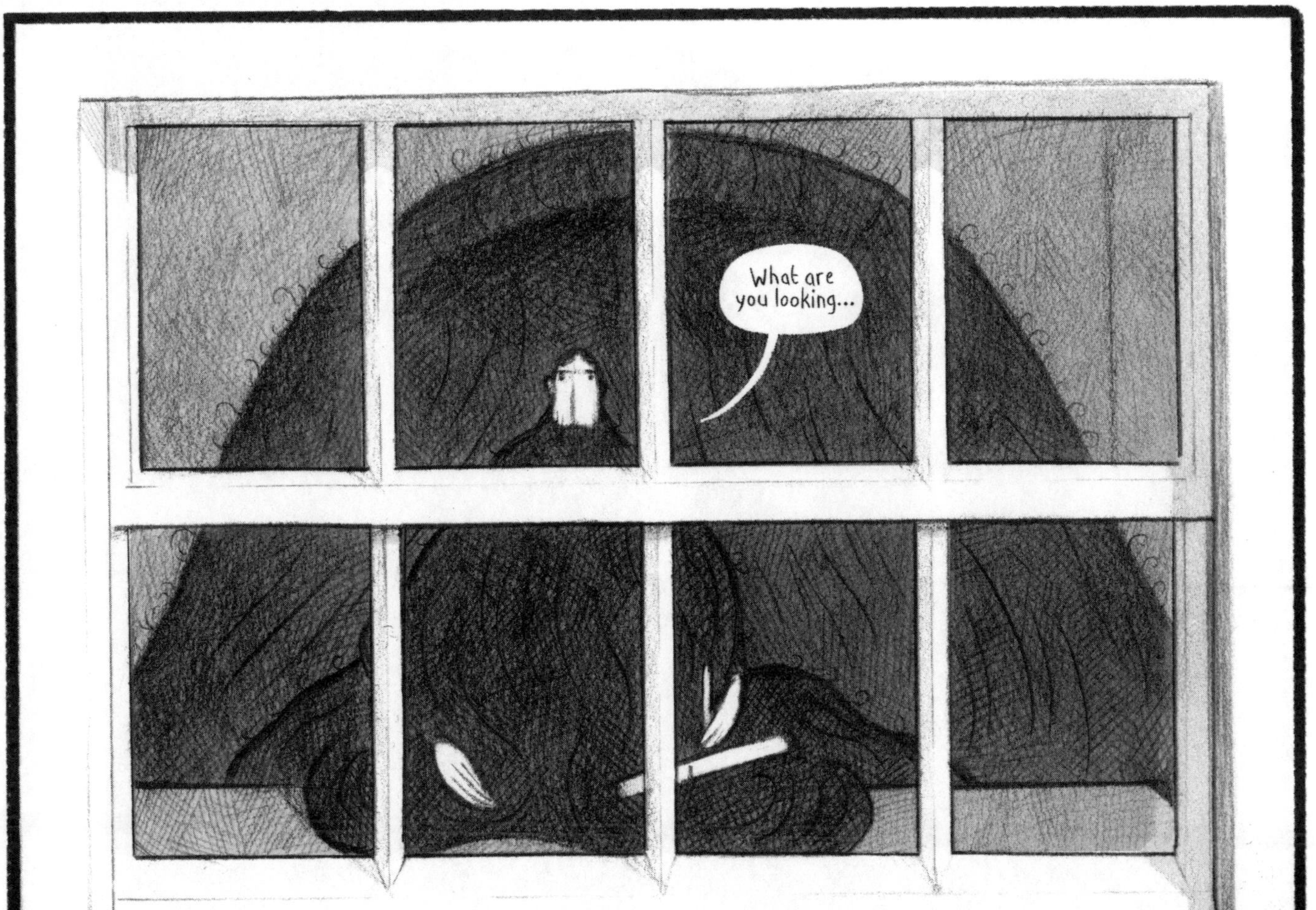
What are you looking...

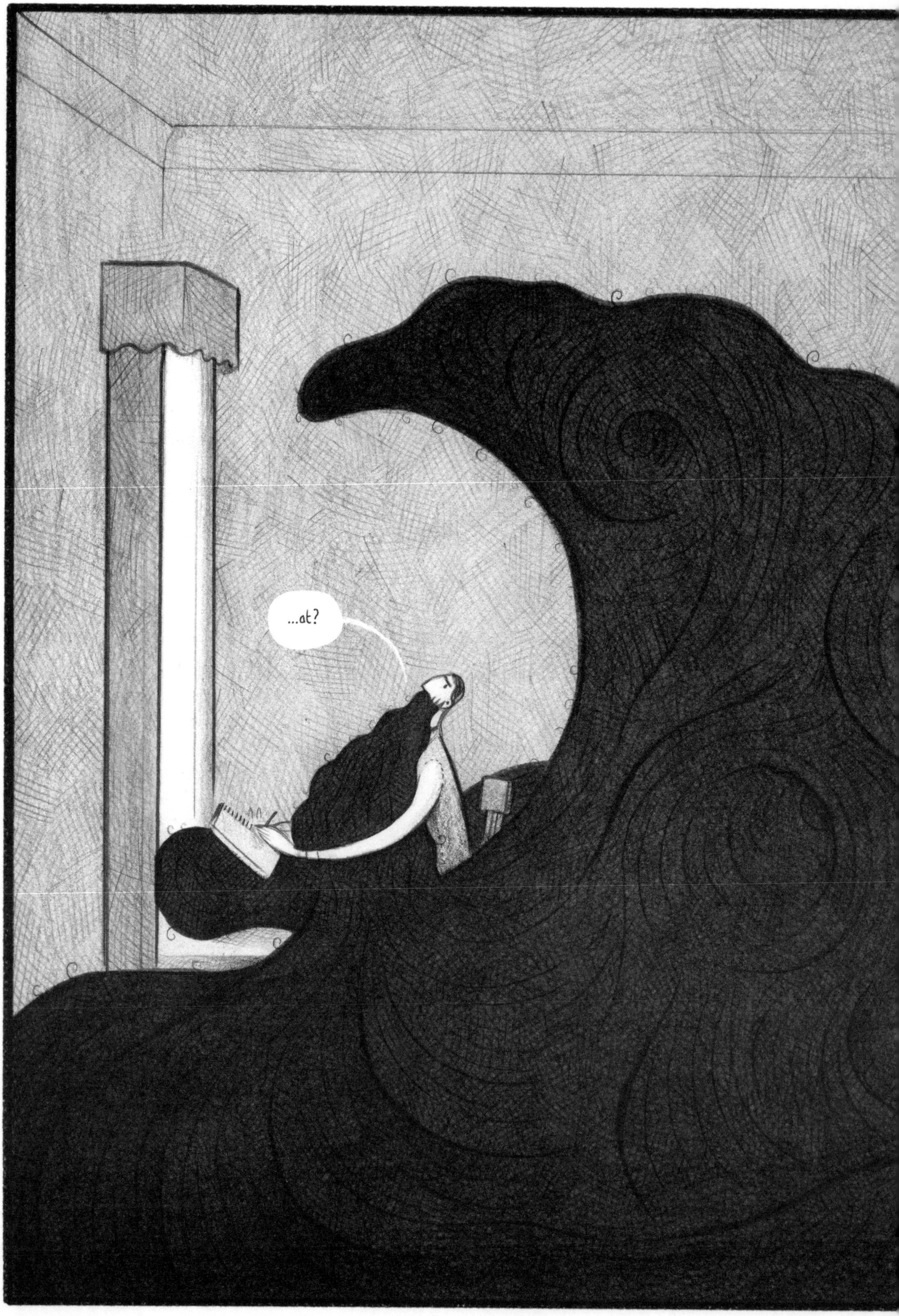
...at?

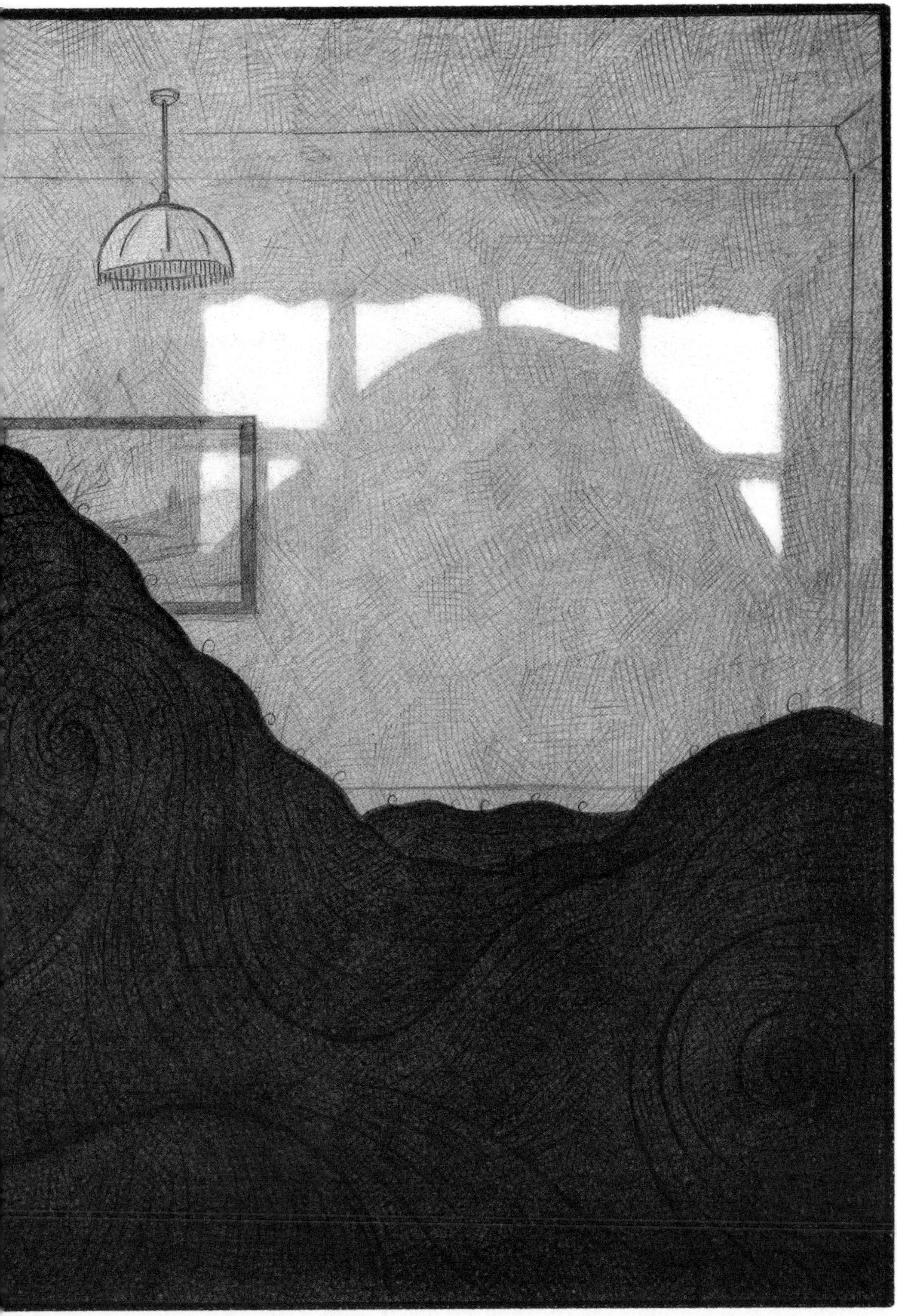

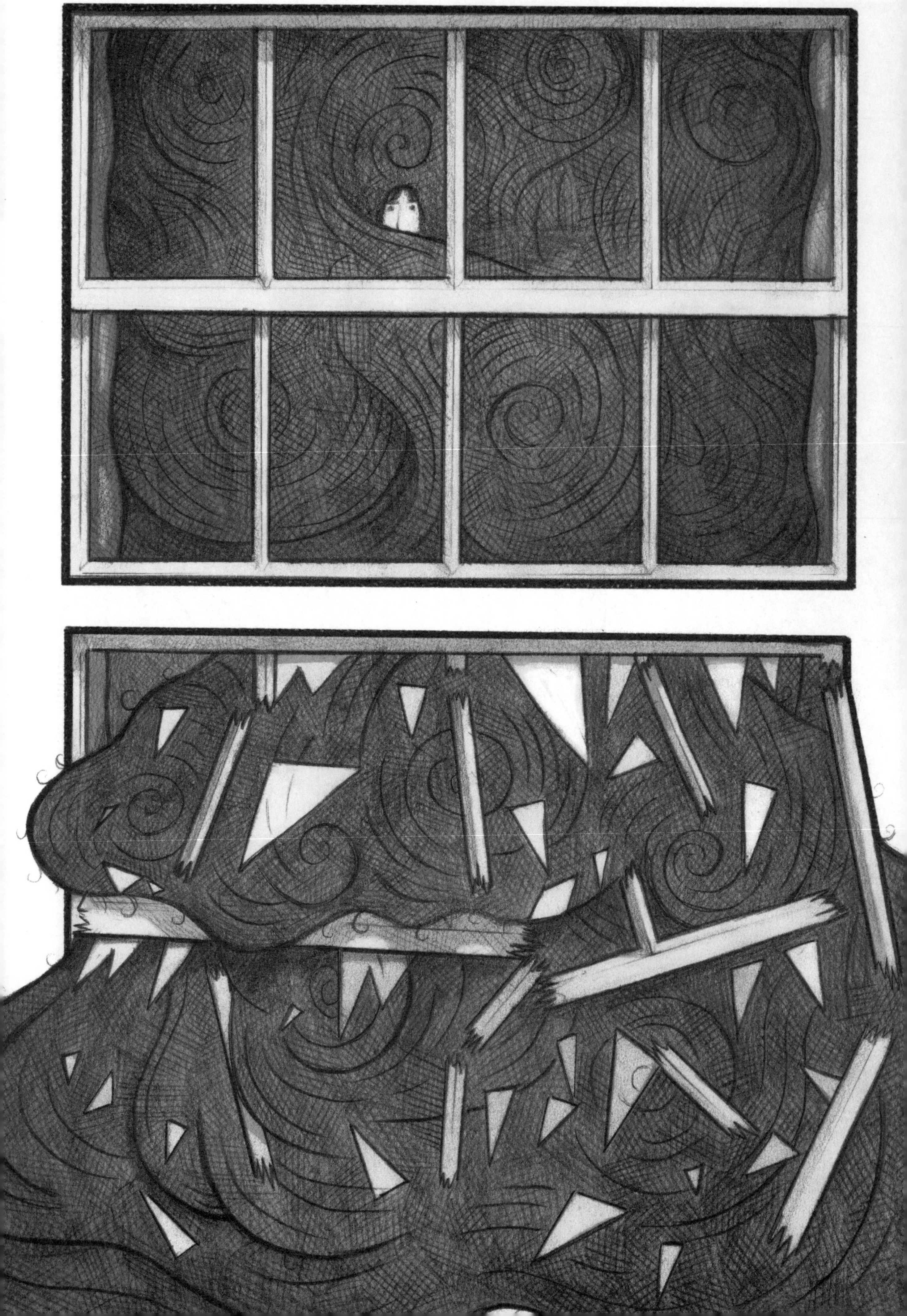

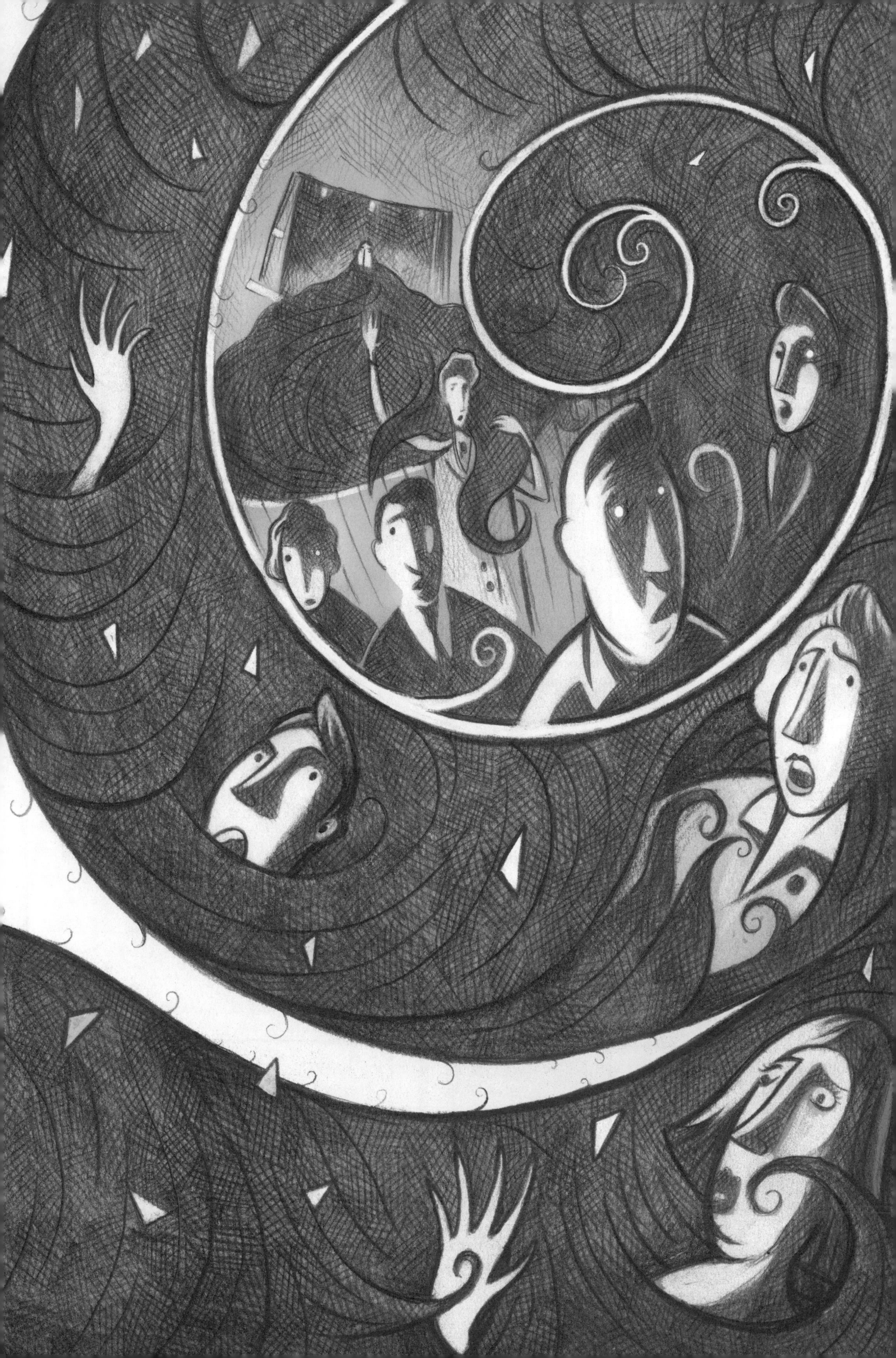

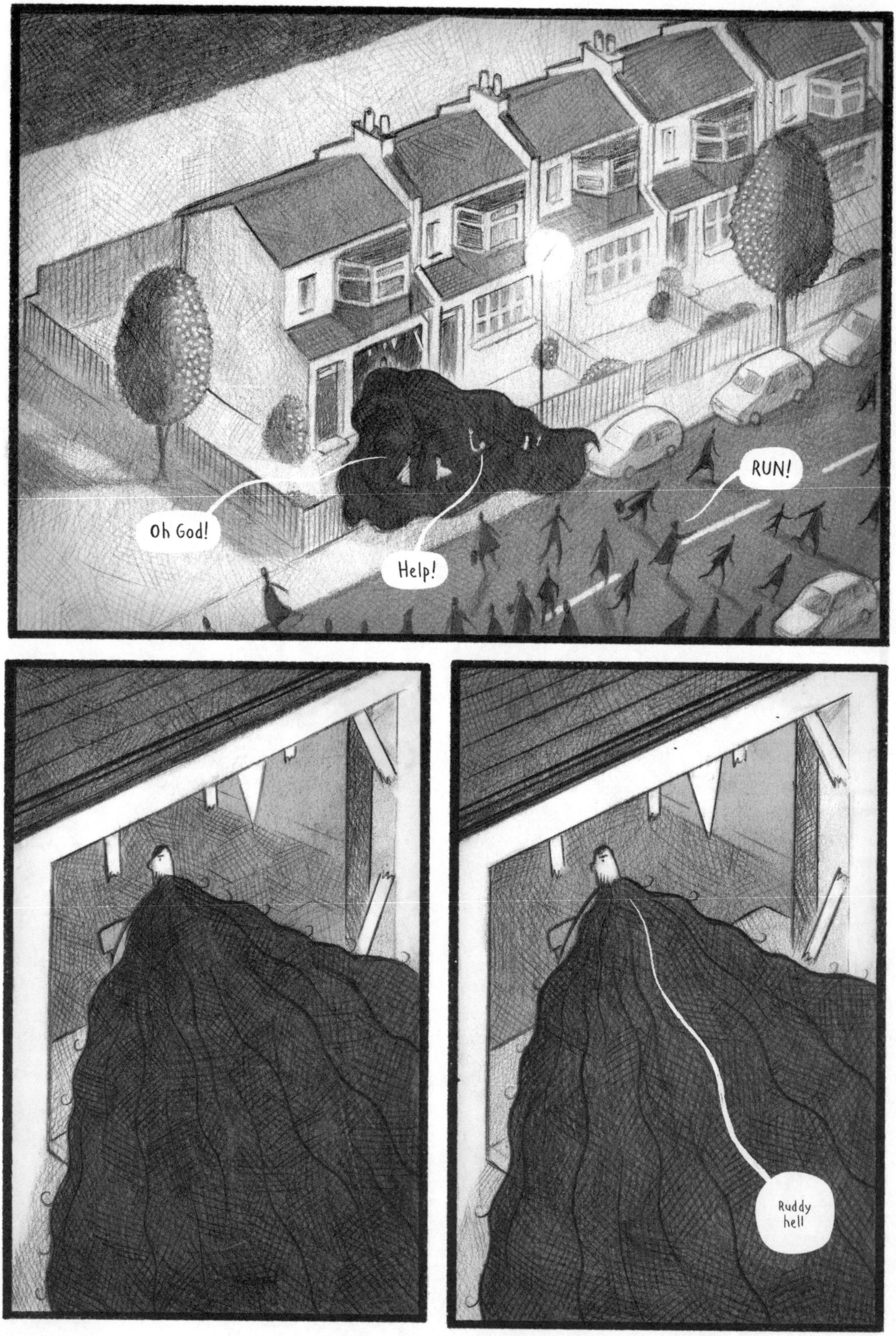
Oh God!
Help!
RUN!
Ruddy hell

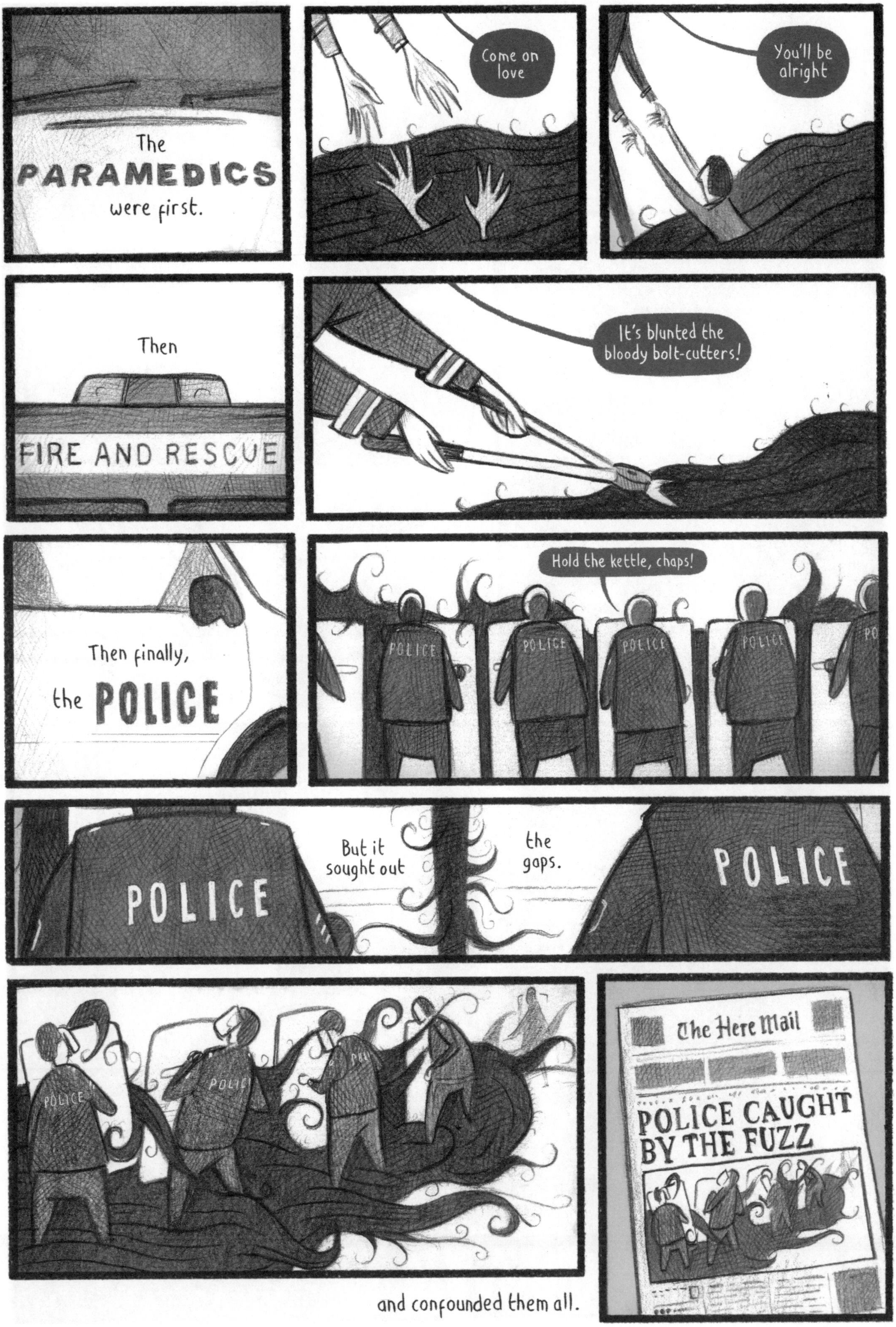
The PARAMEDICS were first.
Come on love
You'll be alright
Then
FIRE AND RESCUE
It's blunted the bloody bolt-cutters!
Then finally, the POLICE
Hold the kettle, chaps!
POLICE
POLICE
POLICE
POLICE
POLICE
But it sought out the gaps.
POLICE
POLICE
POLICE
POLICE
and confounded them all.
The Here Mail
POLICE CAUGHT BY THE FUZZ

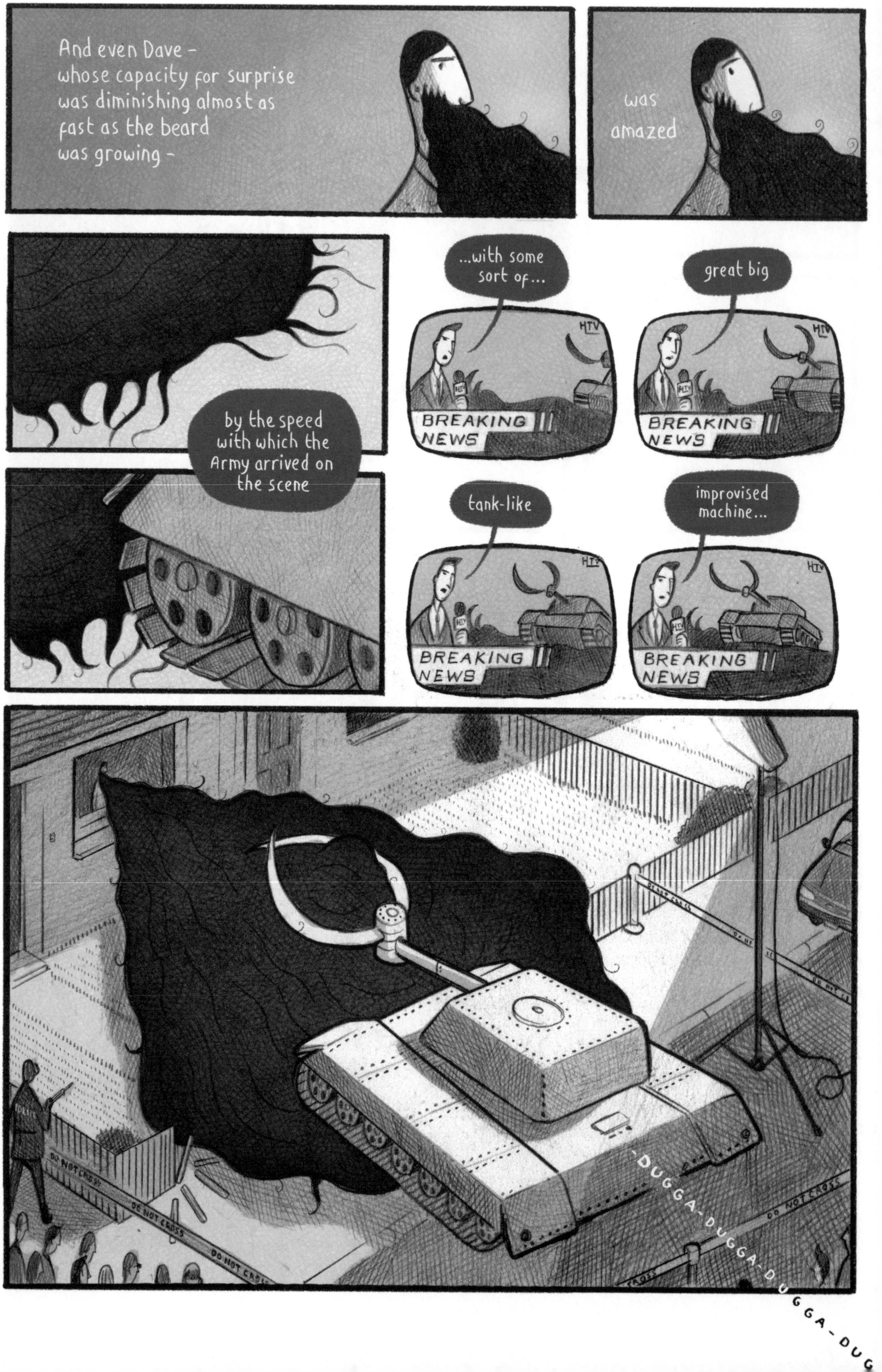
And even Dave – whose capacity for surprise was diminishing almost as fast as the beard was growing –
was amazed
by the speed with which the Army arrived on the scene
...with some sort of...
BREAKING NEWS
great big
BREAKING NEWS
tank-like
BREAKING NEWS
improvised machine...
BREAKING NEWS
DO NOT CROSS
DUGGA-DUGGA-DUGGA-DUG

He was also surprised

-DUGGA-DUGGA-DUGG

JGGA-DUGGA-DUGGA-DUGGA-

DUGGA-DUGGA-DUGGA-DUGGA-DUGGA-

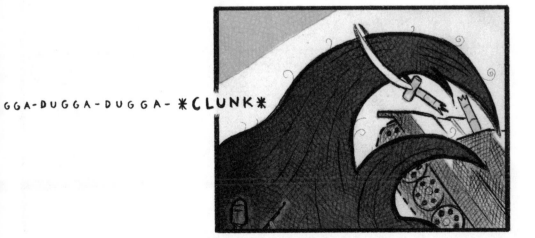

GGA-DUGGA-DUGGA- *CLUNK*

by how quickly
it defeated them.

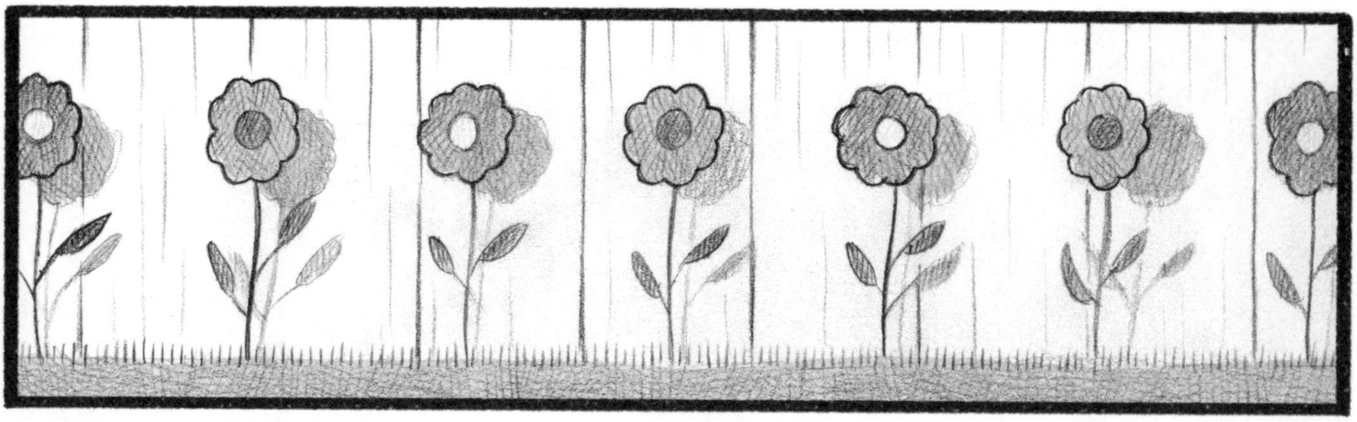

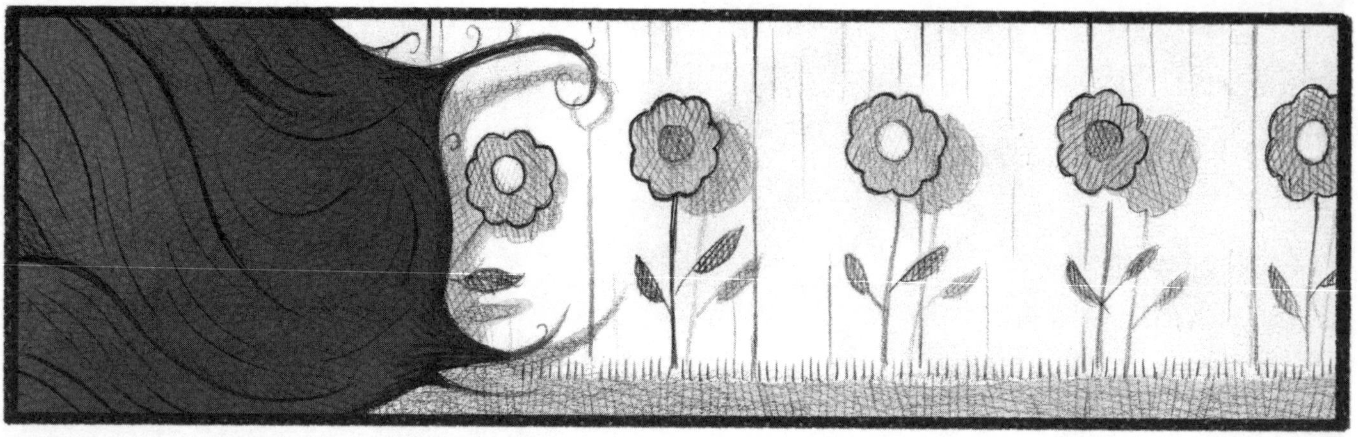

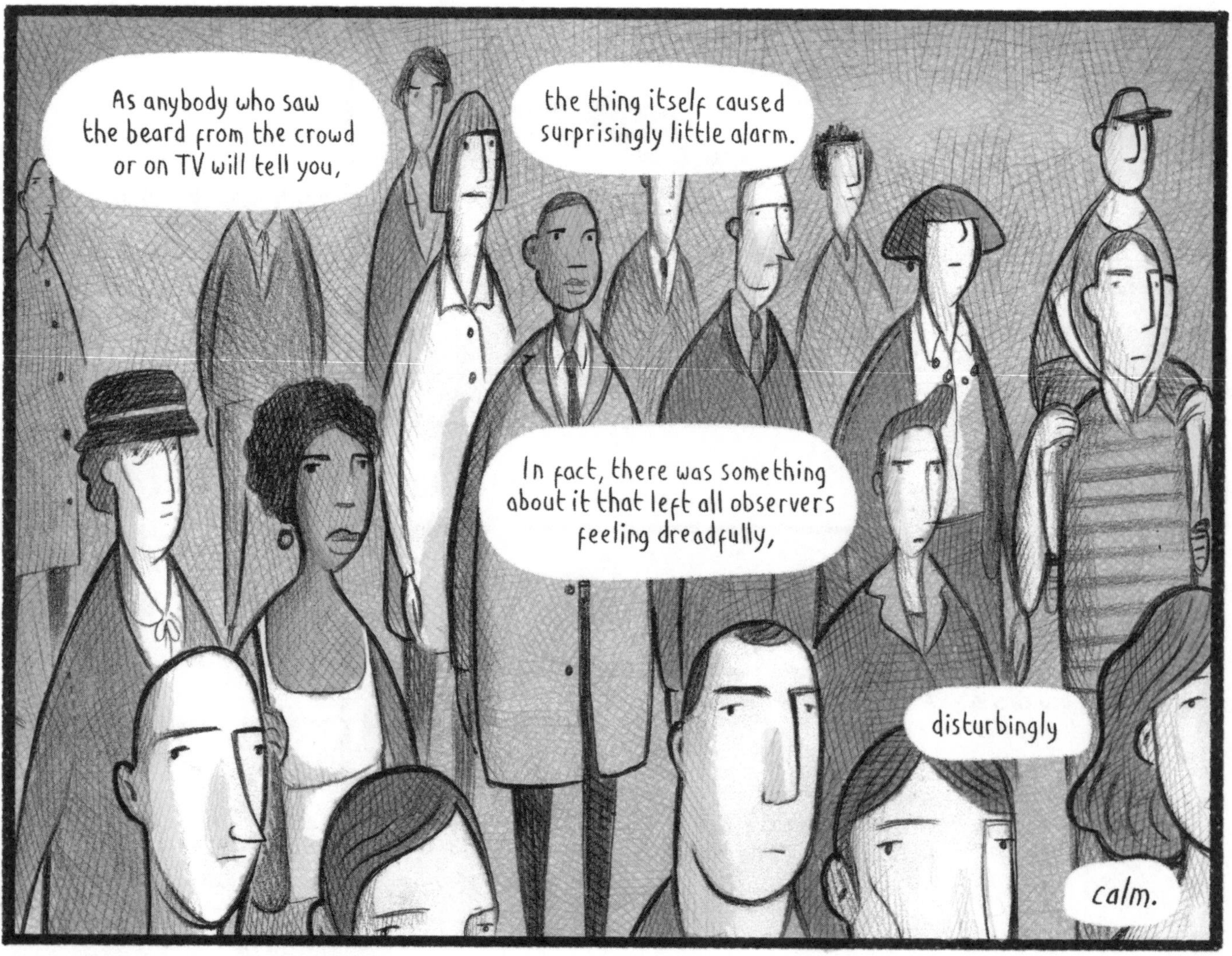

As anybody who saw the beard from the crowd or on TV will tell you,
the thing itself caused surprisingly little alarm.
In fact, there was something about it that left all observers feeling dreadfully,
disturbingly
calm.

Its blackness seemed to drown all thought.

People found themselves watching it for hours

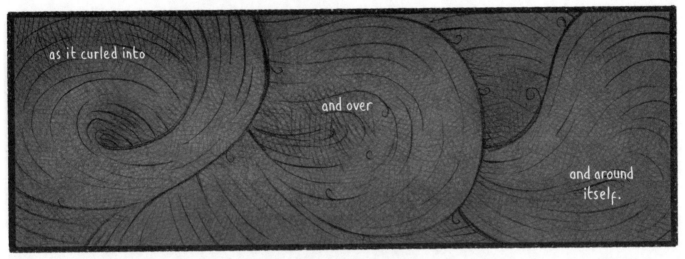

as it curled into and over and around itself.

It seemed to evade *definition* somehow,

for its top side was its underside its right side was its left side and its inside was its outside.

In fact, when people looked at it closely,

they couldn't even tell where it stopped.

Soon enough, observers reported strange psychological phenomena

such as hypnosis

or a disconcerting feeling

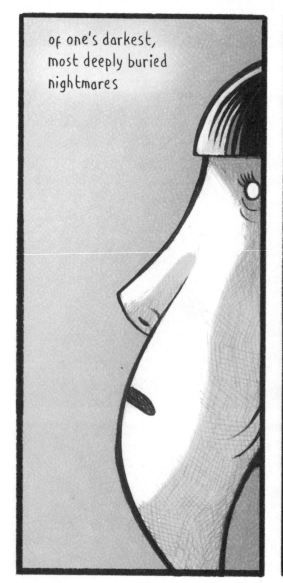

of one's darkest, most deeply buried nightmares

migrating to the surface

And strangest of all, a distinct sense

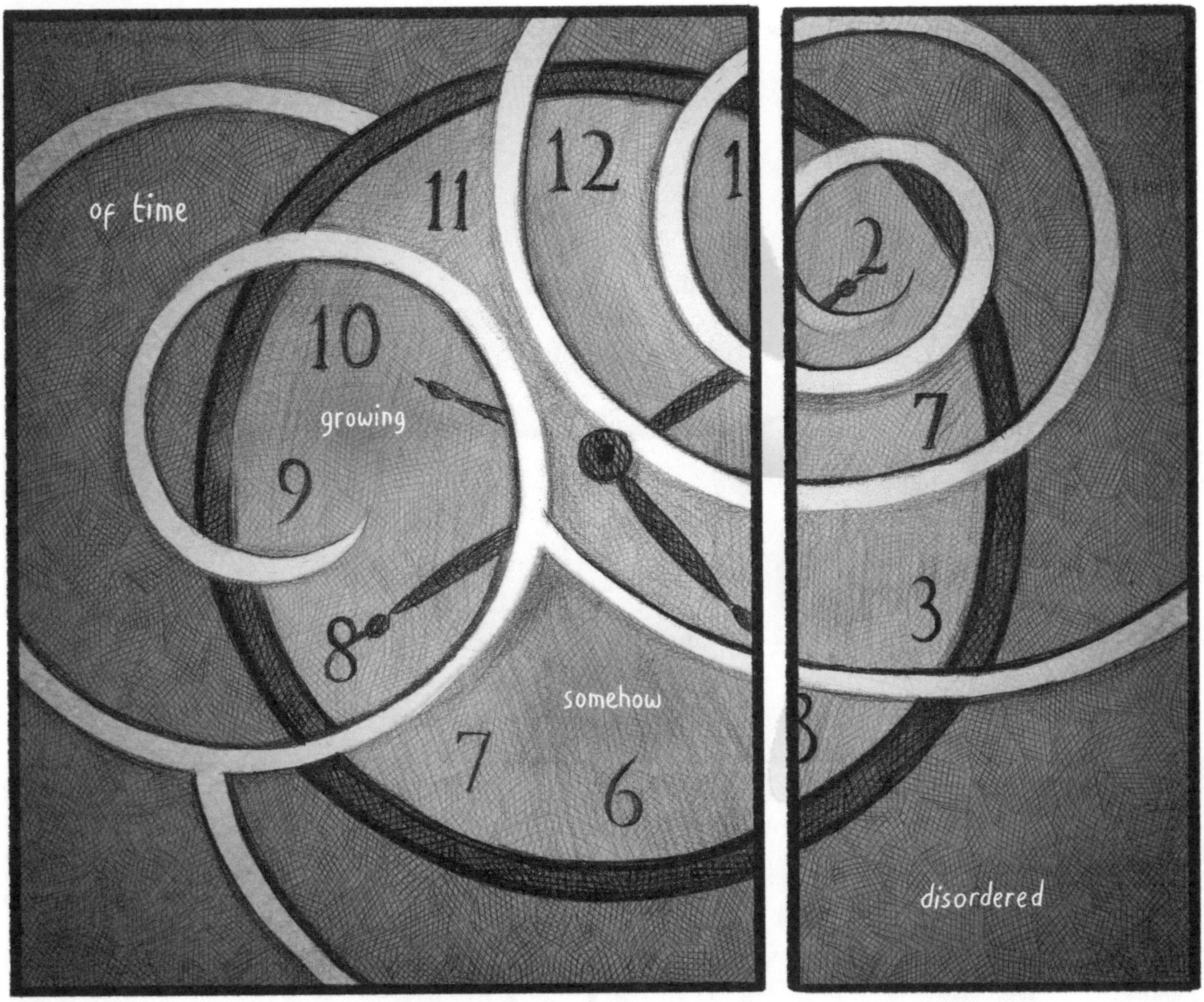
of time
growing
somehow
disordered

to the point where reality seemed to run...

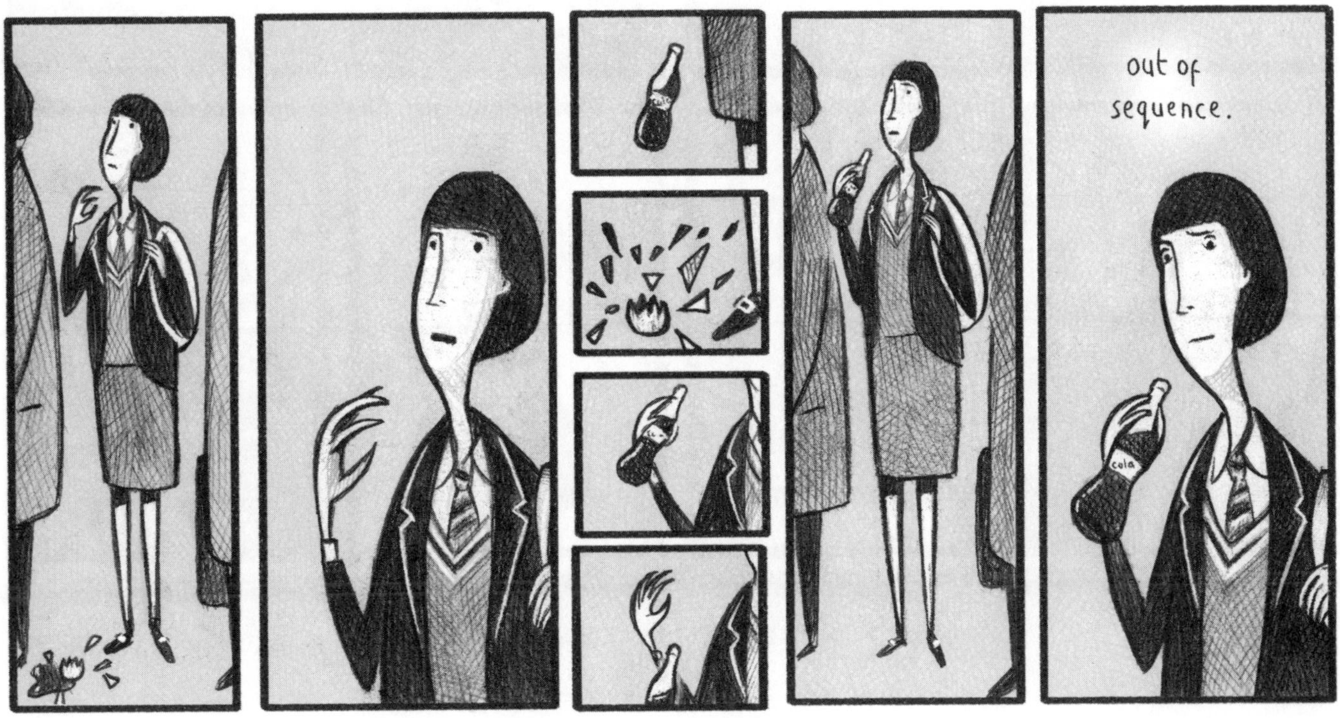
out of
sequence.

They said:

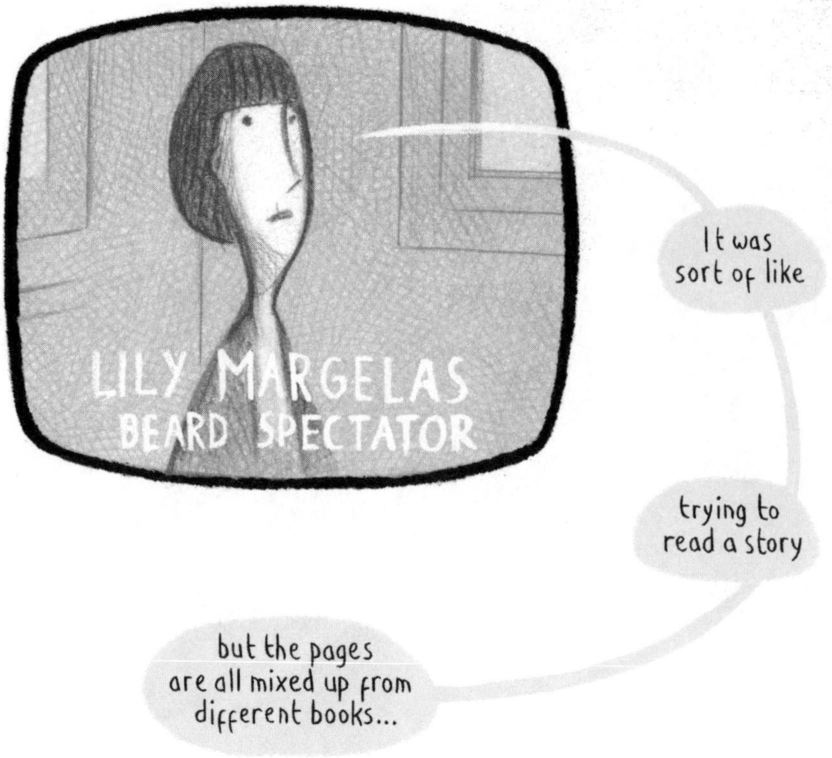

LILY MARGELAS
BEARD SPECTATOR
It was sort of like
trying to read a story
but the pages are all mixed up from different books...

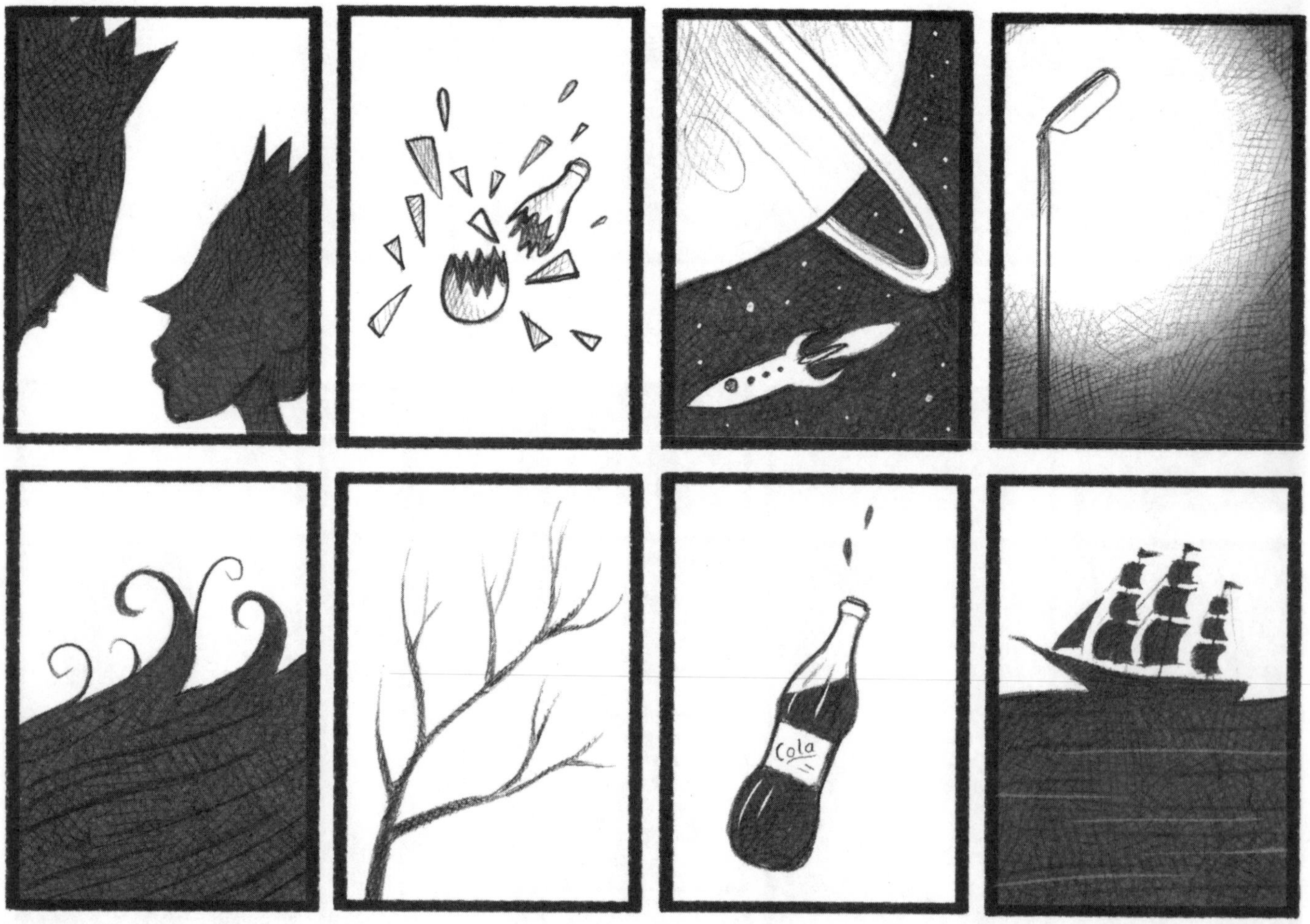

Cola

...so that it can't be read. Y'know?

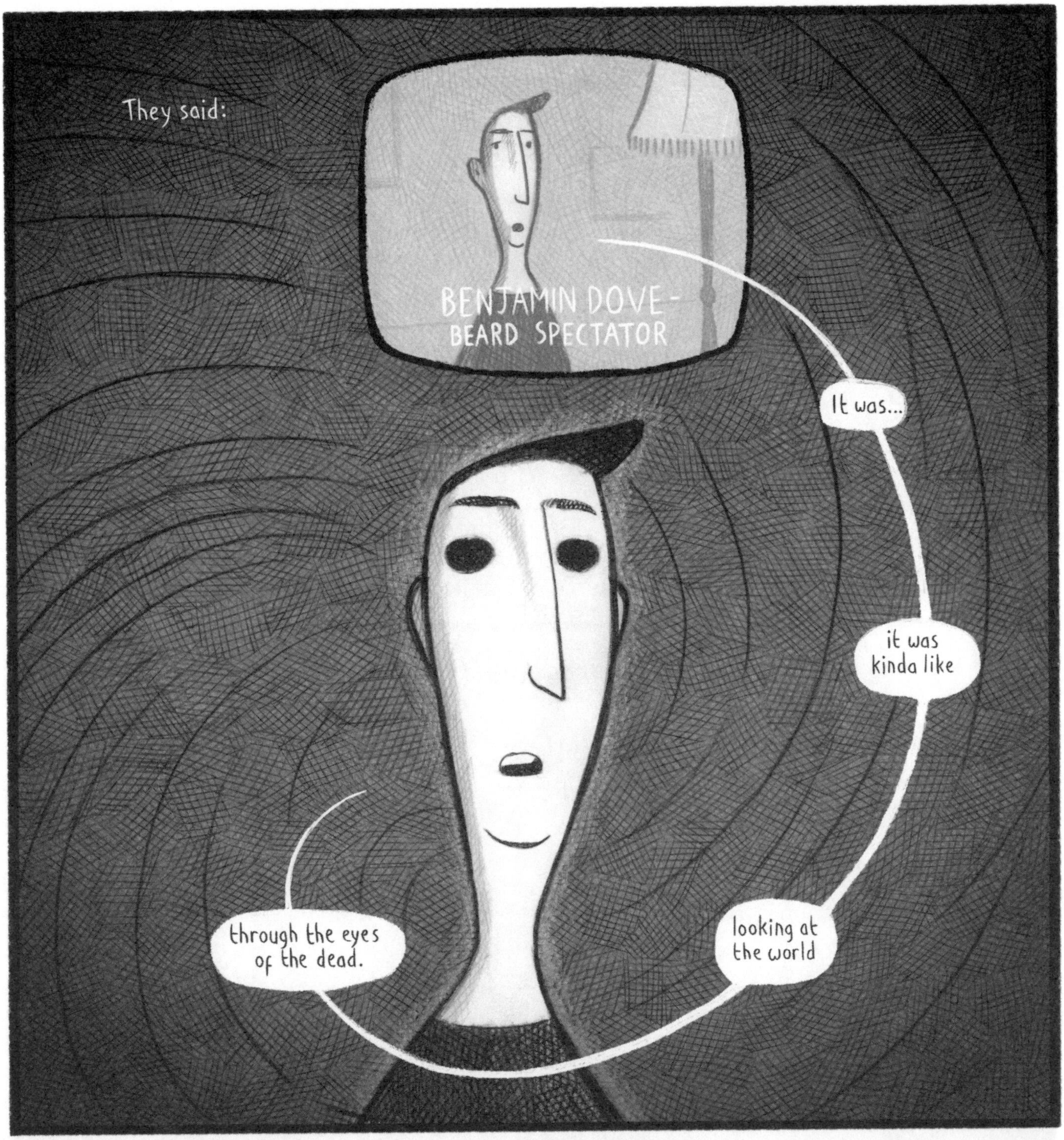
They said:
BENJAMIN DOVE-
BEARD SPECTATOR
It was...
it was kinda like
looking at the world
through the eyes of the dead.

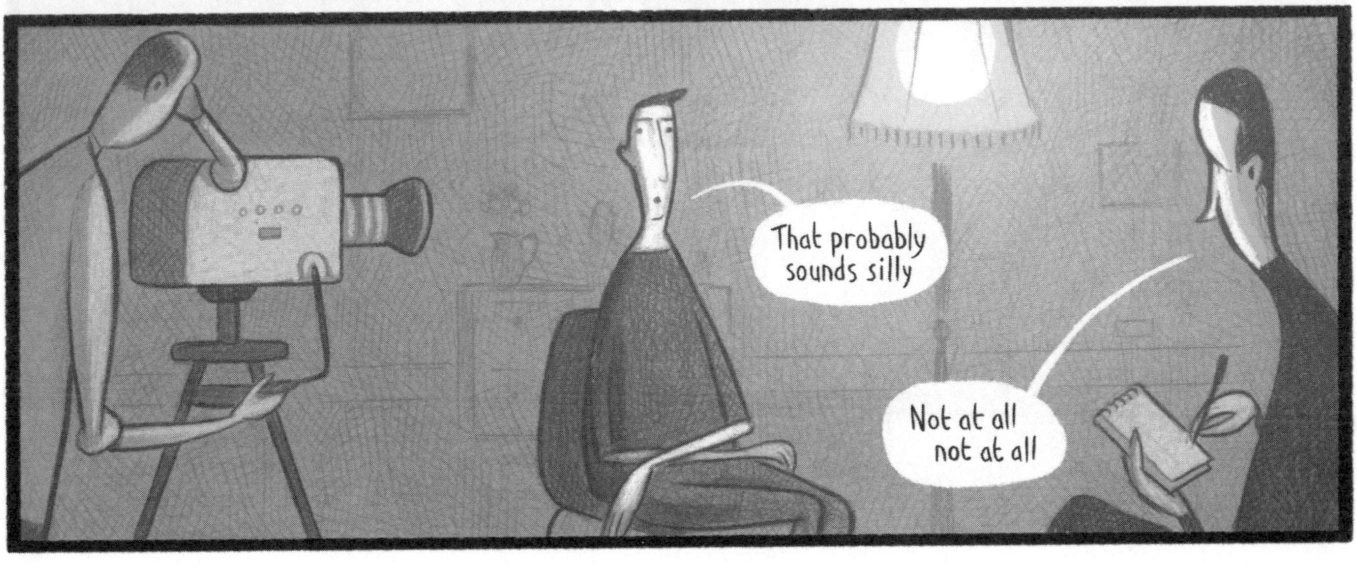
That probably sounds silly
Not at all not at all

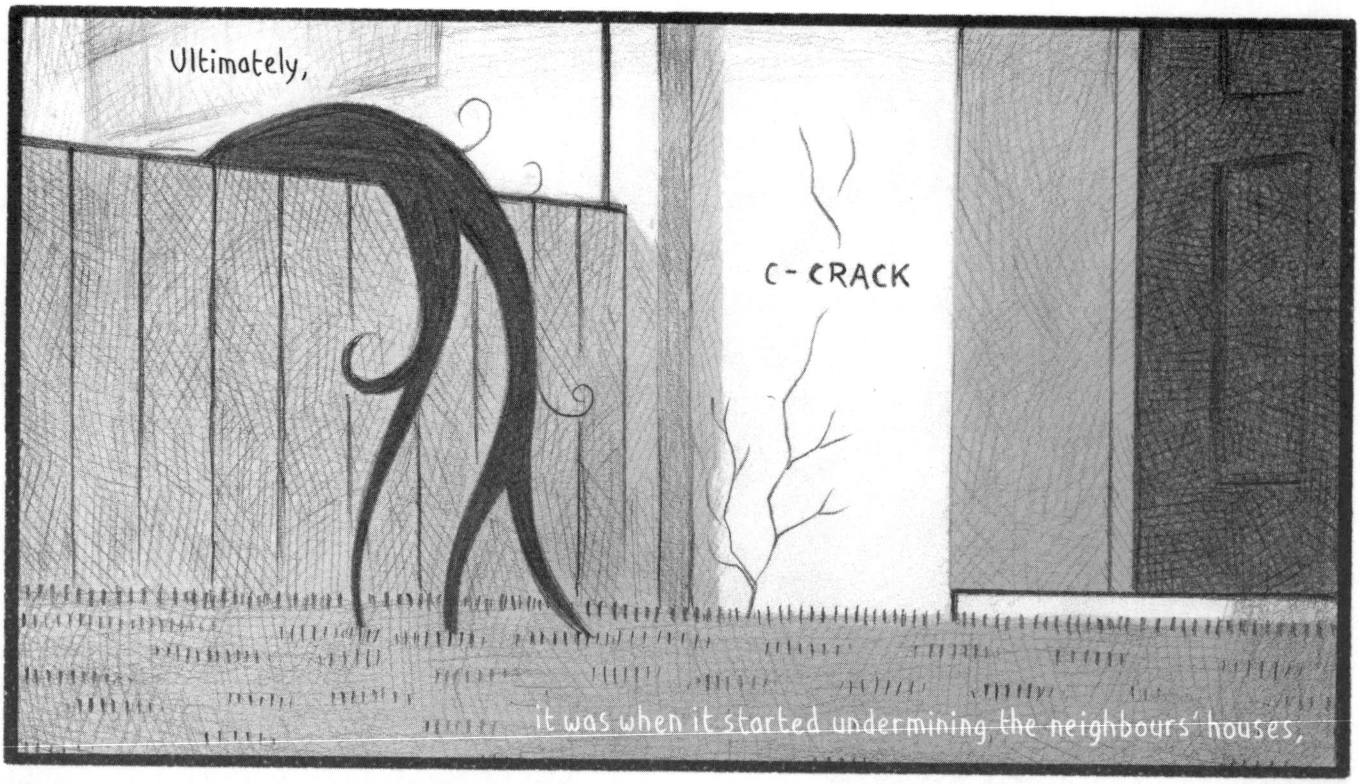
Ultimately,
C-CRACK
it was when it started undermining the neighbours' houses,

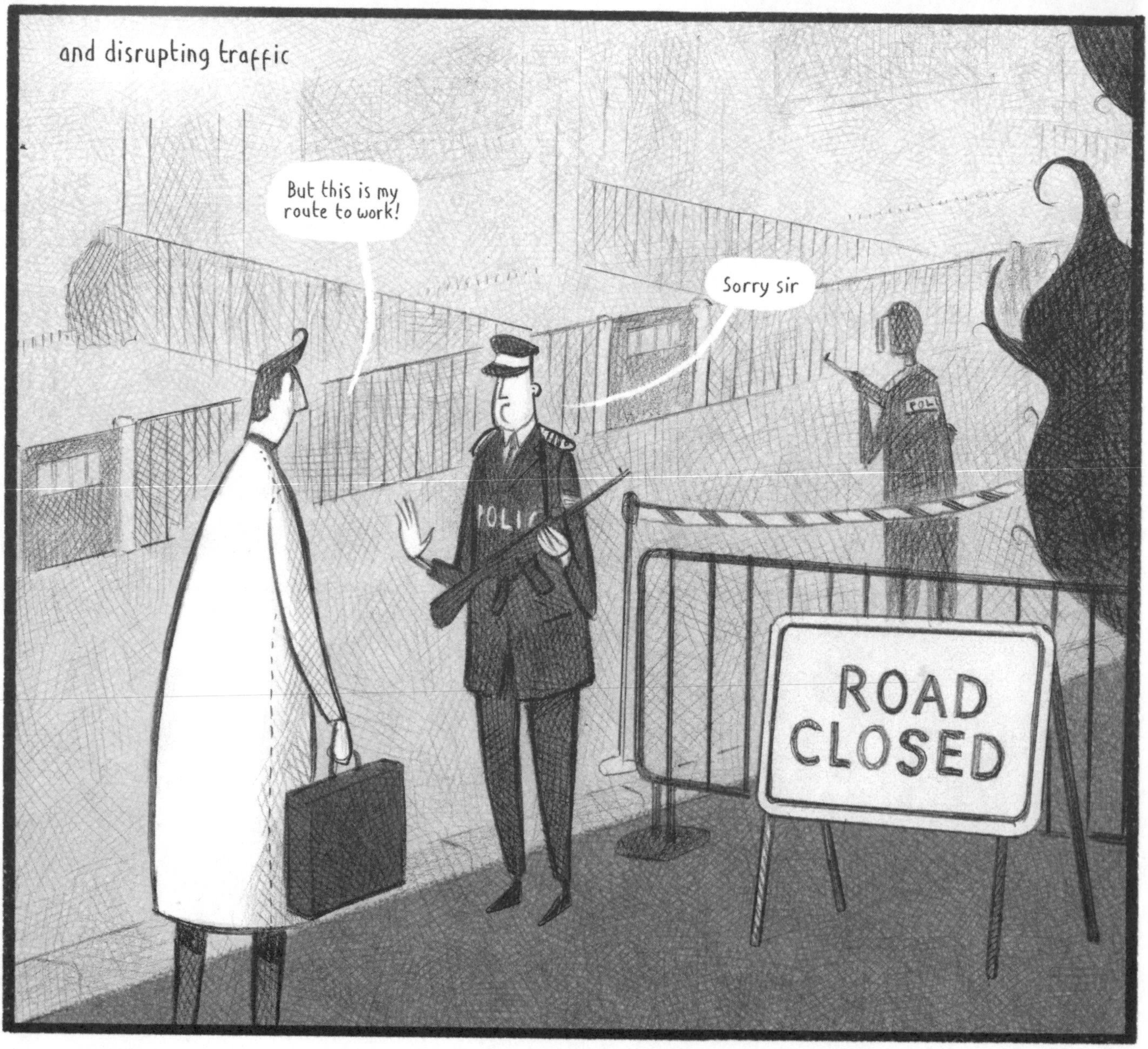
and disrupting traffic
But this is my route to work!
Sorry sir
ROAD CLOSED

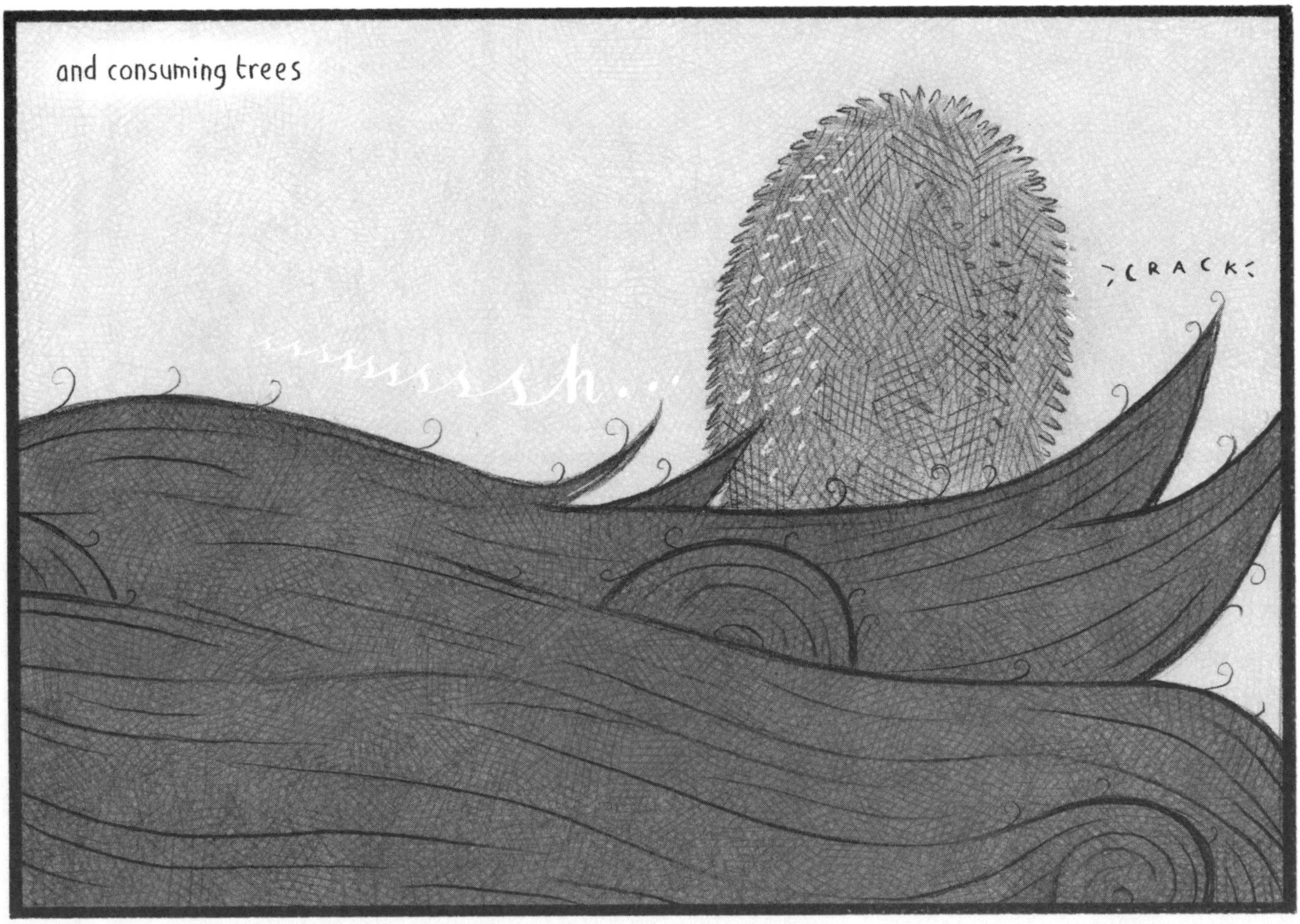
and consuming trees
CRACK

and attracting wildlife

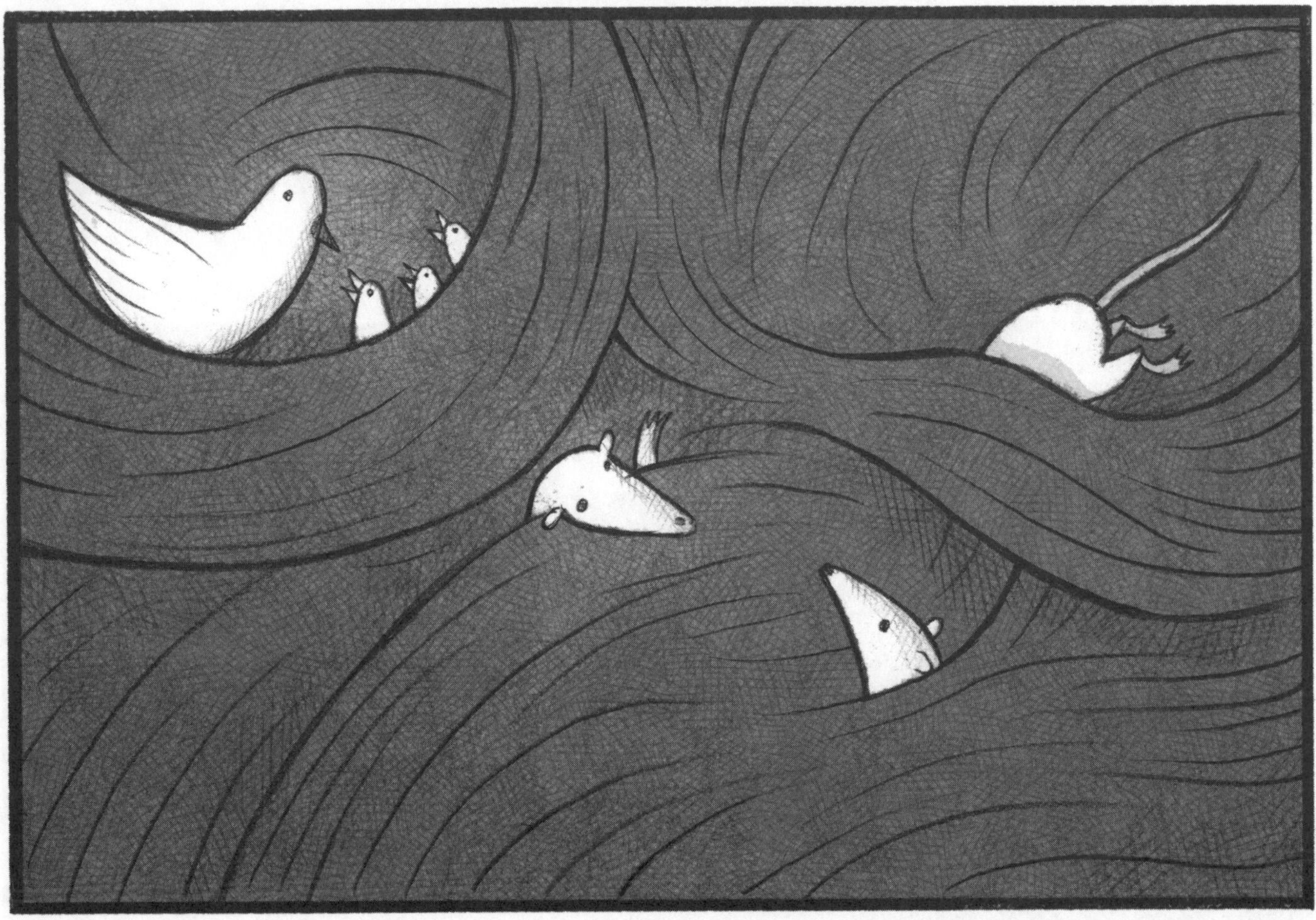

...that the Government finally decided on more drastic action.

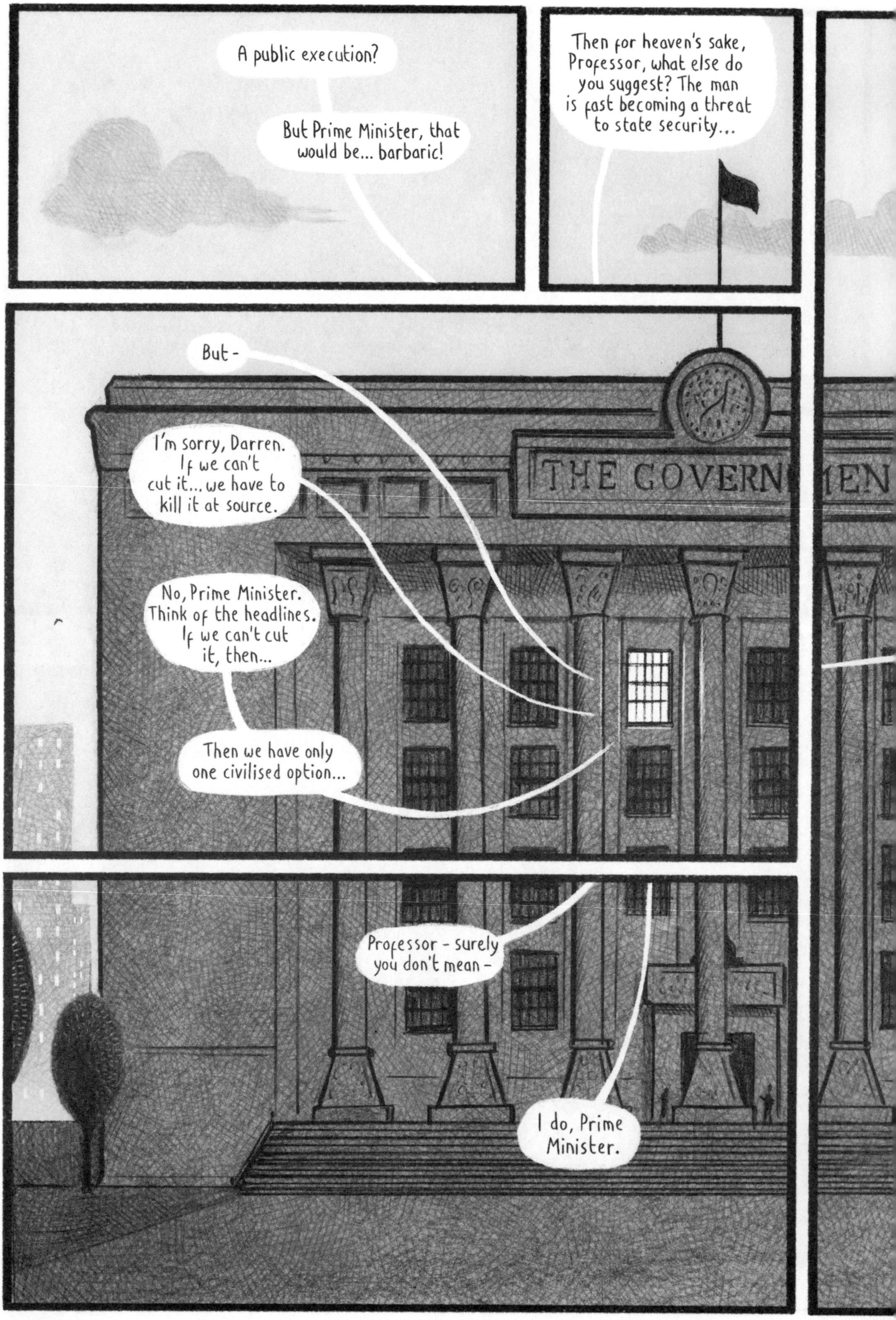
A public execution?
But Prime Minister, that would be... barbaric!
Then for heaven's sake, Professor, what else do you suggest? The man is fast becoming a threat to state security...
THE GOVERN MEN
But-
I'm sorry, Darren. If we can't cut it... we have to kill it at source.
No, Prime Minister. Think of the headlines. If we can't cut it, then...
Then we have only one civilised option...
Professor - surely you don't mean -
I do, Prime Minister.

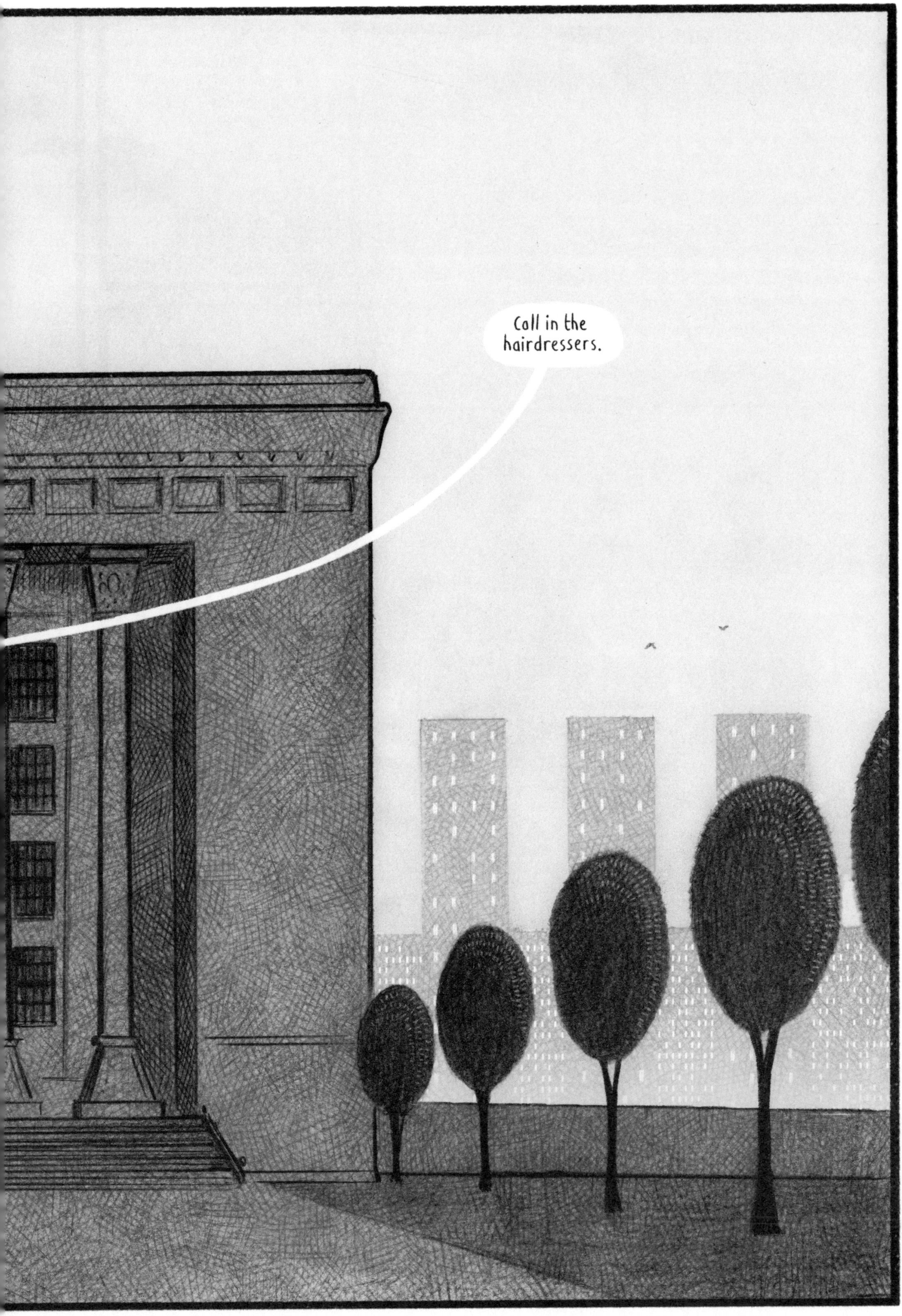
Call in the
hairdressers.

Three
months
later.

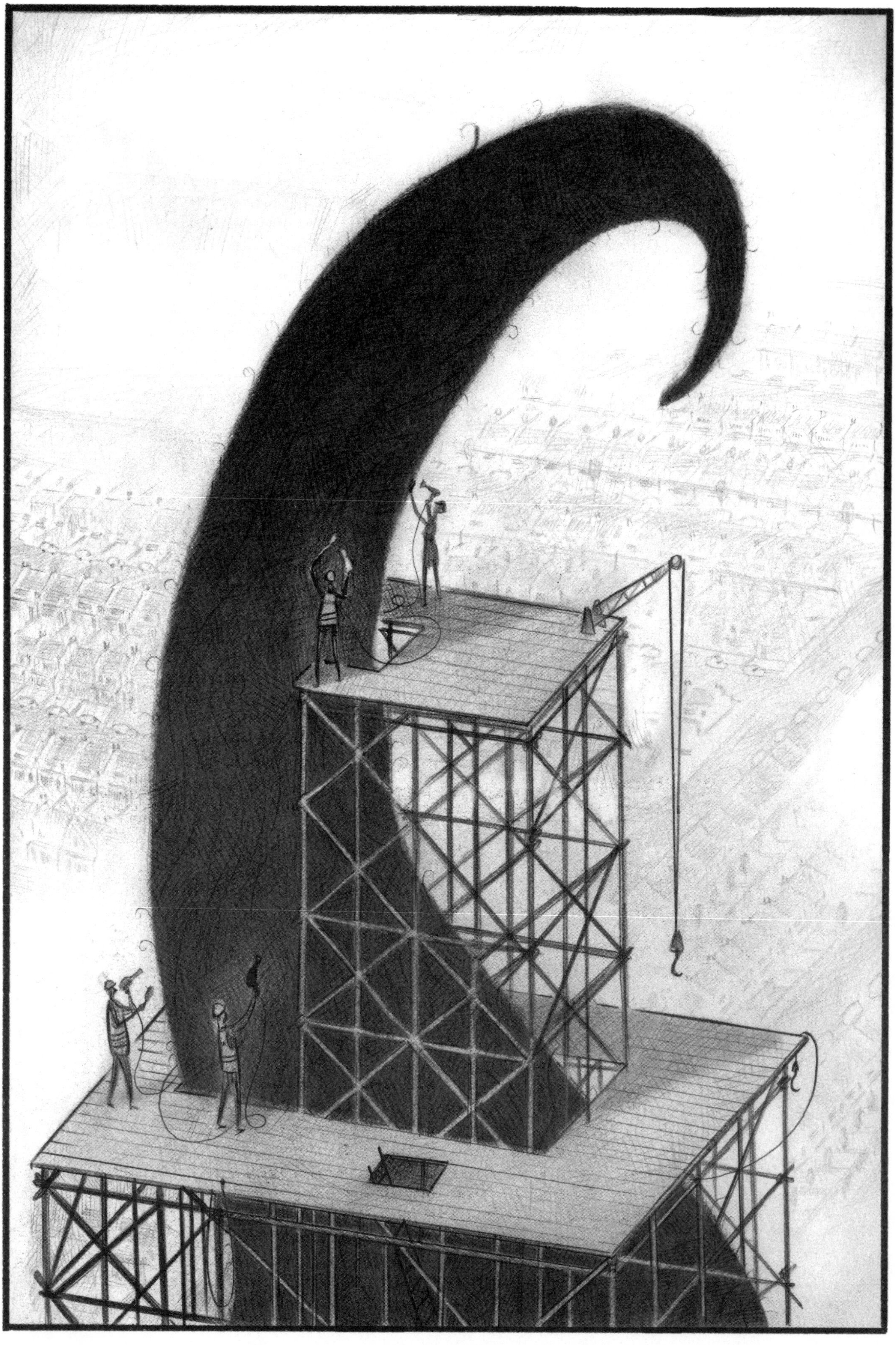

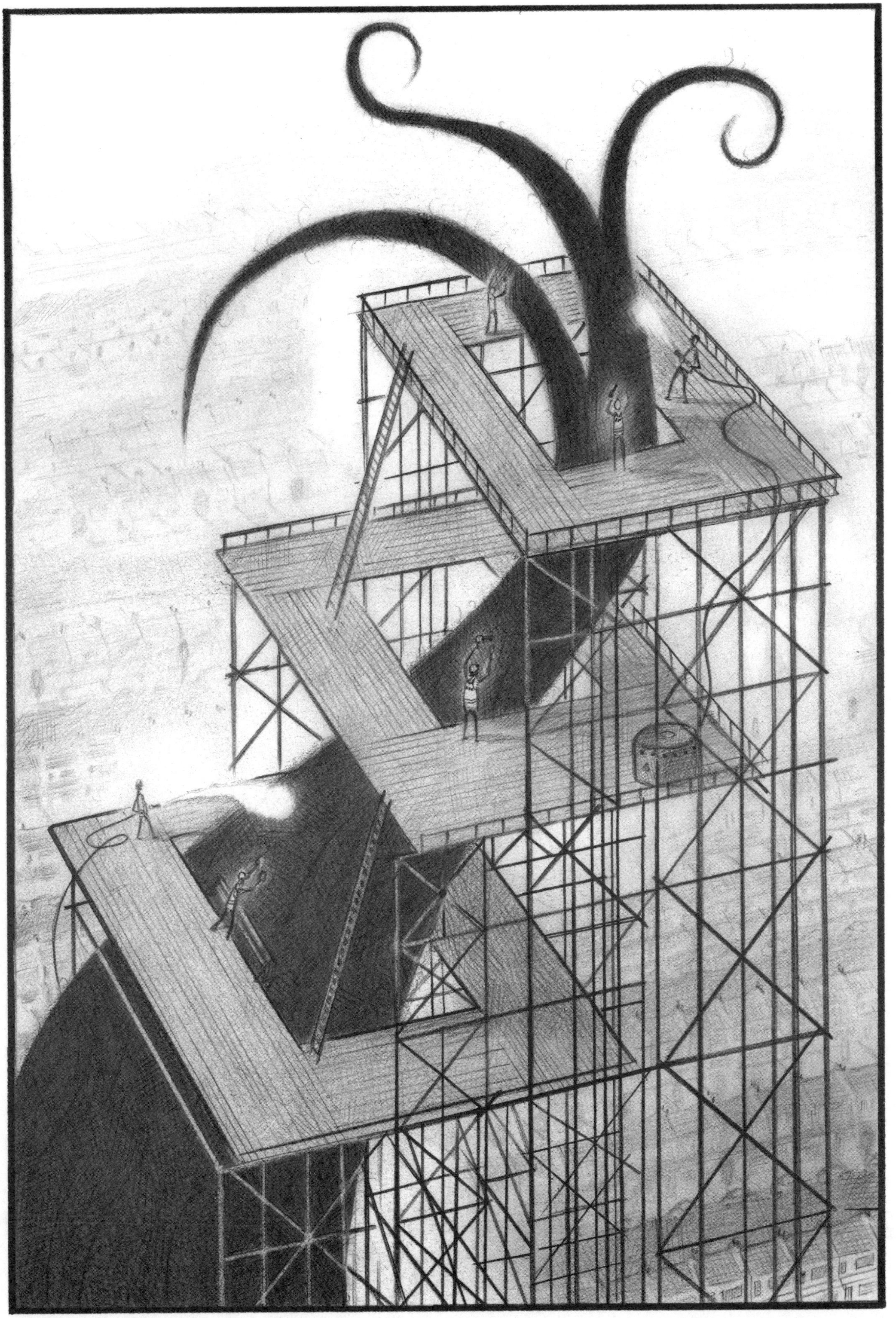

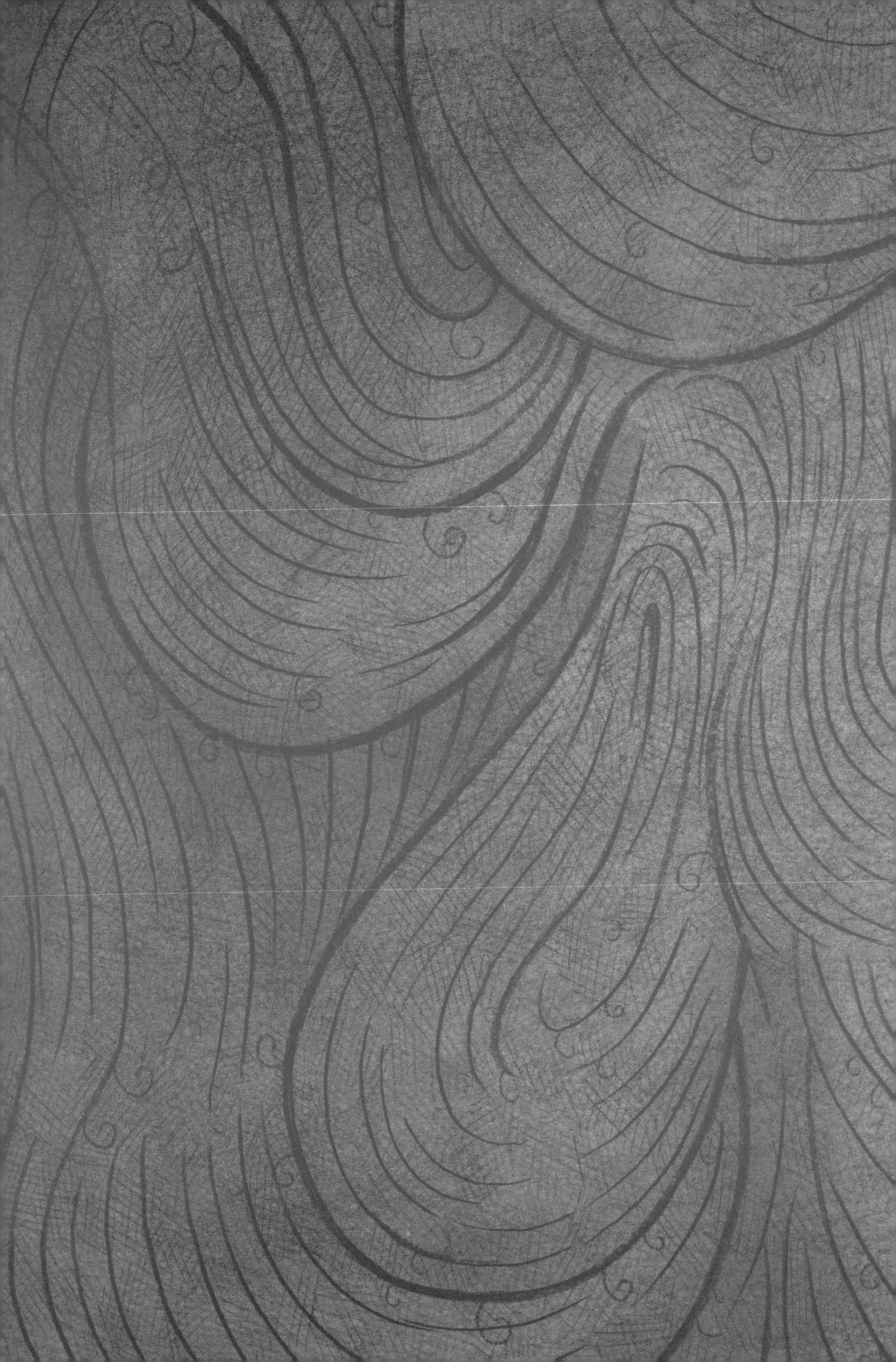

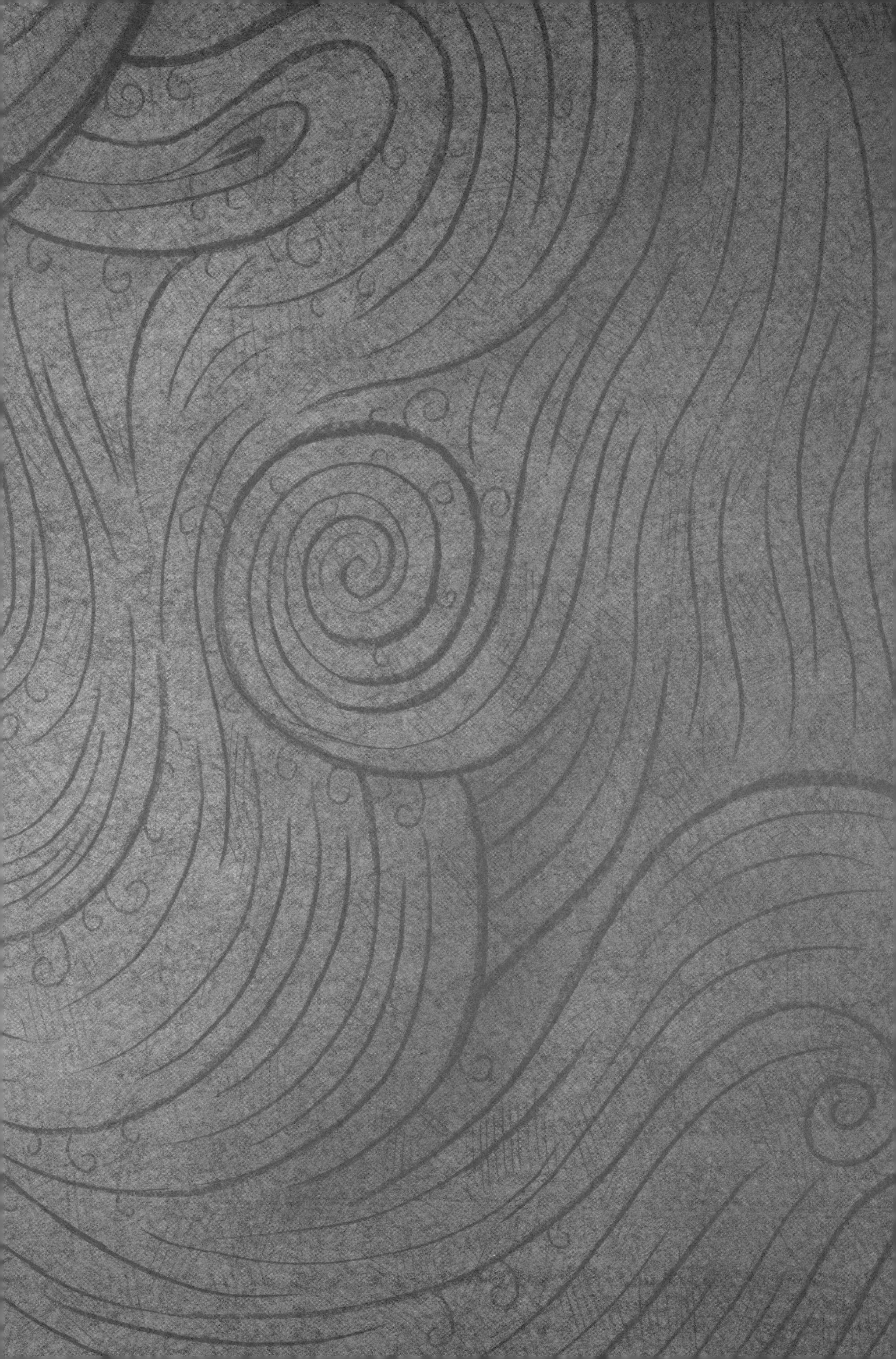

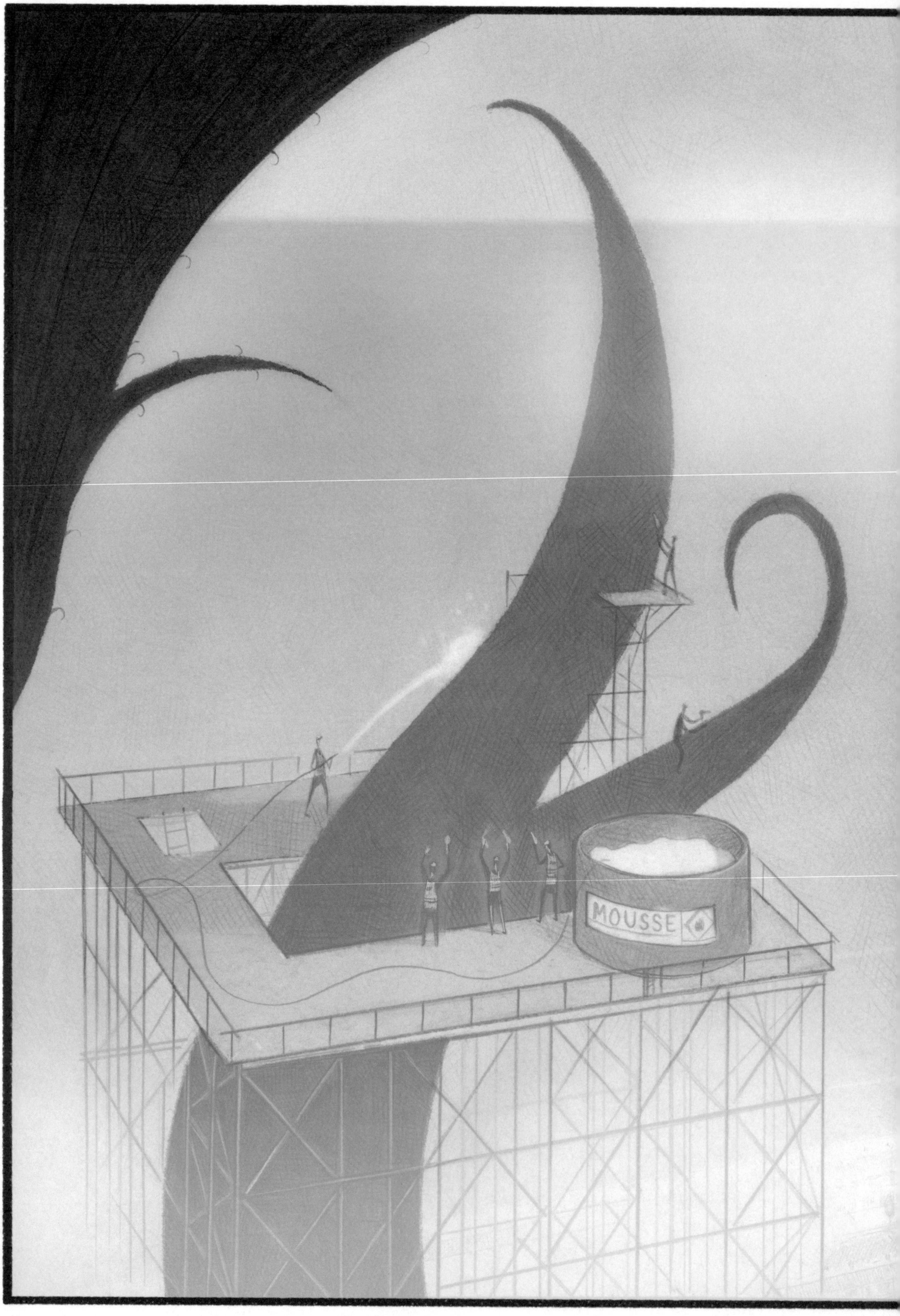
MOUSSE

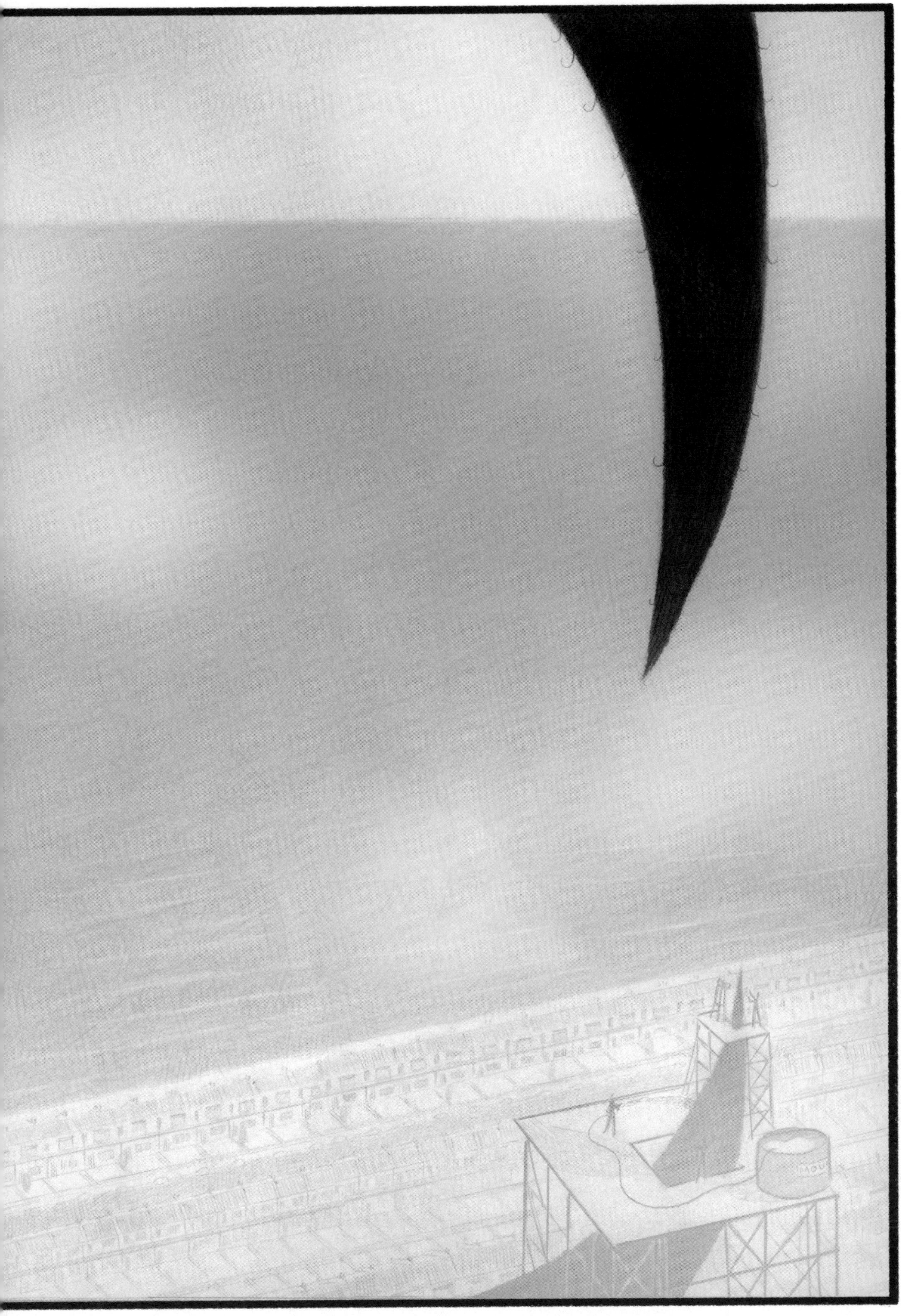

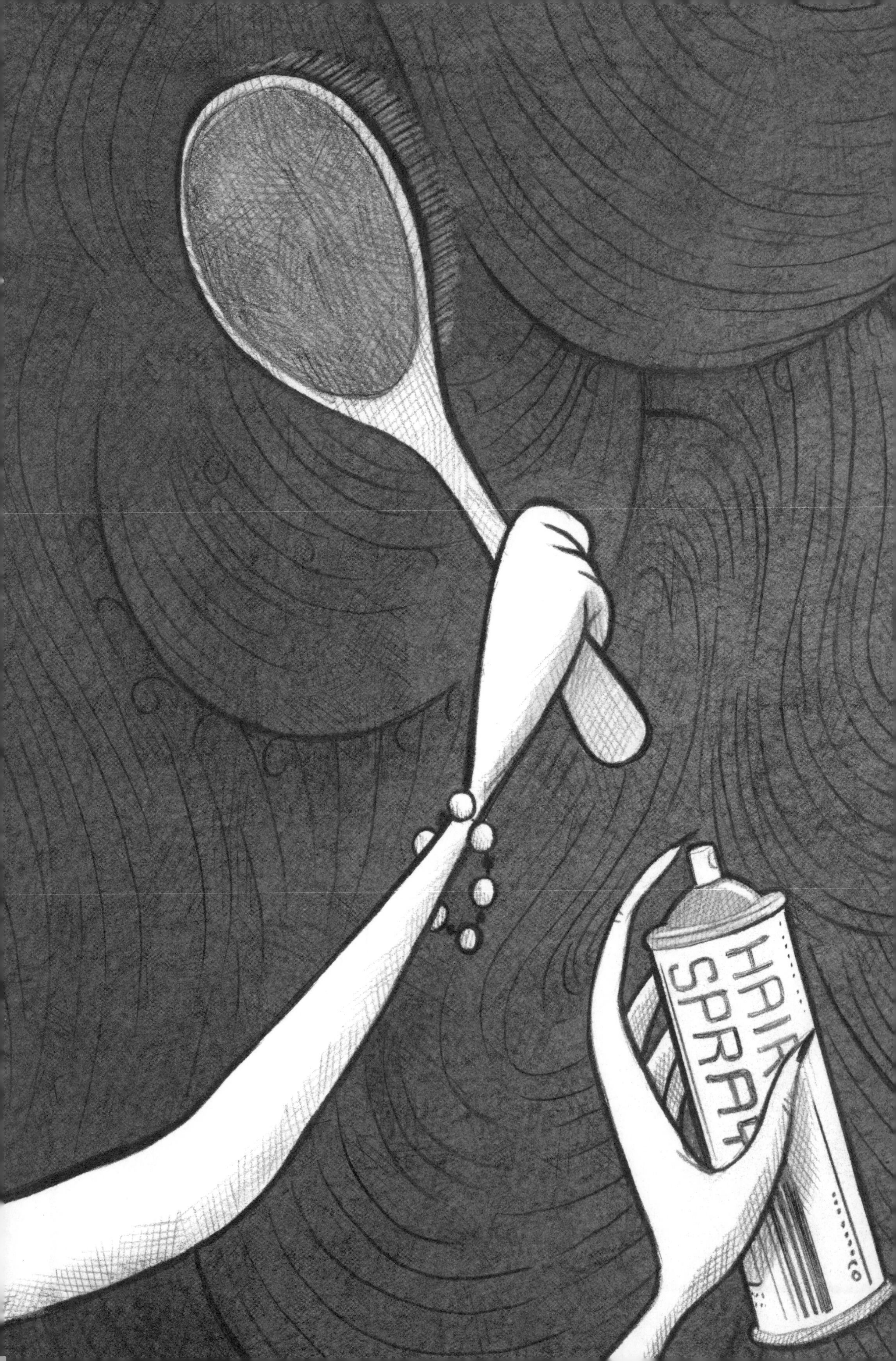
HAIR SPRAY

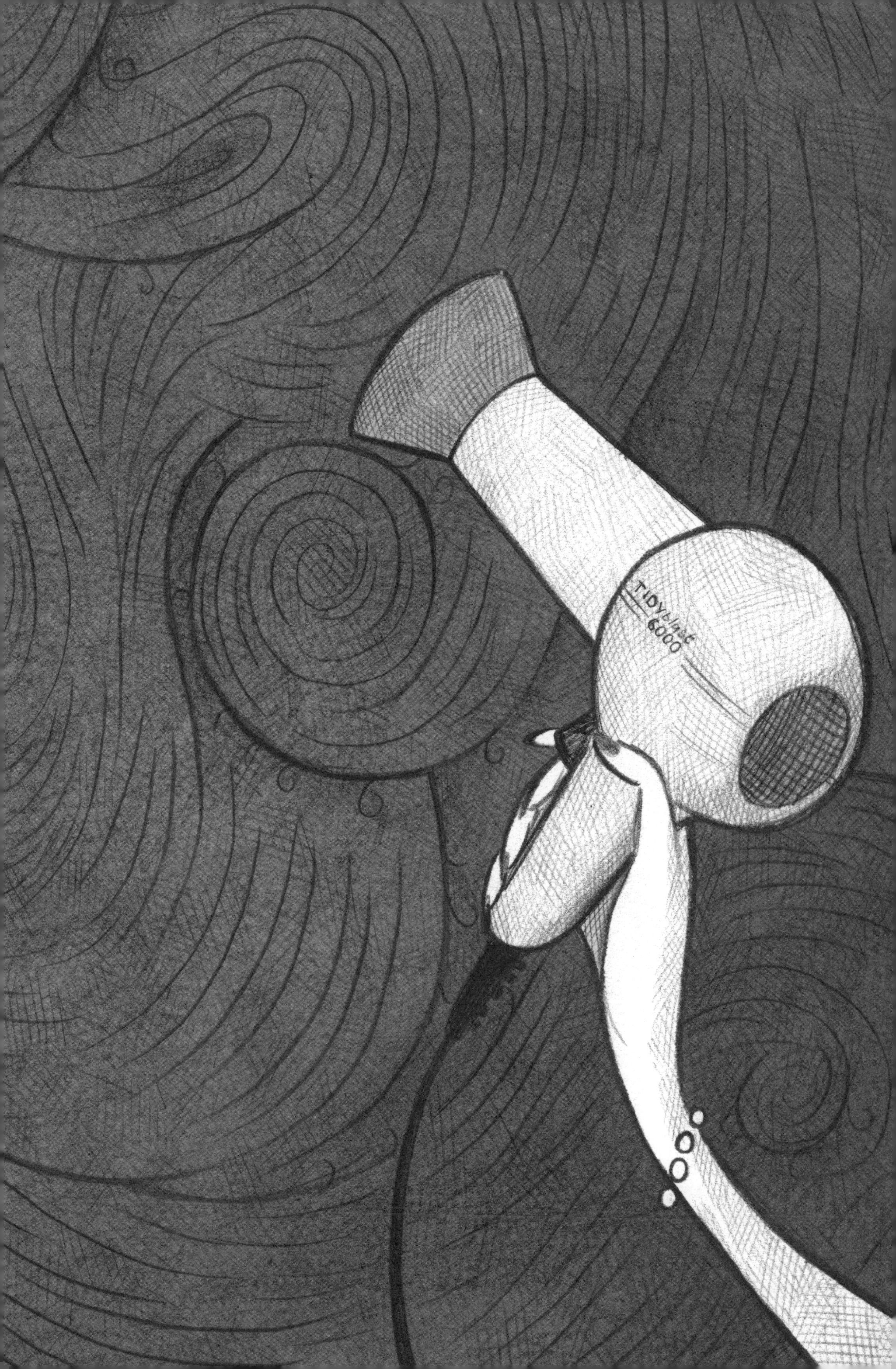
TIDYblast
6000

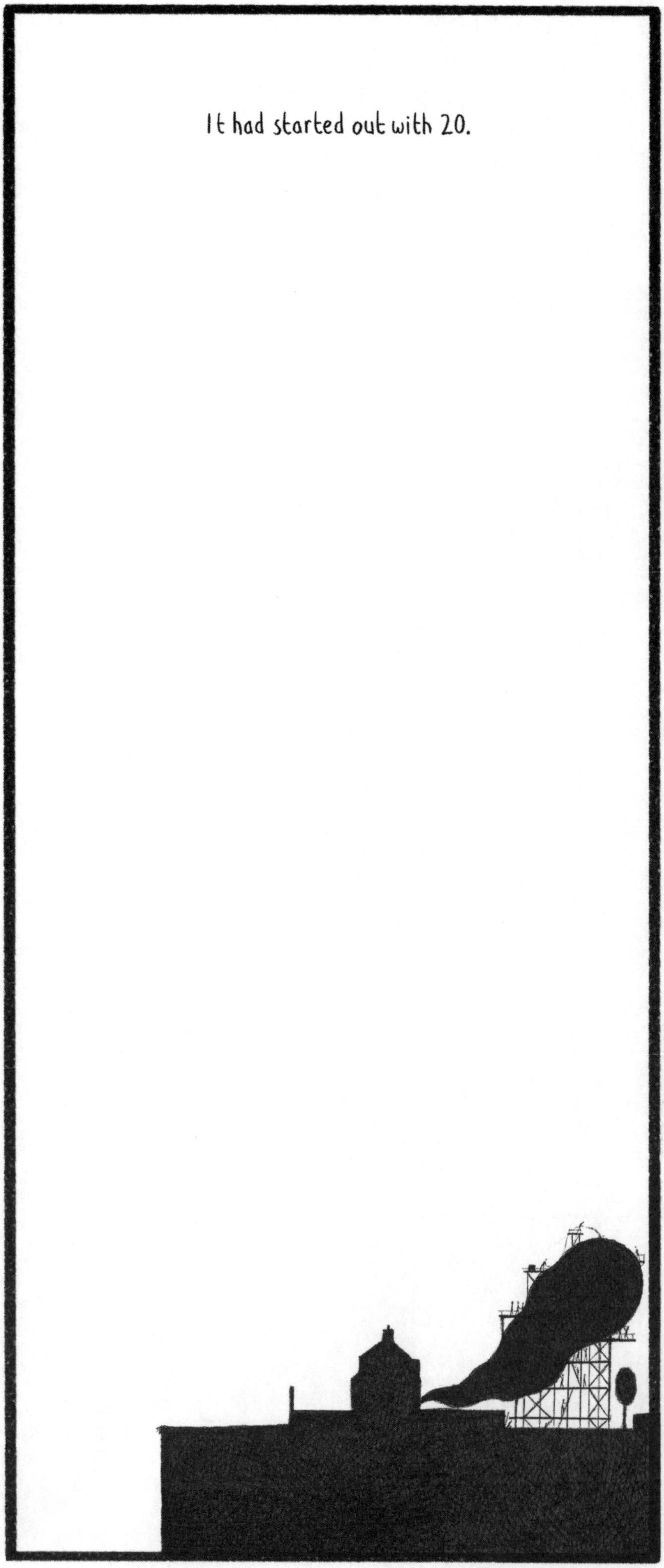
It had started out with 20.

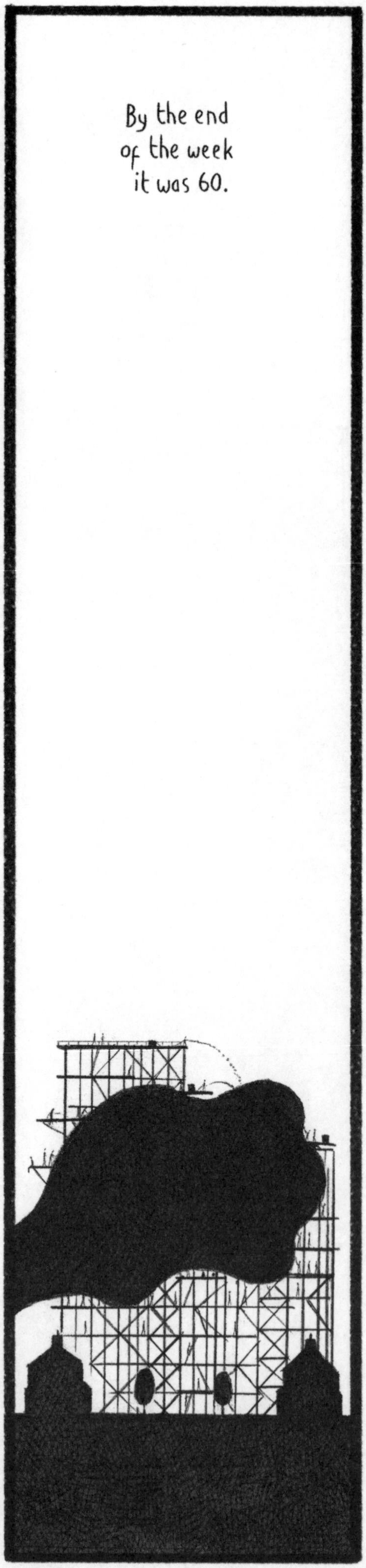
By the end
of the week
it was 60.

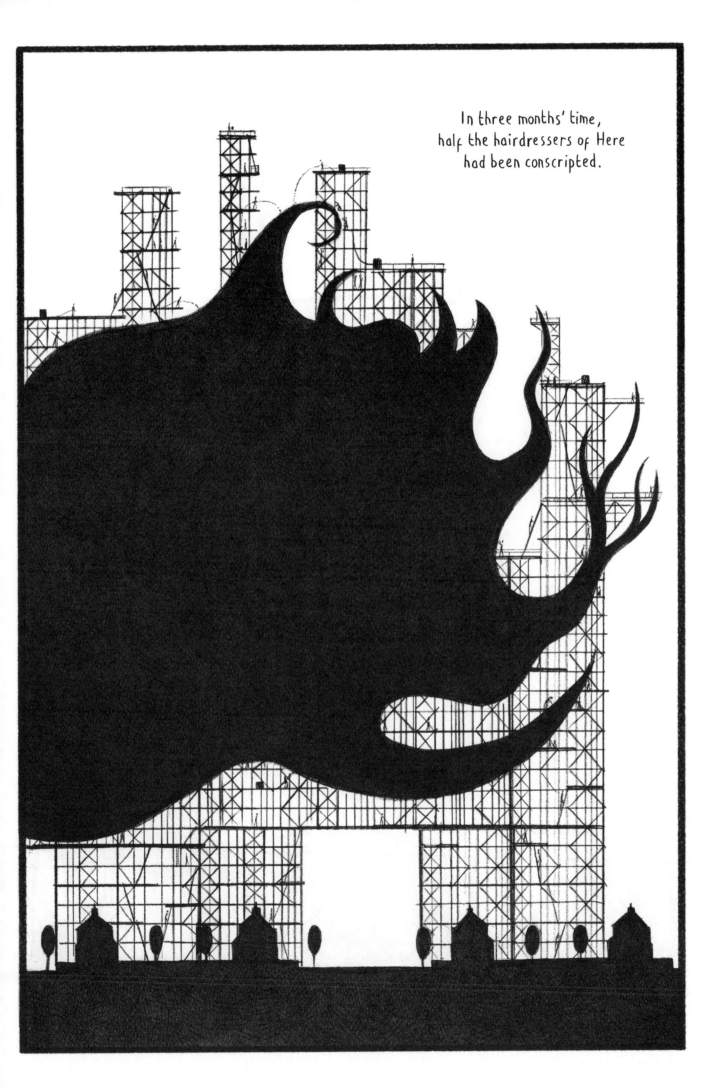

In three months' time,
half the hairdressers of Here
had been conscripted.

The Government's official line was thought up by a hastily-appointed consultant:

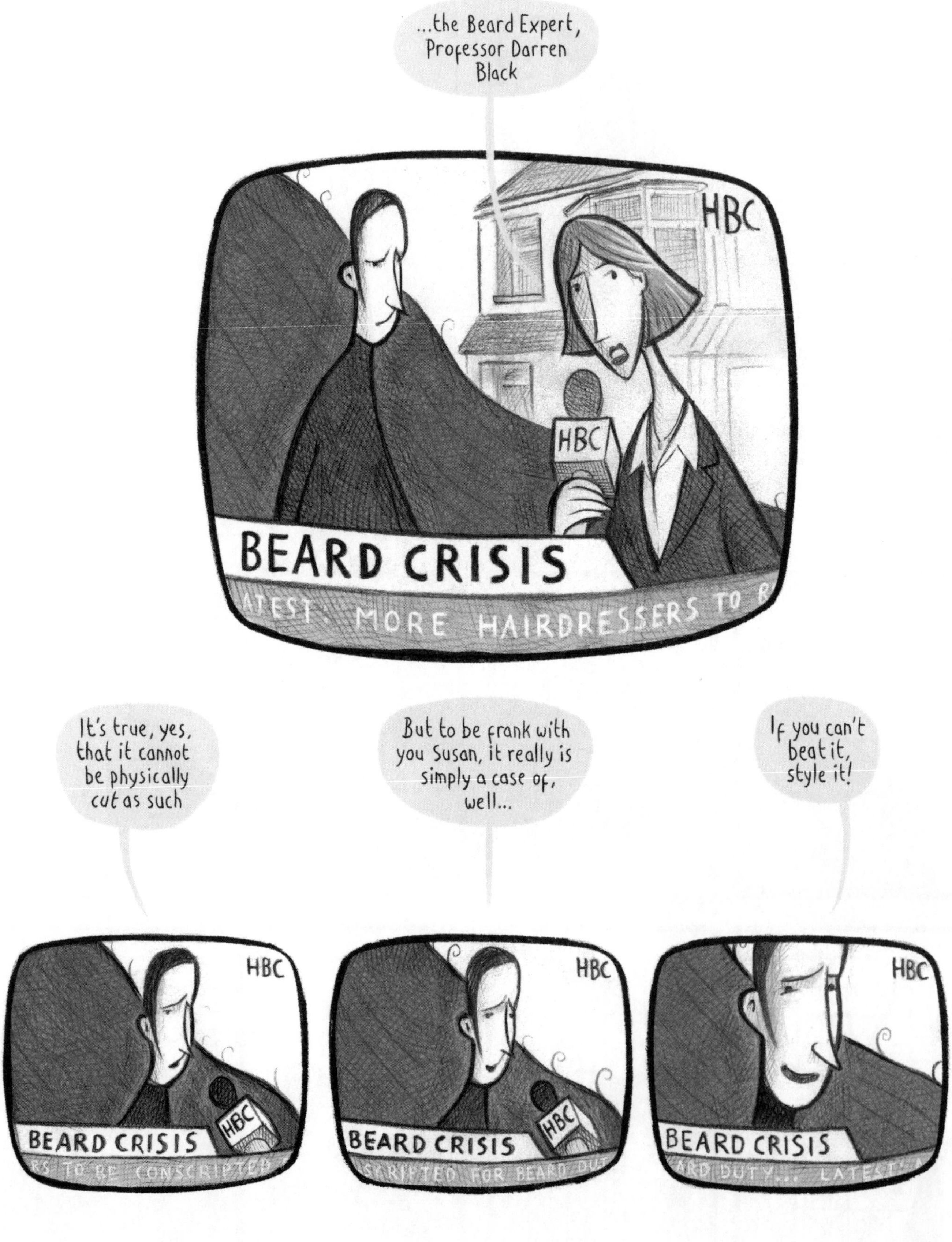
...the Beard Expert, Professor Darren Black
HBC
HBC
BEARD CRISIS
MORE HAIRDRESSERS
It's true, yes, that it cannot be physically *cut* as such
But to be frank with you Susan, it really is simply a case of, well...
If you can't beat it, style it!
HBC
HBC
BEARD CRISIS
HBC
HBC
BEARD CRISIS
HBC
BEARD CRISIS

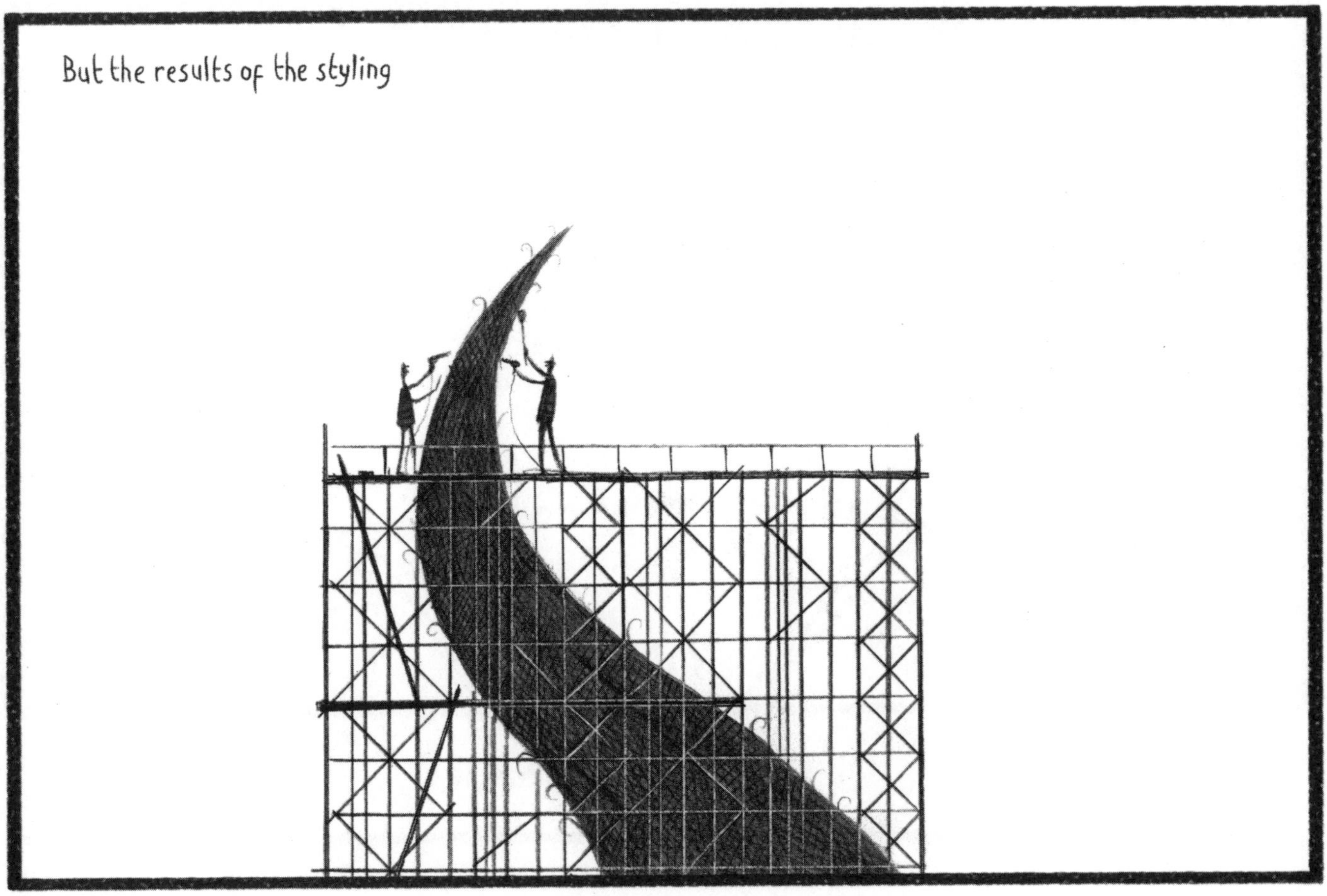
But the results of the styling

were as much of a surprise to the hairdressers
as they were to everyone else.

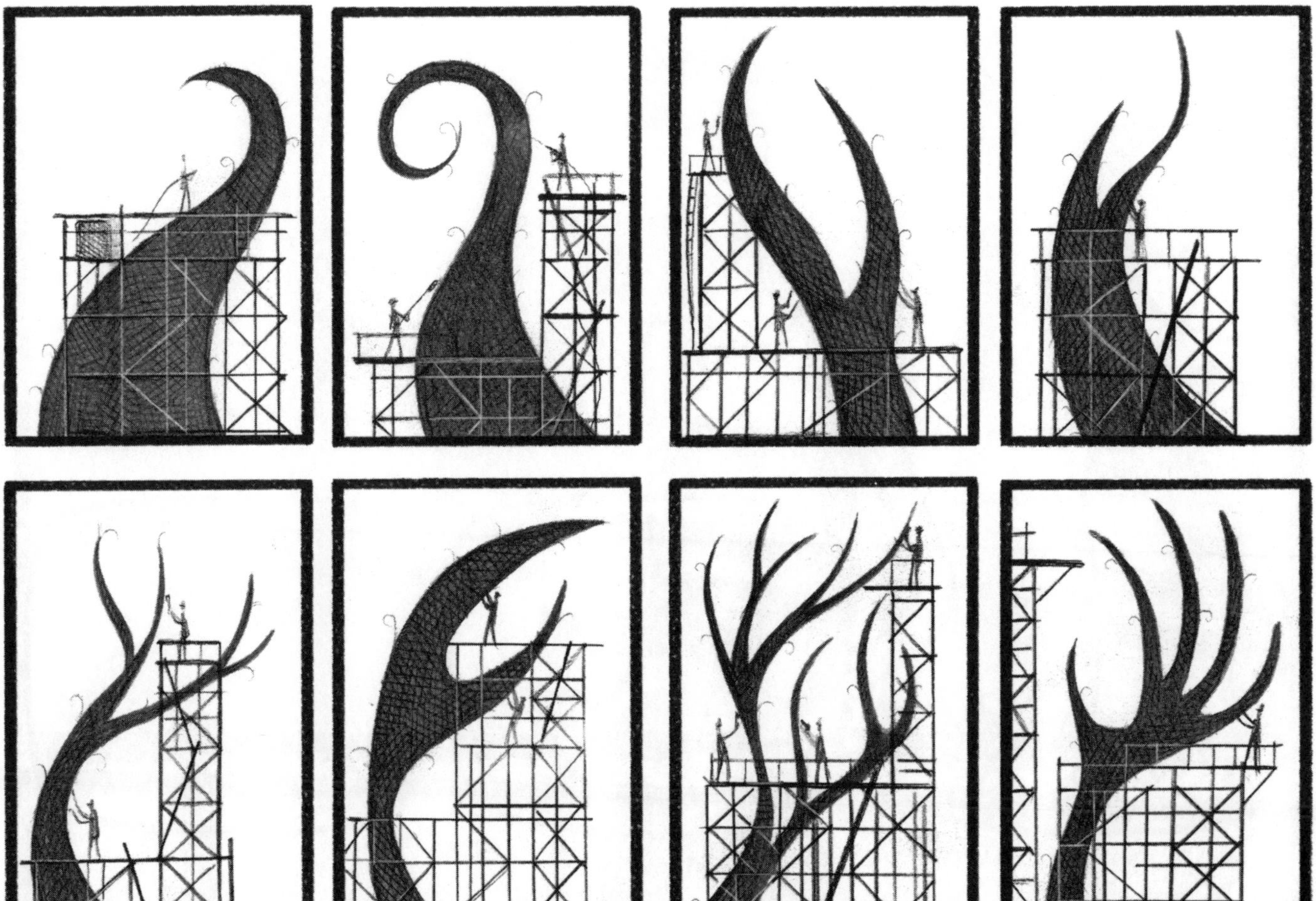

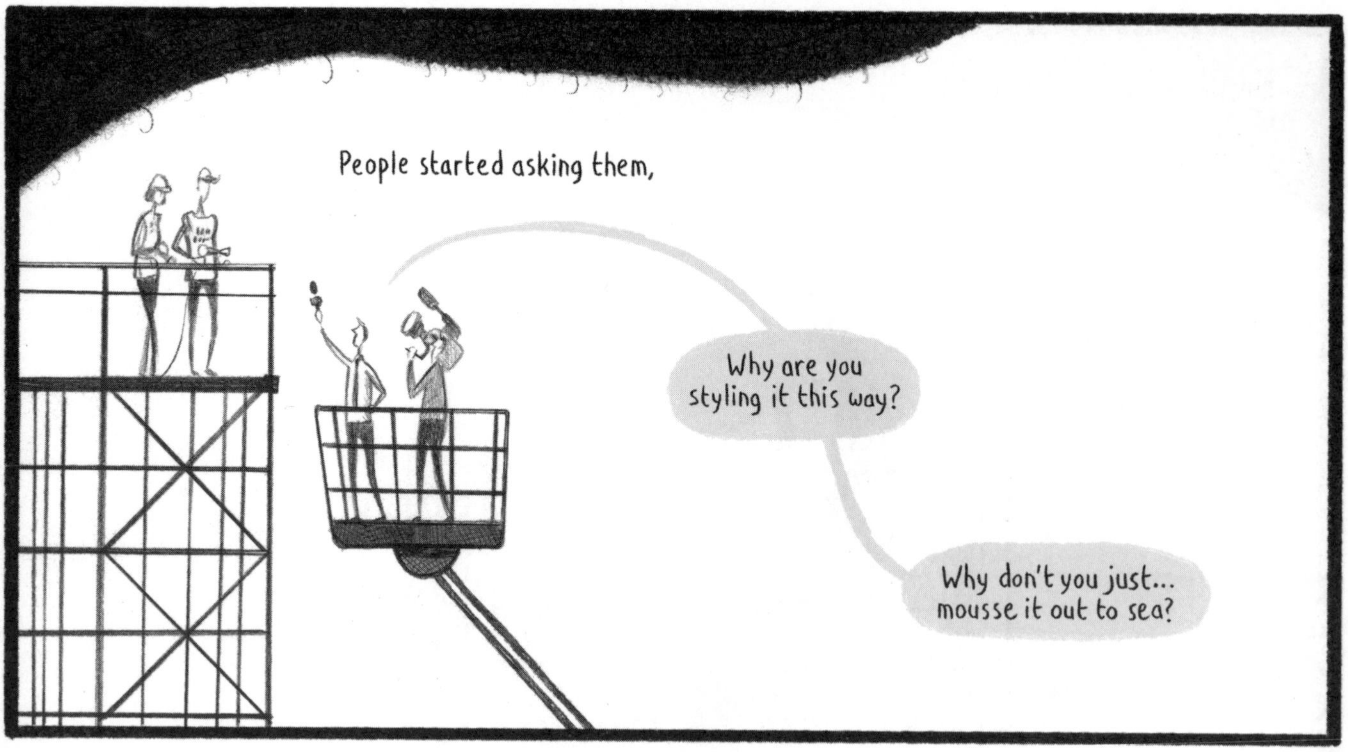
People started asking them,
Why are you styling it this way?
Why don't you just... mousse it out to sea?

To which they could only reply,

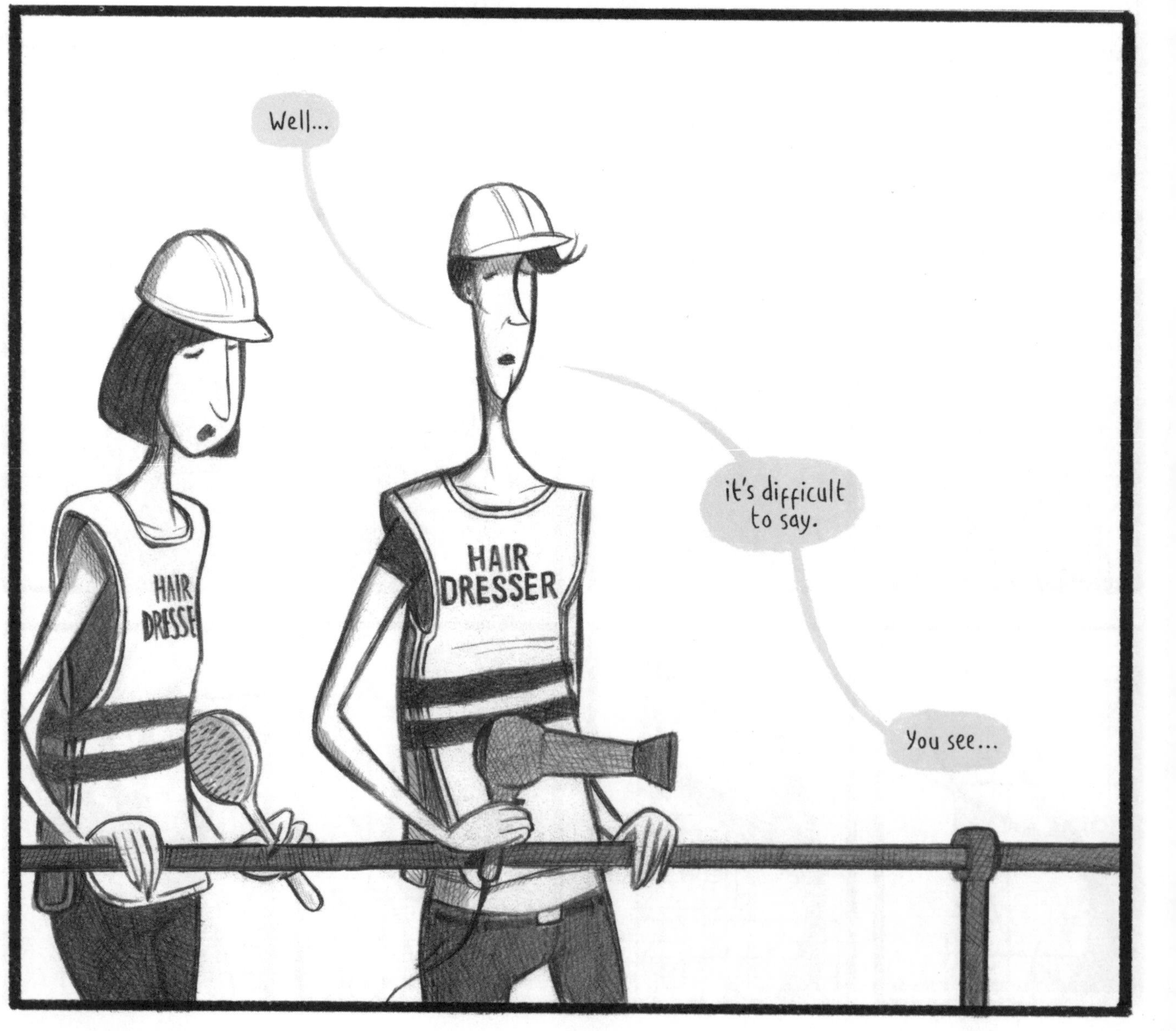
Well...
it's difficult to say.
You see...
HAIR DRESSER
HAIR DRESSER

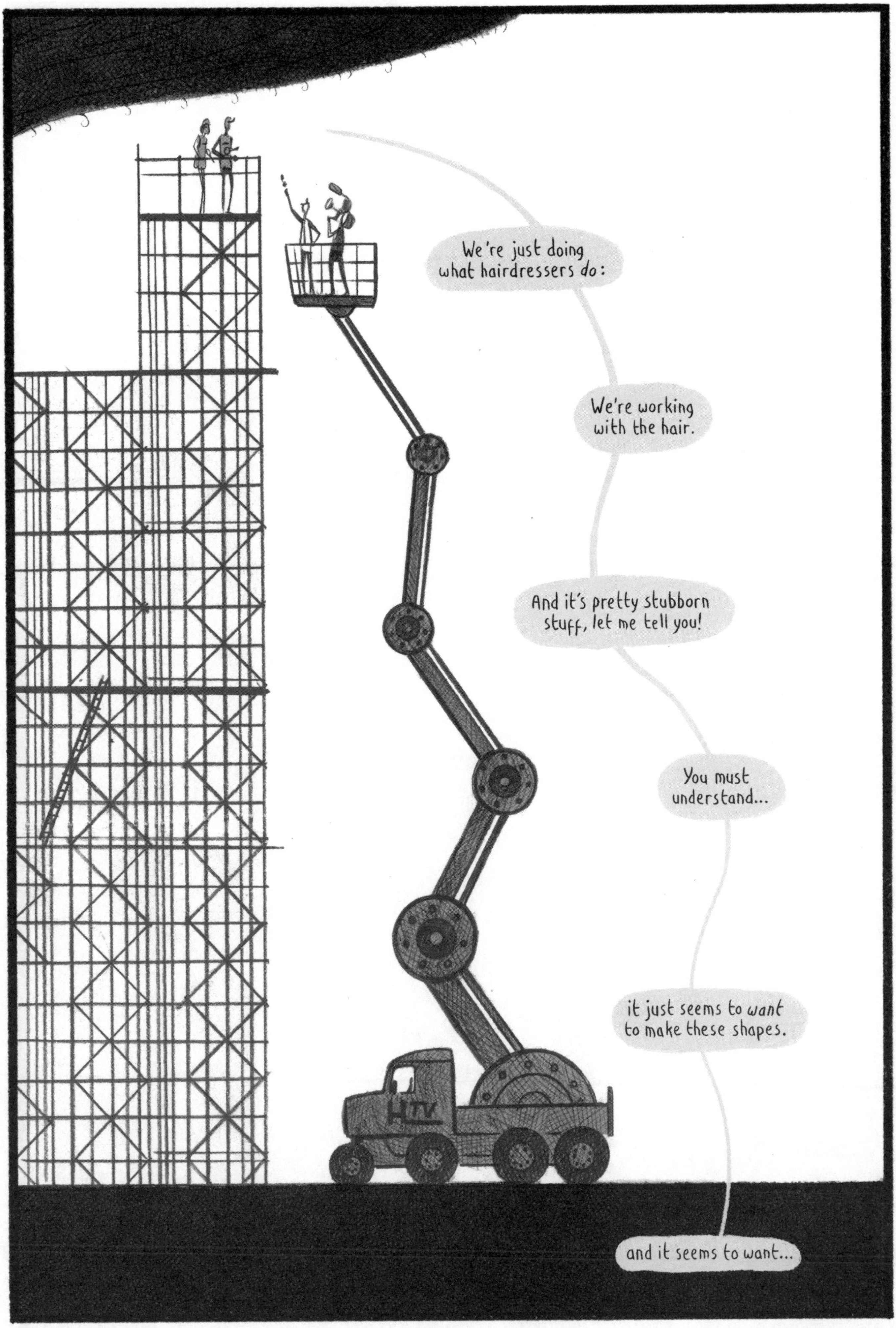
We're just doing what hairdressers do:
We're working with the hair.
And it's pretty stubborn stuff, let me tell you!
You must understand...
it just seems to *want* to make these shapes.
and it seems to want...
HTV

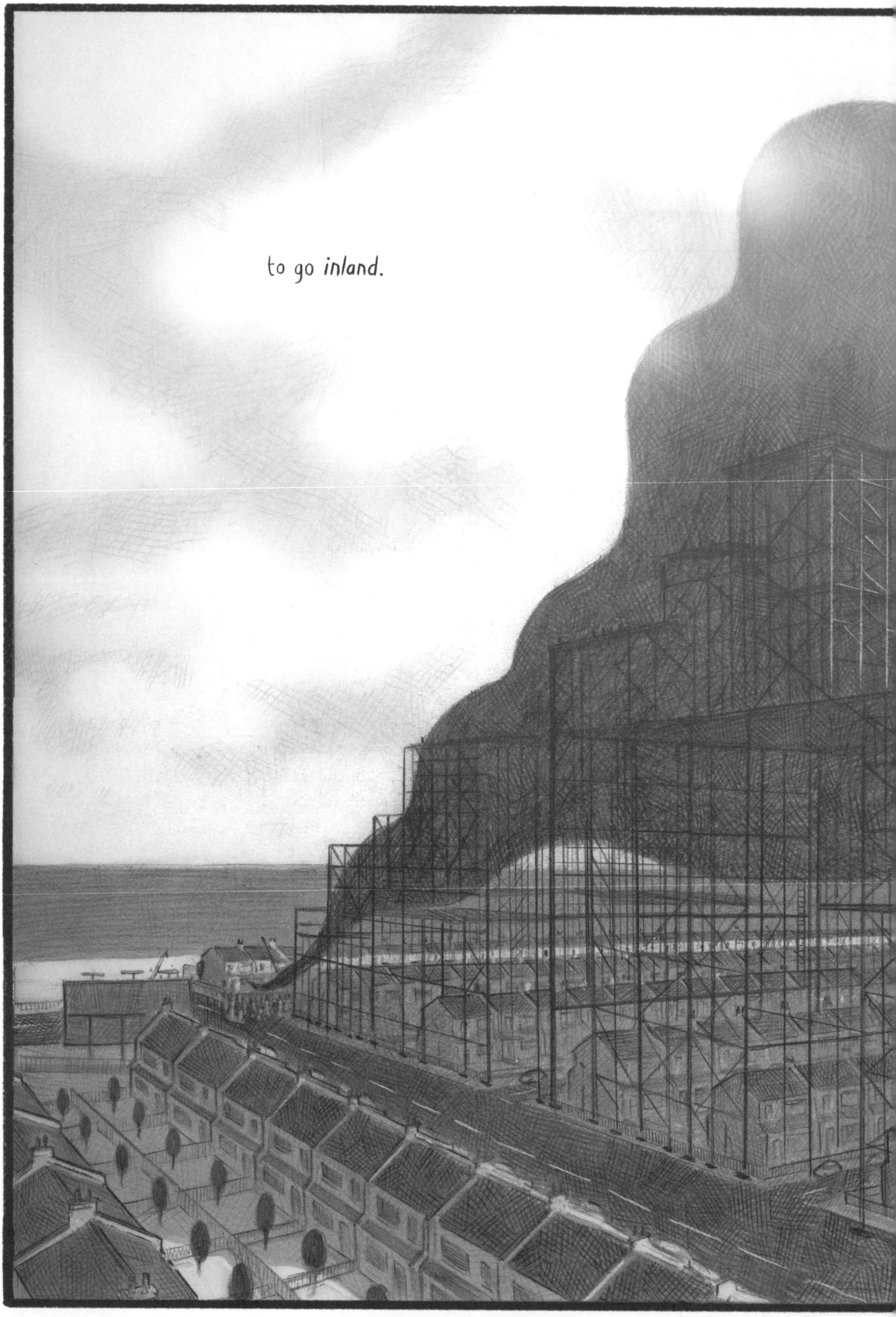
to go *inland.*

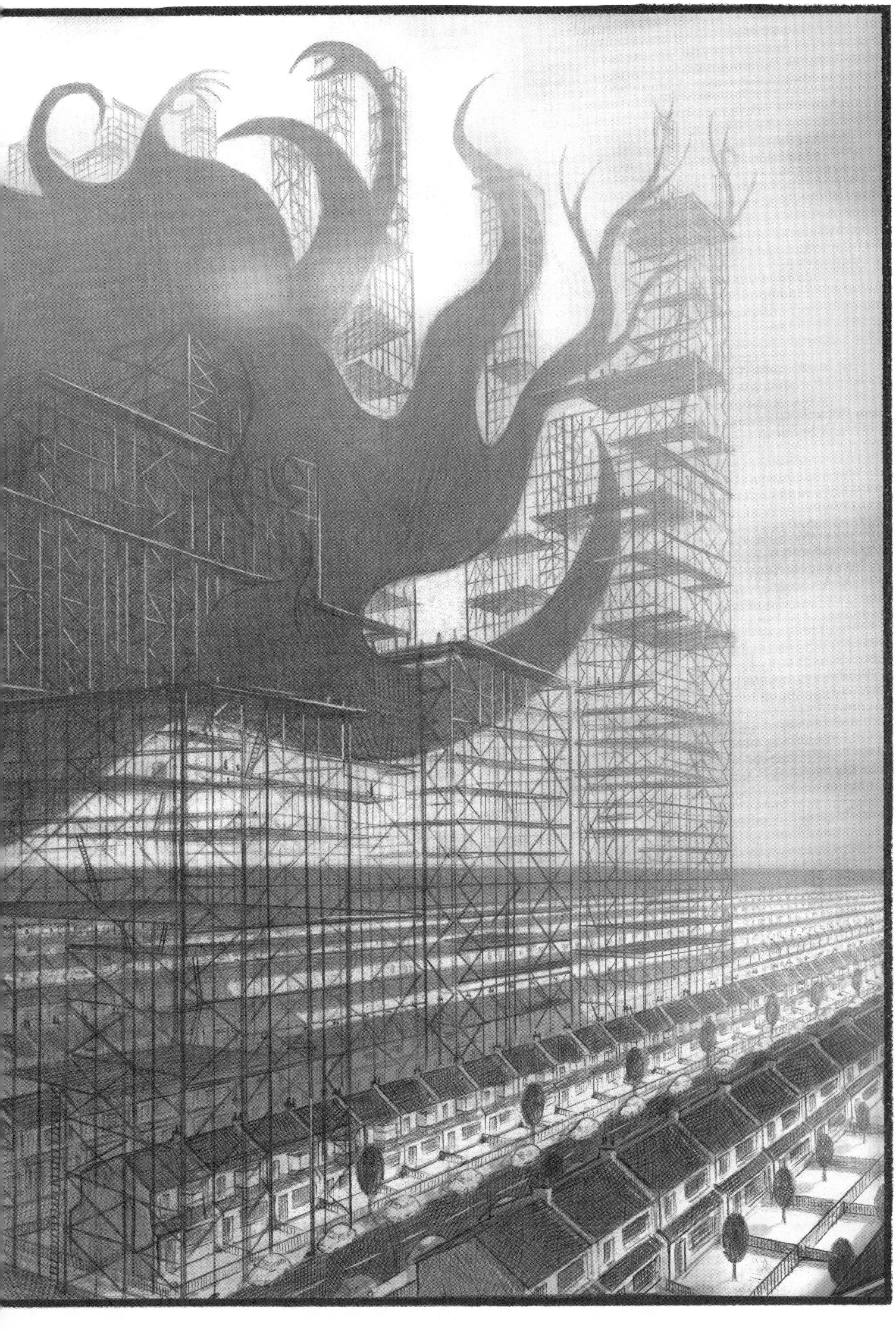

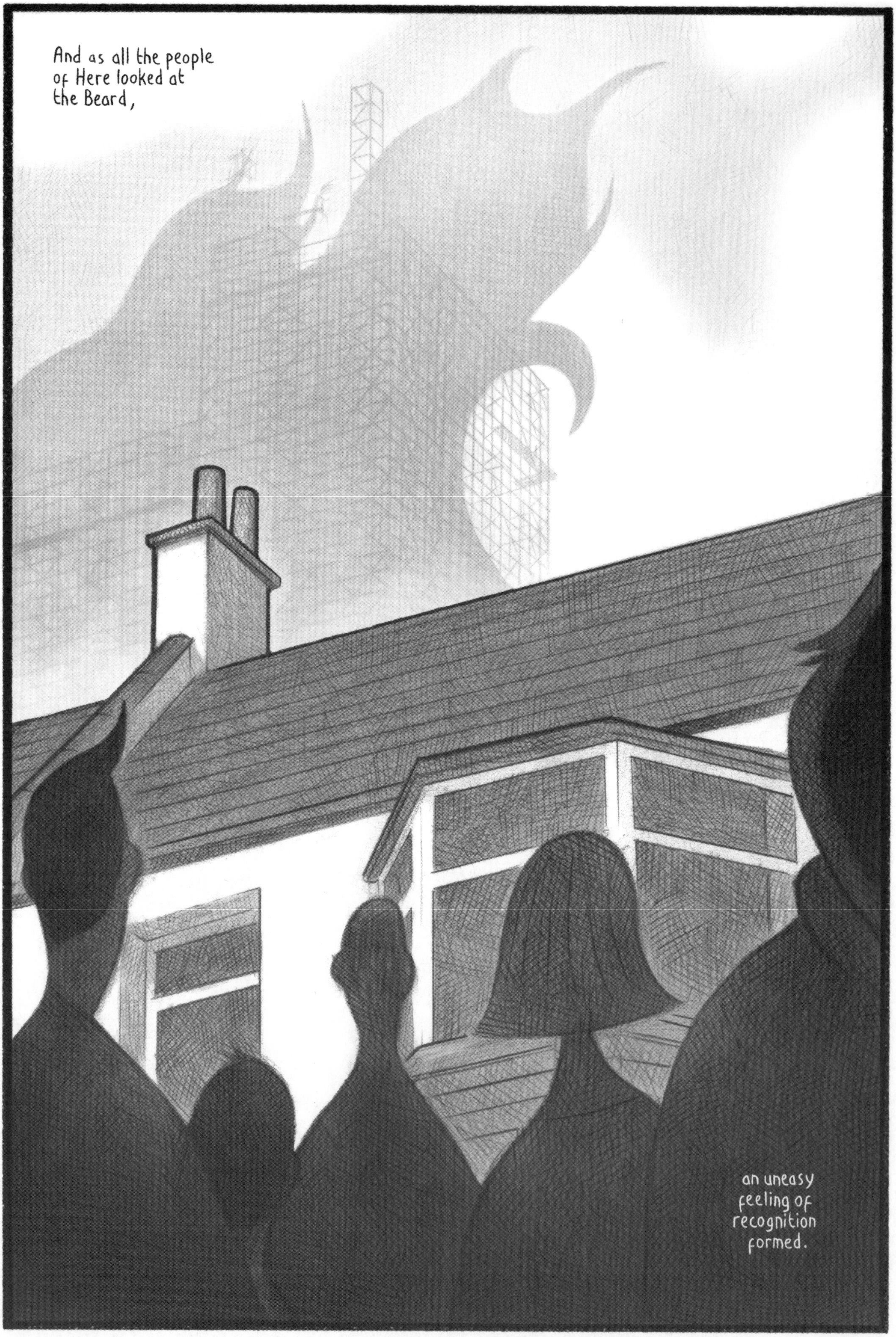
And as all the people of Here looked at the Beard,
an uneasy feeling of recognition formed.

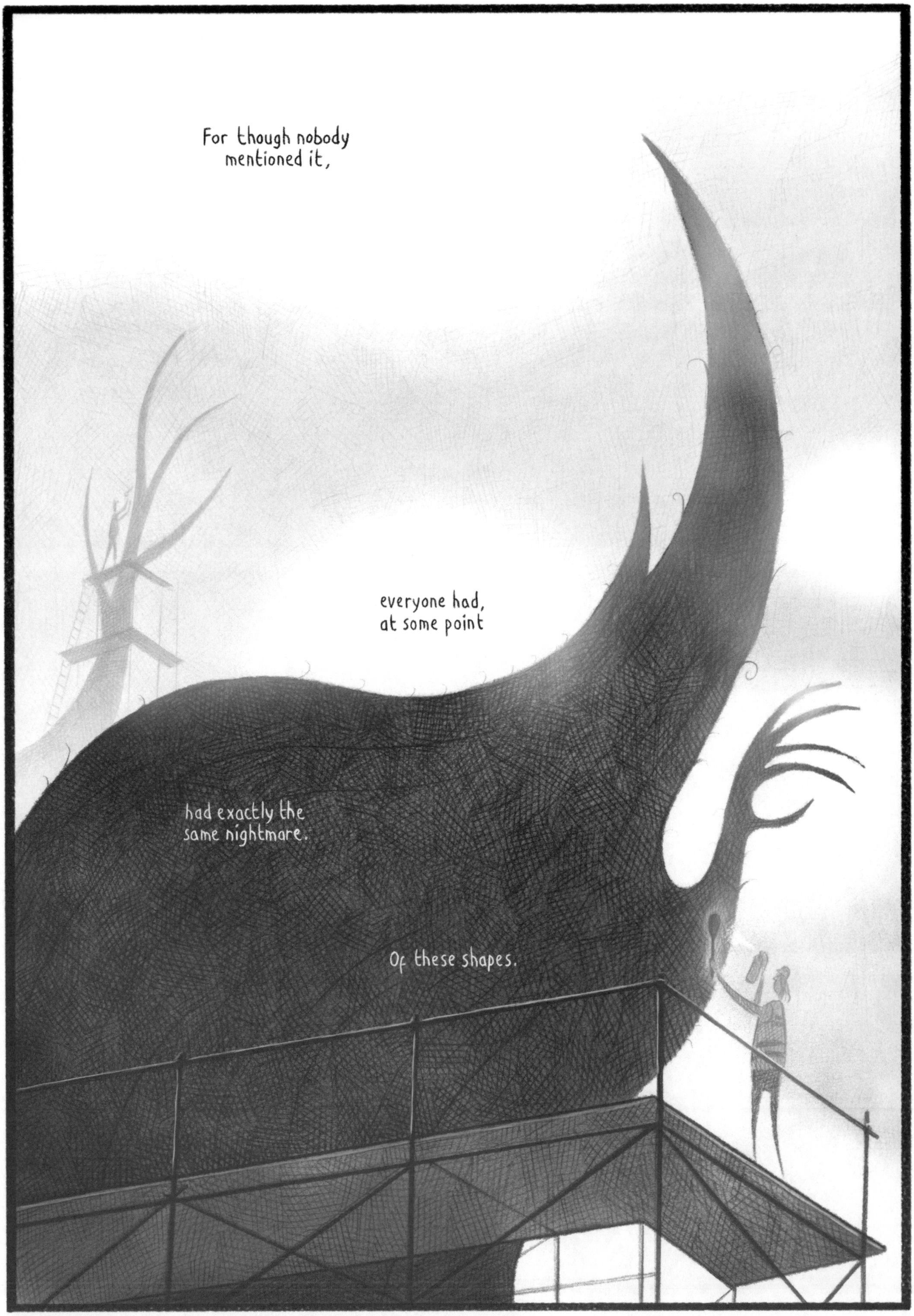
For though nobody mentioned it,
everyone had, at some point
had exactly the same nightmare.
Of these shapes.

Of There.

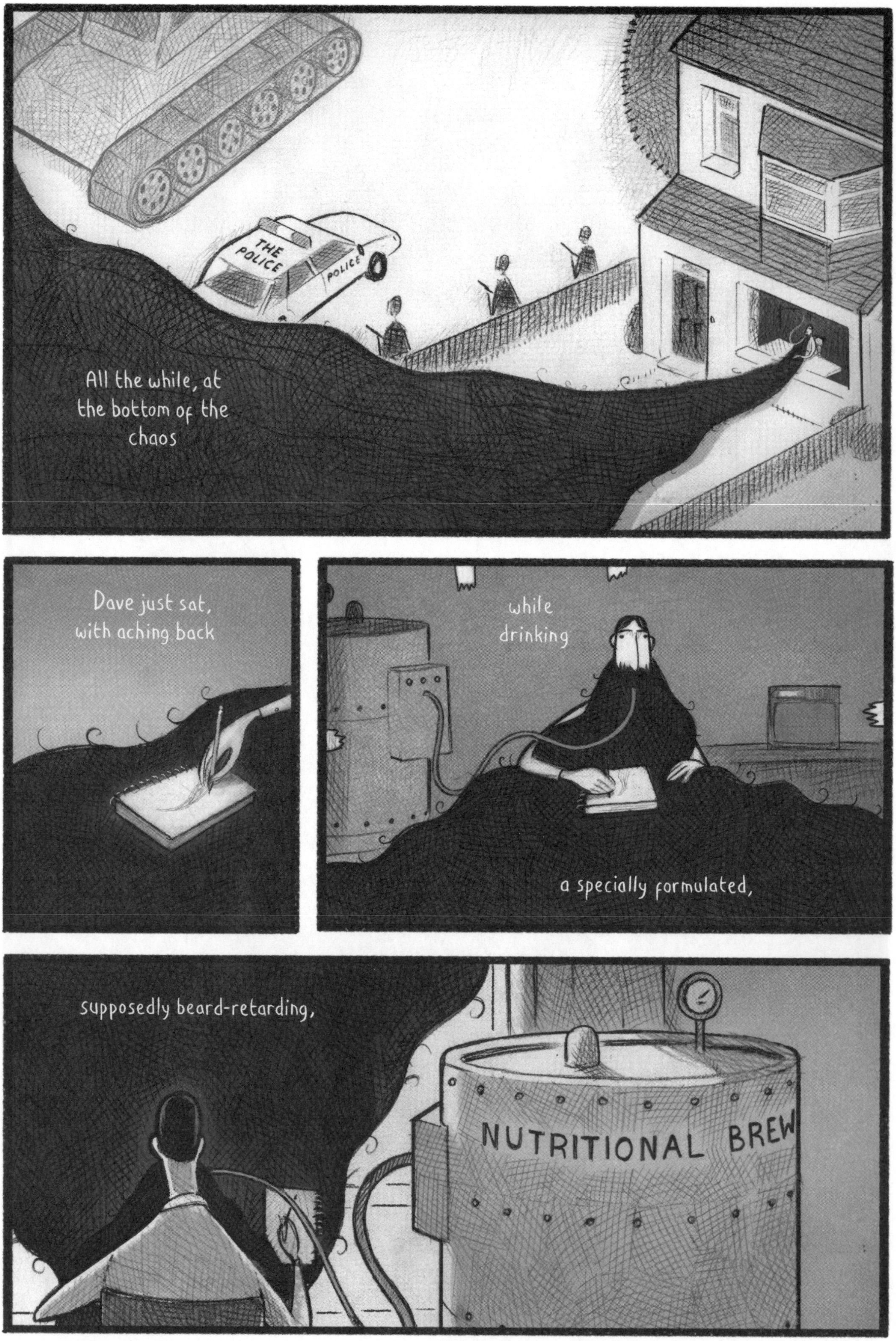

THE POLICE
POLICE
All the while, at the bottom of the chaos
Dave just sat, with aching back
while drinking
a specially formulated,
supposedly beard-retarding,
NUTRITIONAL BREW

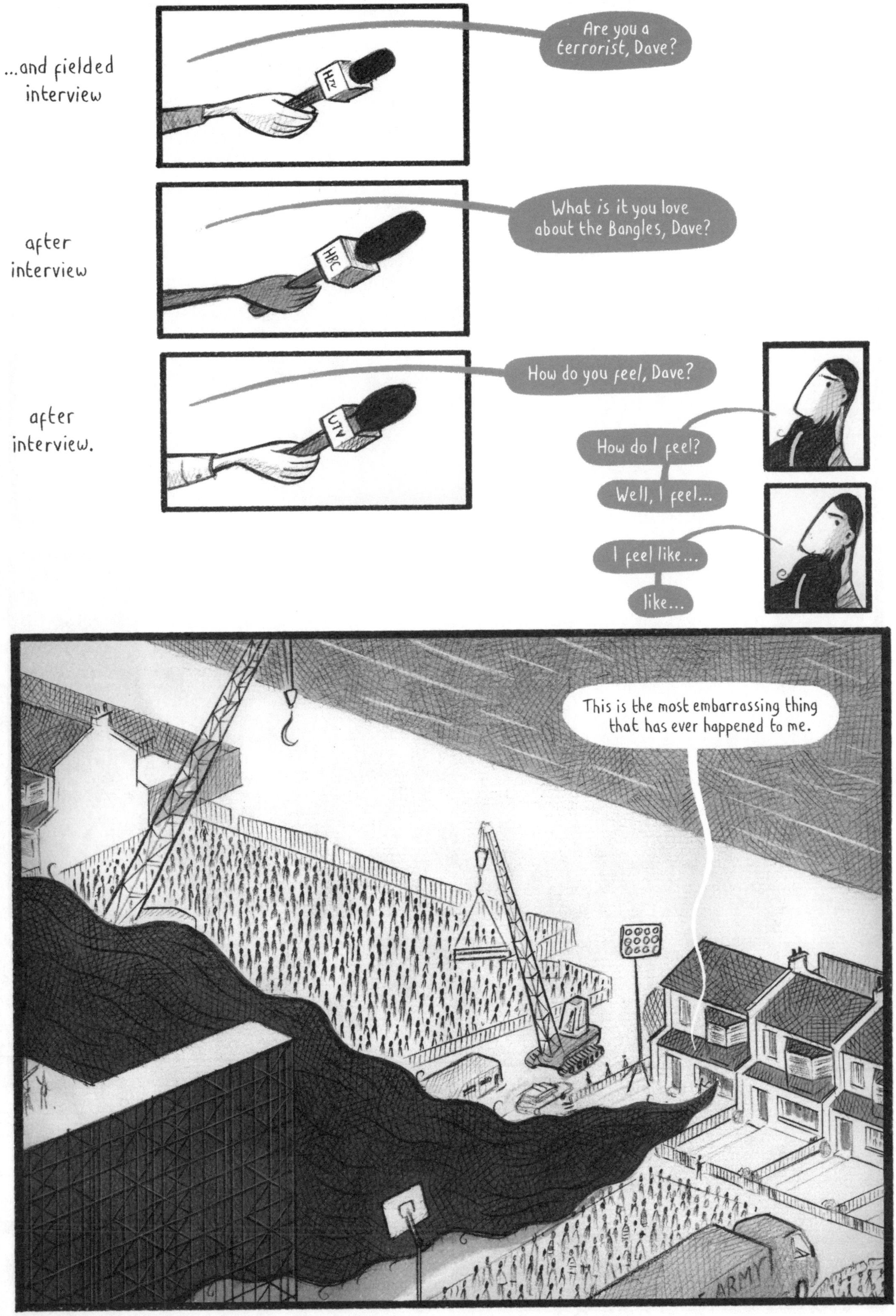
...and fielded interview
Are you a terrorist, Dave?
after interview
What is it you love about the Bangles, Dave?
after interview.
How do you feel, Dave?
How do I feel?
Well, I feel...
I feel like...
like...
This is the most embarrassing thing that has ever happened to me.

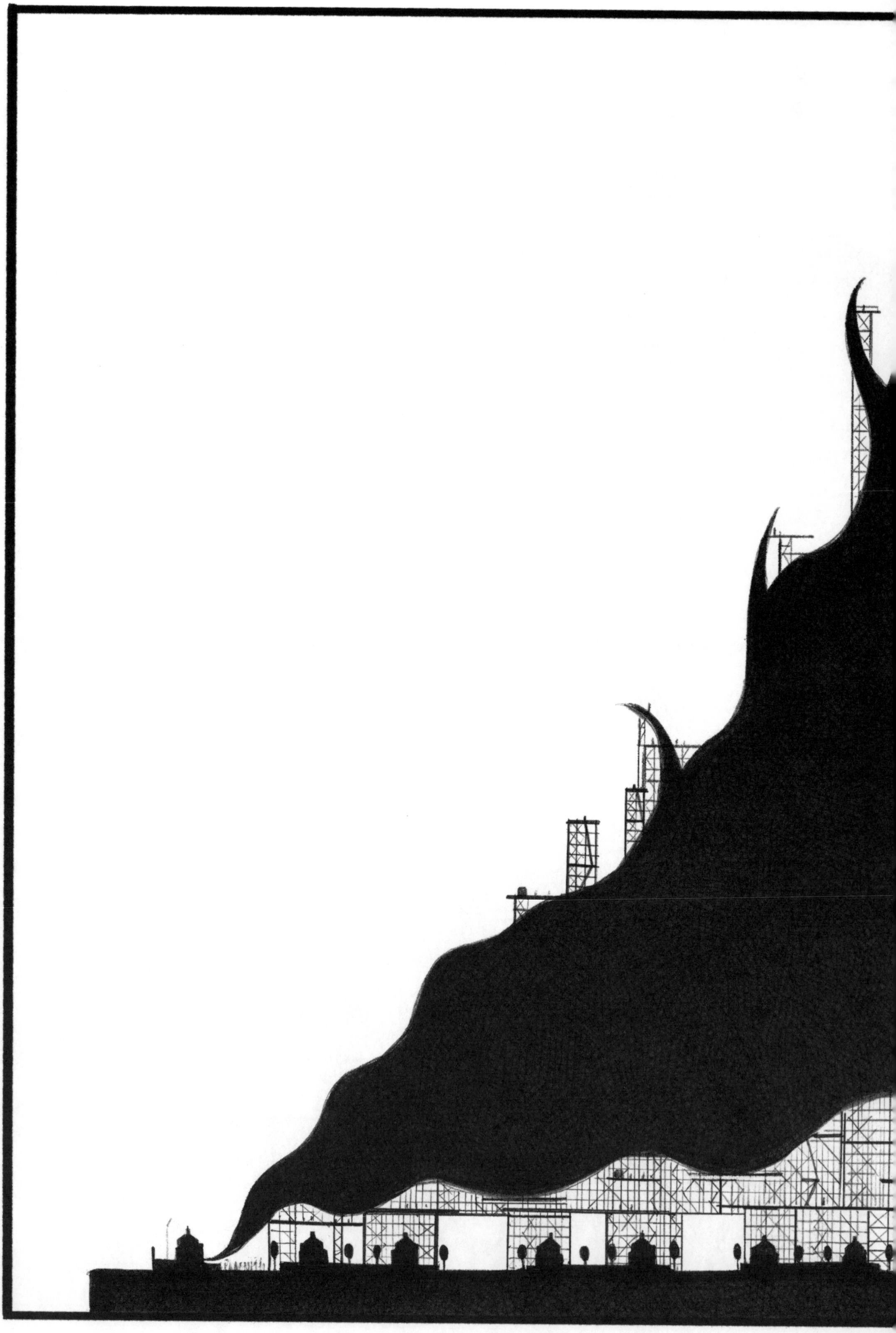

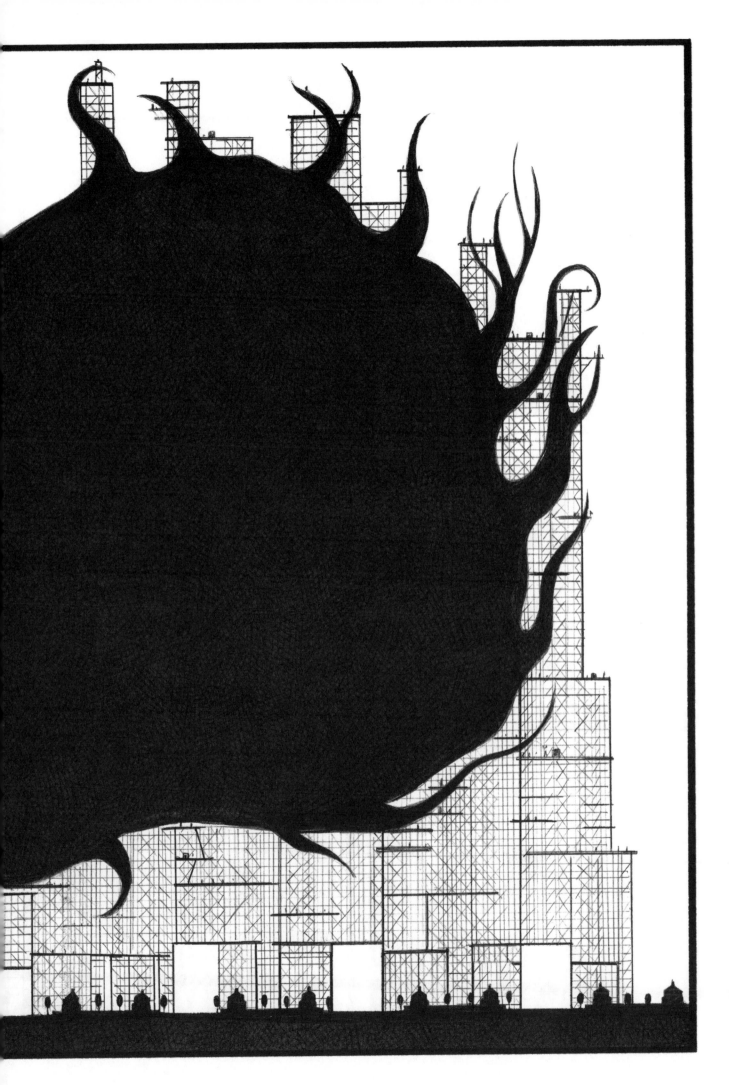

The Untidiness, as it later came to be known

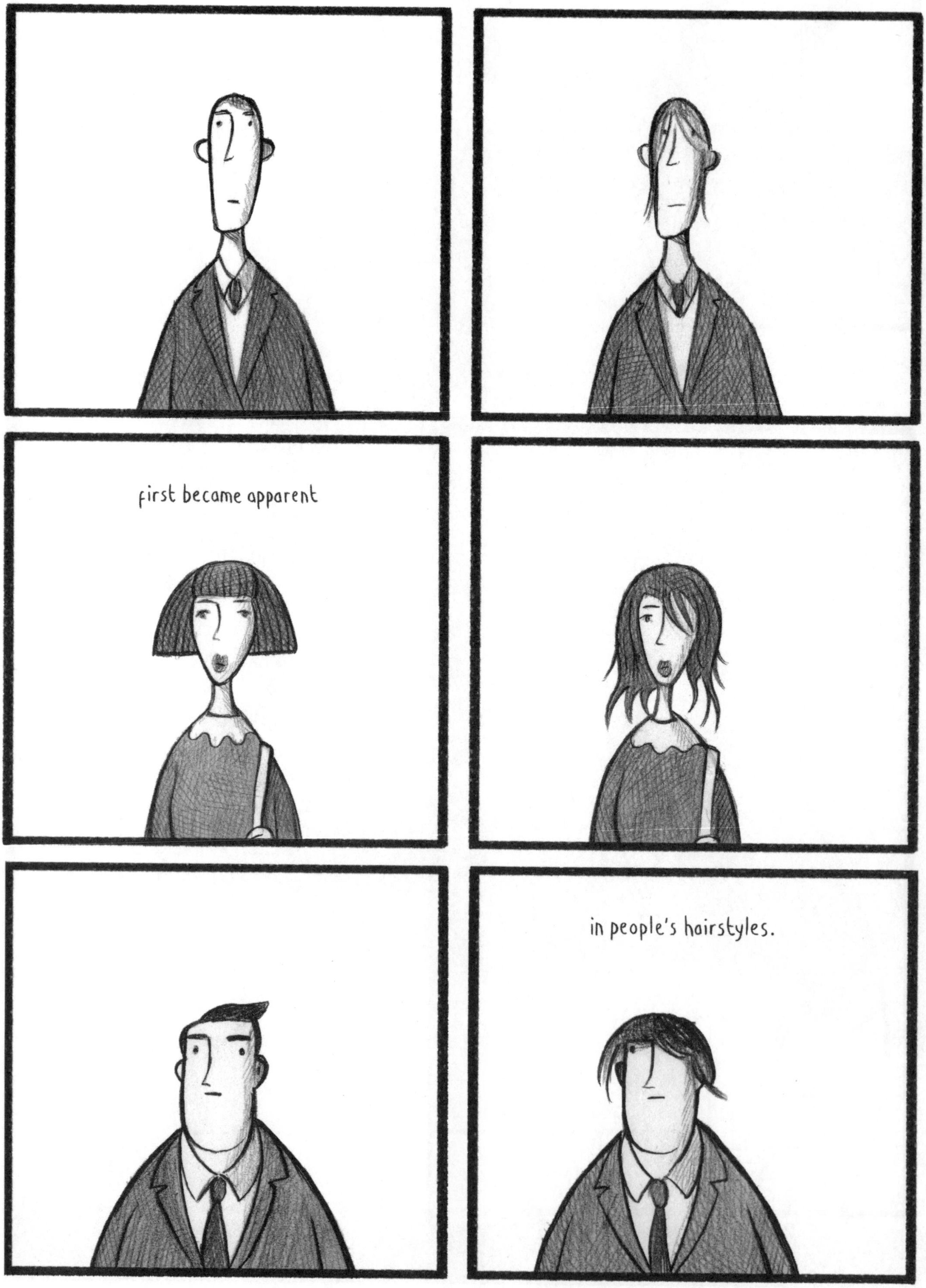
first became apparent
in people's hairstyles.

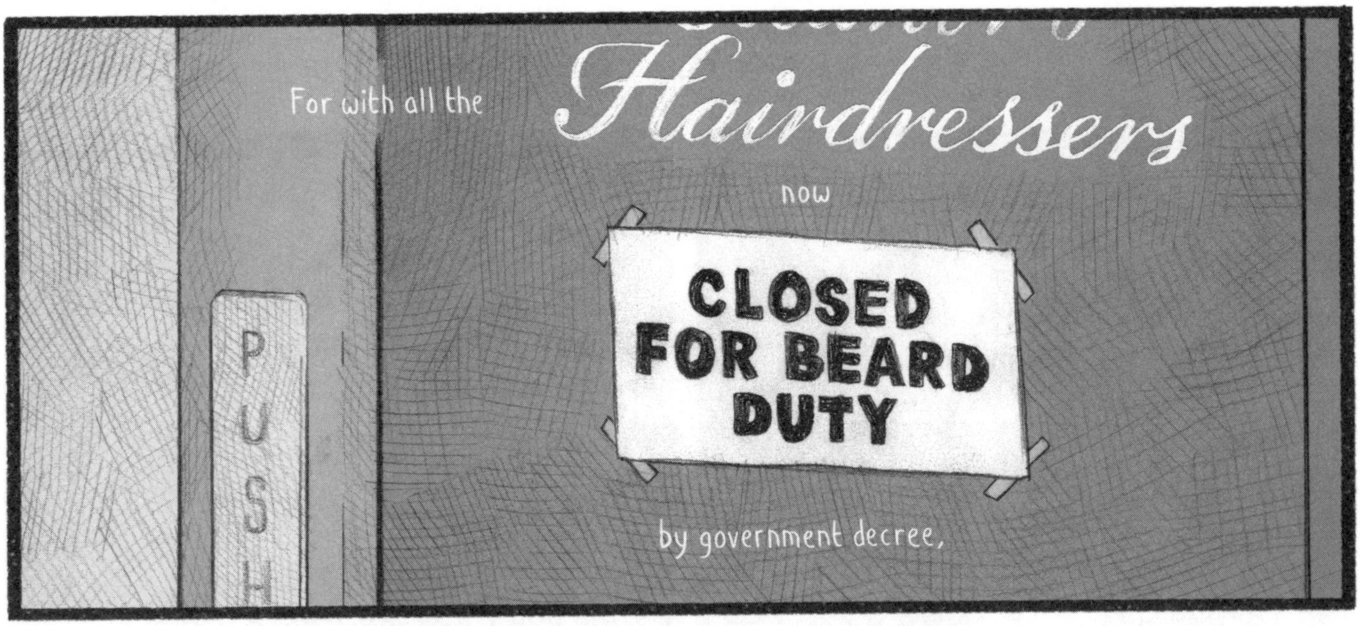
For with all the
Hairdressers
now
CLOSED FOR BEARD DUTY
by government decree,

everyone soon realised they would
have to cut their own hair -

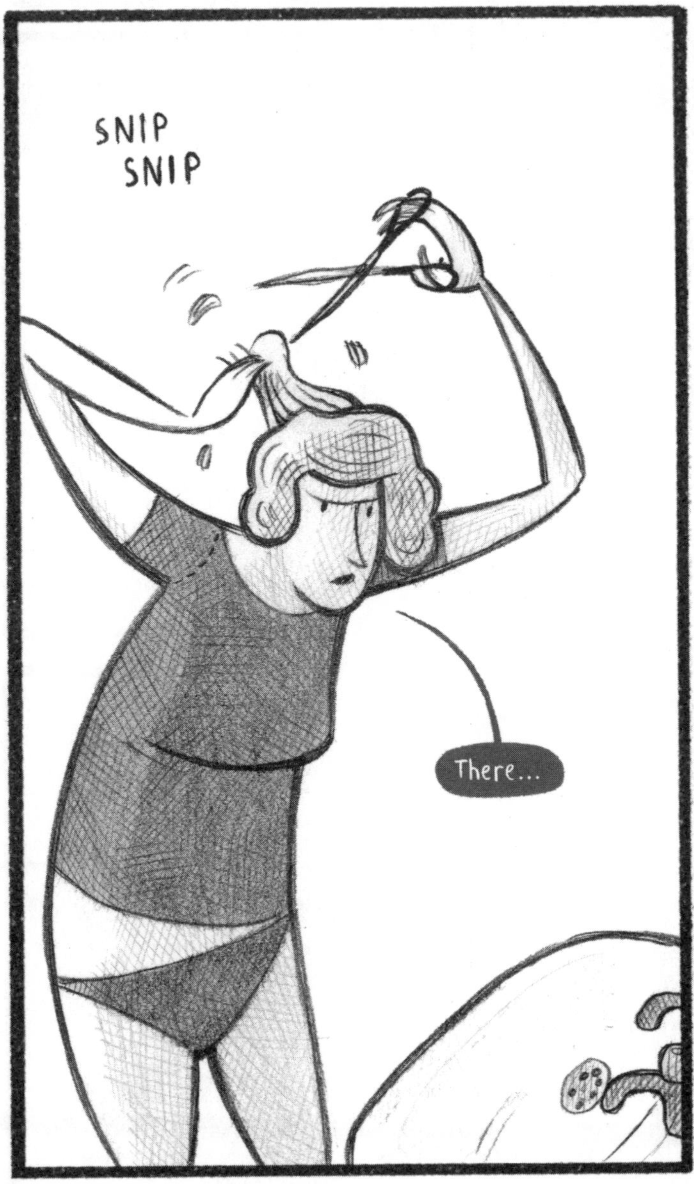
SNIP
SNIP
There...

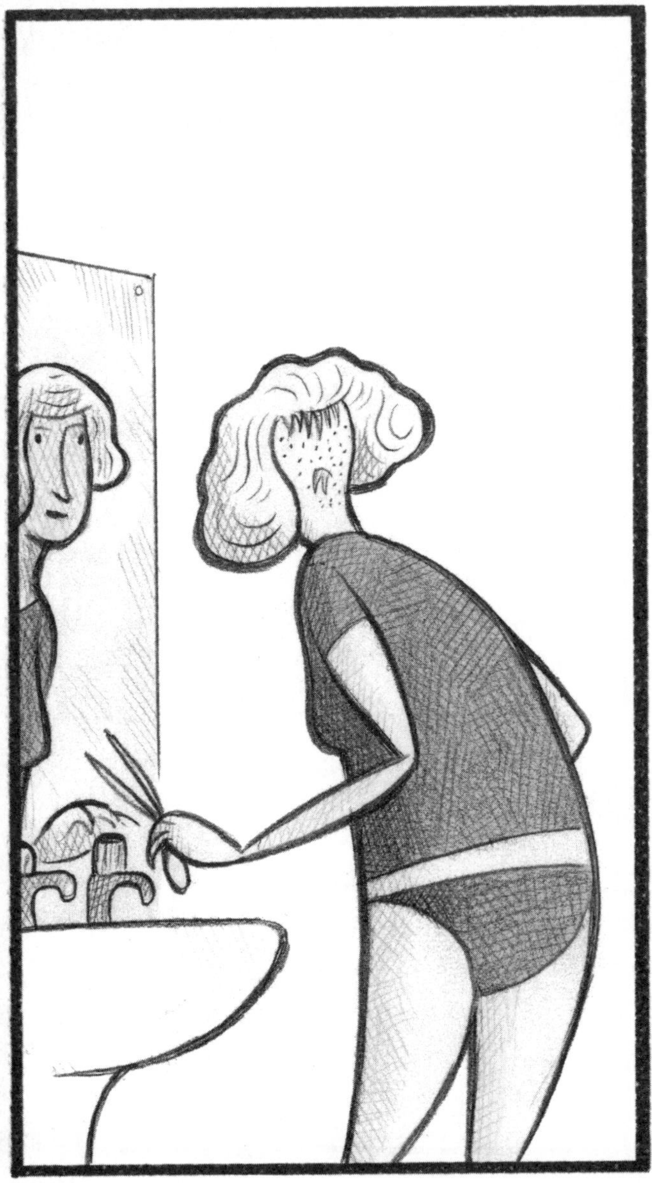

with differing results.

Consequently,
for the first time in his life

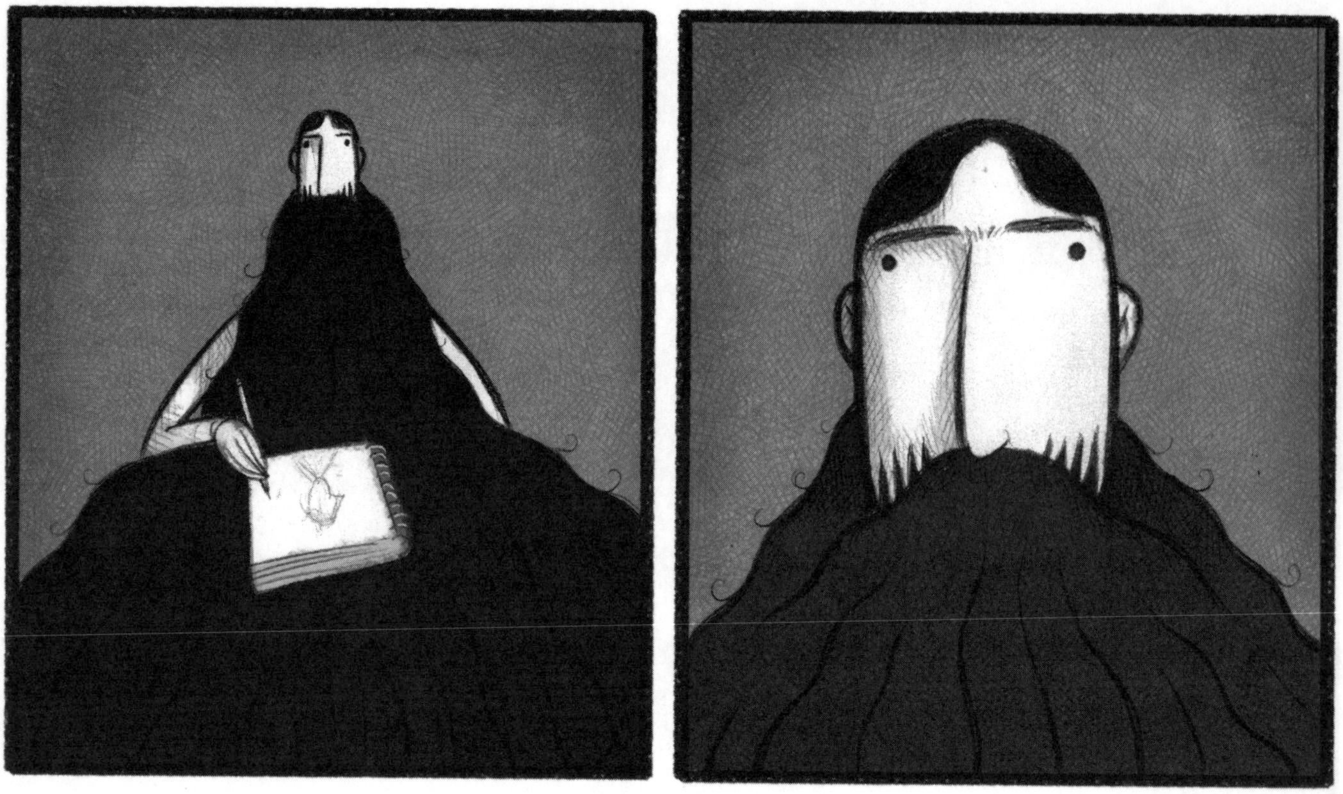

Dave found that
the people he drew outside his house

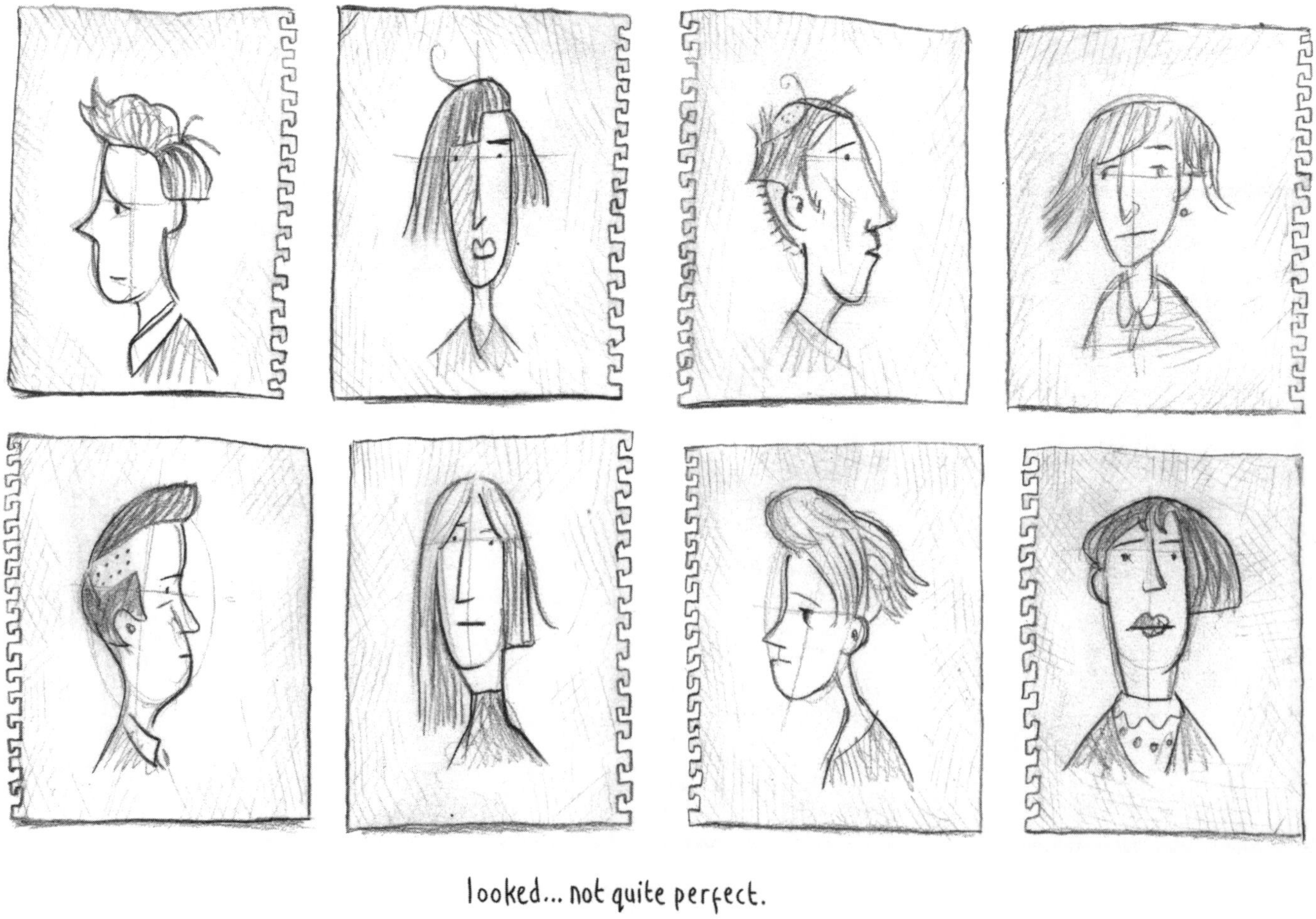

looked... not quite perfect.

And when there were no more
hairdressers to enlist,

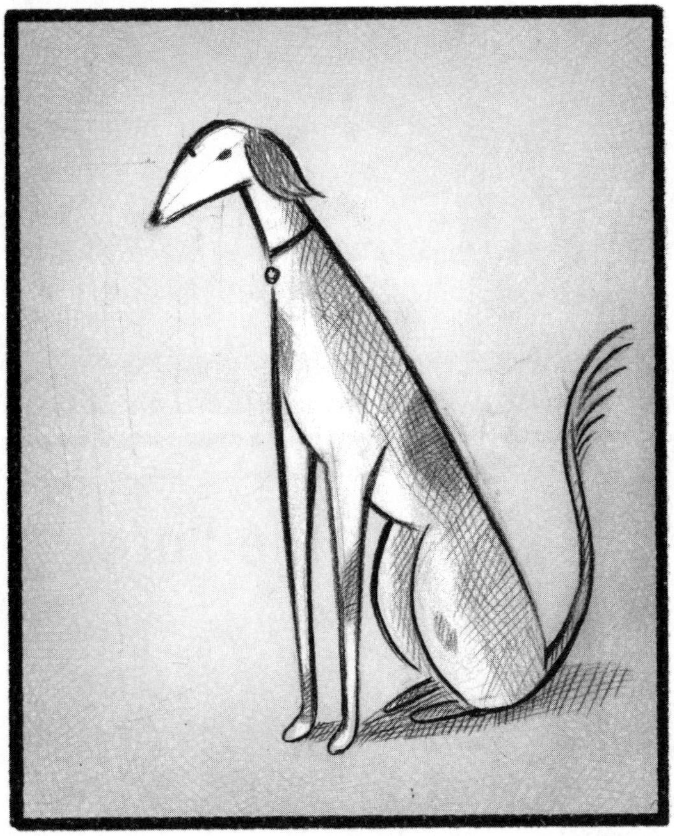

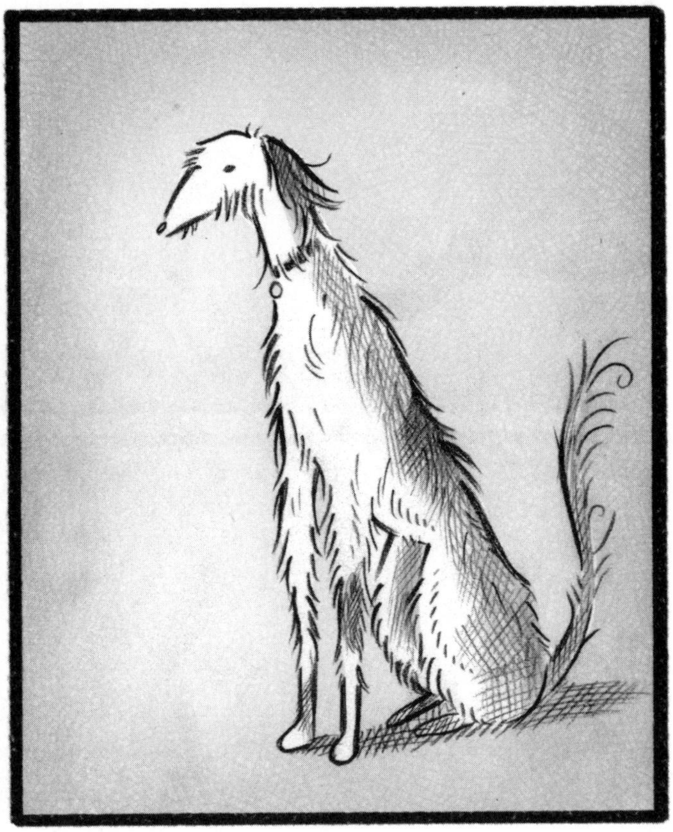

the dog groomers were called in.

And when there were no more dog groomers,

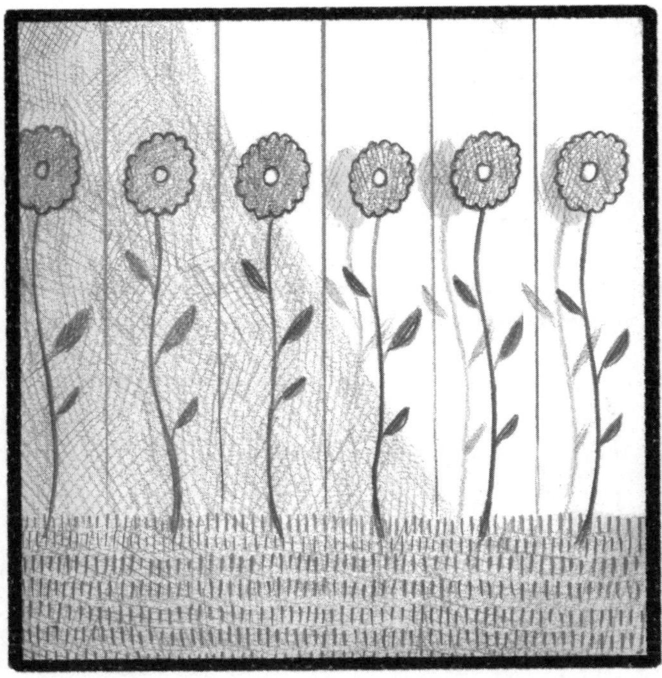

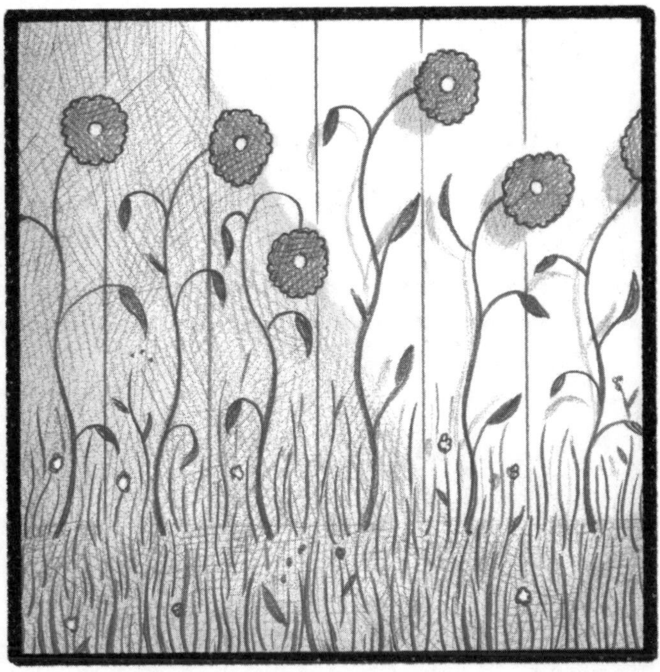

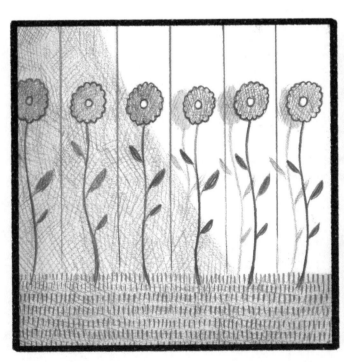

the gardeners were summoned too.

Until, in the space of just four months

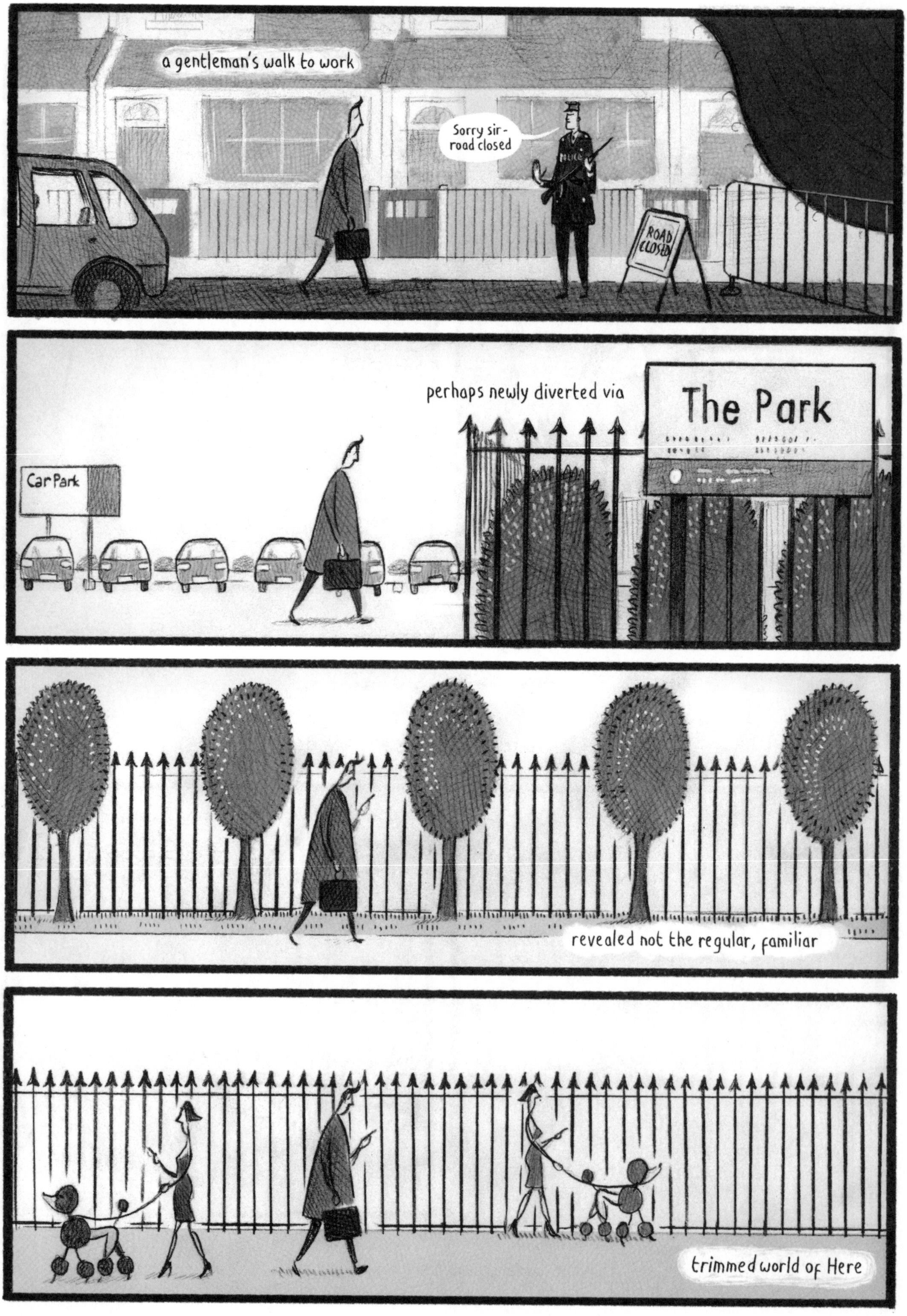
a gentleman's walk to work
Sorry sir-
road closed
ROAD
CLOSED
perhaps newly diverted via
The Park
Car Park
revealed not the regular, familiar
trimmed world of Here

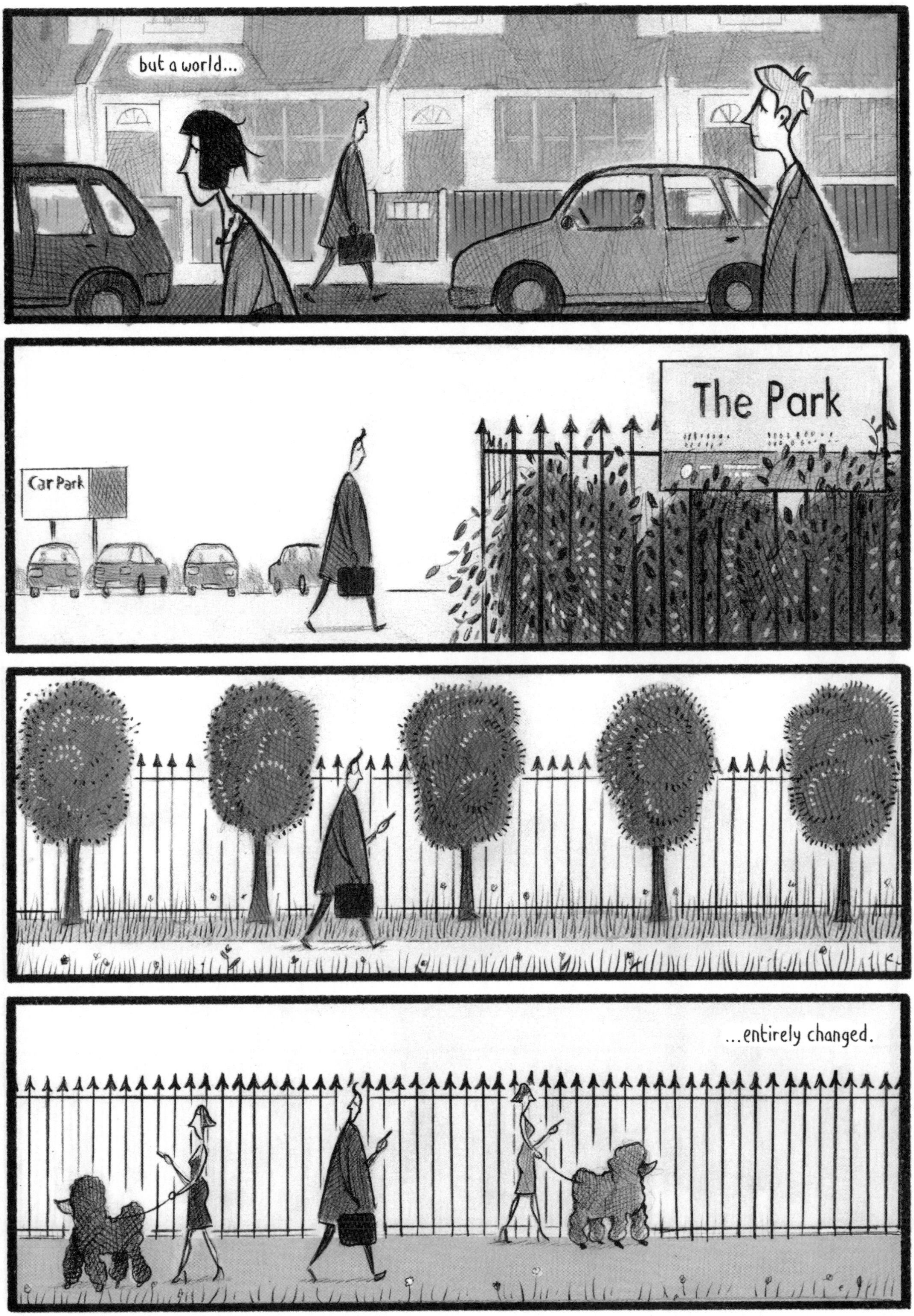
but a world...
Car Park
The Park
...entirely changed.

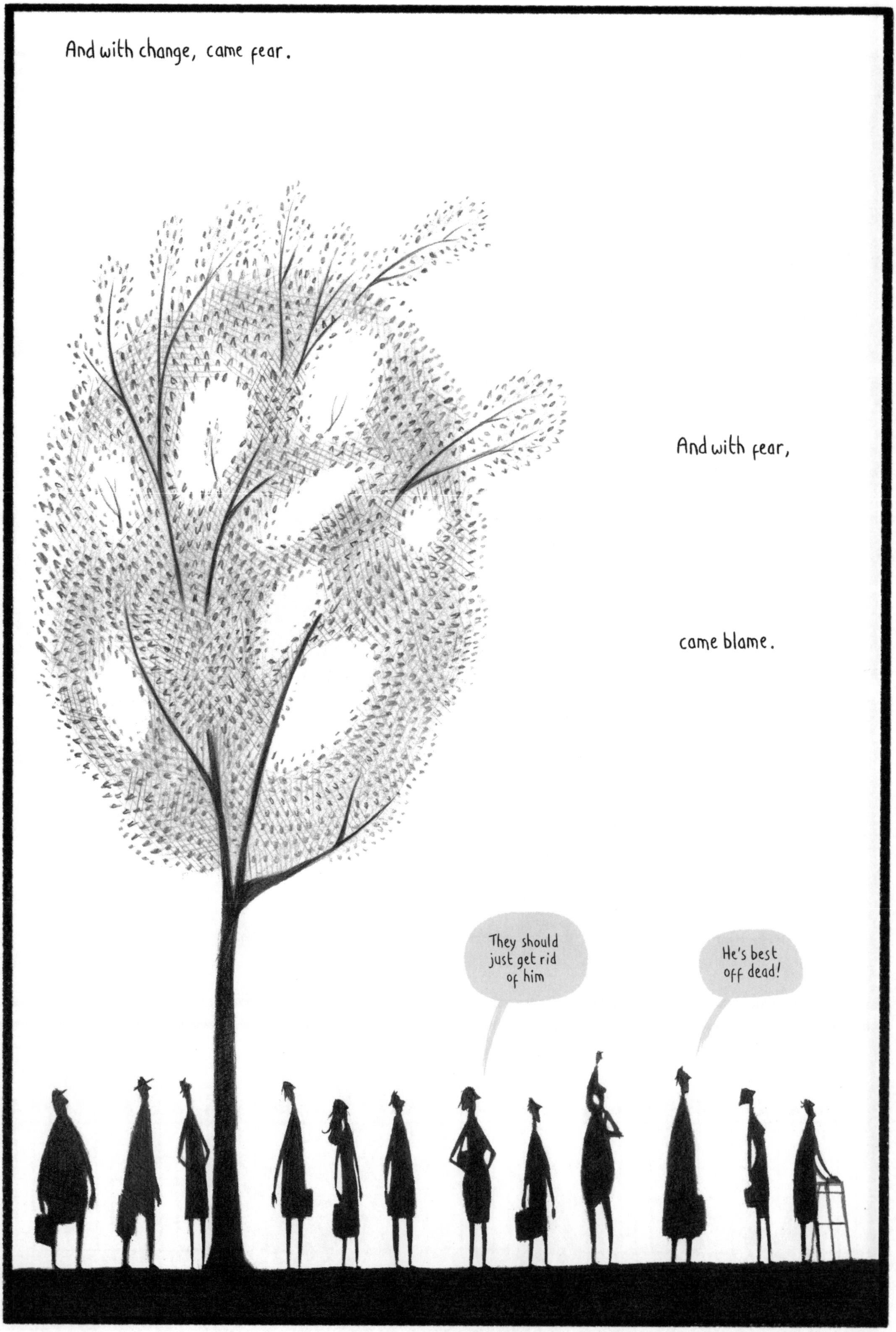
And with change, came fear.
And with fear,
came blame.
They should just get rid of him
He's best off dead!

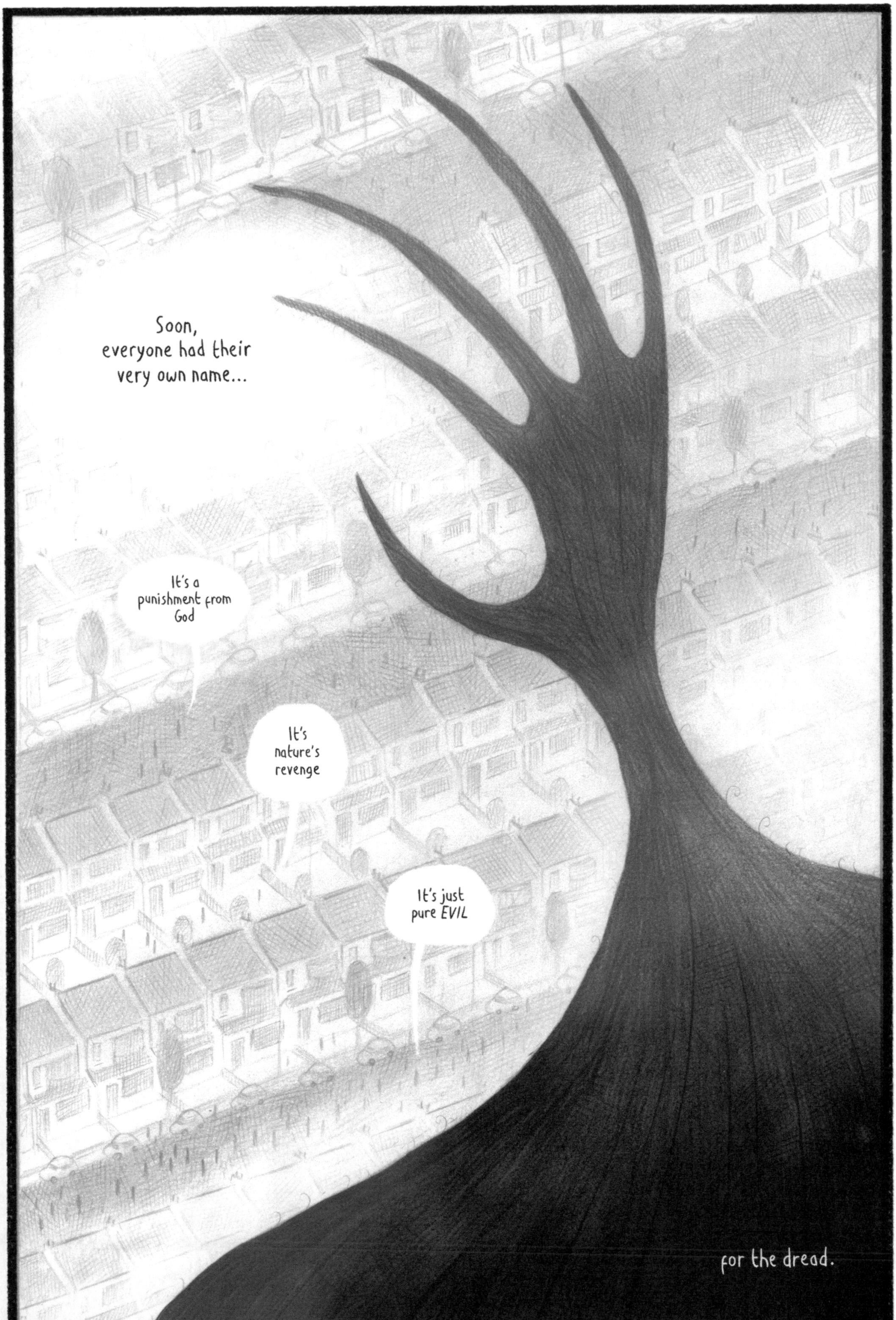
Soon, everyone had their very own name...
It's a punishment from God
It's nature's revenge
It's just pure EVIL
for the dread.

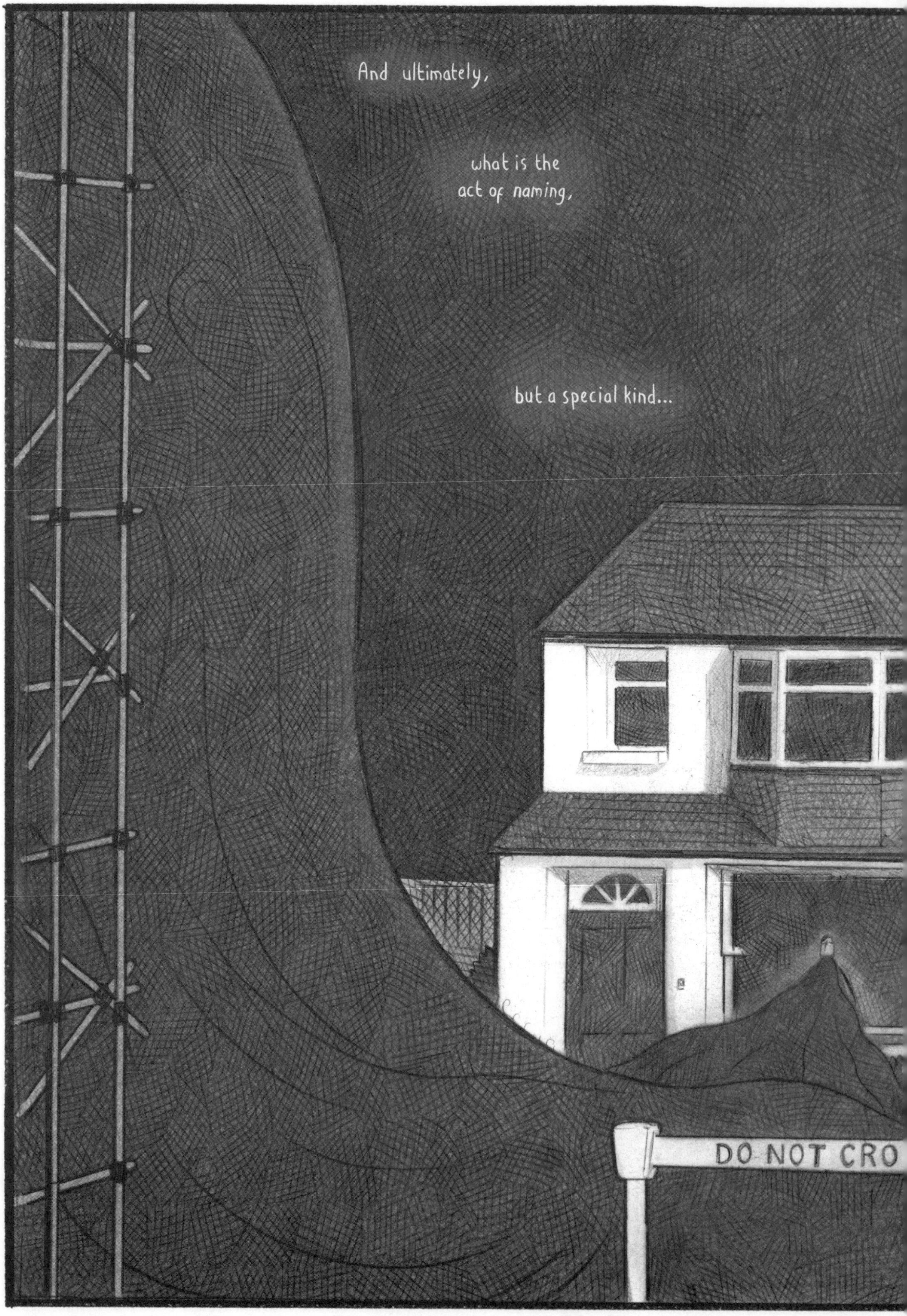
And ultimately,
what is the
act of naming,
but a special kind...
DO NOT CRO

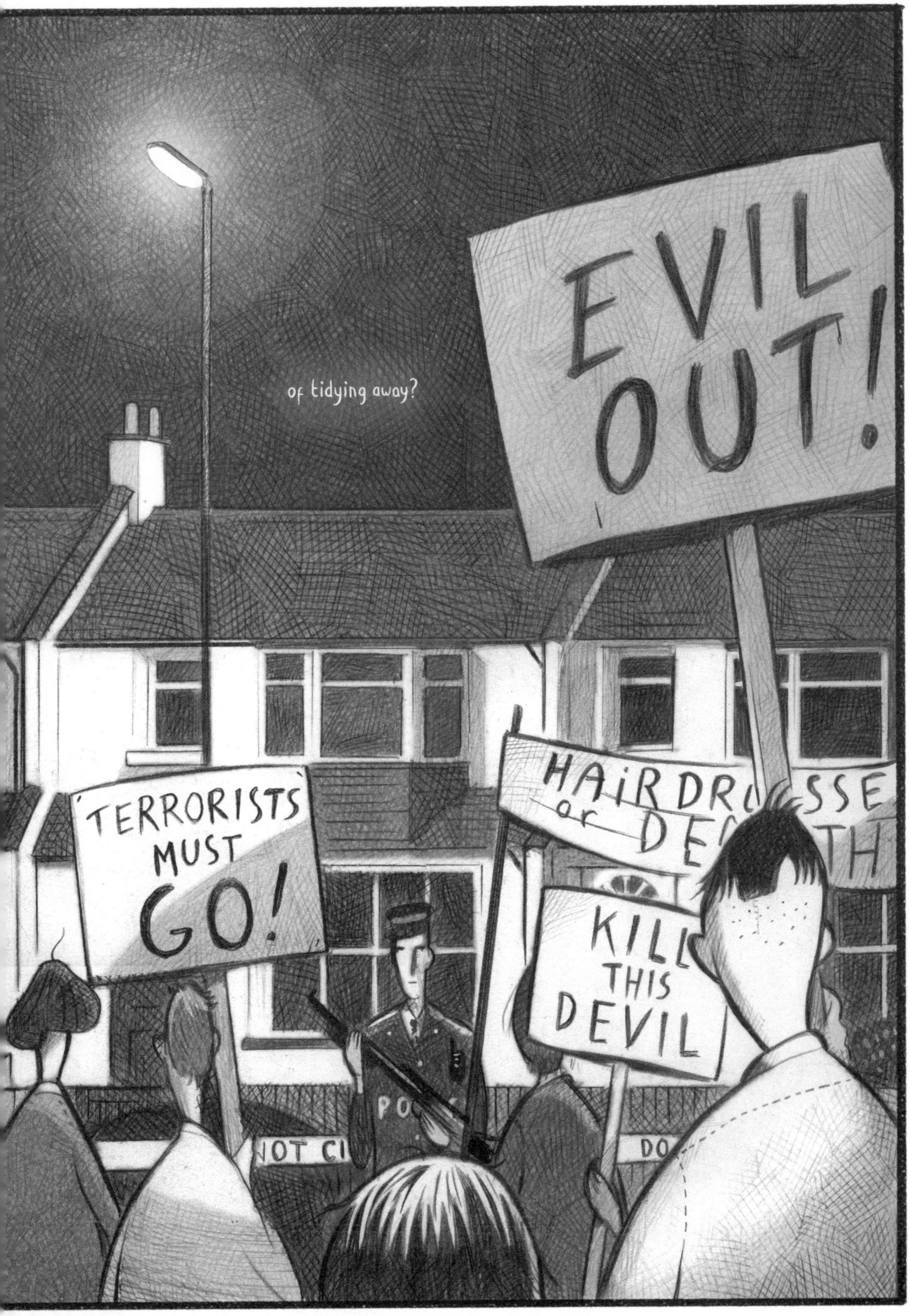
of tidying away?
EVIL OUT!
TERRORISTS MUST GO!
HAiR DR SSE
or DE TH
KILL THIS DEVIL

It had to end somewhere.

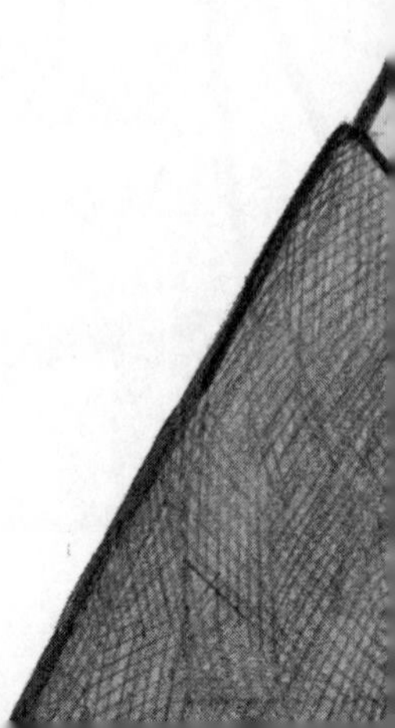

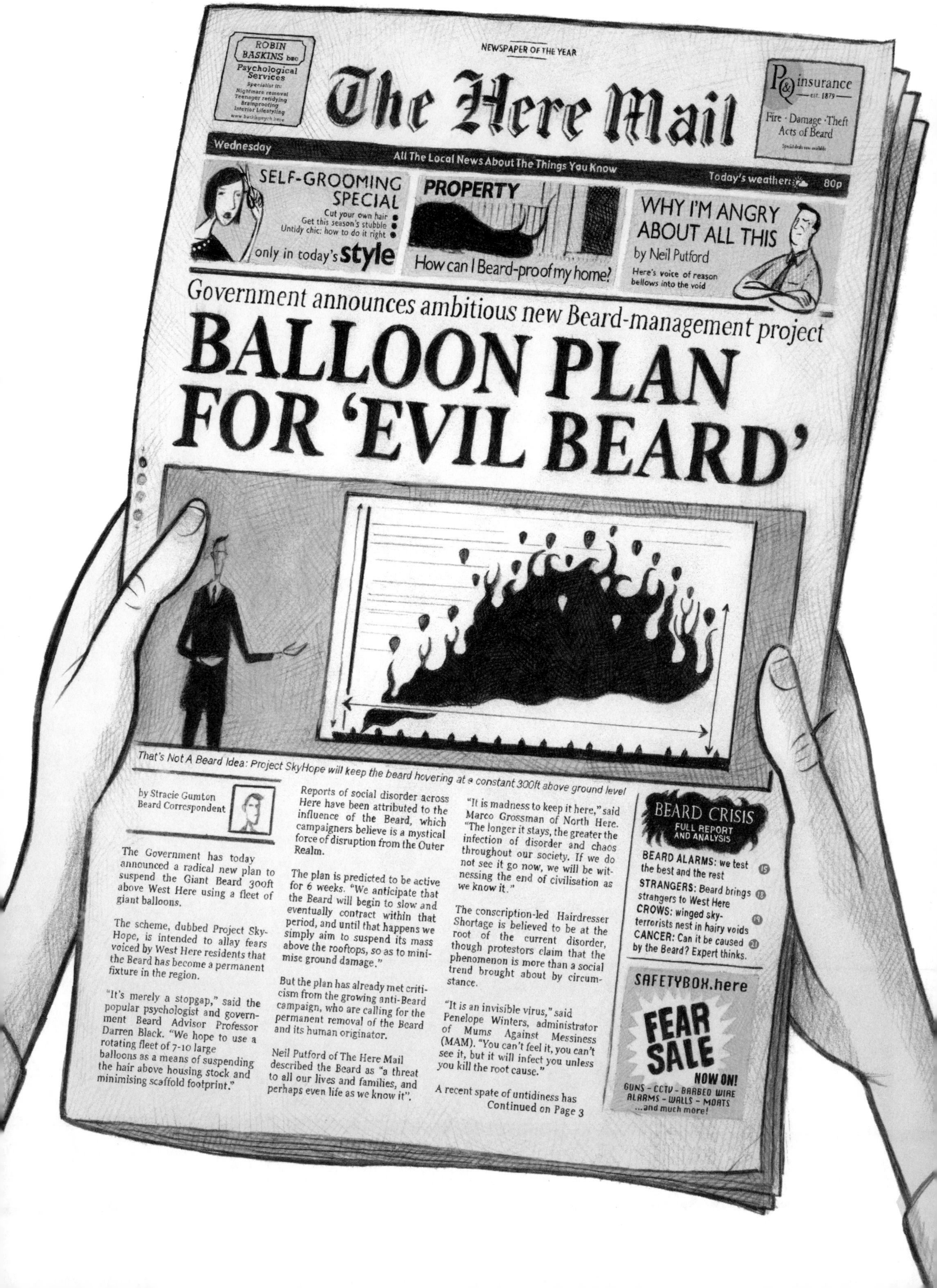
ROBIN BASKINS bsc
Psychological Services
Specialist in:
Nightmare removal
Teenager retidying
Brainproofing
Interior Lifestyling
www.baskinpsych.here
NEWSPAPER OF THE YEAR
The Here Mail
P&Q insurance
est. 1879
Fire · Damage · Theft
Acts of Beard
Wednesday
All The Local News About The Things You Know
Today's weather:
80p
SELF-GROOMING SPECIAL
Cut your own hair
Get this season's stubble
Untidy chic: how to do it right
only in today's style
PROPERTY
How can I Beard-proof my home?
WHY I'M ANGRY ABOUT ALL THIS
by Neil Putford
Here's voice of reason bellows into the void
Government announces ambitious new Beard-management project
BALLOON PLAN FOR 'EVIL BEARD'
That's Not A Beard Idea: Project SkyHope will keep the beard hovering at a constant 300ft above ground level
by Stracie Gumton
Beard Correspondent
The Government has today announced a radical new plan to suspend the Giant Beard 300ft above West Here using a fleet of giant balloons.
The scheme, dubbed Project Sky-Hope, is intended to allay fears voiced by West Here residents that the Beard has become a permanent fixture in the region.
"It's merely a stopgap," said the popular psychologist and government Beard Advisor Professor Darren Black. "We hope to use a rotating fleet of 7-10 large balloons as a means of suspending the hair above housing stock and minimising scaffold footprint."
Reports of social disorder across Here have been attributed to the influence of the Beard, which campaigners believe is a mystical force of disruption from the Outer Realm.
The plan is predicted to be active for 6 weeks. "We anticipate that the Beard will begin to slow and eventually contract within that period, and until that happens we simply aim to suspend its mass above the rooftops, so as to minimise ground damage."
But the plan has already met criticism from the growing anti-Beard campaign, who are calling for the permanent removal of the Beard and its human originator.
Neil Putford of The Here Mail described the Beard as "a threat to all our lives and families, and perhaps even life as we know it".
"It is madness to keep it here," said Marco Grossman of North Here. "The longer it stays, the greater the infection of disorder and chaos throughout our society. If we do not see it go now, we will be witnessing the end of civilisation as we know it."
The conscription-led Hairdresser Shortage is believed to be at the root of the current disorder, though protestors claim that the phenomenon is more than a social trend brought about by circumstance.
"It is an invisible virus," said Penelope Winters, administrator of Mums Against Messiness (MAM). "You can't feel it, you can't see it, but it will infect you unless you kill the root cause."
A recent spate of untidiness has
Continued on Page 3
BEARD CRISIS
FULL REPORT AND ANALYSIS
BEARD ALARMS: we test the best and the rest 15
STRANGERS: Beard brings strangers to West Here 18
CROWS: winged sky-terrorists nest in hairy voids 19
CANCER: Can it be caused by the Beard? Expert thinks. 21
SAFETYBOX.here
FEAR SALE
NOW ON!
GUNS – CCTV – BARBED WIRE
ALARMS – WALLS – MOATS
...and much more!

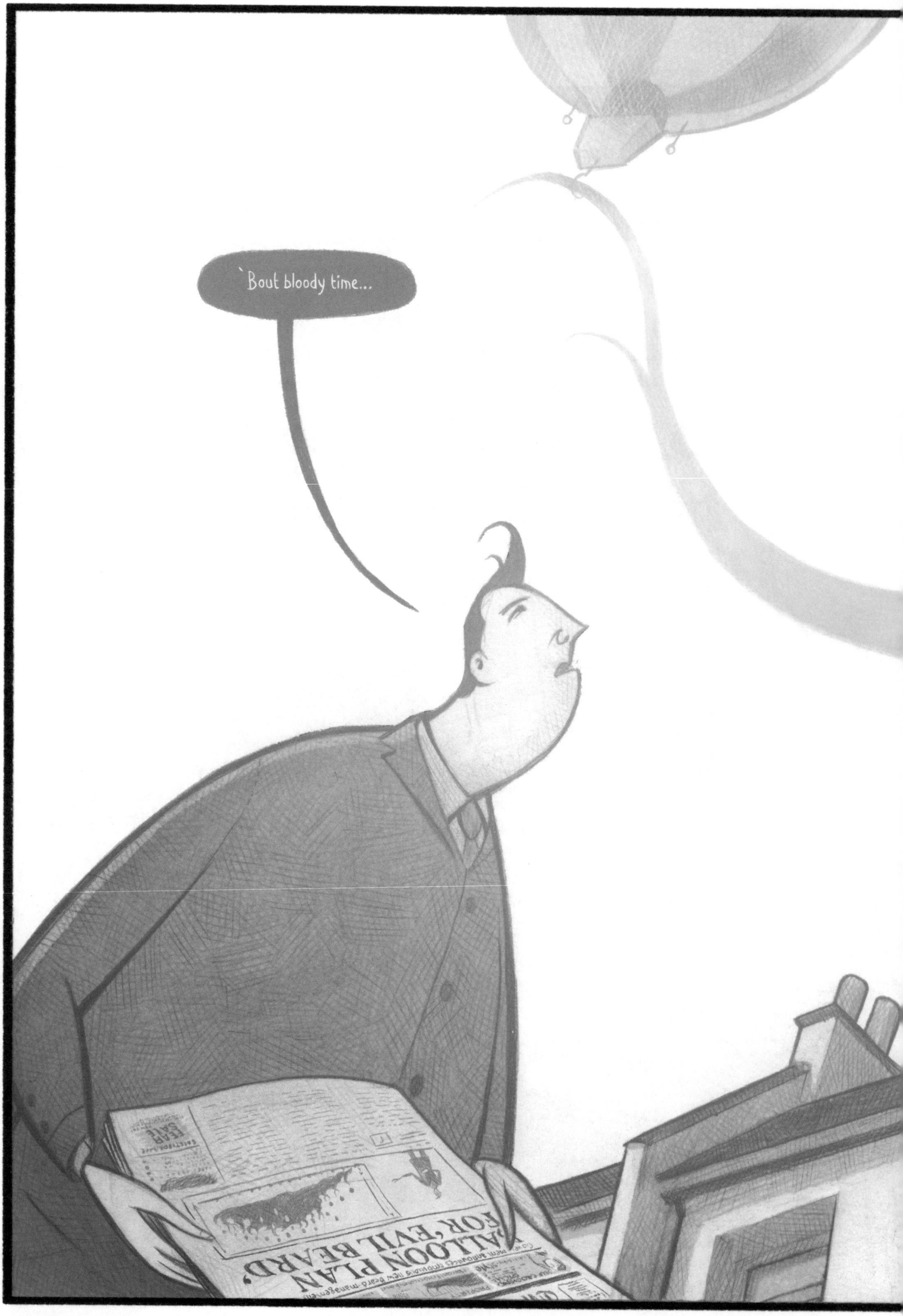
`Bout bloody time...

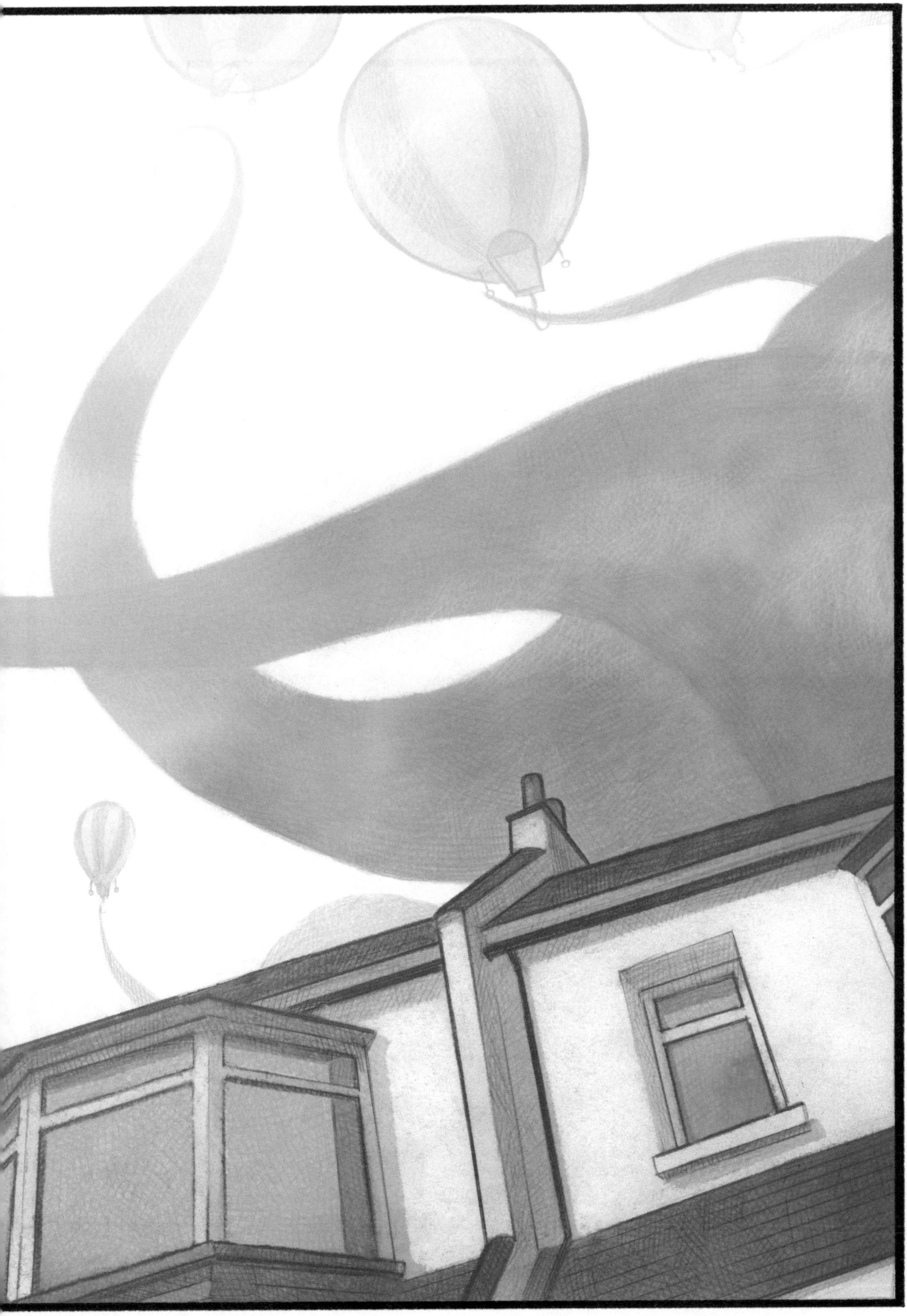

It was, of course, the Government's idea.

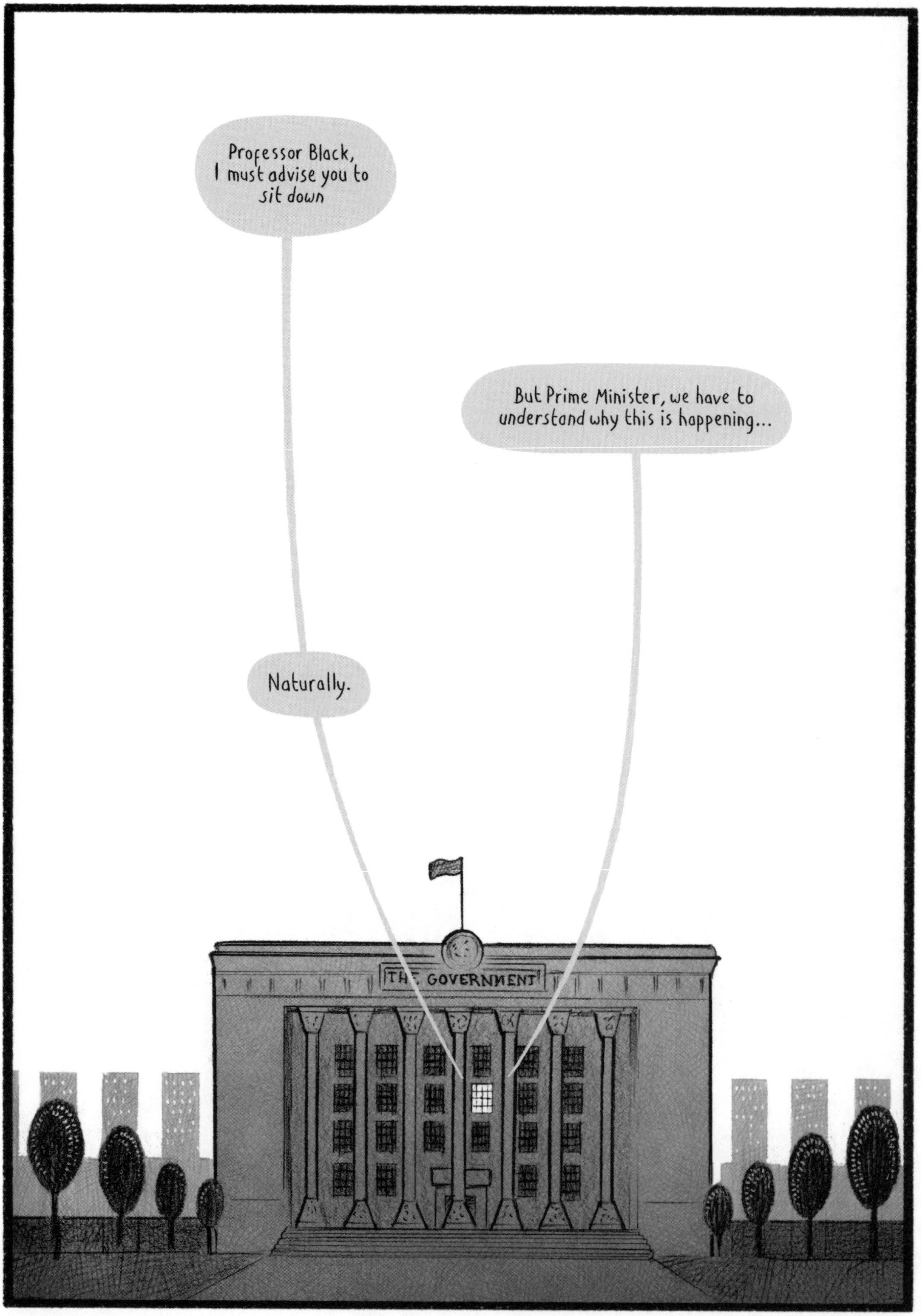
Professor Black, I must advise you to sit down
But Prime Minister, we have to understand why this is happening...
Naturally.
THE GOVERNMENT

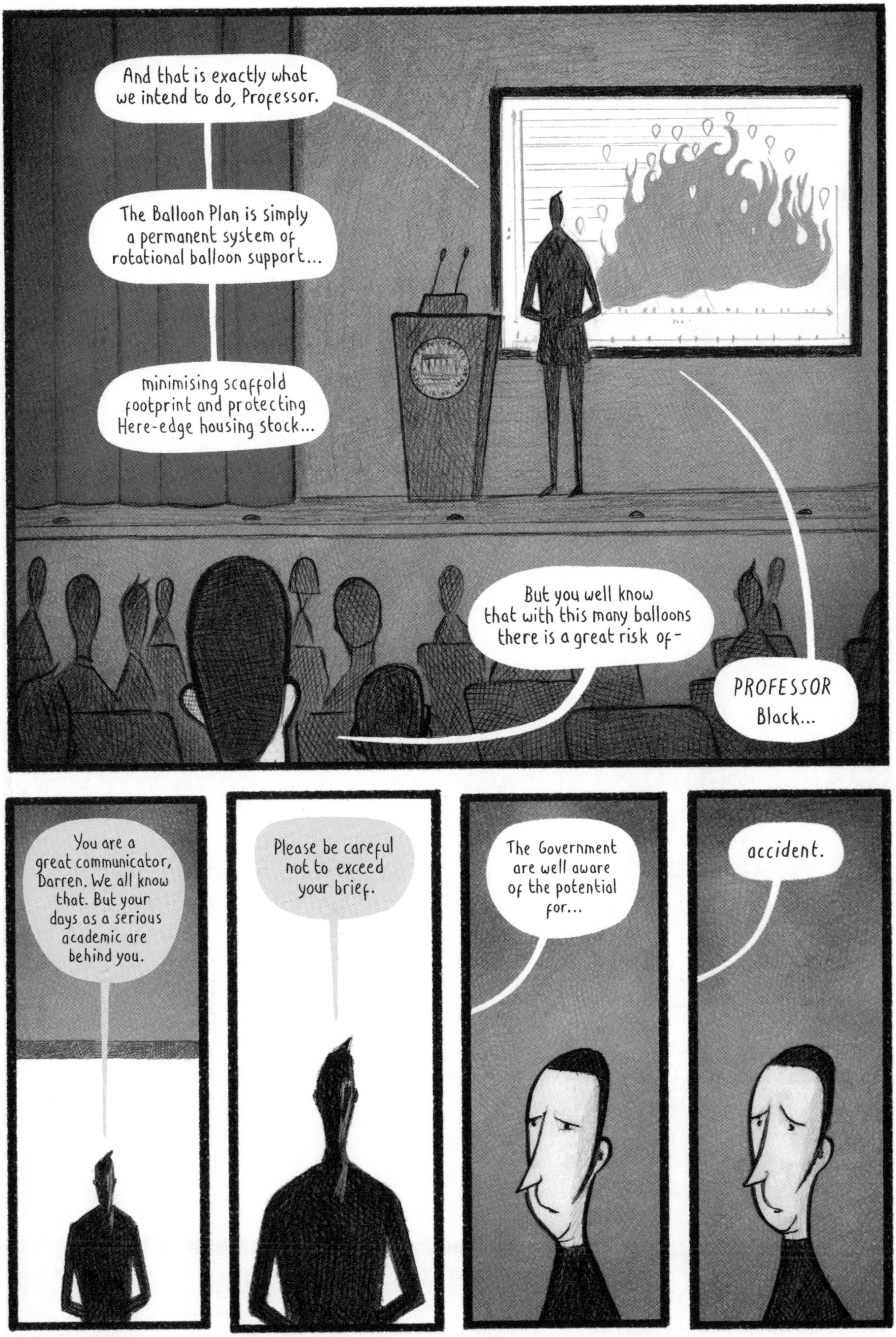
And that is exactly what we intend to do, Professor.
The Balloon Plan is simply a permanent system of rotational balloon support...
minimising scaffold footprint and protecting Here-edge housing stock...
But you well know that with this many balloons there is a great risk of-
PROFESSOR Black...
You are a great communicator, Darren. We all know that. But your days as a serious academic are behind you.
Please be careful not to exceed your brief.
The Government are well aware of the potential for...
accident.

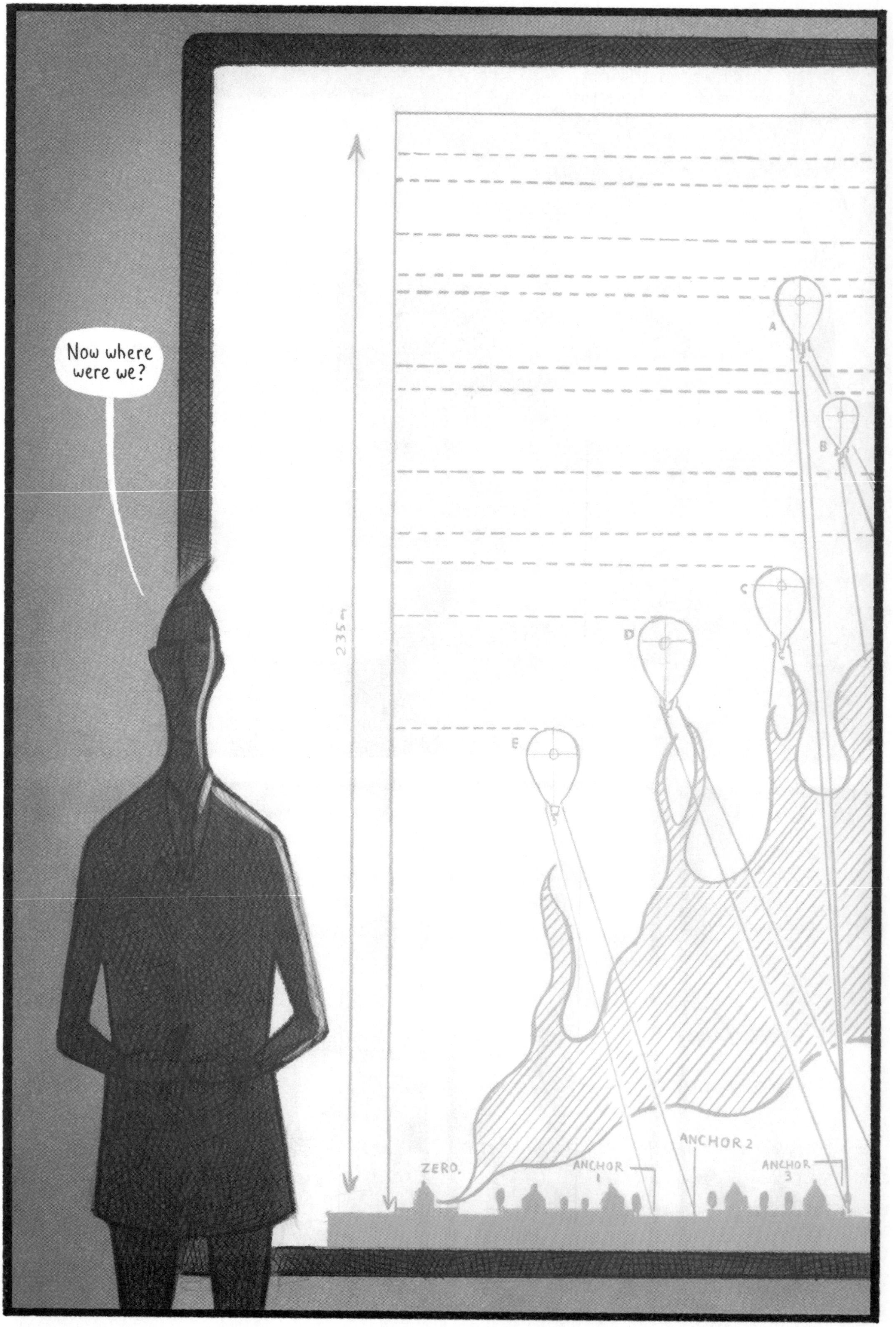
Now where were we?
A
B
C
D
E
235m
ZERO.
ANCHOR 1
ANCHOR 2
ANCHOR 3

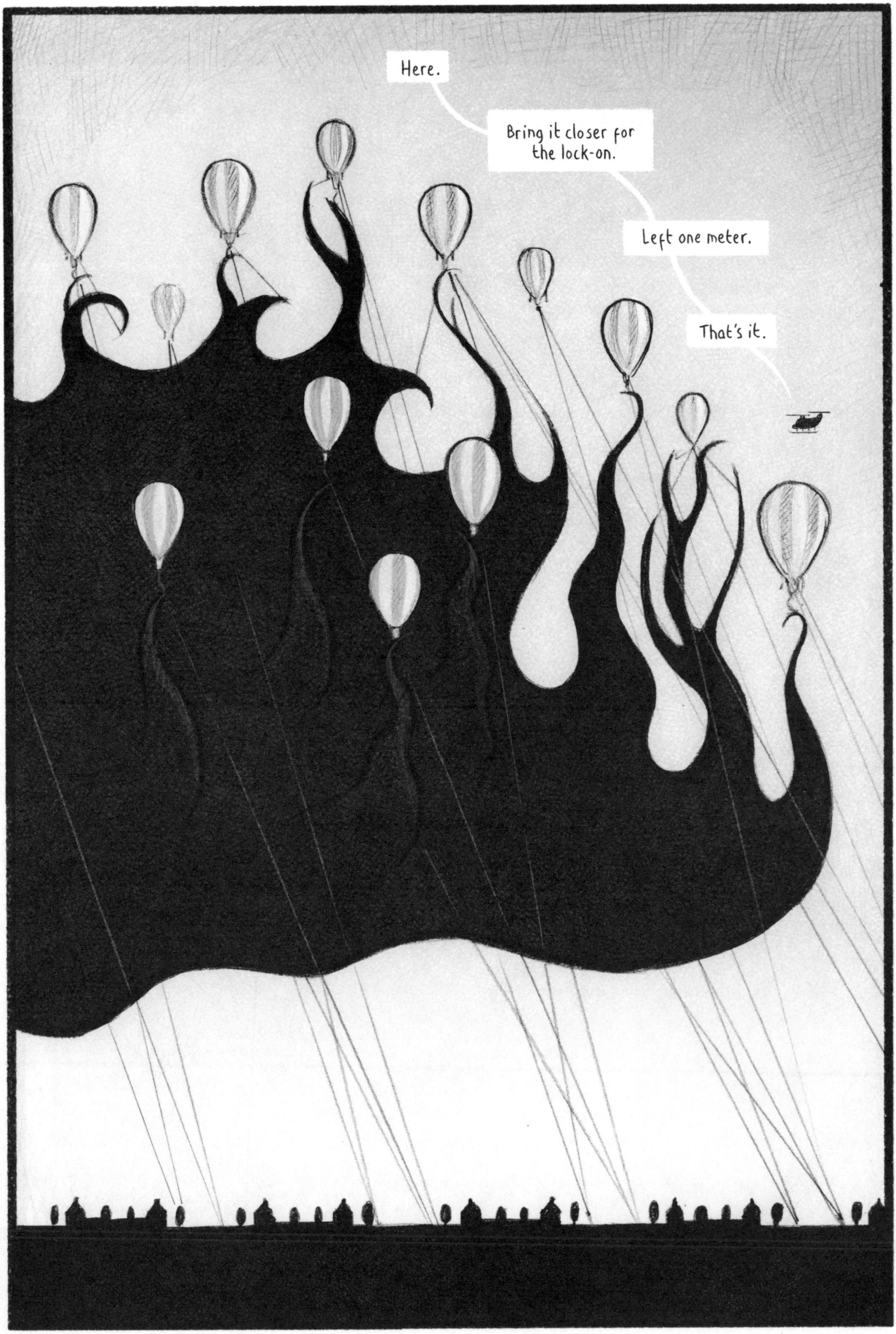
Here.
Bring it closer for the lock-on.
Left one meter.
That's it.

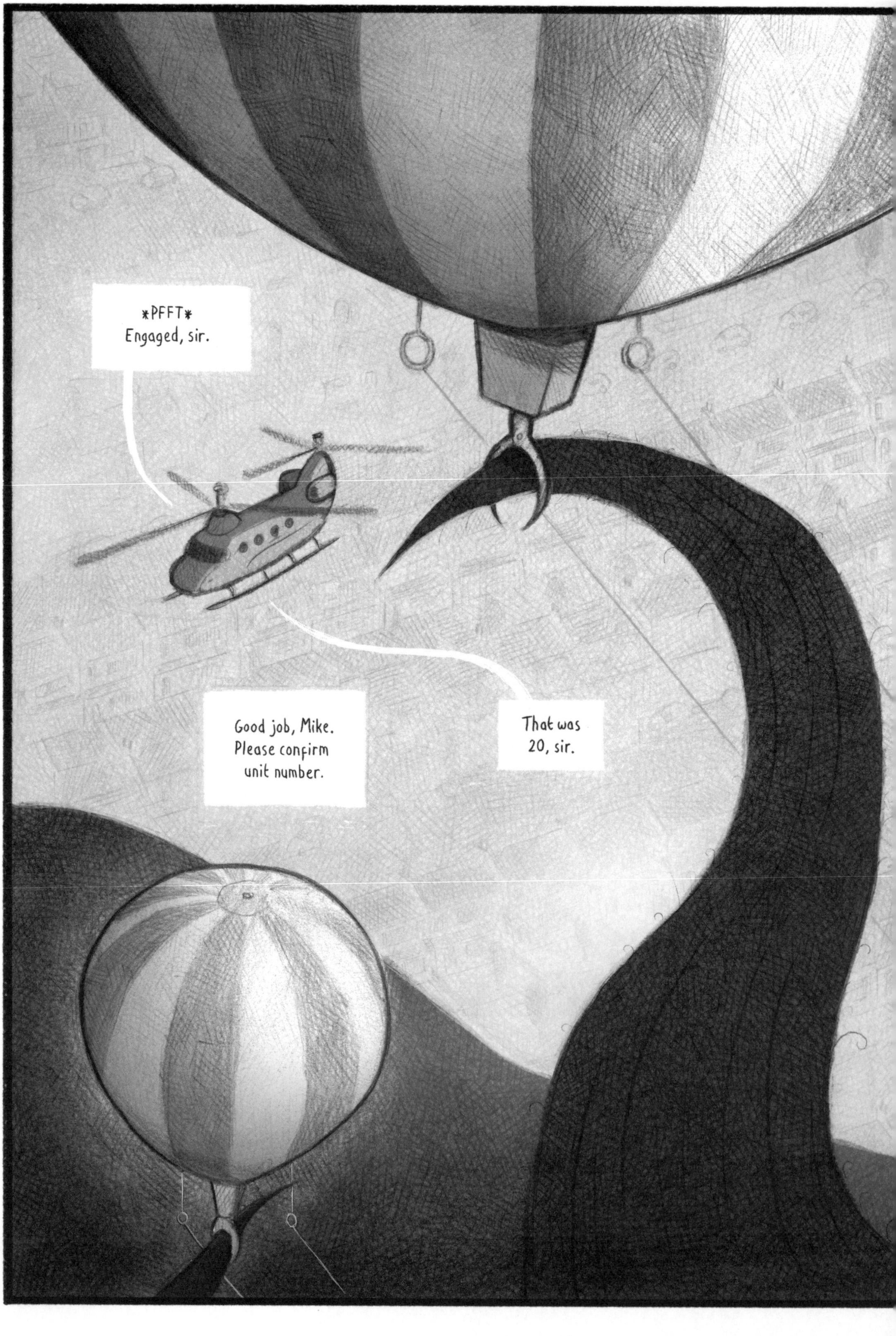
PFFT
Engaged, sir.
Good job, Mike.
Please confirm
unit number.
That was
20, sir.

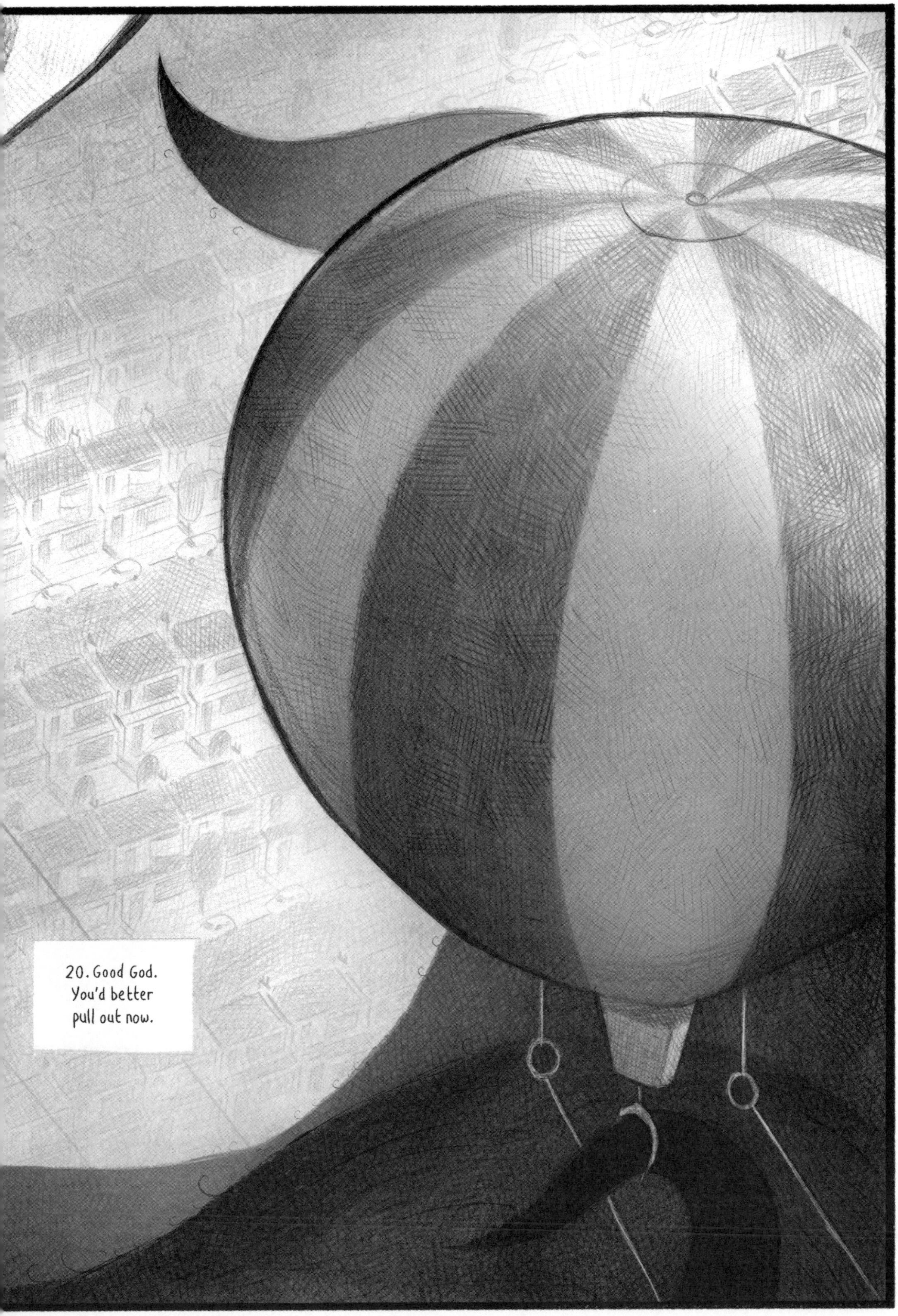
20. Good God.
You'd better
pull out now.

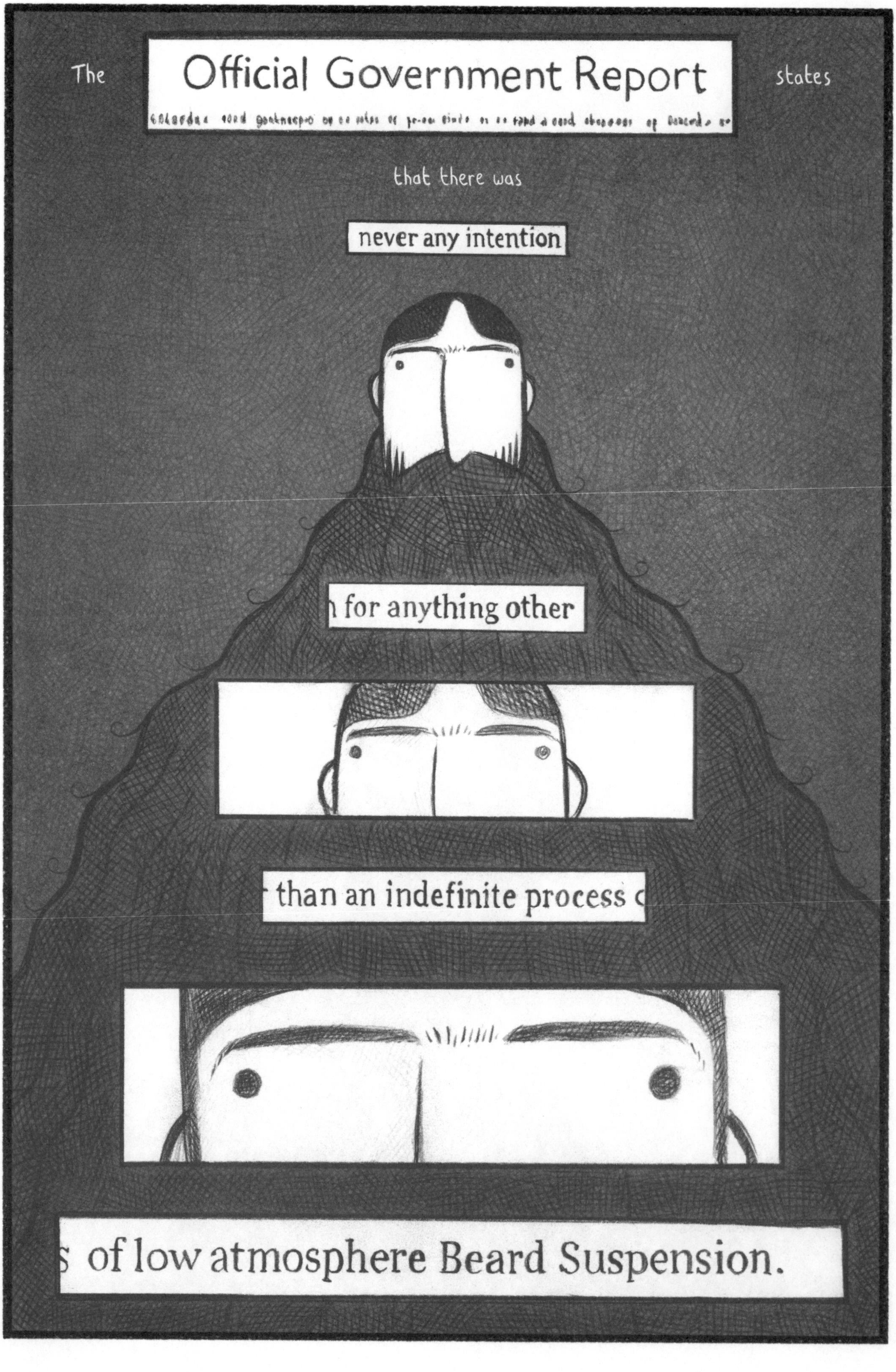

Official Government Report

that there was

never any intention

for anything other

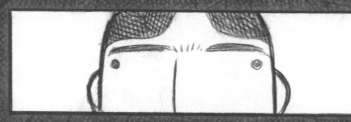

than an indefinite process

of low atmosphere Beard Suspension.

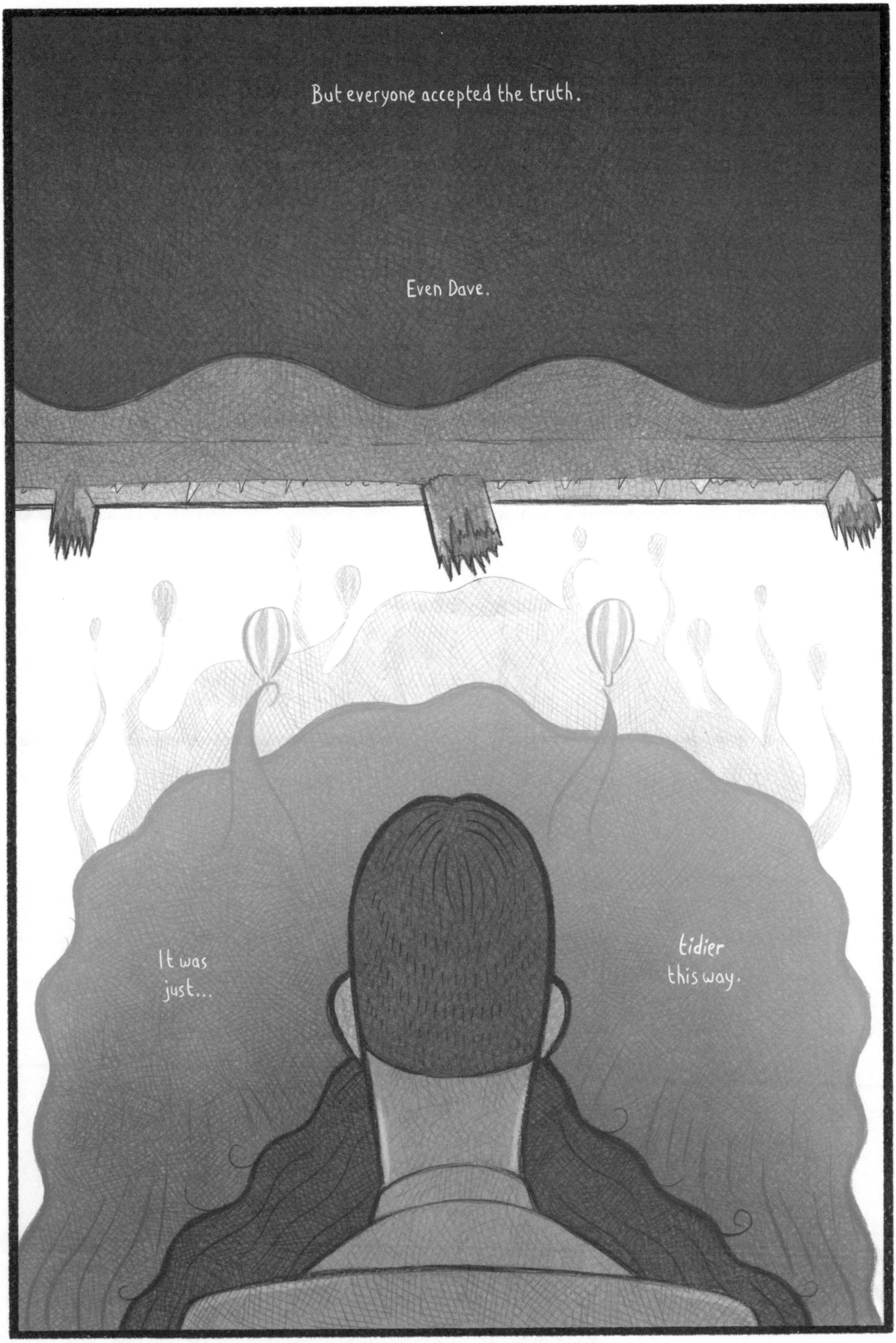
But everyone accepted the truth.
Even Dave.
It was just...
tidier this way.

And all witnesses concur
that as the Beard began to lift

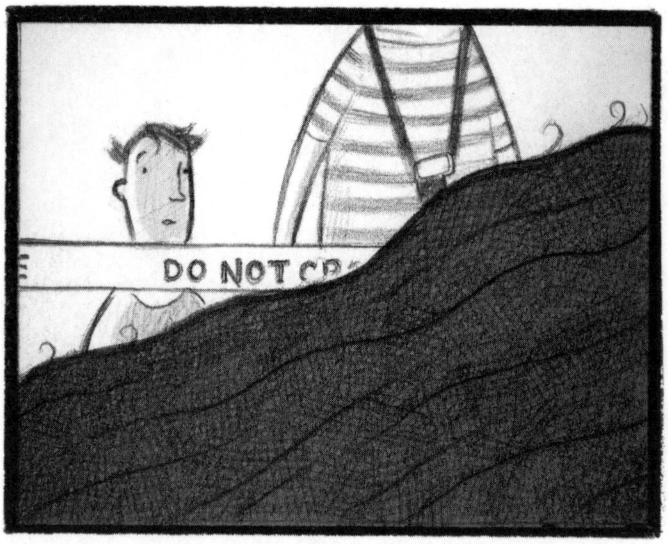
DO NOT CR

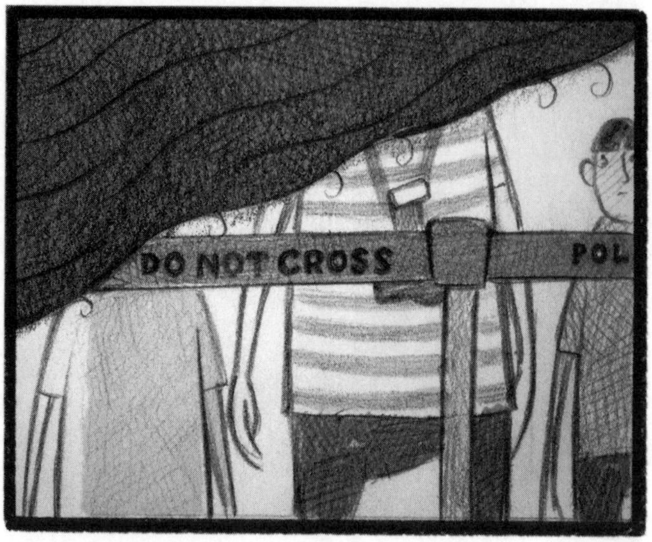
DO NOT CROSS
POL

and the tethers began to

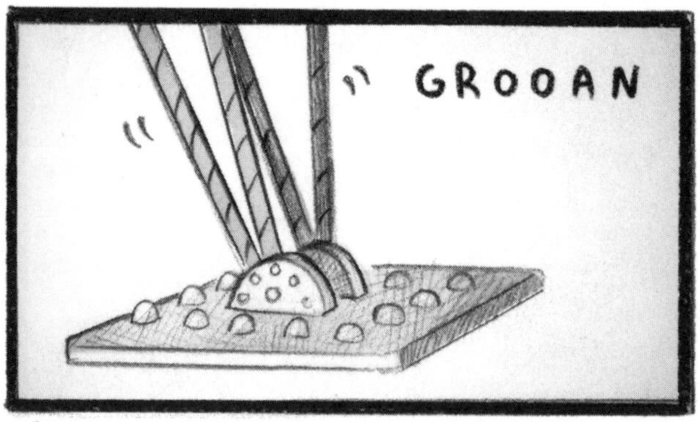
GROOAN

and

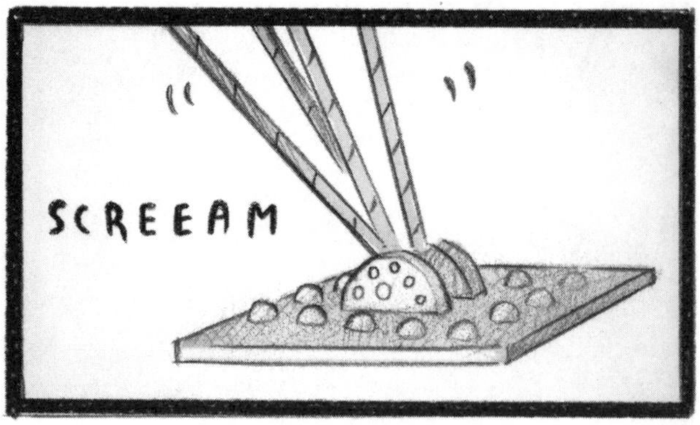
SCREEAM

Dave looked

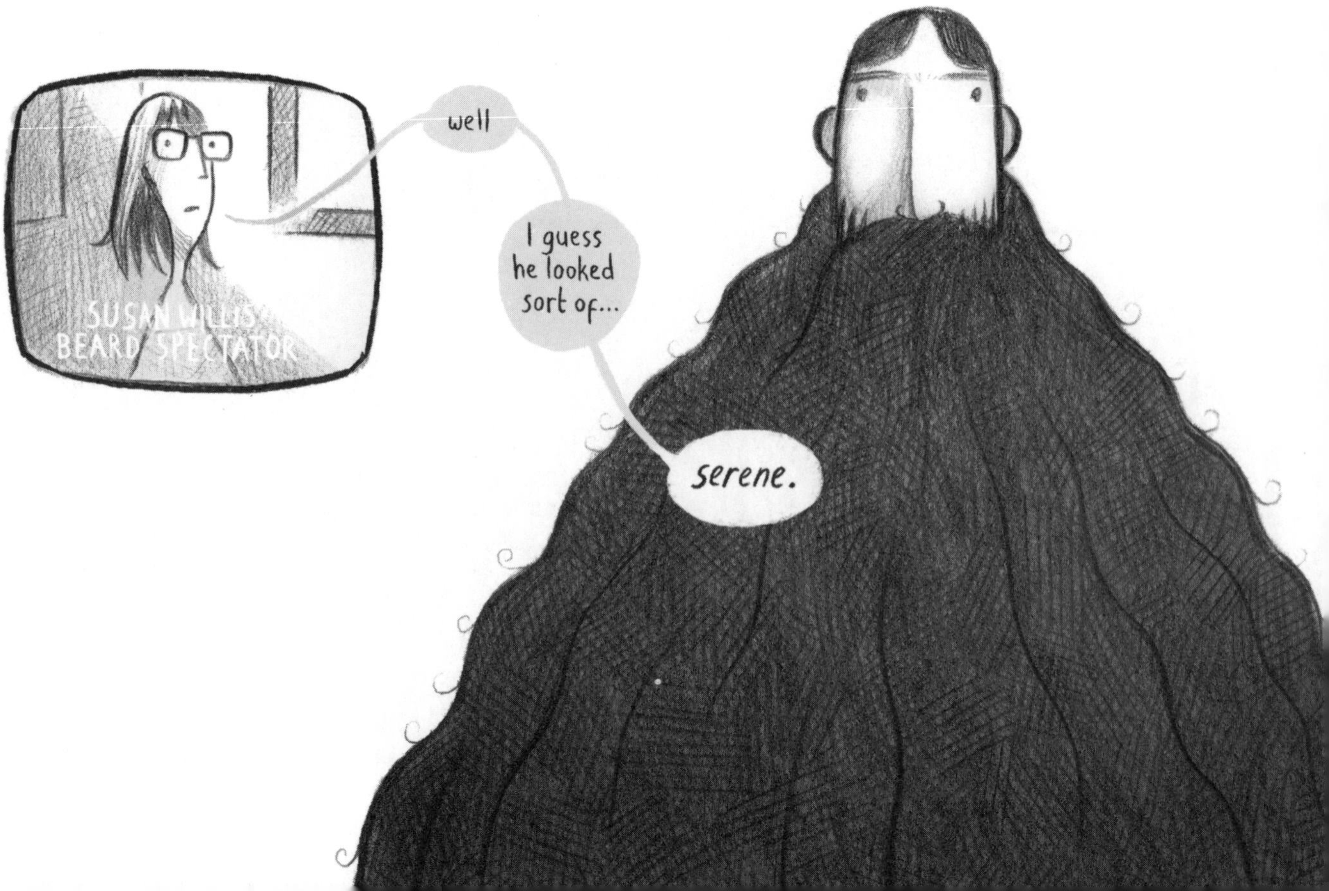
SUSAN WILLIS
BEARD SPECTATOR
well
I guess he looked sort of...
serene.

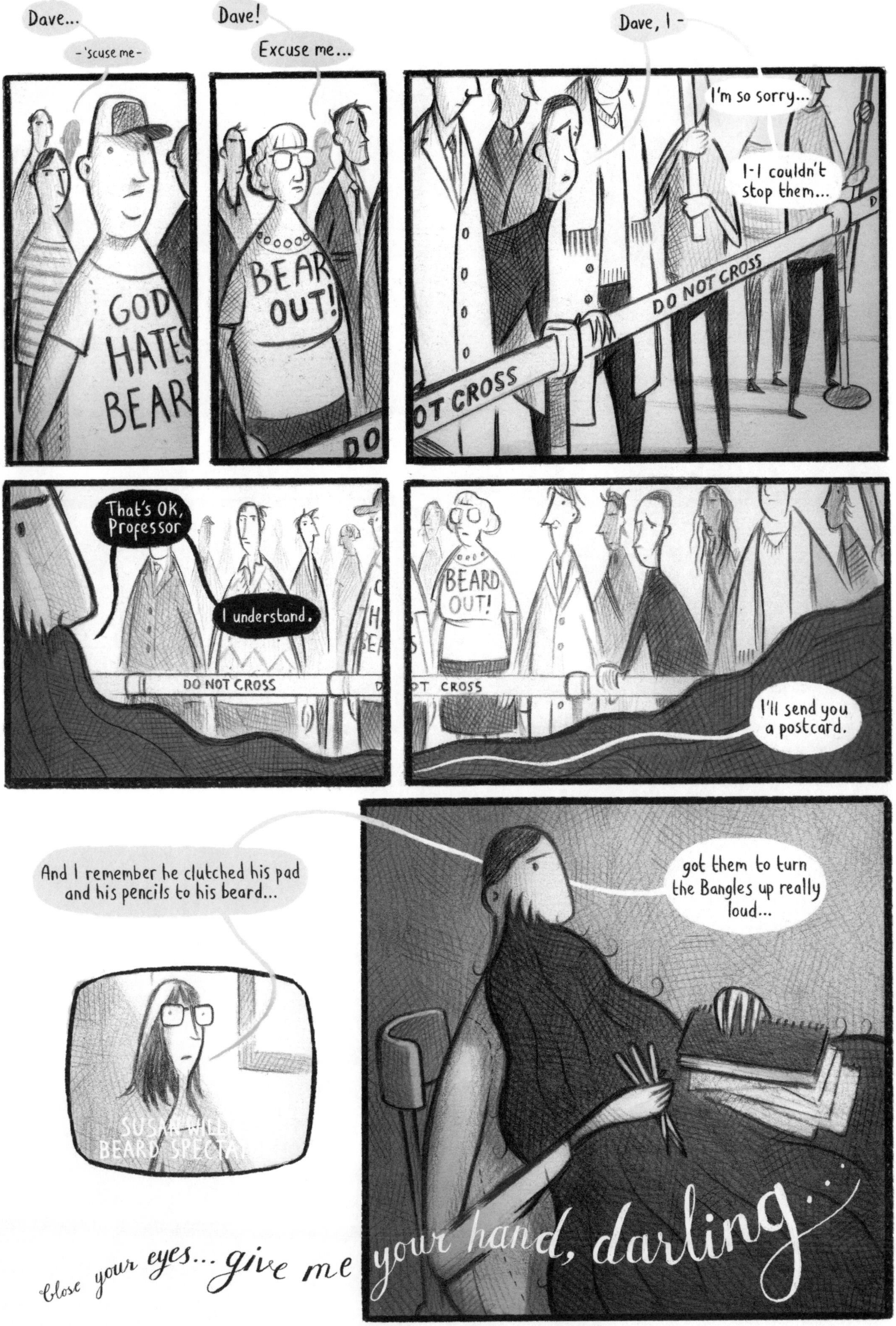
Dave...
-'scuse me-
GOD HATES BEAR
Dave!
Excuse me...
BEAR OUT!
Dave, I -
I'm so sorry...
I-I couldn't stop them...
DO NOT CROSS
DO NOT CROSS
DO
That's OK, Professor
I understand.
DO NOT CROSS
BEARD OUT!
I'll send you a postcard.
And I remember he clutched his pad and his pencils to his beard...
got them to turn the Bangles up really loud...
Close your eyes... give me your hand, darling...

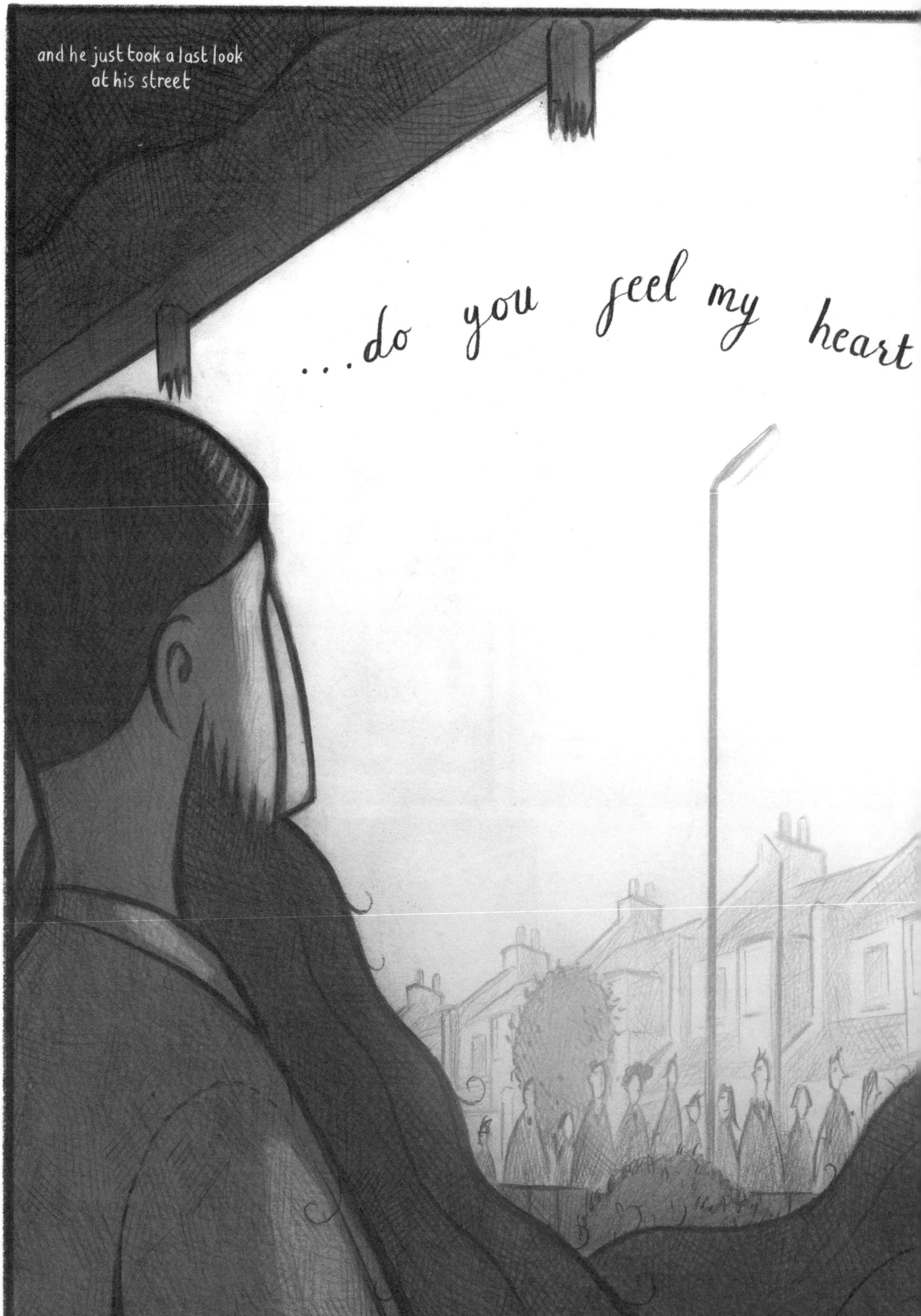
and he just took a last look at his street
...do you feel my heart

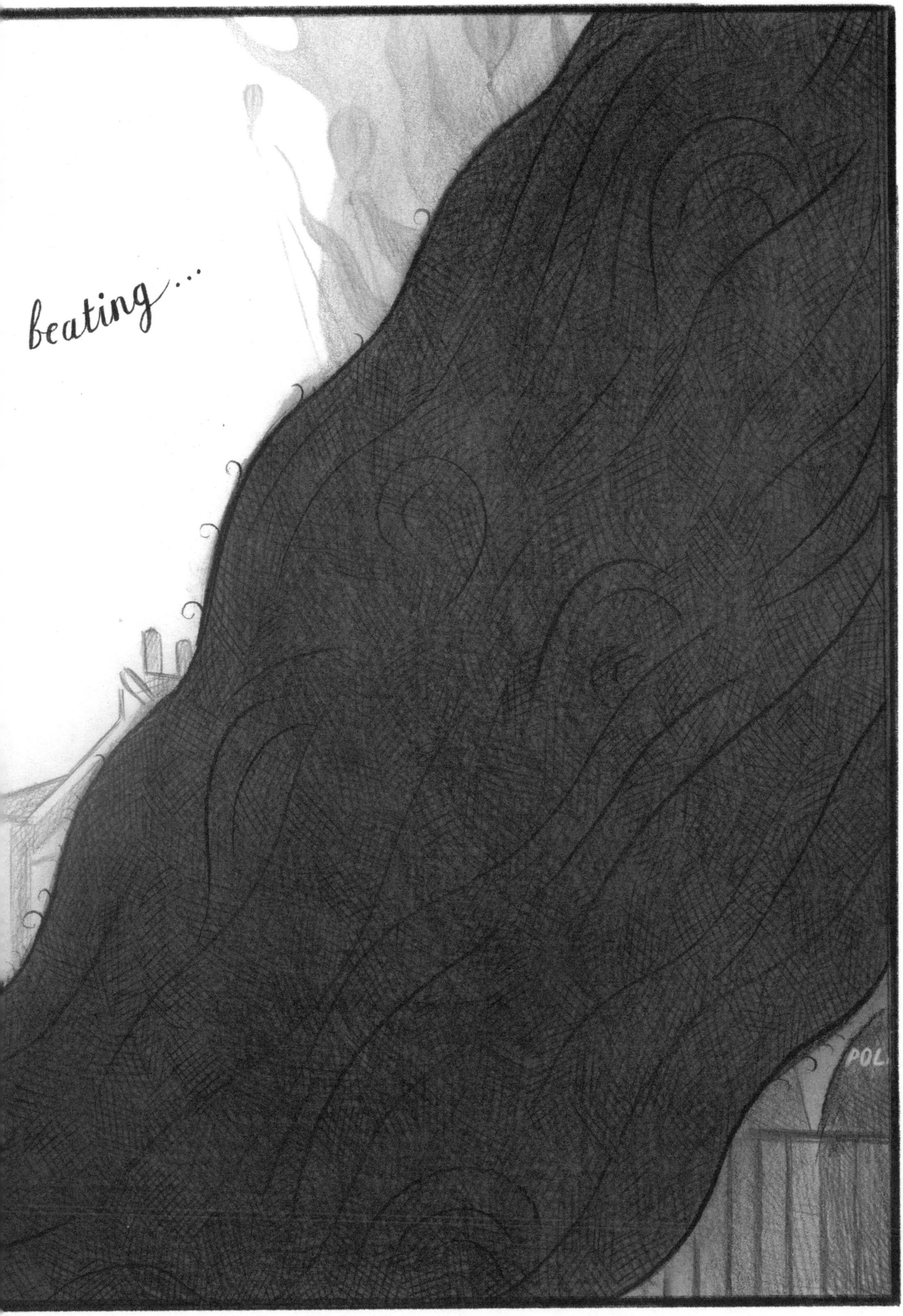
beating...
POL

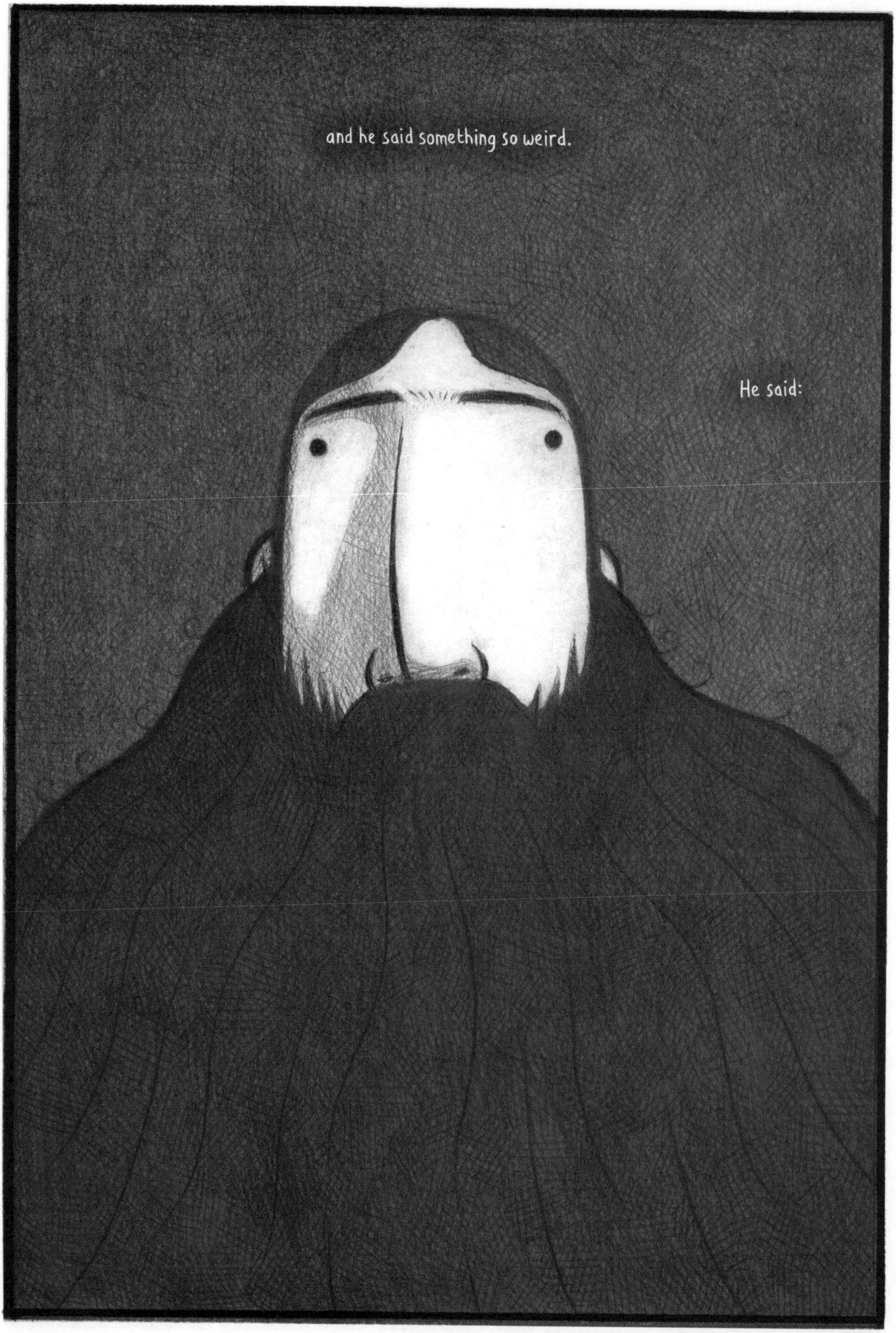
and he said something so weird.
He said:

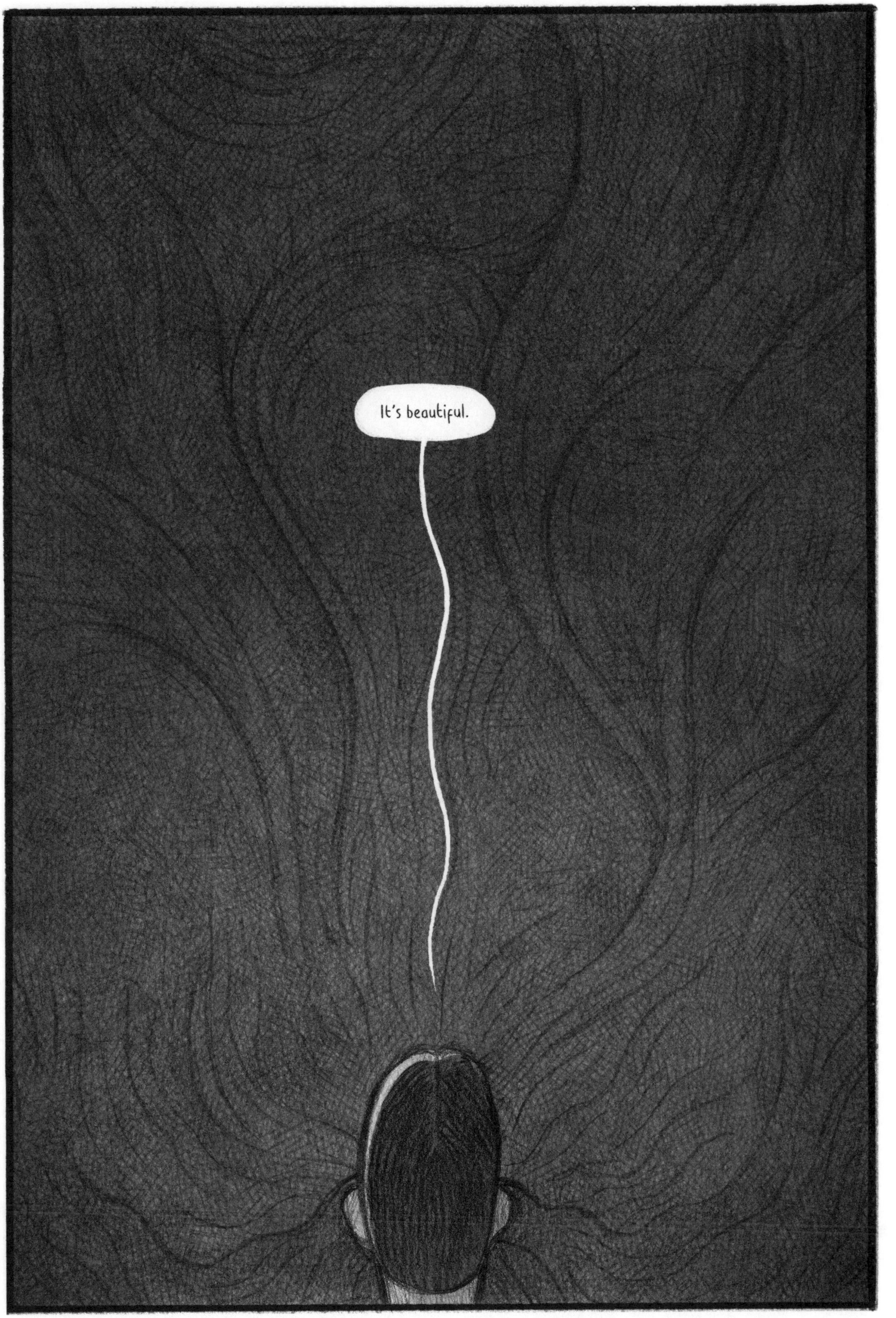
It's beautiful.

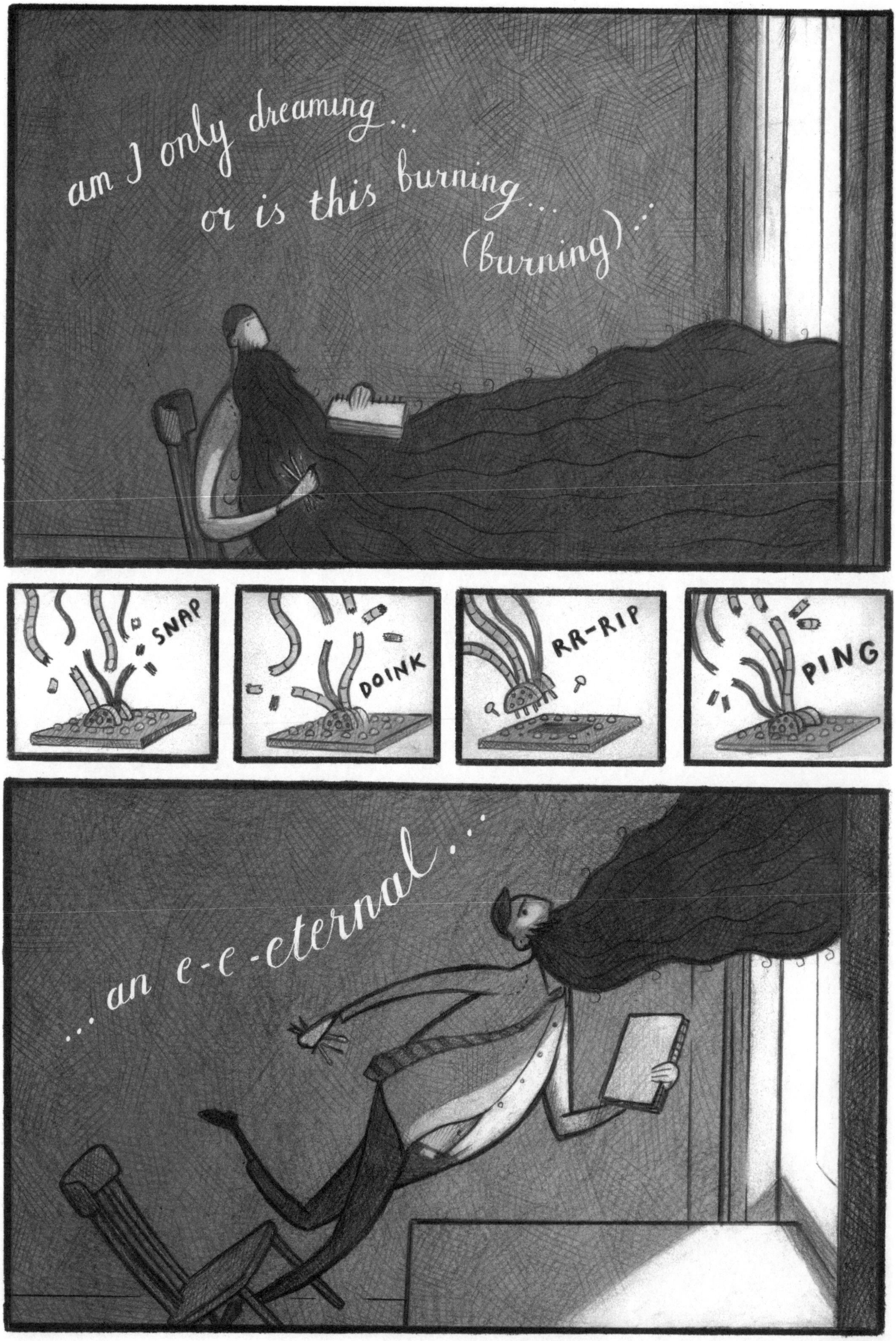
am I only dreaming...
or is this burning...
(burning)...
SNAP
DOINK
RR-RIP
PING
...an e-e-eternal...

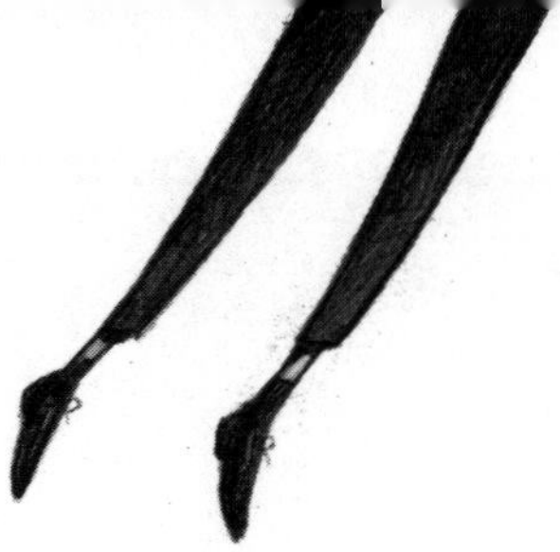

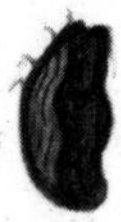

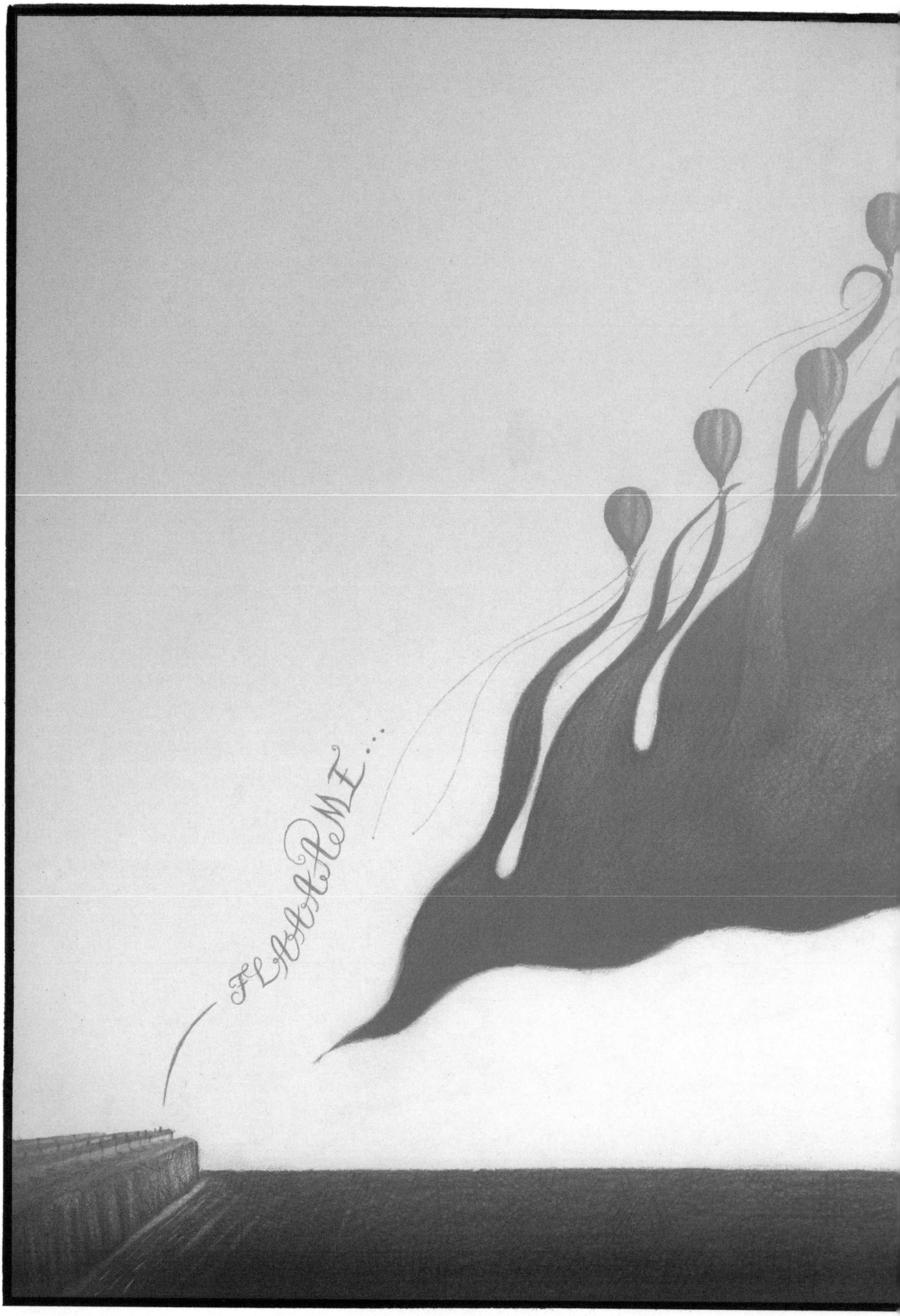
—FLAARME...

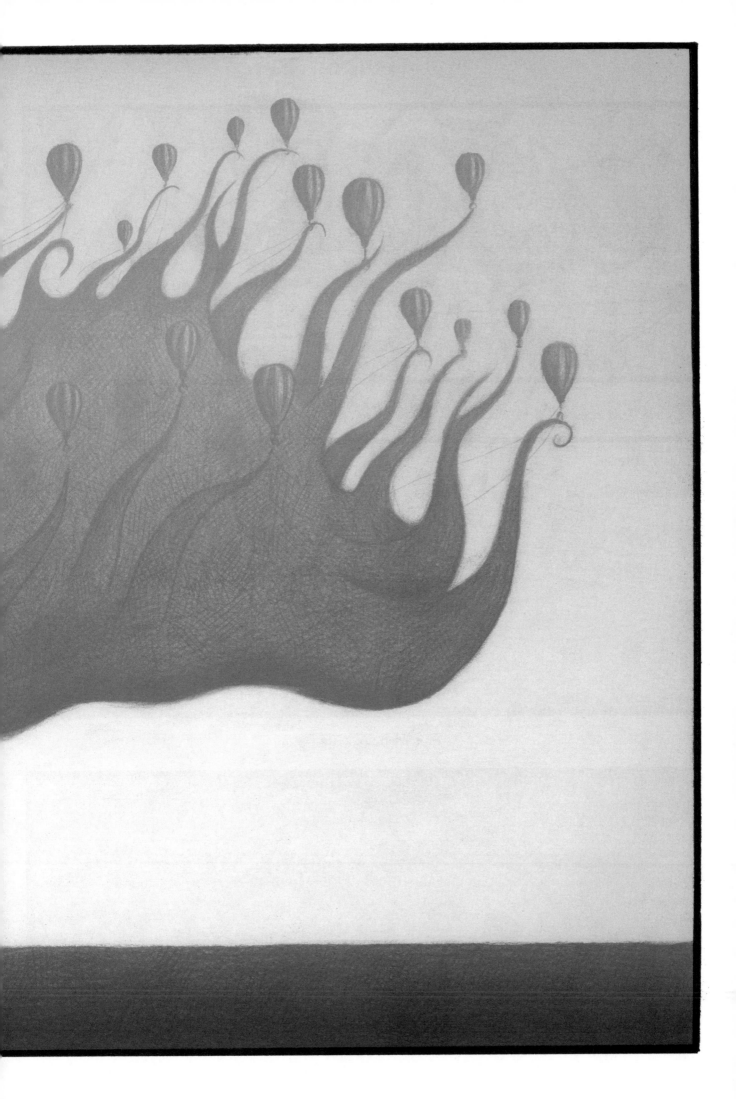

It wasn't pretty, that was true.

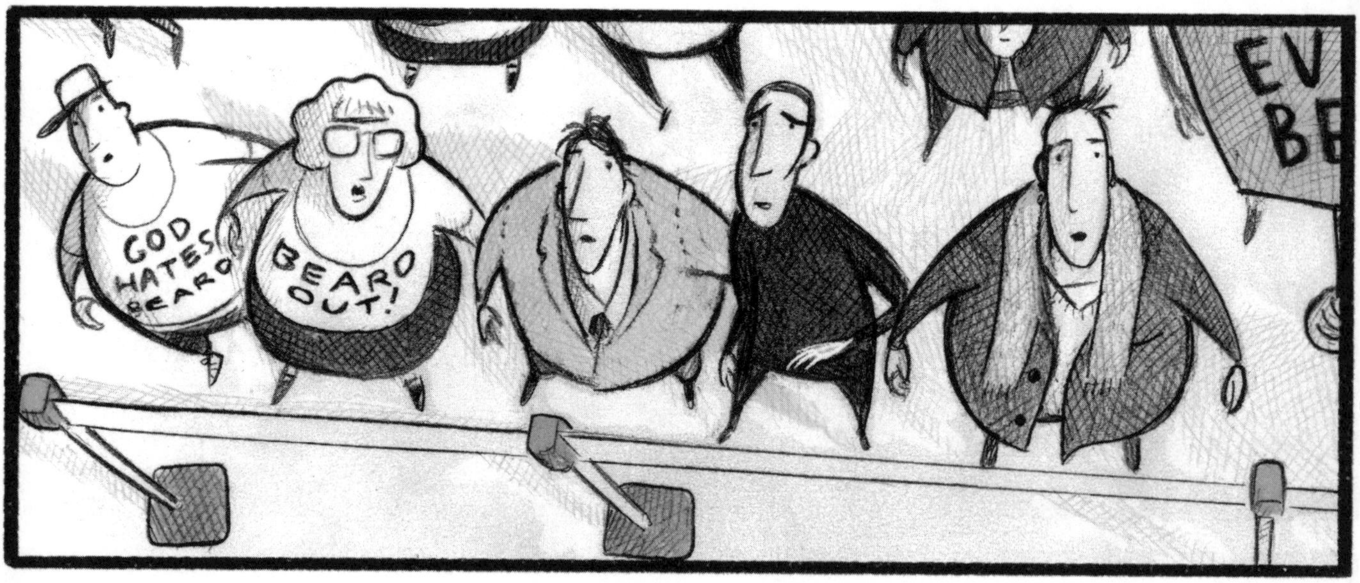
GOD HATES BEARD
BEARD OUT!

But it looked like an ending.

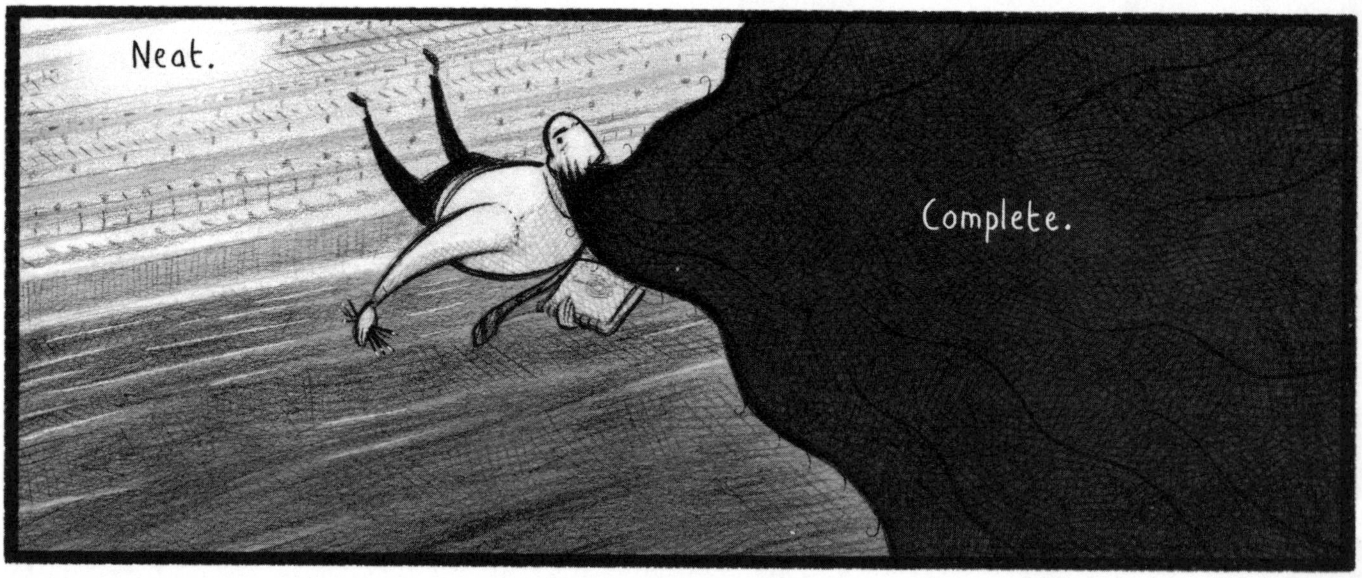
Neat.
Complete.

And as Dave sailed away

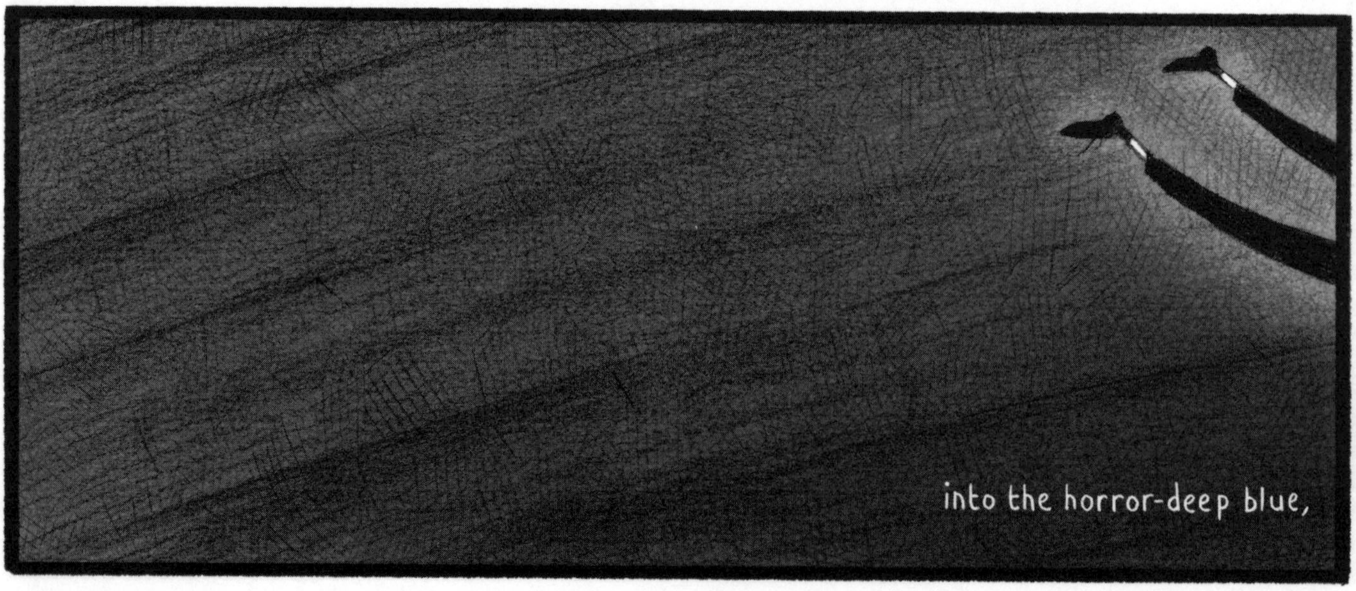
into the horror-deep blue,

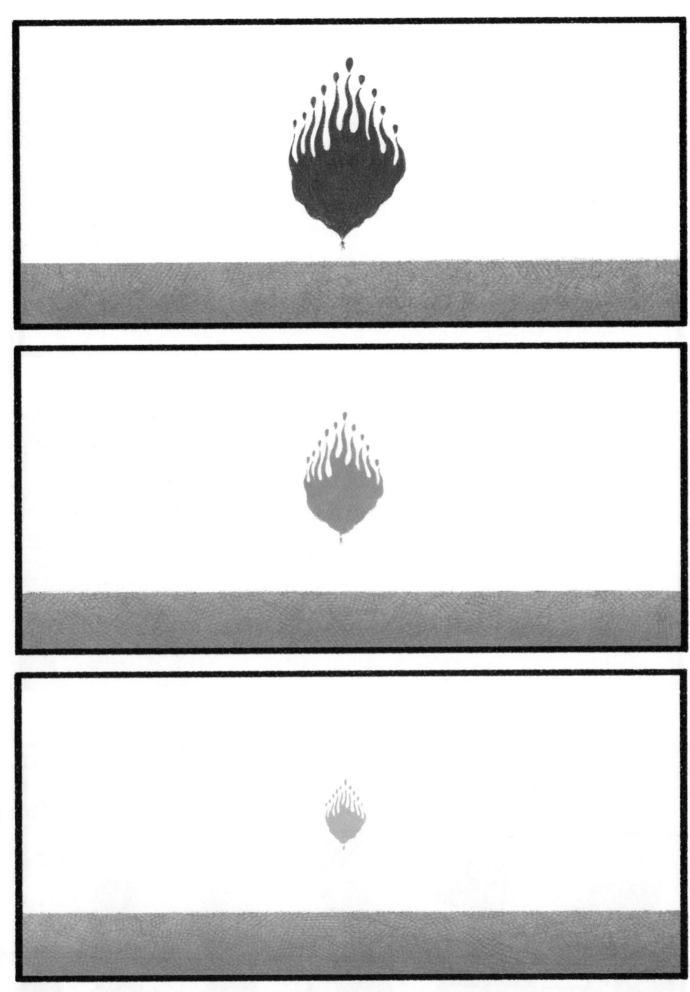

everyone knew:

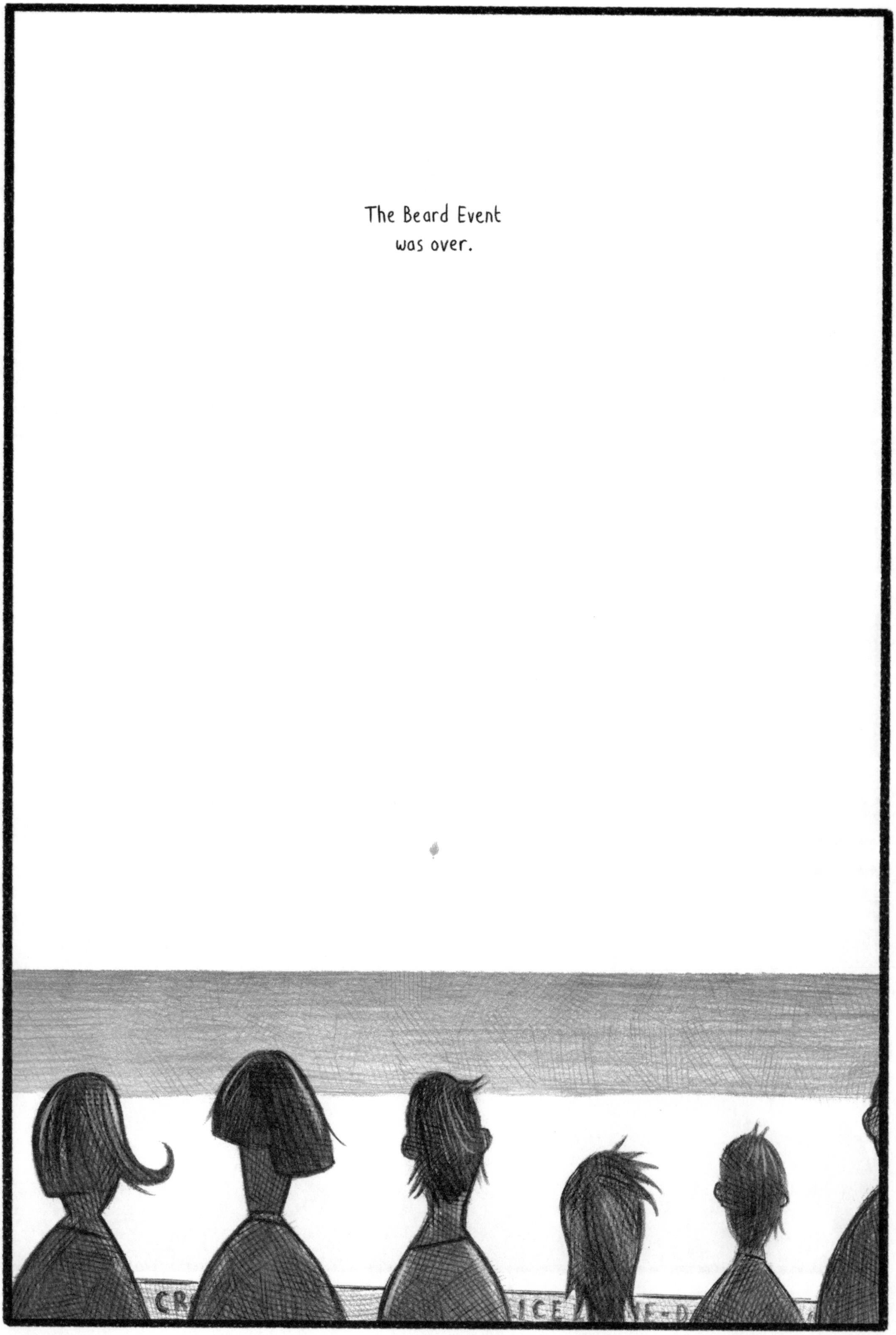
The Beard Event
was over.

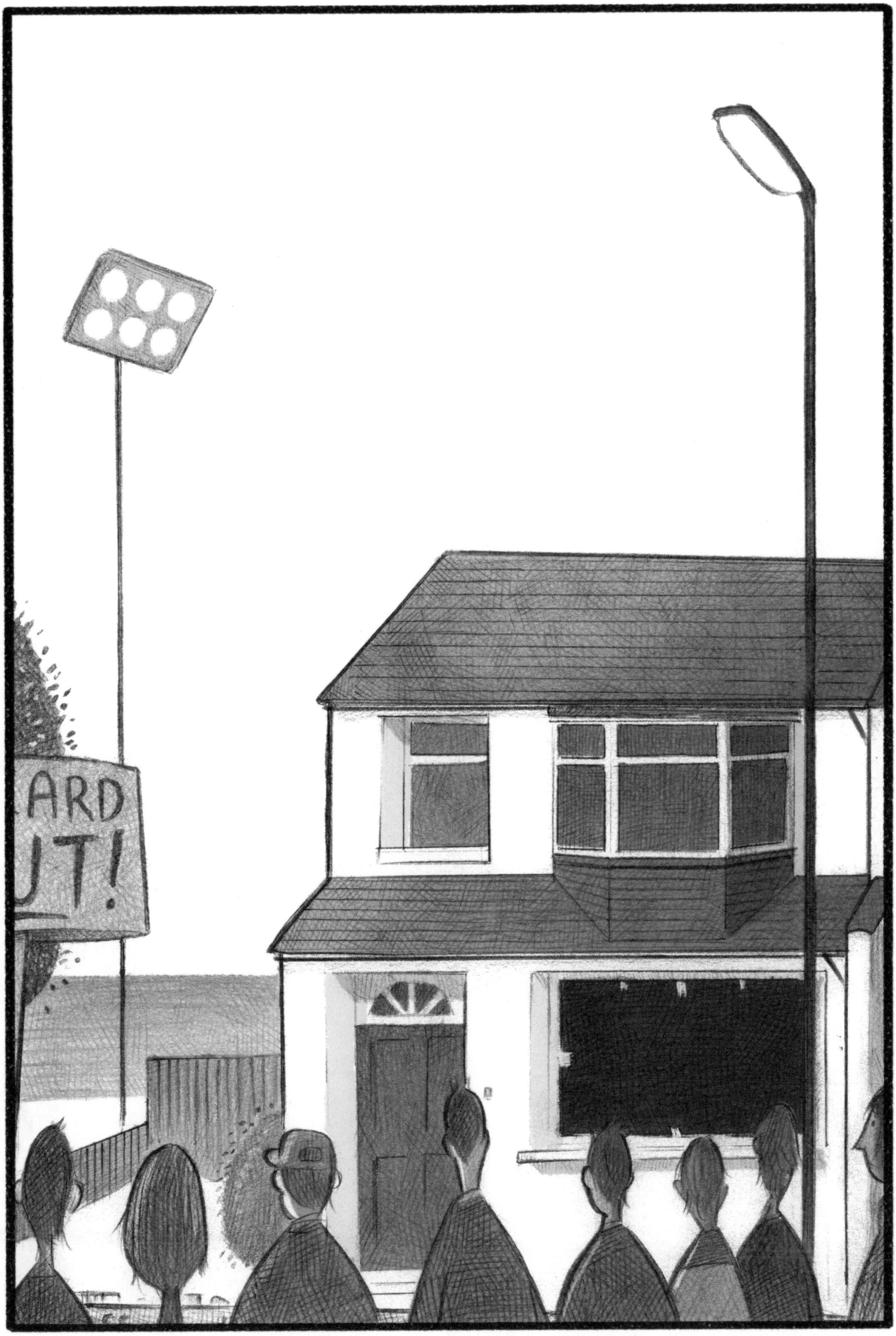
ARD
UT!

4.

THERE

#1 HEREWIDE BESTSELLER

The
THERE EQUATION

How a Little Bit of Chaos
Can Make Everything Much Tidier

by

Professor Darren Black

author of ETERNAL FLAME

"A fascinating book which basically
explains everything" - HERE MAIL

reads:

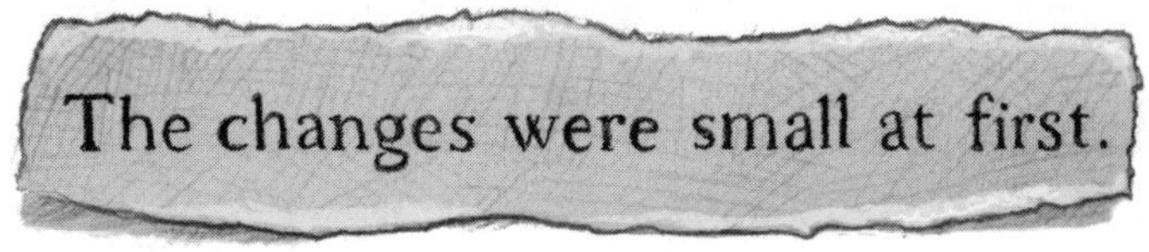
The changes were small at first.

For some, it began with a new self-administered hairstyle...

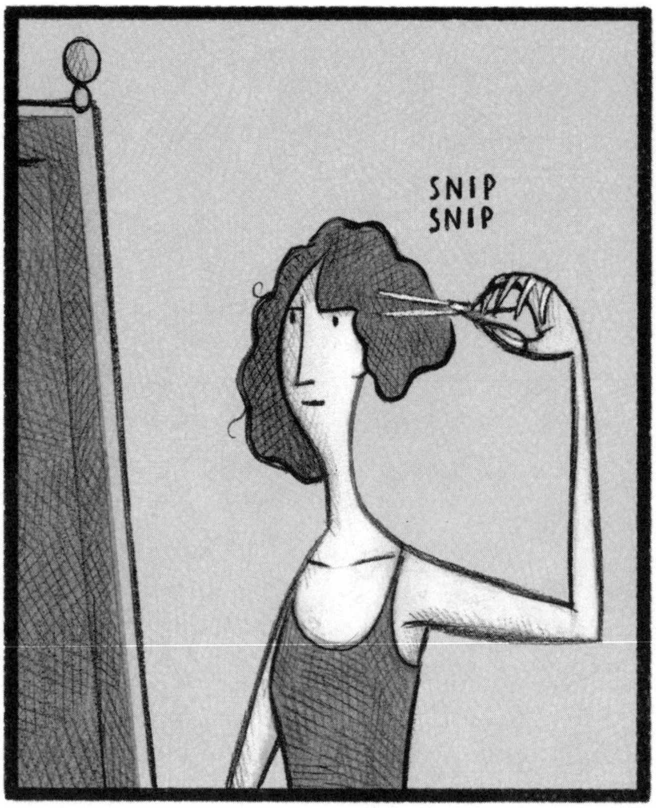
SNIP
SNIP

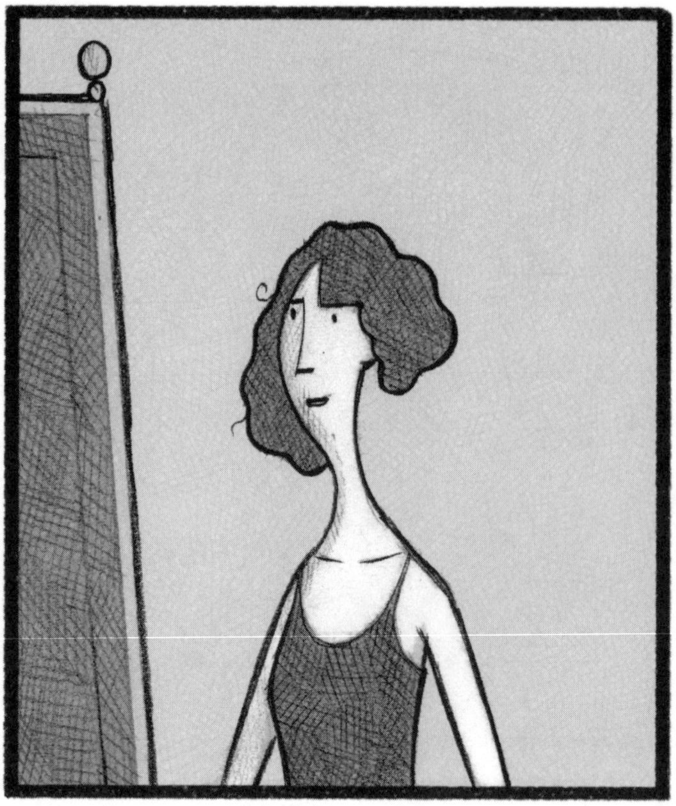

...which just kind of grew on them.

For others, it was a slightly less tidy 'look'...

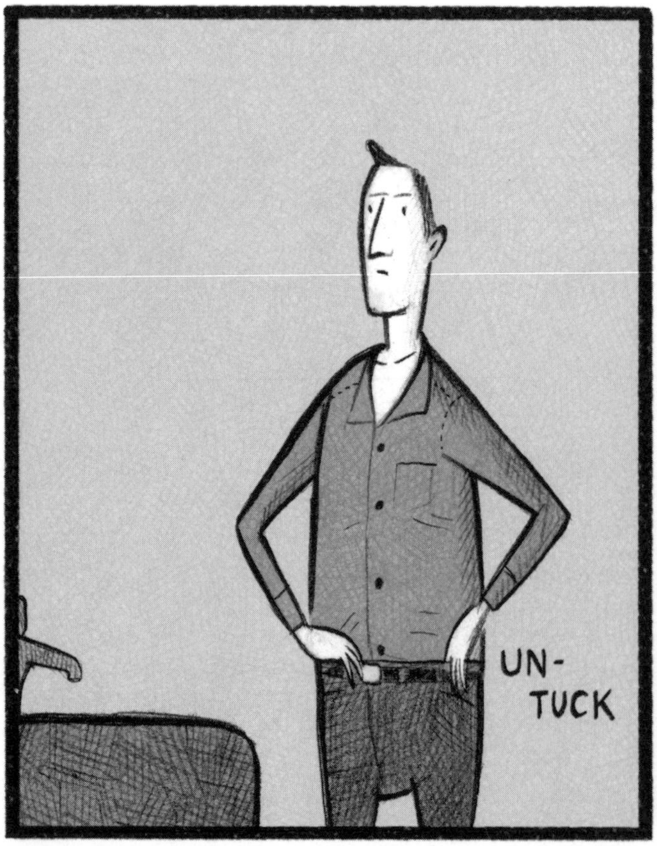
UN-
TUCK

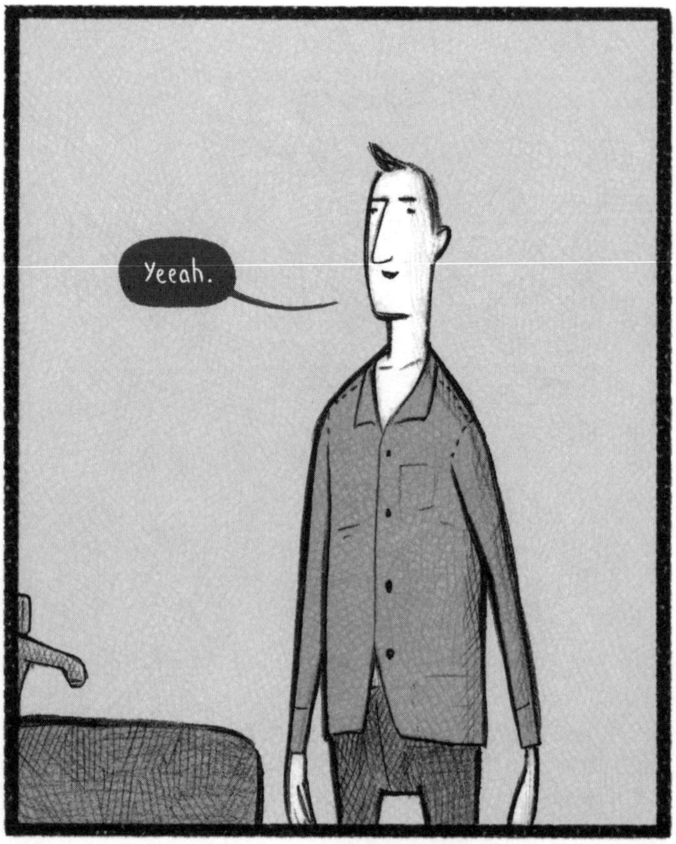
Yeeah.

...that just kind of stuck.

Pubescent sproutings
started growing

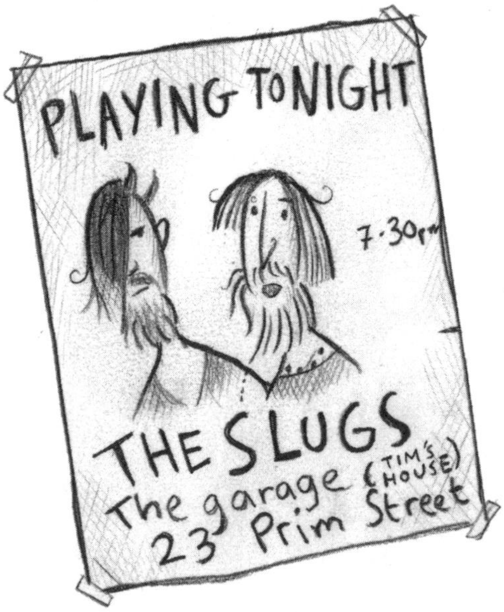
PLAYING TONIGHT
7.30pm
THE SLUGS
The garage (TIM'S HOUSE)
23 Prim Street

to become
movements

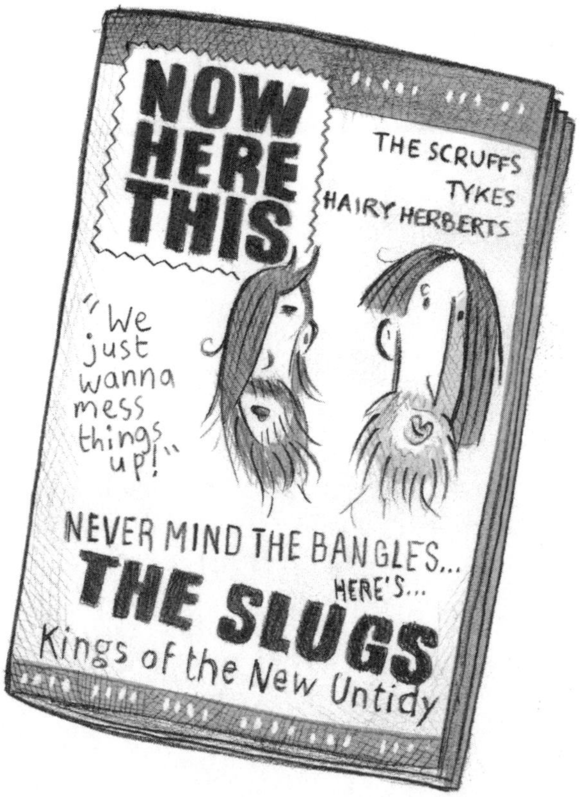
NOW HERE THIS
THE SCRUFFS
TYKES
HAIRY HERBERTS
"We just wanna mess things up!"
NEVER MIND THE BANGLES...
HERE'S...
THE SLUGS
Kings of the New Untidy

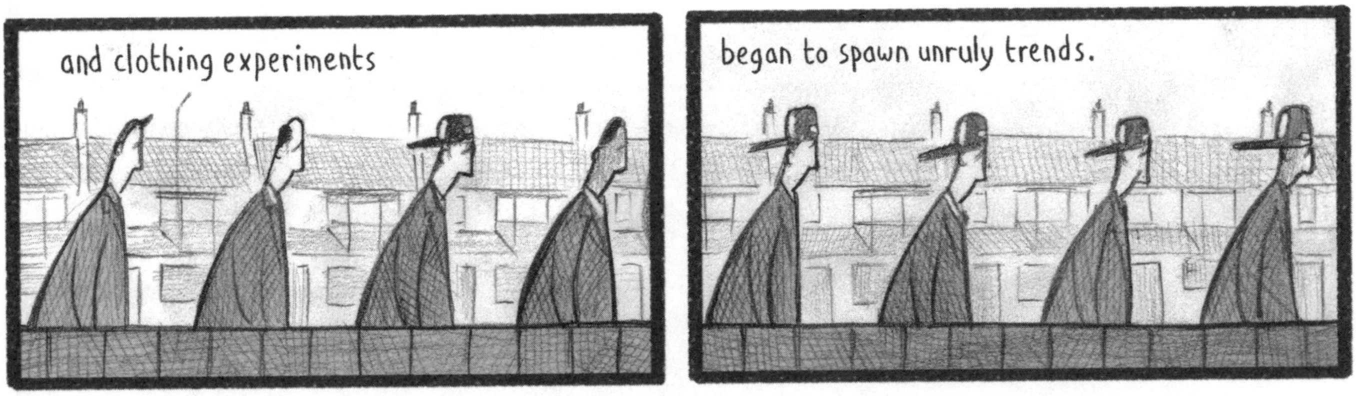
and clothing experiments
began to spawn unruly trends.

There was even a trickle of ex-beard spectators, who

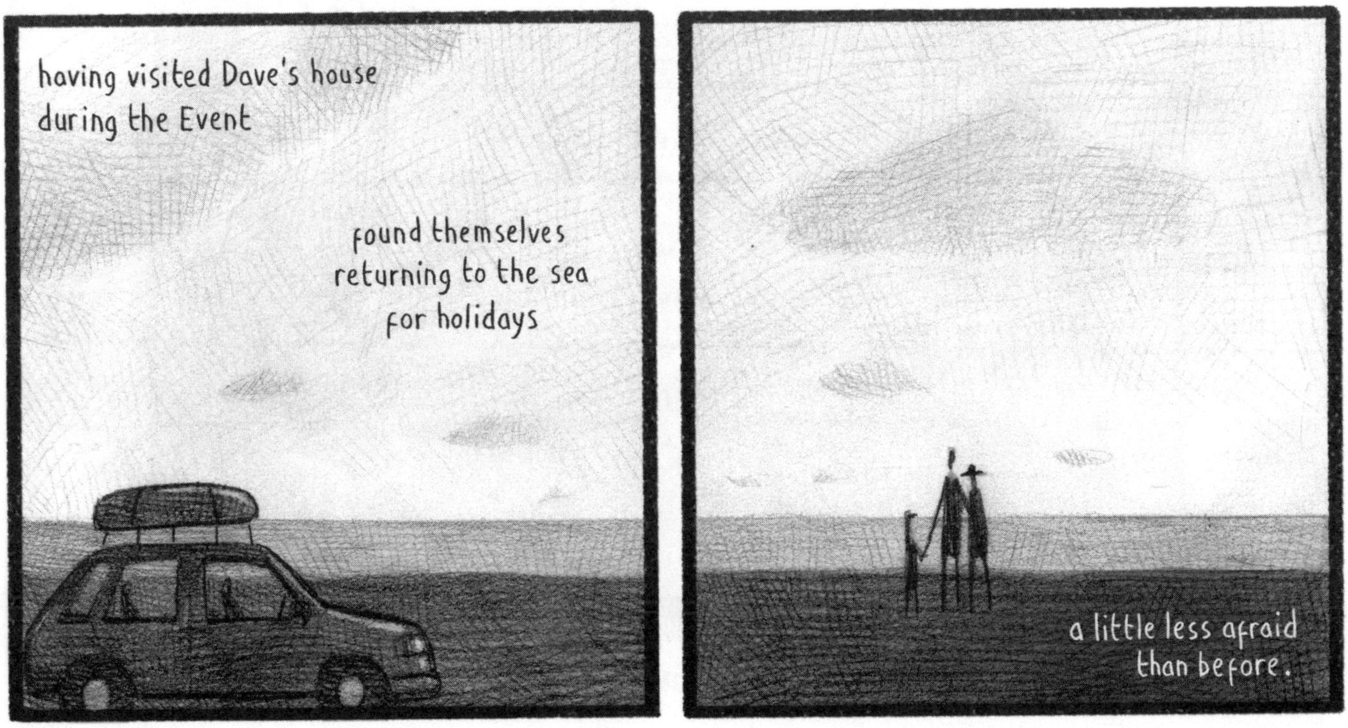
having visited Dave's house
during the Event
found themselves
returning to the sea
for holidays
a little less afraid
than before.

The local architecture of the old Beard Zone also displayed changes,

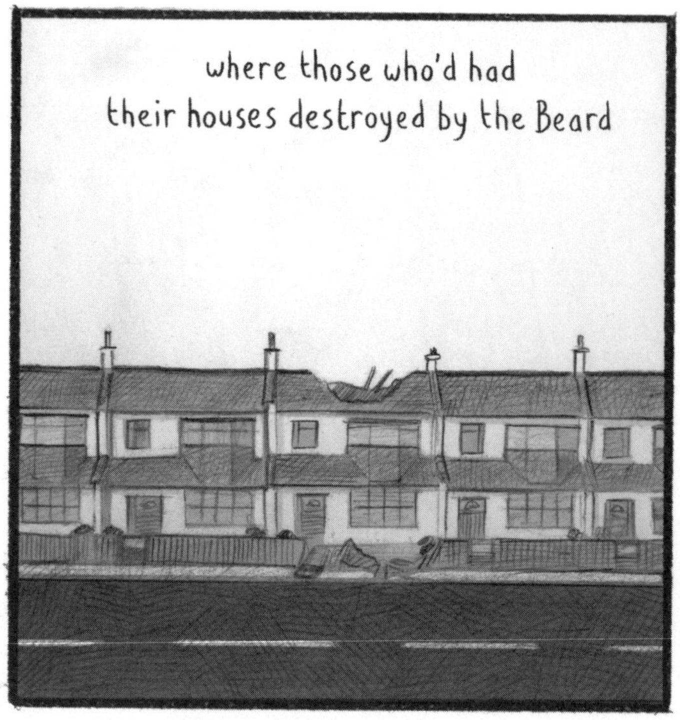
where those who'd had
their houses destroyed by the Beard

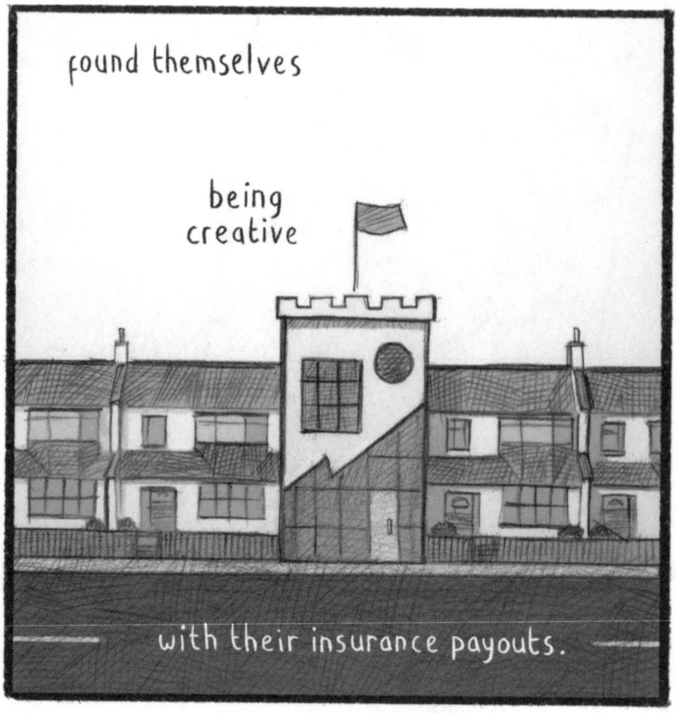
found themselves
being
creative
with their insurance payouts.

And commuters who had once been forced

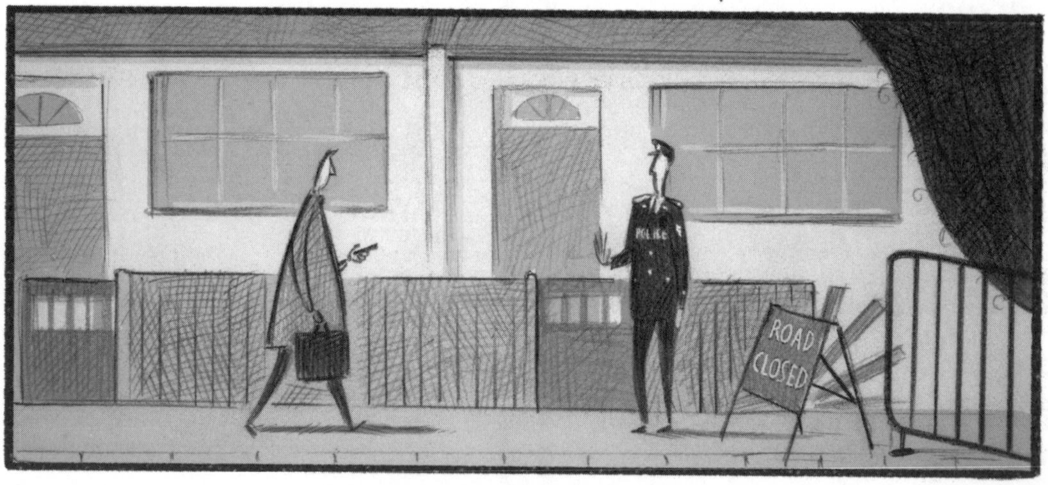
ROAD
CLOSED

to try new routes to work

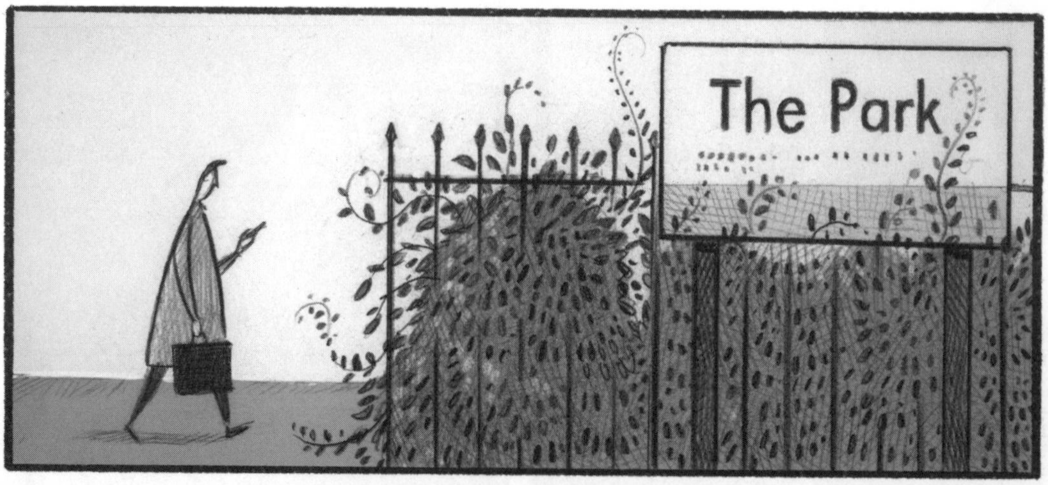
The Park

nowadays found themselves doing so

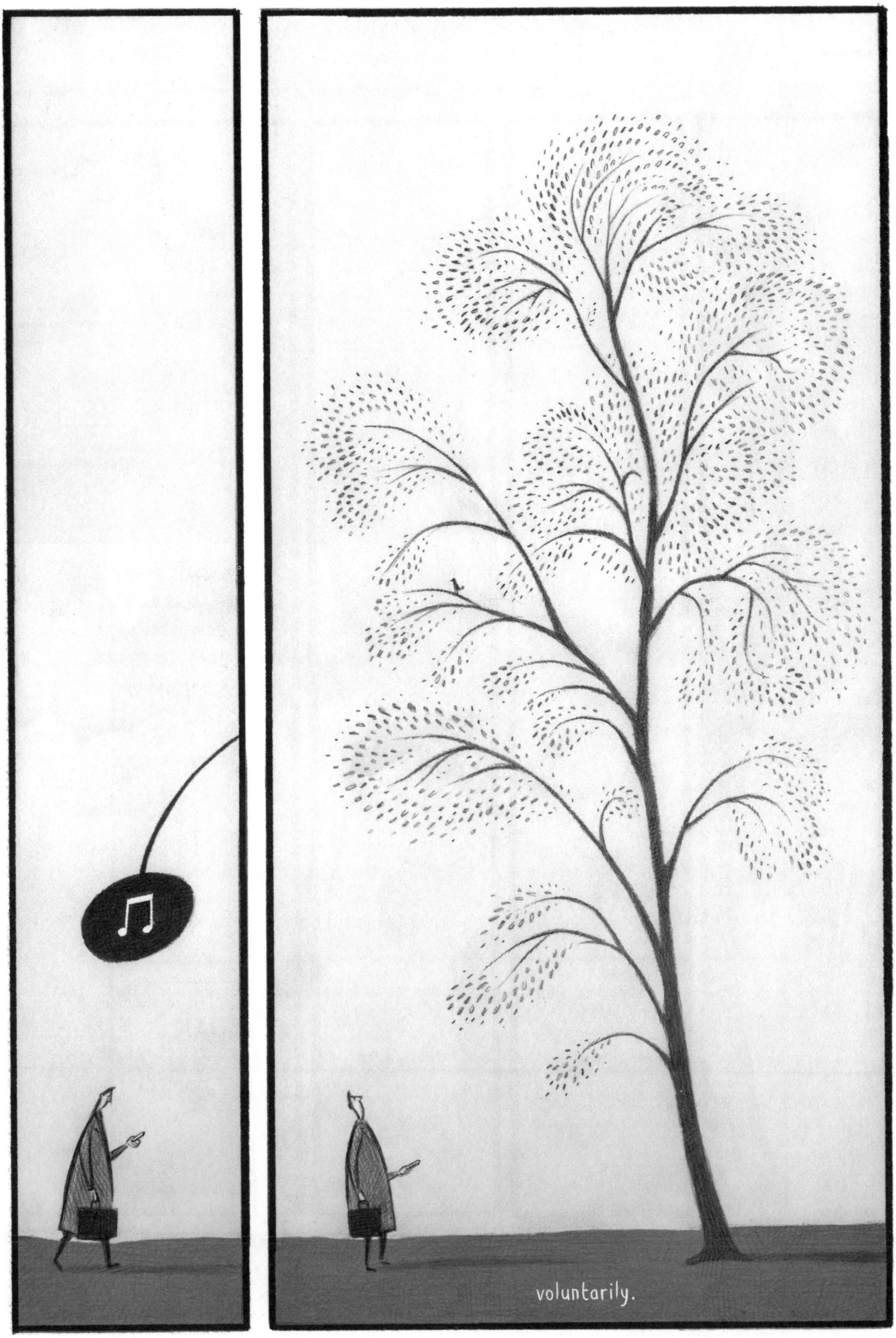
voluntarily.

It was the fear that people noticed most, though.

Or rather, its absence.

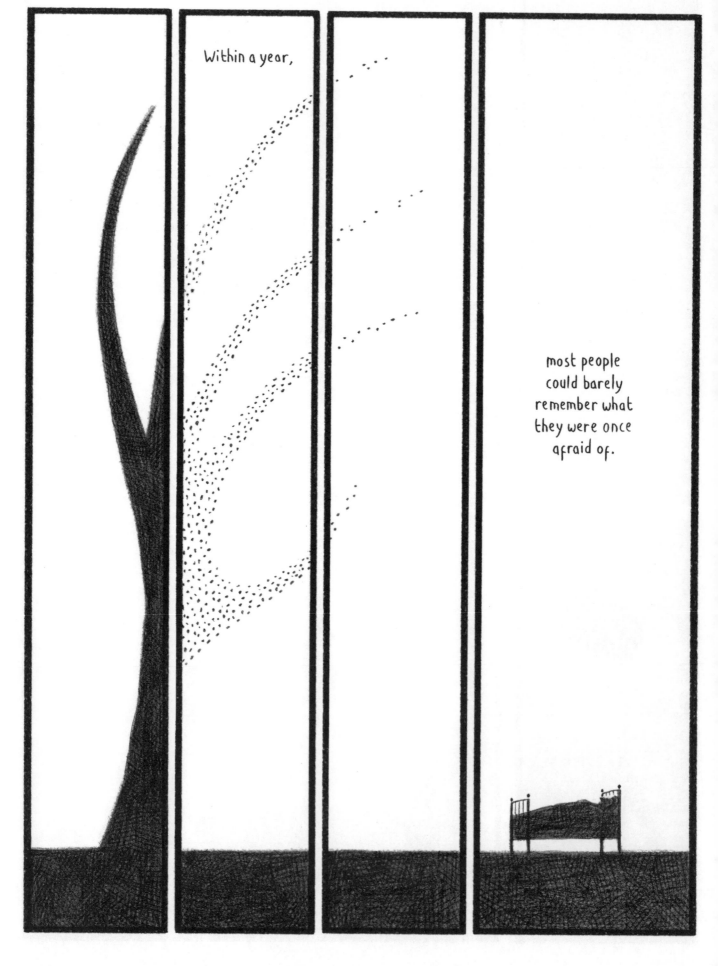

Within a year,

most people
could barely
remember what
they were once
afraid of.

And by the end of the decade,

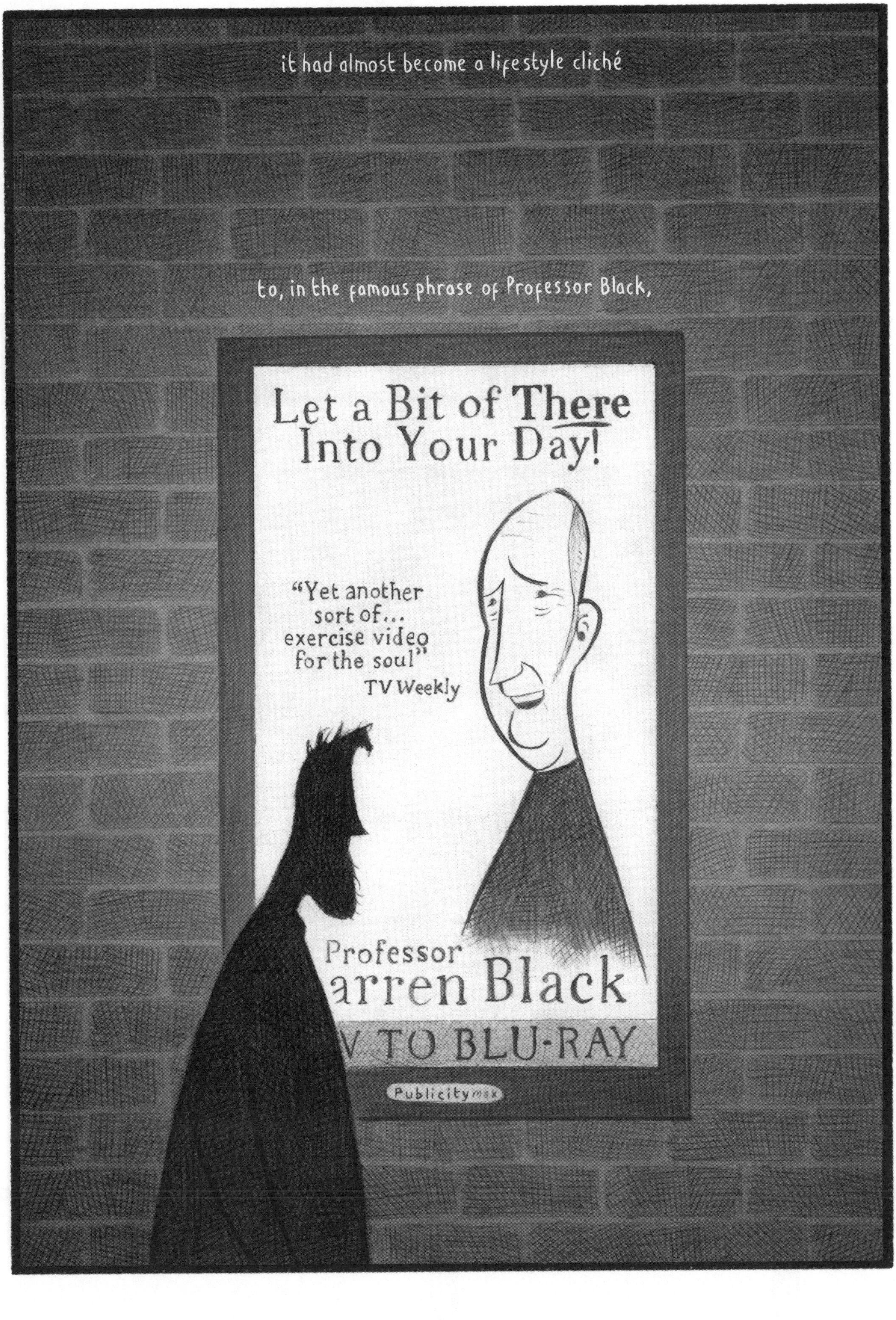
it had almost become a lifestyle cliché
to, in the famous phrase of Professor Black,
Let a Bit of There Into Your Day!
"Yet another sort of... exercise video for the soul"
TV Weekly
Professor
arren Black
V TO BLU-RAY
Publicitymax

And as the years went by

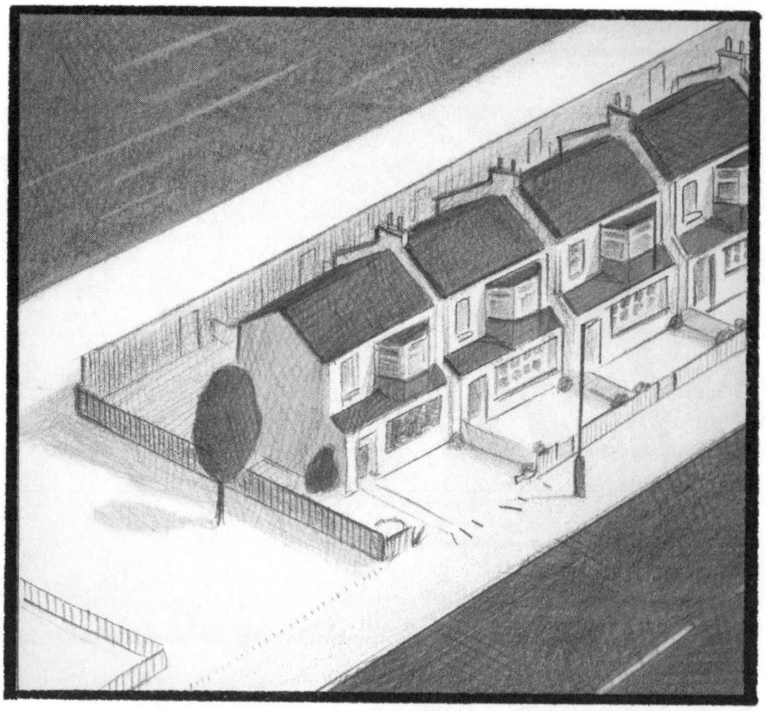

with no further Beard-like events,

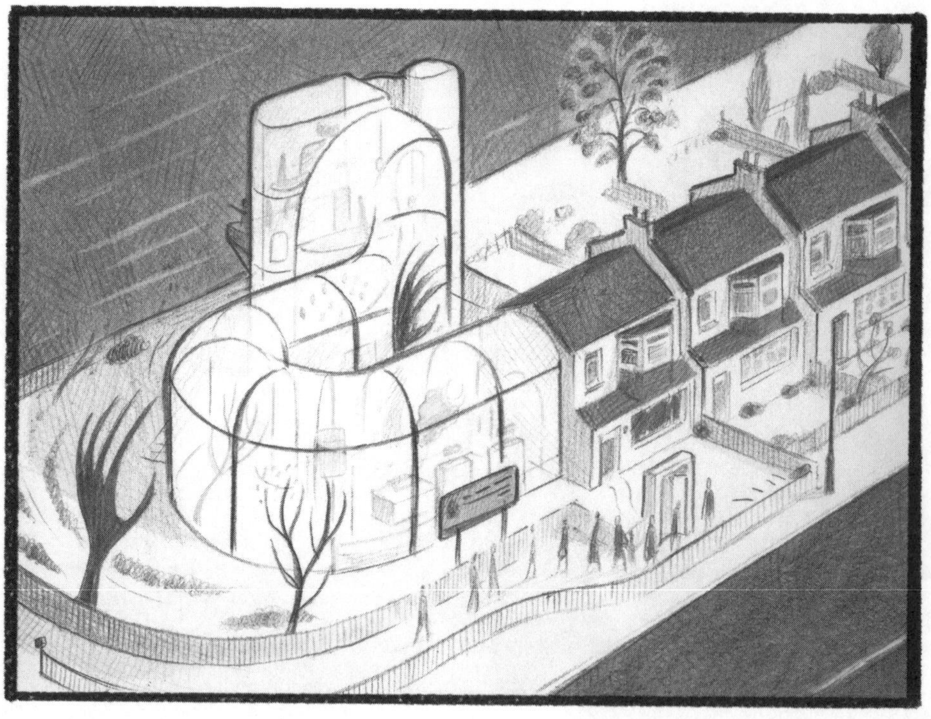

what happened to Dave

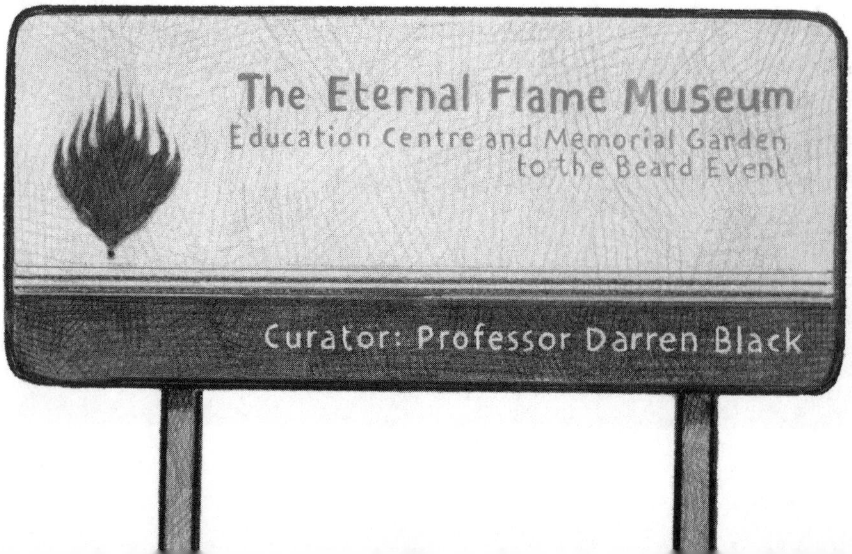
The Eternal Flame Museum
Education Centre and Memorial Garden to the Beard Event
Curator: Professor Darren Black

became *past.*

Nobody noticed

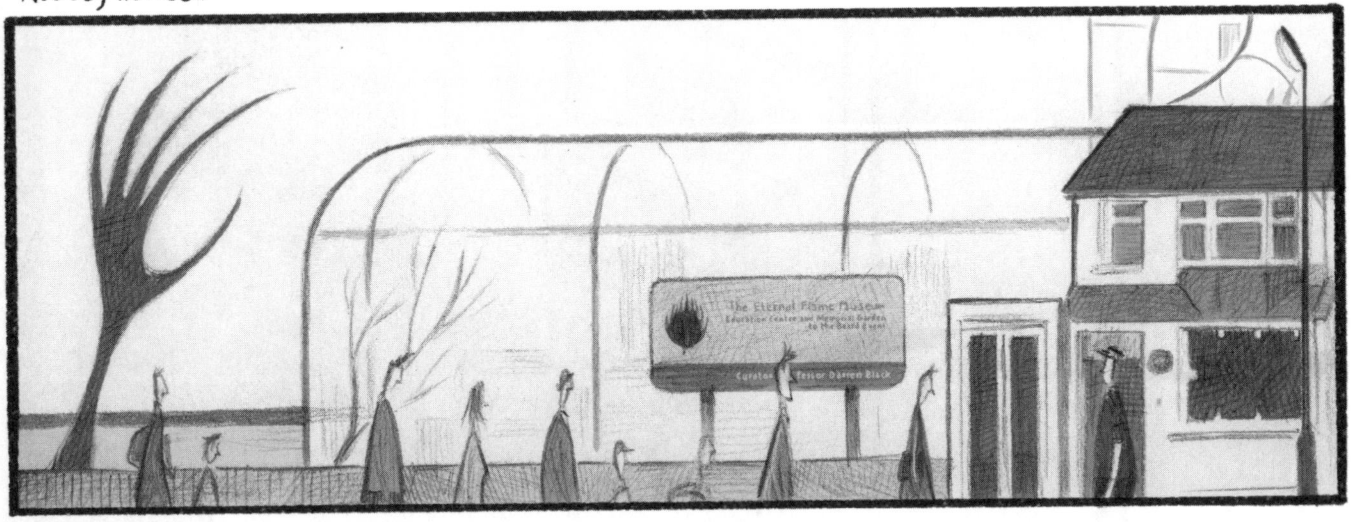

The Eternal Flame Museum

that this most extraordinary of happenings

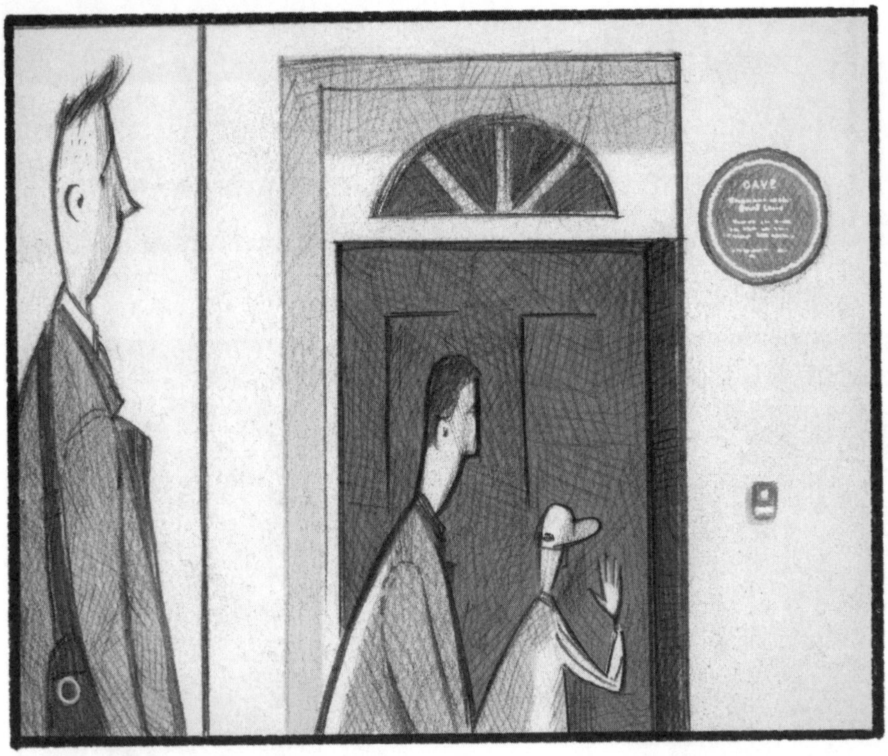

had been absorbed

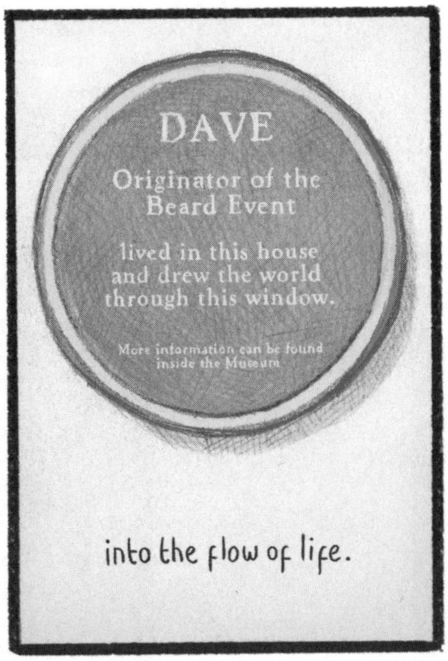

DAVE
Originator of the Beard Event
lived in this house and drew the world through this window.
More information can be found inside the Museum
into the flow of life.

As familiar

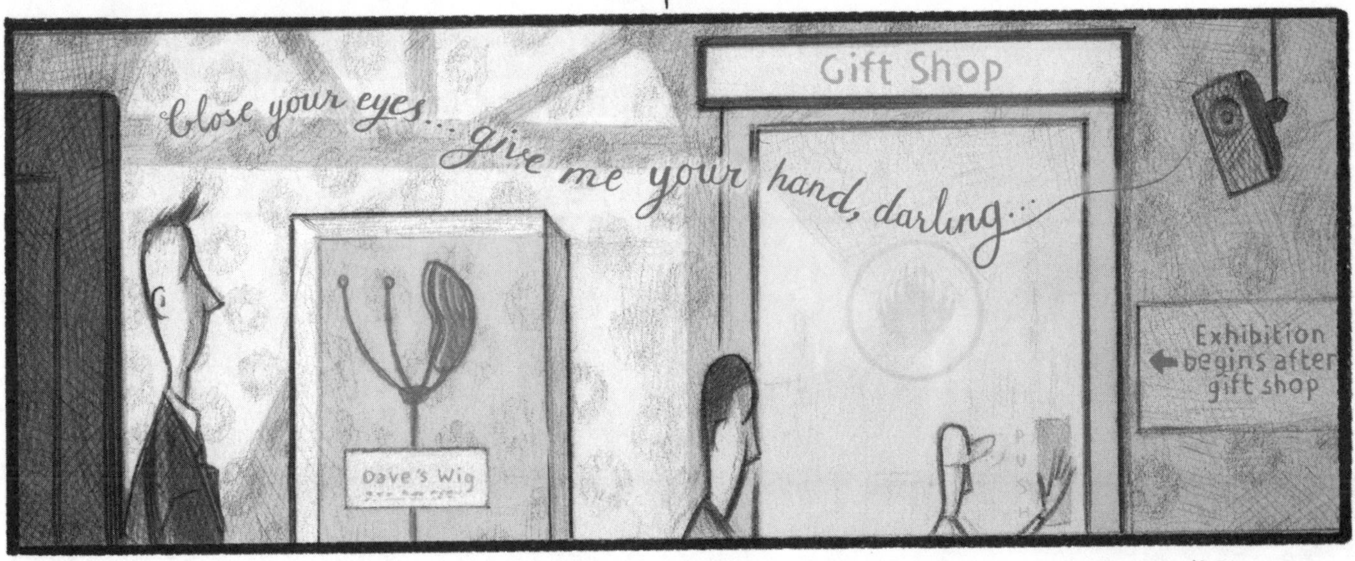

Gift Shop
Close your eyes... give me your hand, darling...
Dave's Wig
Exhibition begins after gift shop

as a well-known song.

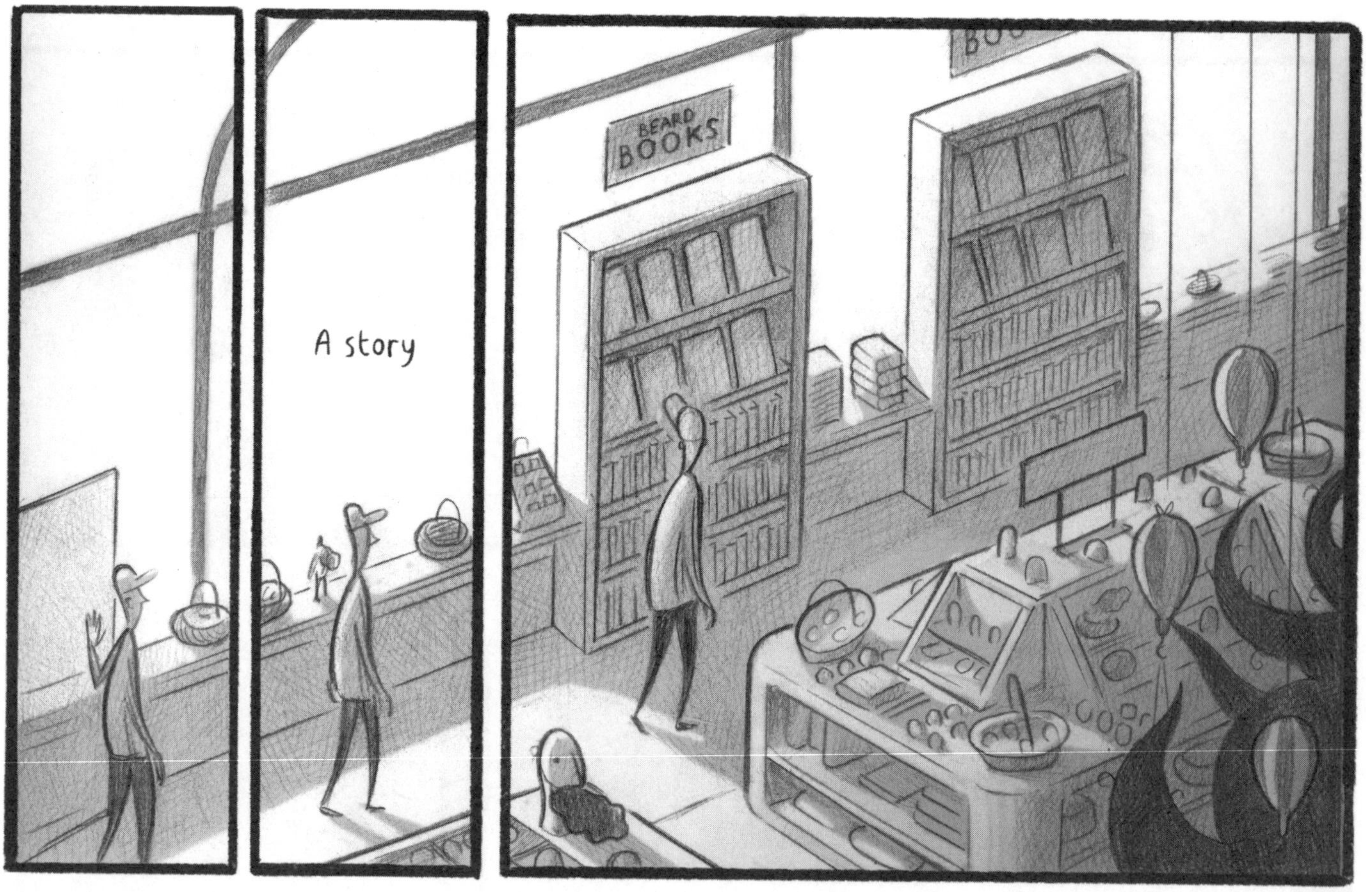
A story
BEARD
BOOKS

many times retold

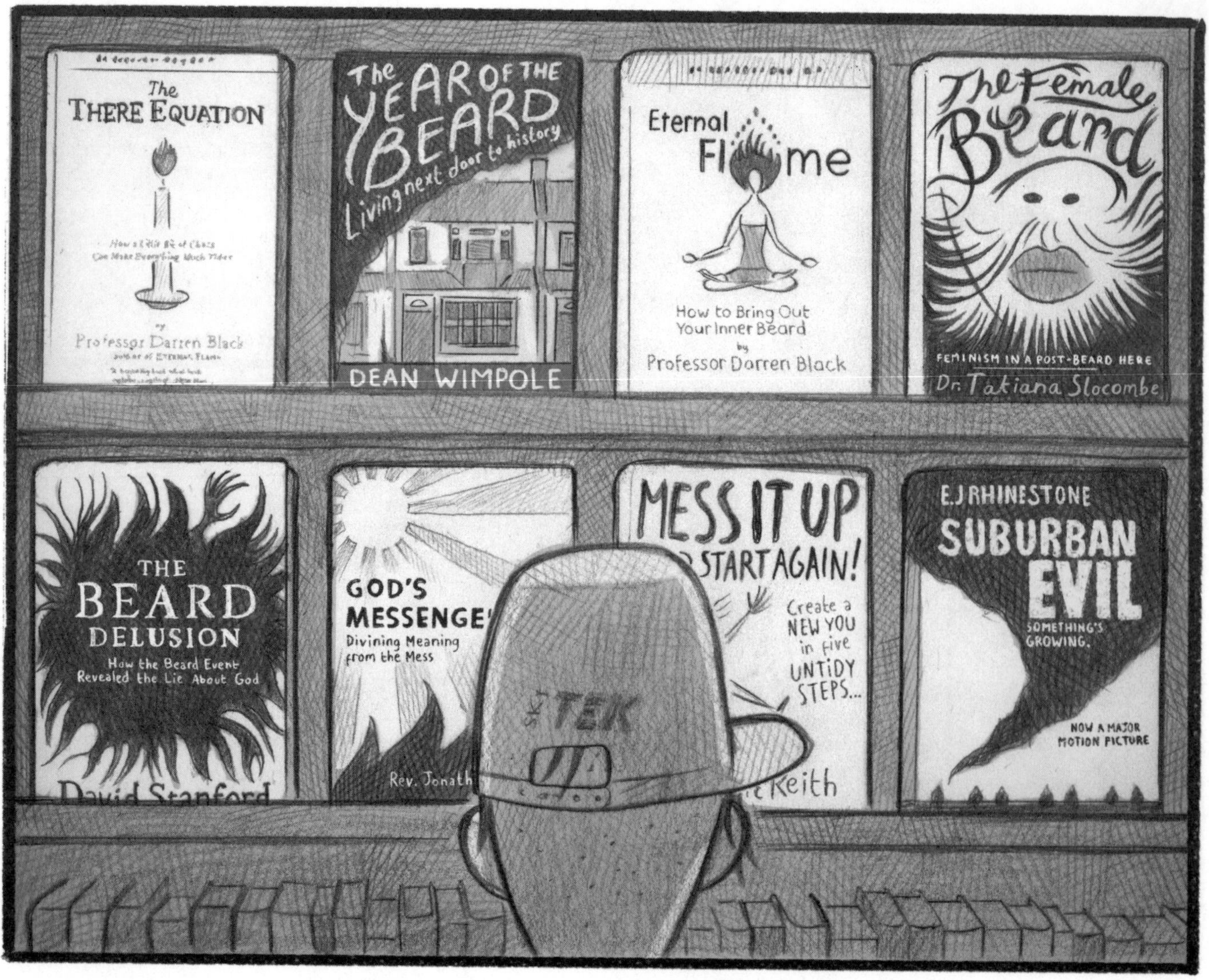
The
THERE EQUATION
Professor Darren Black
The YEAR OF THE BEARD
Living next door to history
DEAN WIMPOLE
Eternal Flame
How to Bring Out
Your Inner Beard
by
Professor Darren Black
The Female Beard
FEMINISM IN A POST-BEARD HERE
Dr. Tatiana Slocombe
THE
BEARD
DELUSION
How the Beard Event
Revealed the Lie About God
GOD'S
MESSENGE
Divining Meaning
from the Mess
Rev. Jonath
MESS IT UP
START AGAIN!
Create a
NEW YOU
in five
UNTIDY
STEPS...
Keith
TEK
E.J RHINESTONE
SUBURBAN
EVIL
SOMETHING'S
GROWING.
NOW A MAJOR
MOTION PICTURE

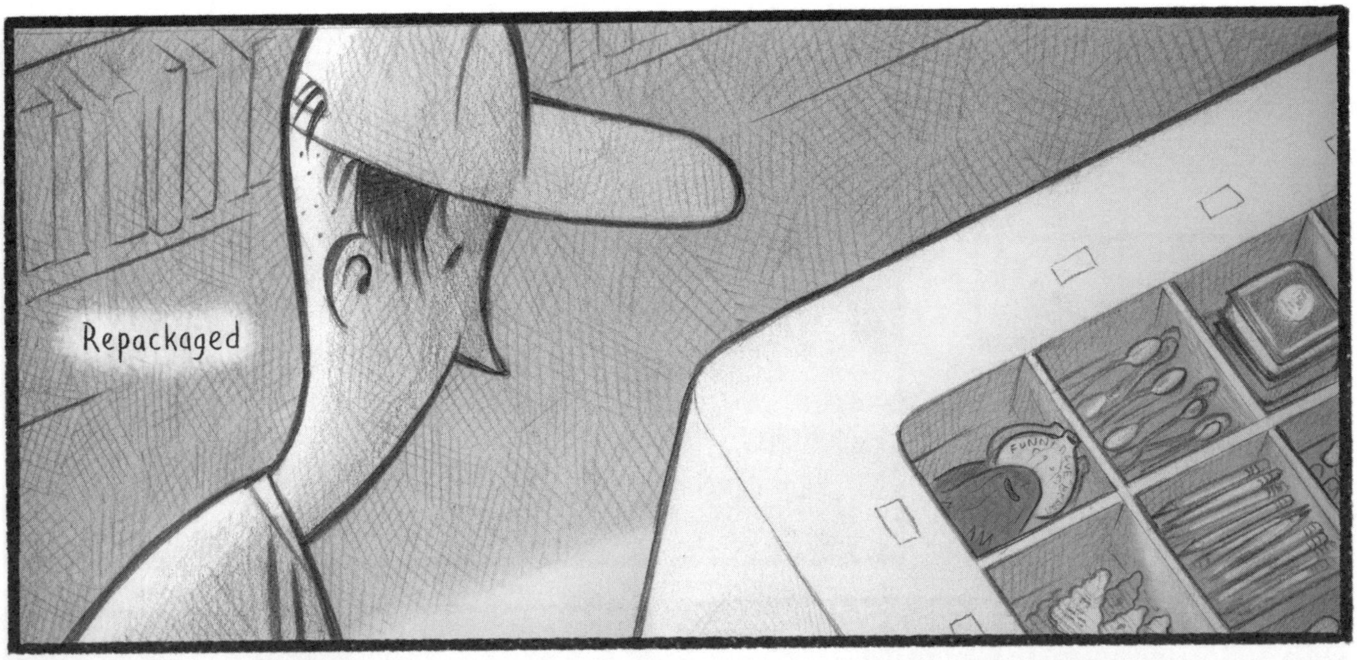
Repackaged

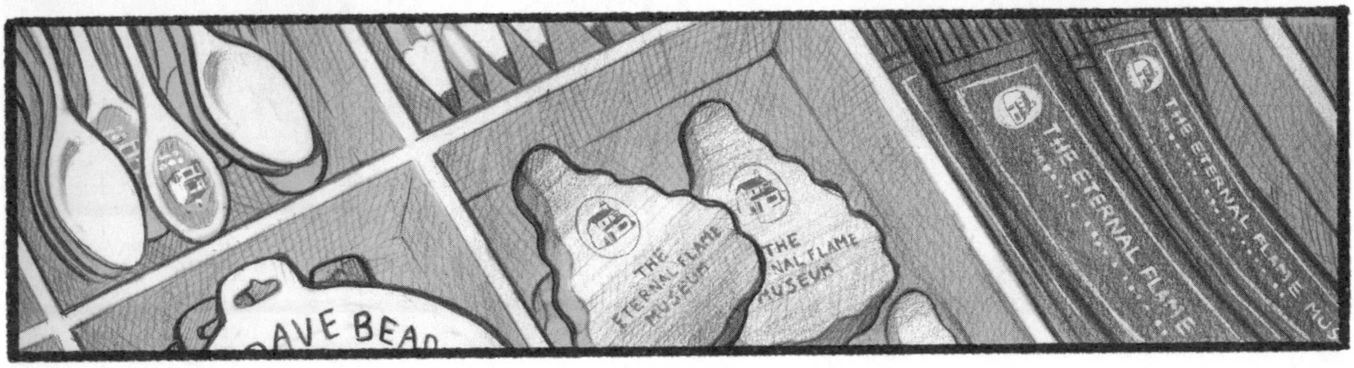
THE ETERNAL FLAME MUSEUM
THE ETERNAL FLAME MUSEUM

and resold.

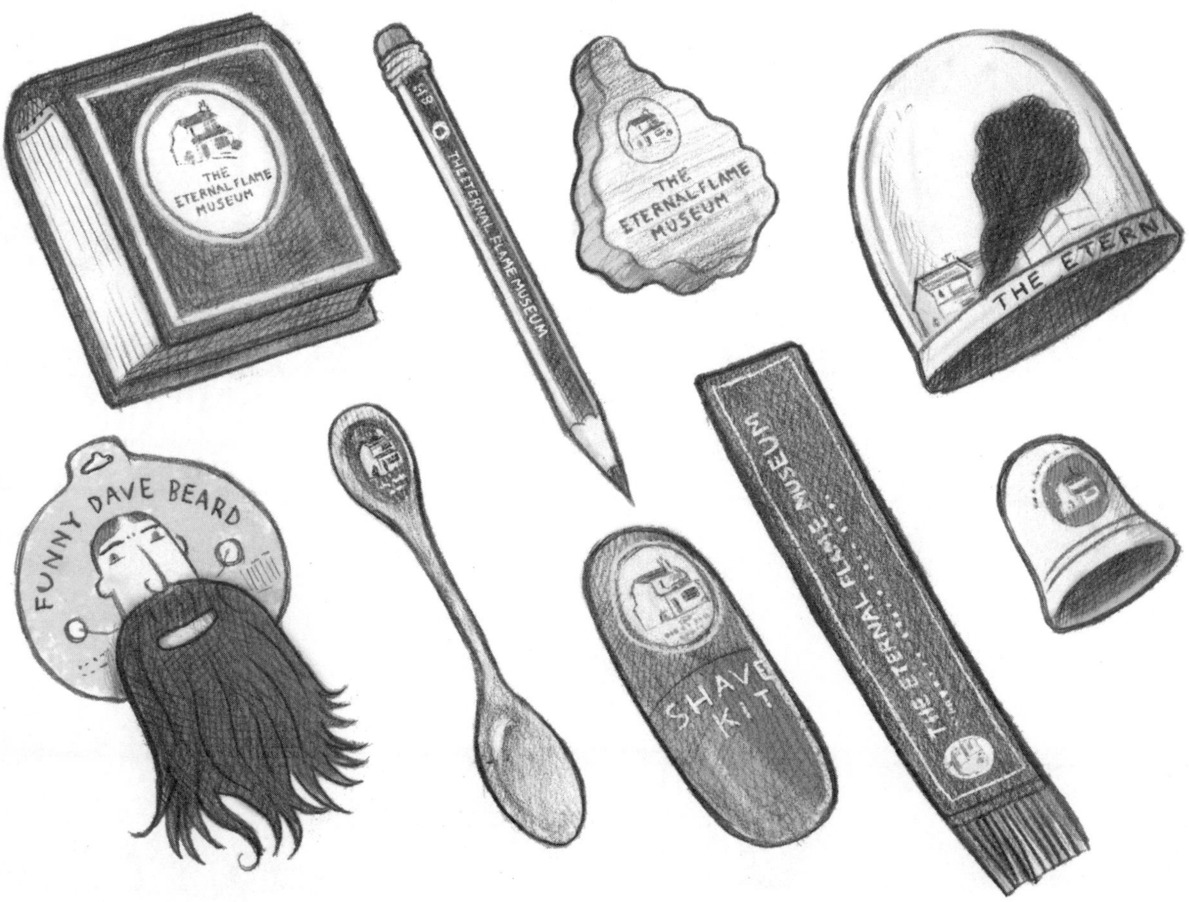
THE ETERNAL FLAME MUSEUM
THE ETERNAL FLAME MUSEUM
THE ETERNAL FLAME MUSEUM
THE ETERN
FUNNY DAVE BEARD
SHAVE KIT
THE ETERNAL FLAME MUSEUM

Reframed

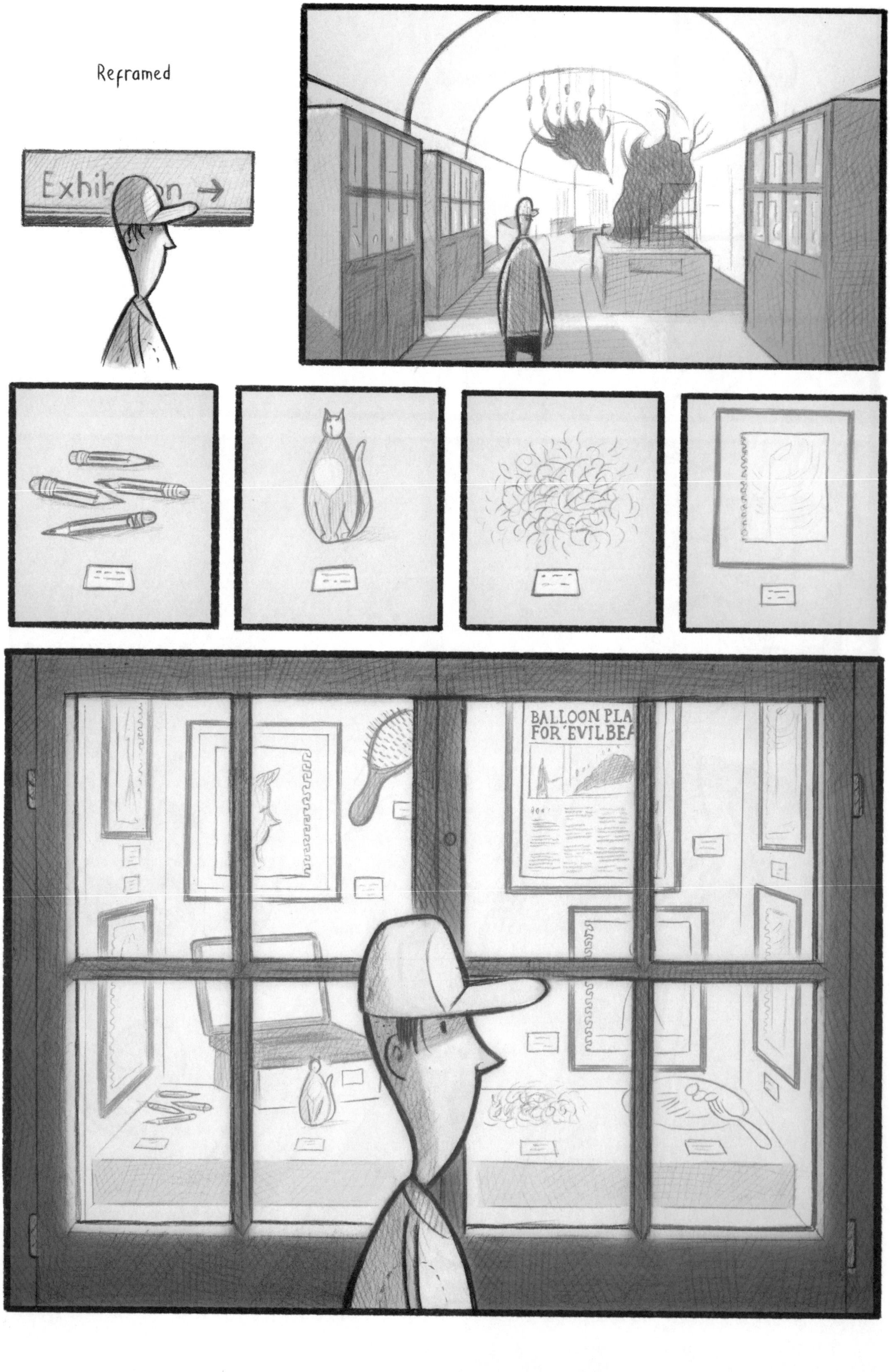
Exhib on →
BALLOON PLA
FOR 'EVILBEA

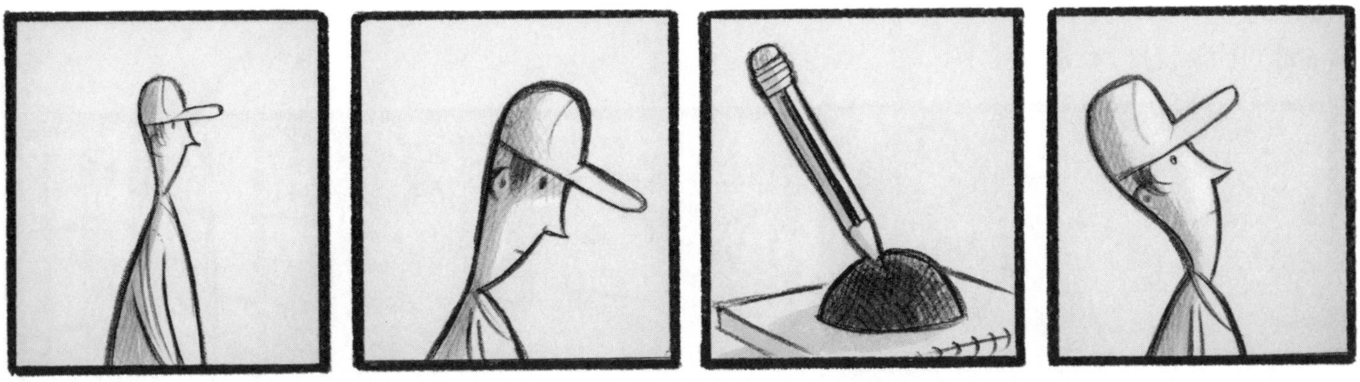

Re-experienced

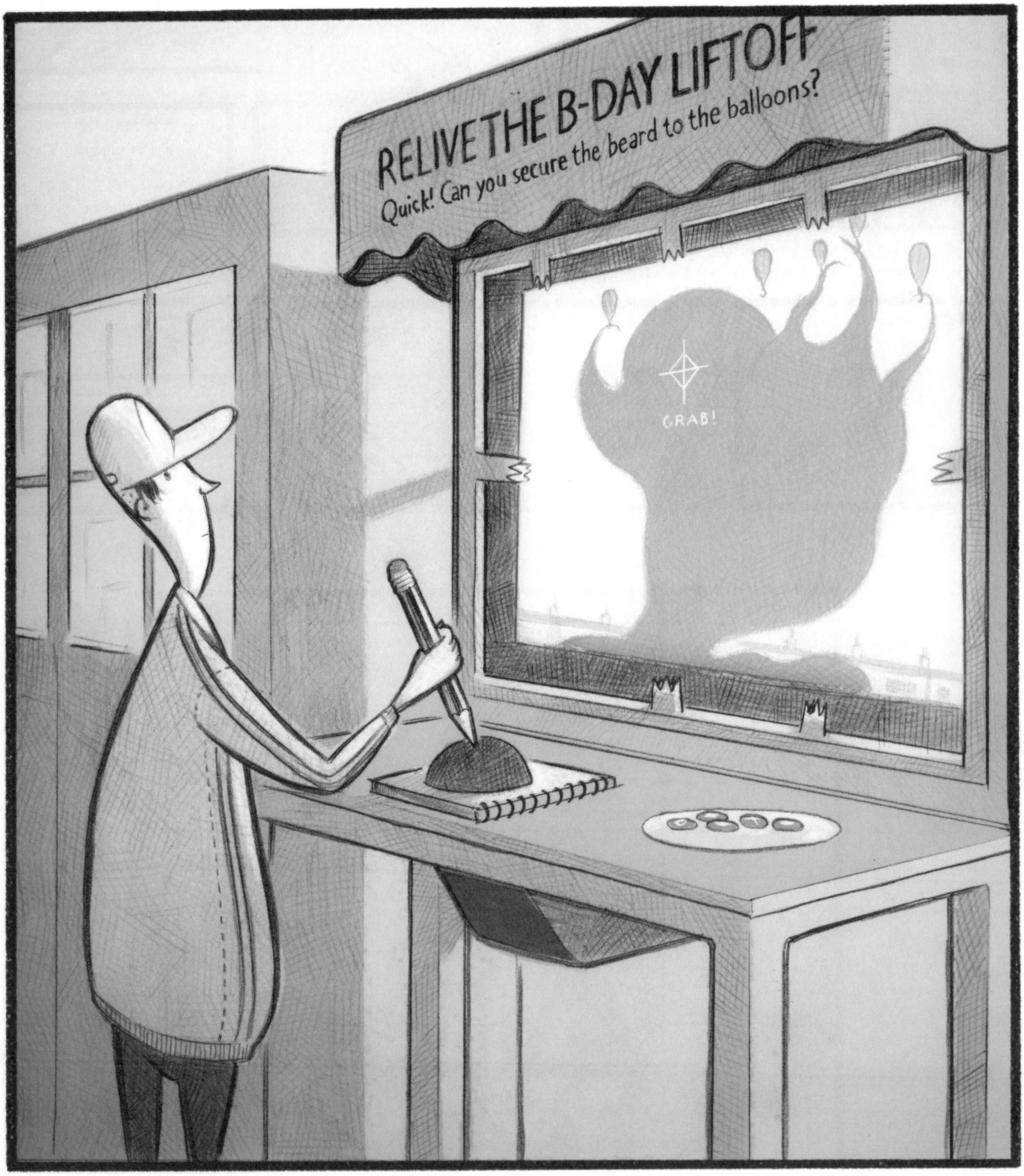
RELIVE THE B-DAY LIFTOFF
Quick! Can you secure the beard to the balloons?
GRAB!

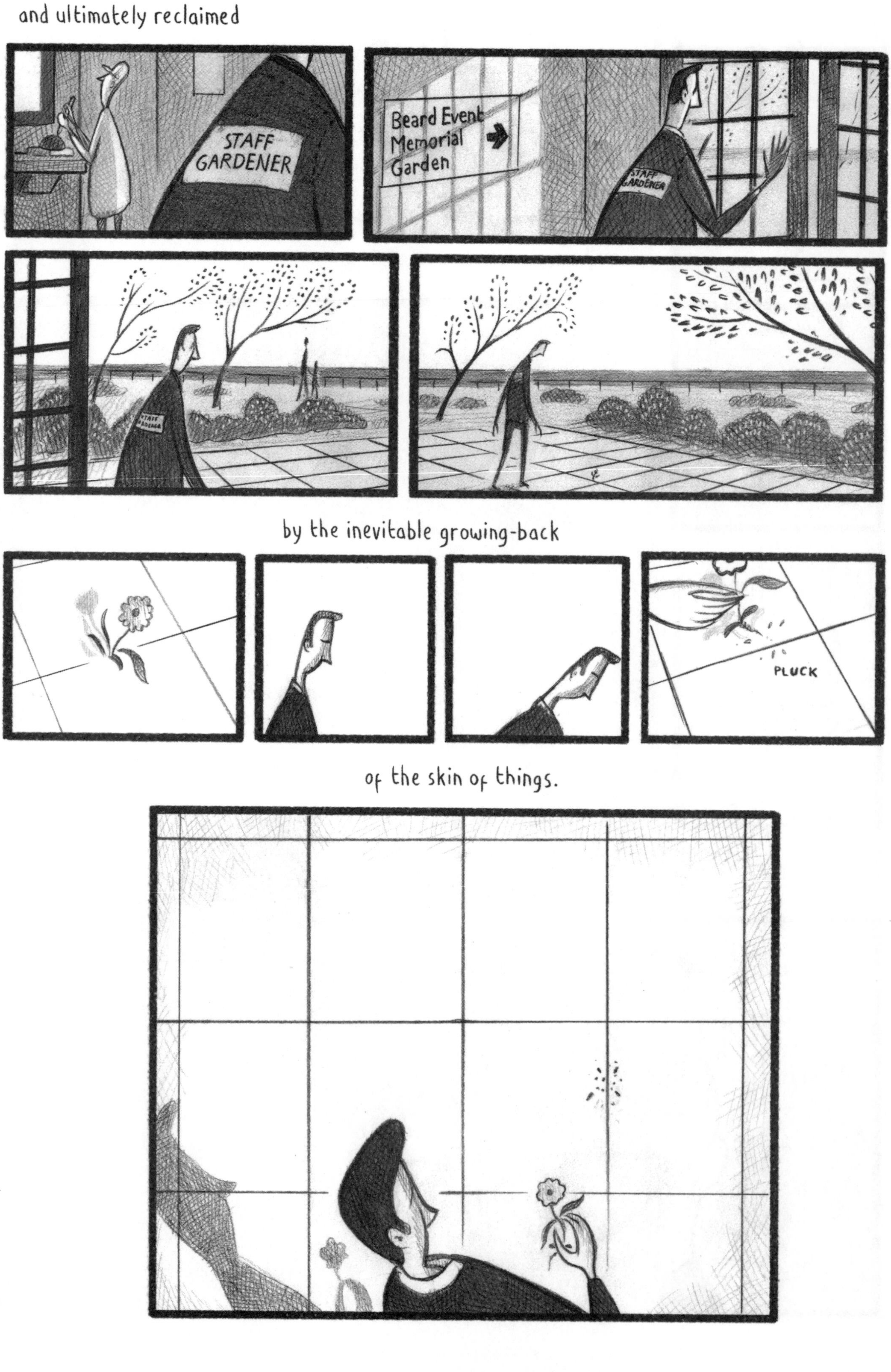
and ultimately reclaimed
STAFF GARDENER
Beard Event Memorial Garden
STAFF GARDENER
by the inevitable growing-back
PLUCK
of the skin of things.

Today people no longer even see a scar.

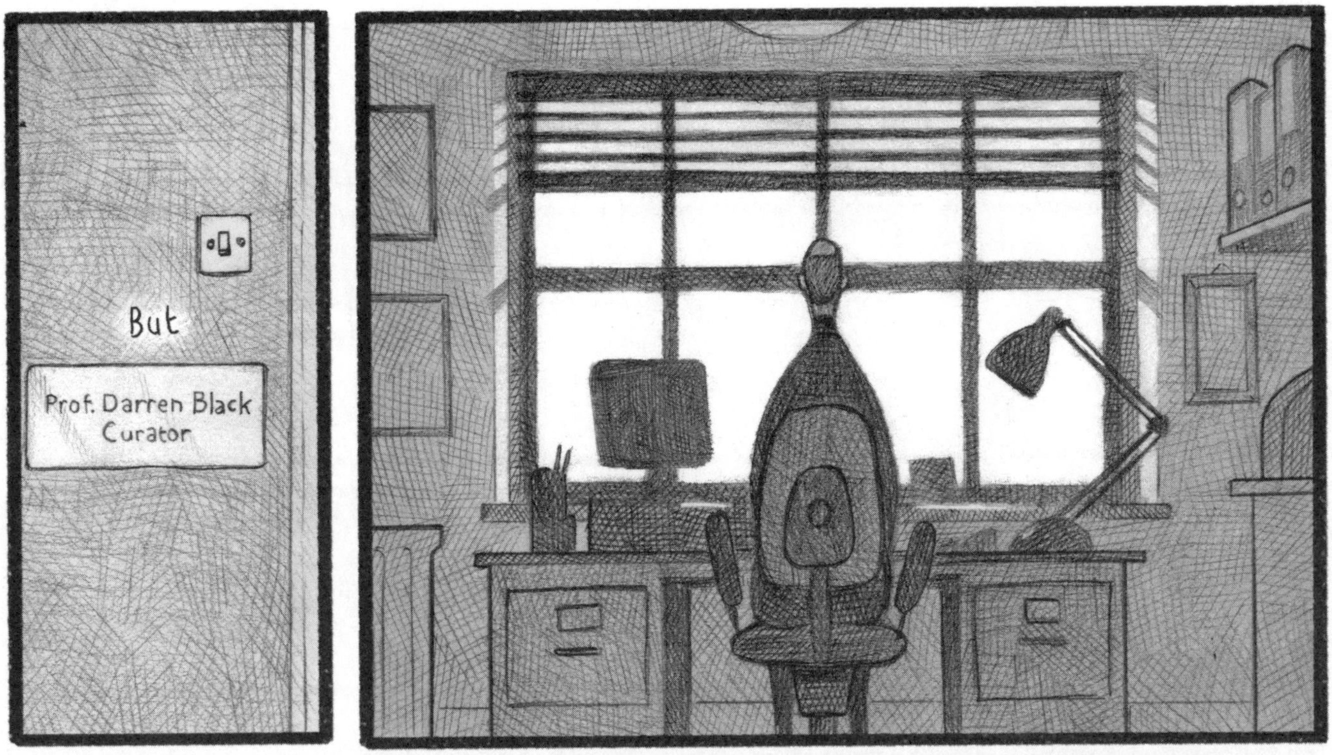
But
Prof. Darren Black
Curator

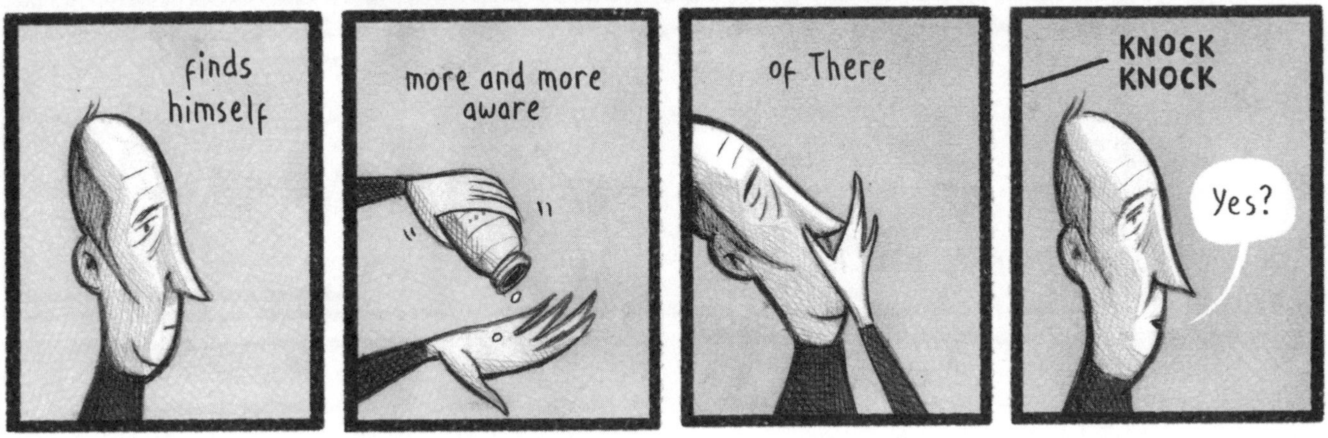
finds himself
more and more aware
of There
KNOCK KNOCK
Yes?

as the years fly past.

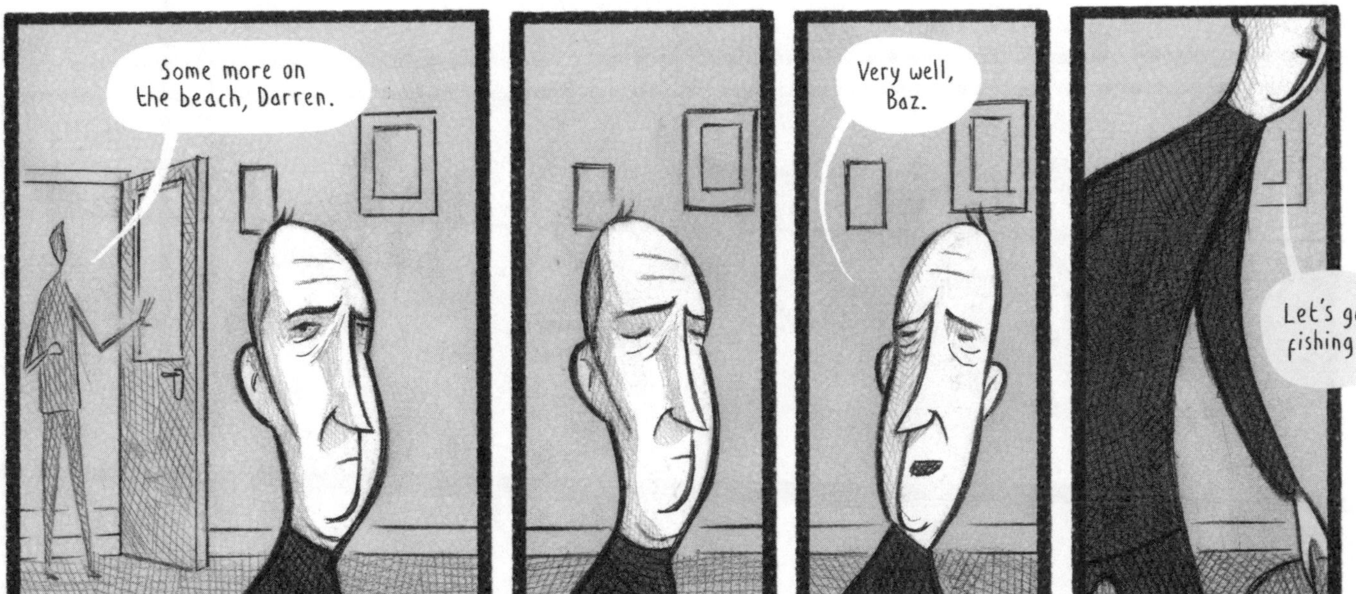
Some more on the beach, Darren.
Very well, Baz.
Let's go fishing.

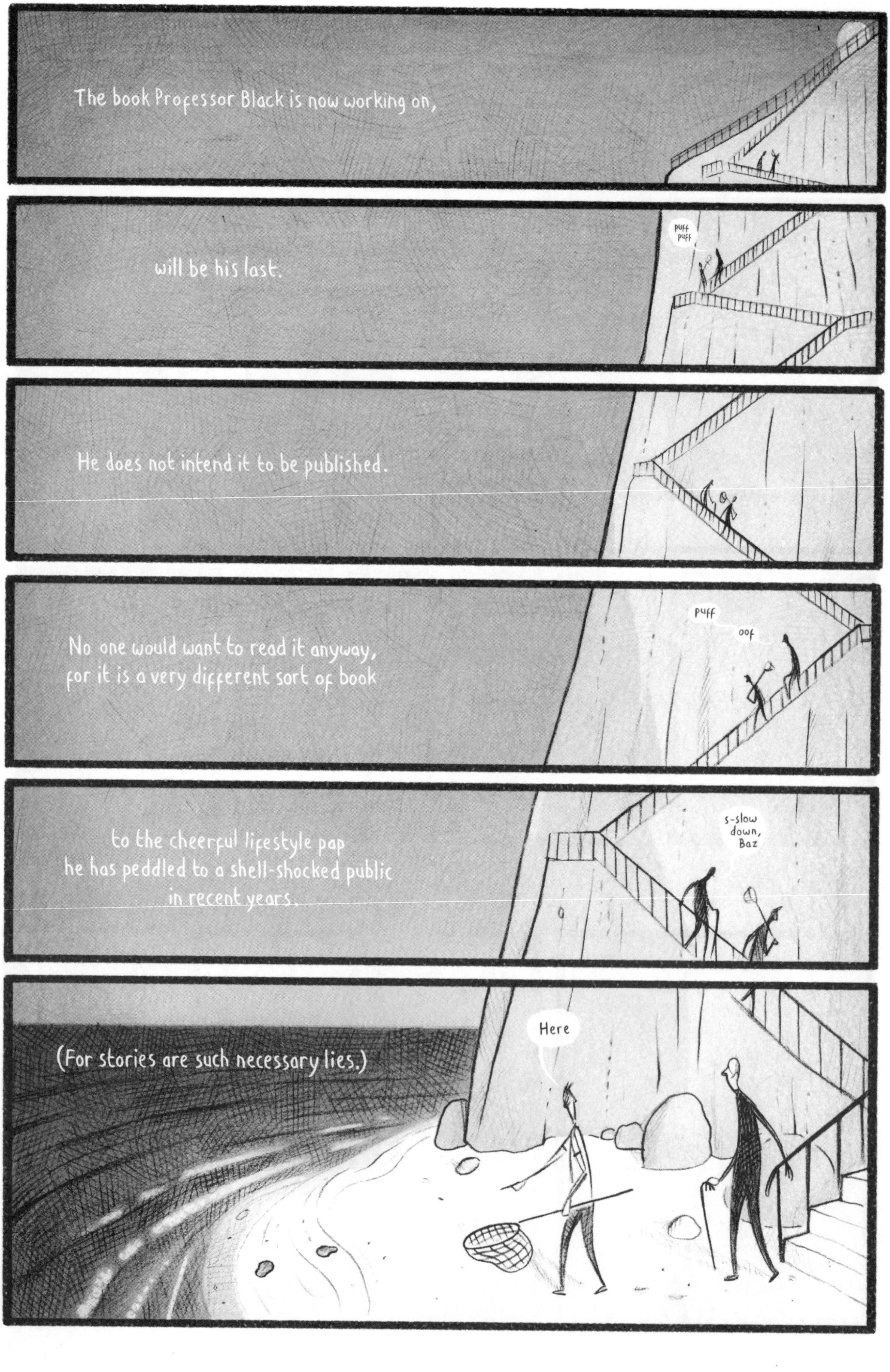
The book Professor Black is now working on,
puff puff
will be his last.
He does not intend it to be published.
puff
oof
No one would want to read it anyway,
for it is a very different sort of book
s-slow down, Baz
to the cheerful lifestyle pap
he has peddled to a shell-shocked public
in recent years.
Here
(For stories are such necessary lies.)

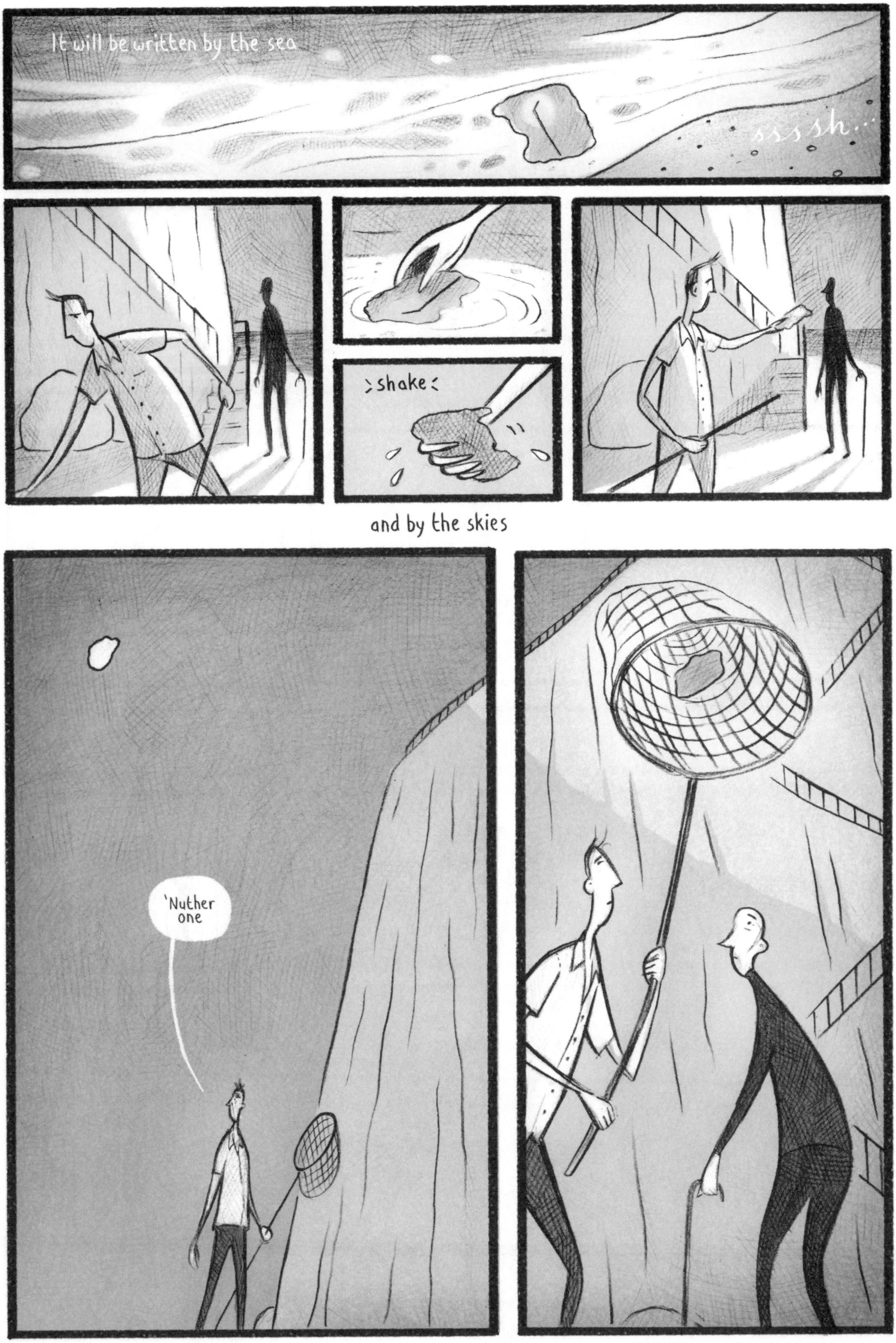
It will be written by the sea
ssssh...
shake
and by the skies
'Nuther one

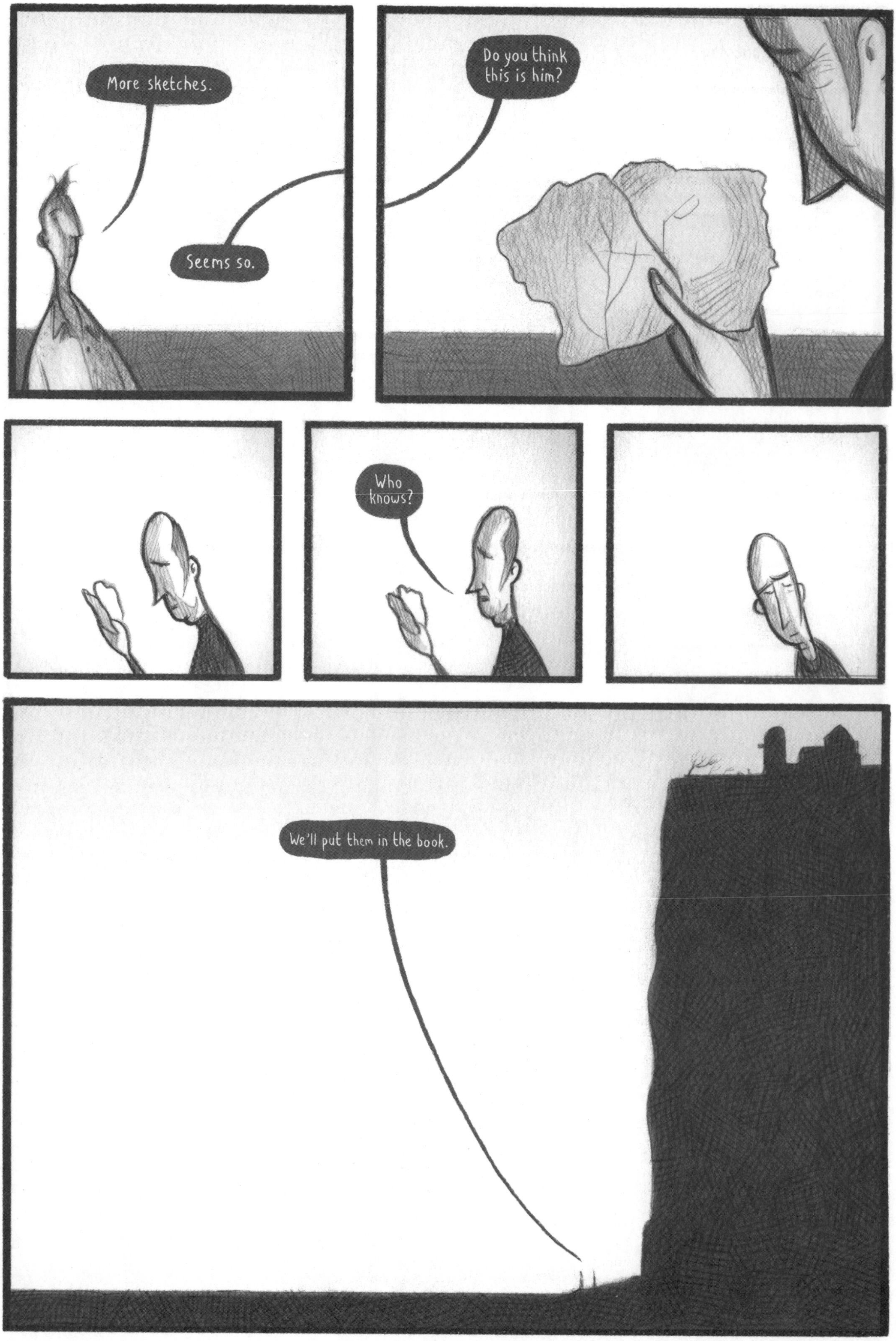
More sketches.
Seems so.
Do you think this is him?
Who knows?
We'll put them in the book.

He hopes that one day

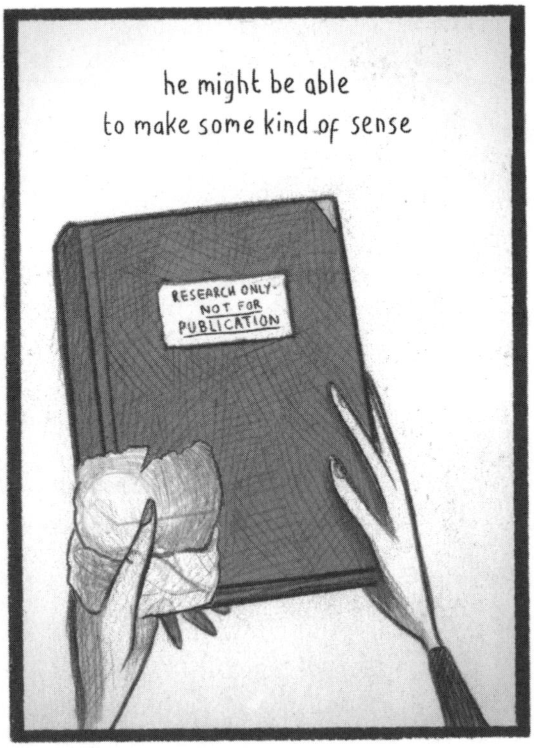
he might be able
to make some kind of sense
RESEARCH ONLY-
NOT FOR
PUBLICATION

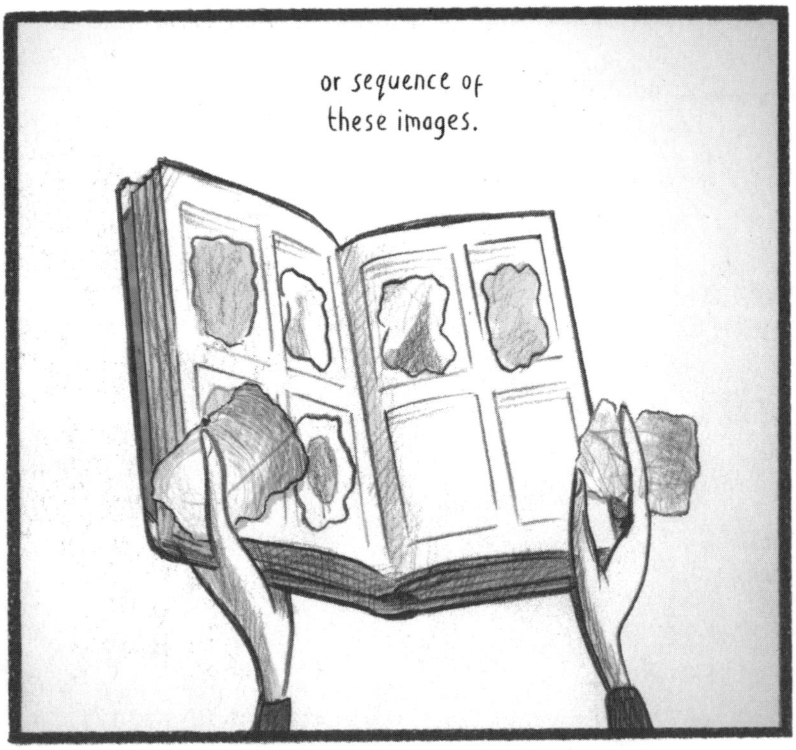
or sequence of
these images.

Maybe even a narrative.

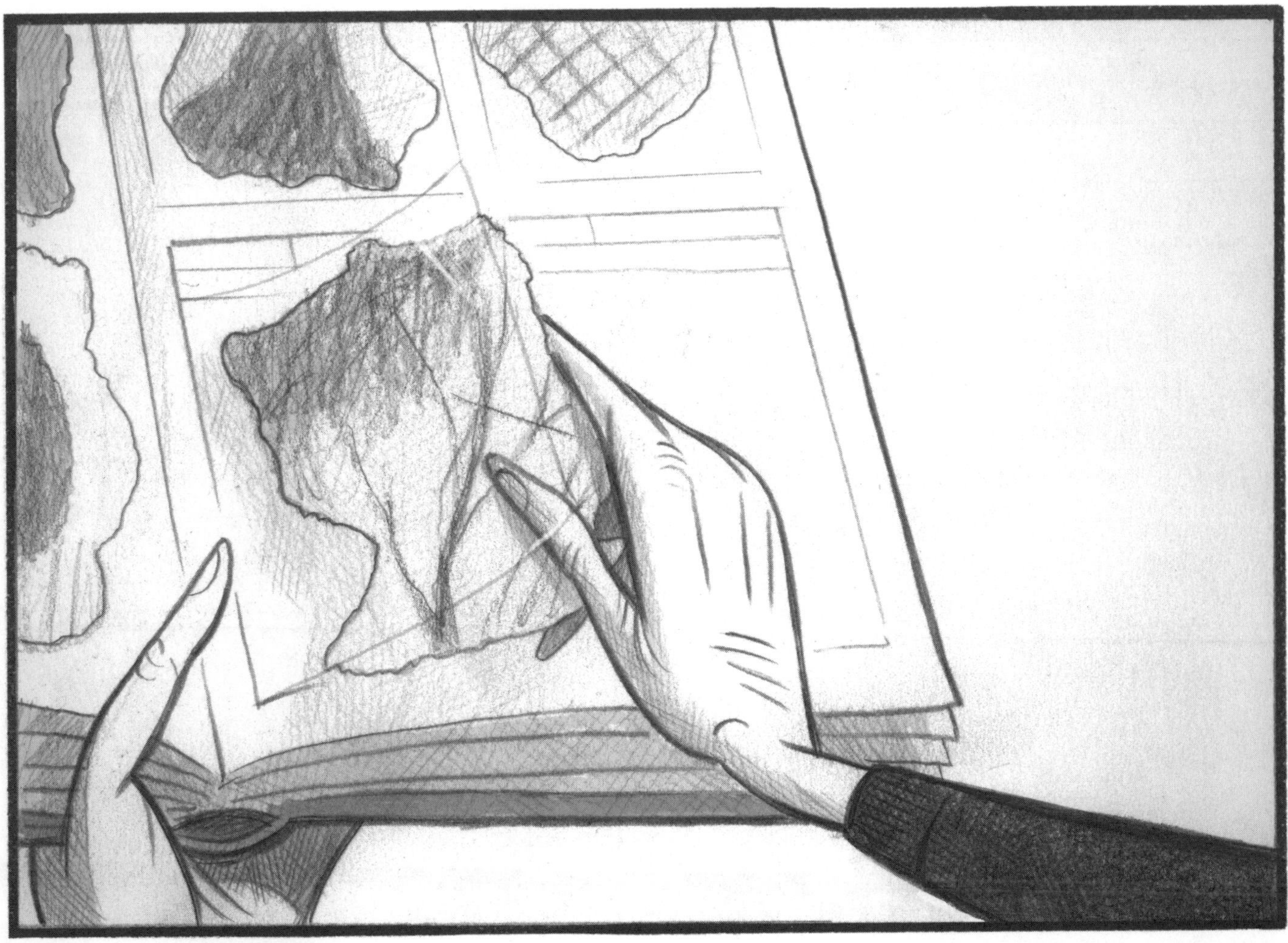

A story from There.

So far, none is apparent.

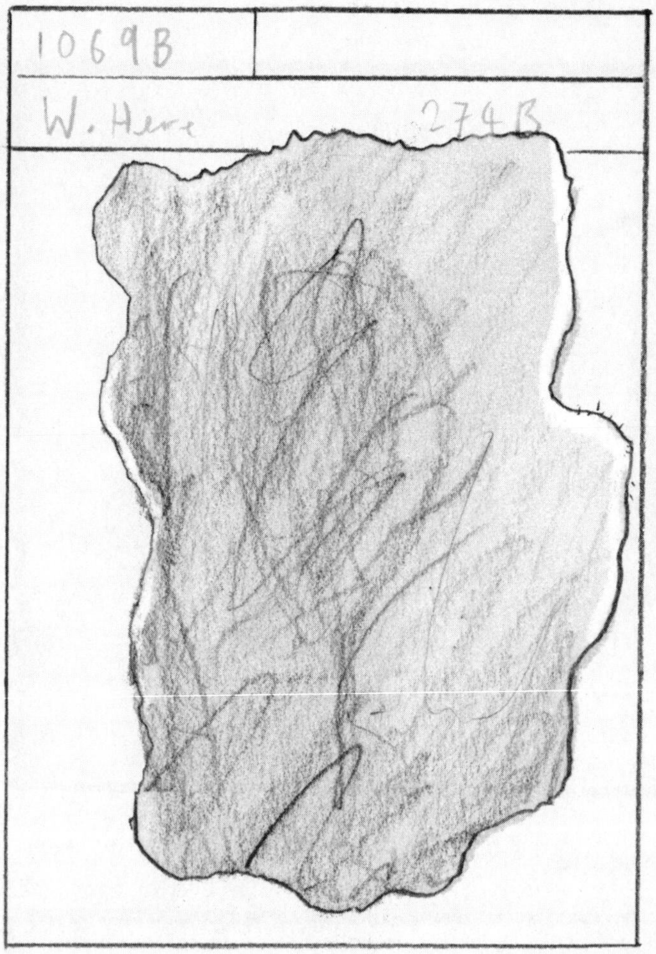
1069B
W. Here
274B

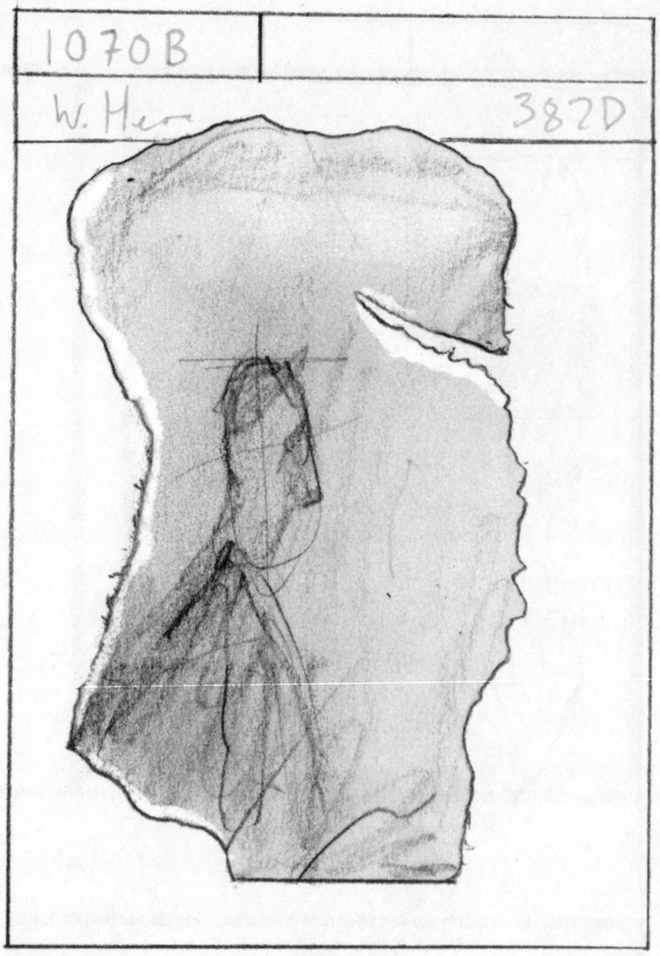
1070B
W. Here
382D

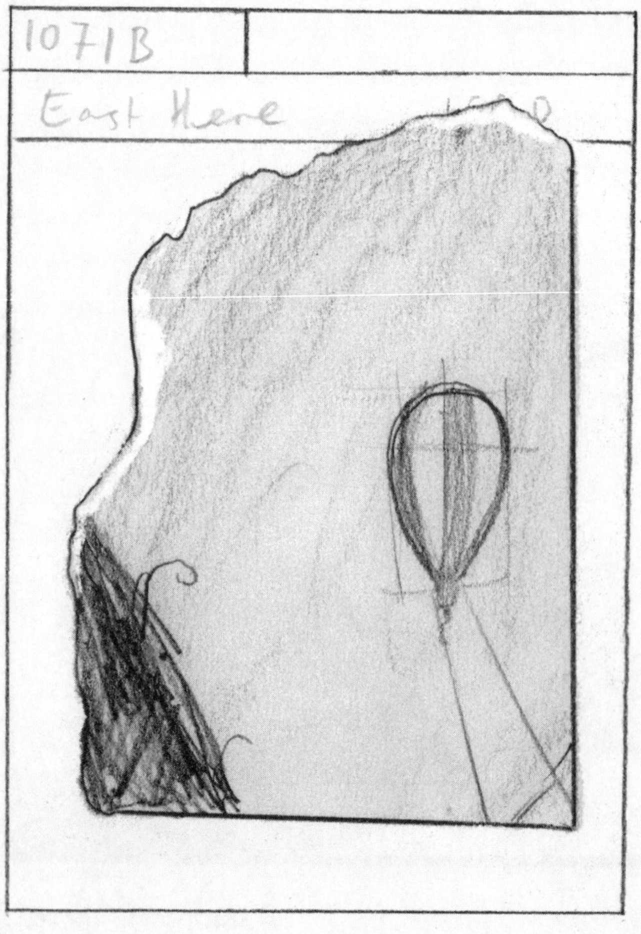
1071B
East Here

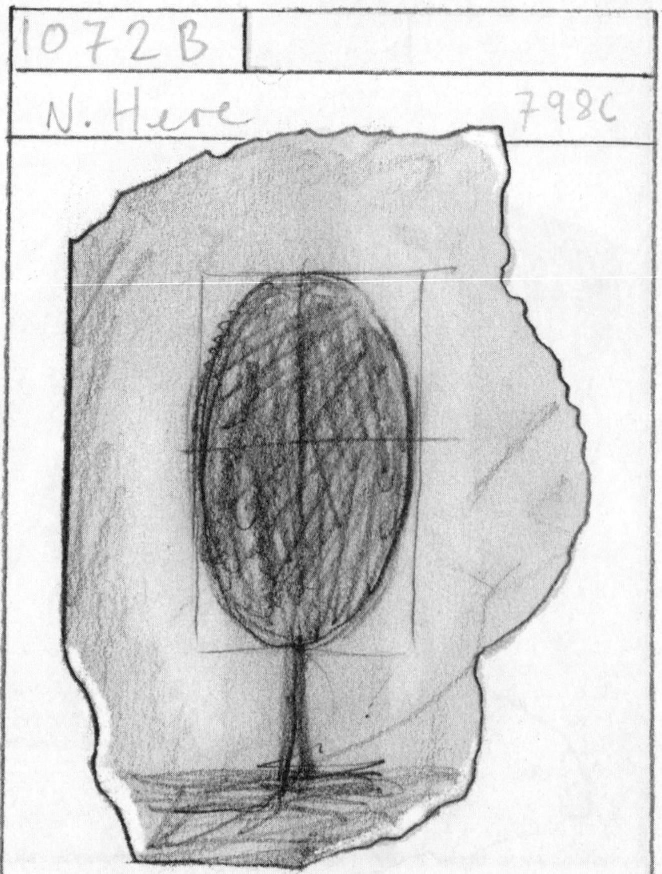
1072B
N. Here
798C

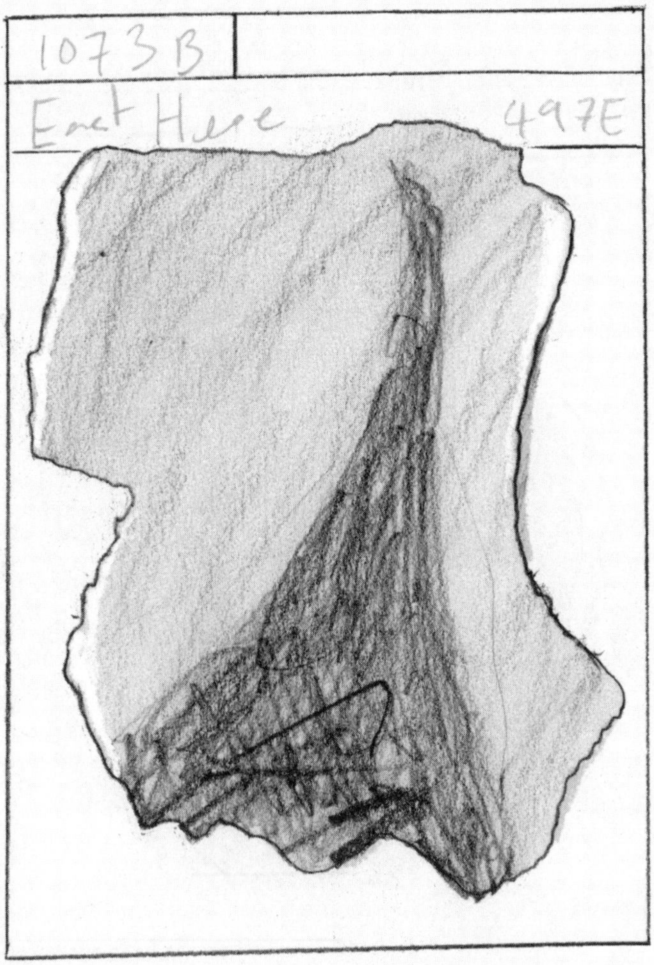
1073B
East Here
497E

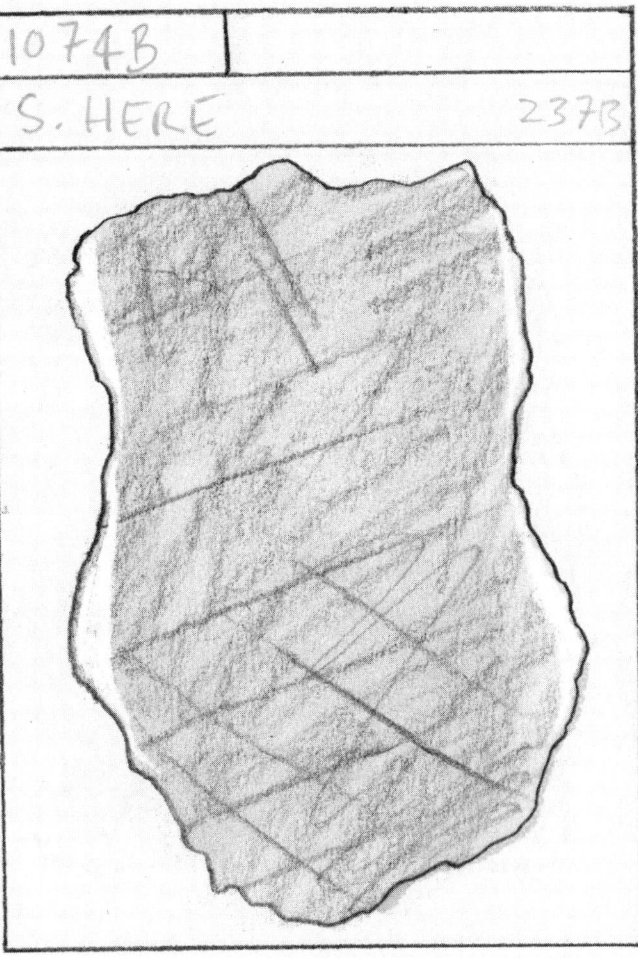
1074B
S. HERE
237B

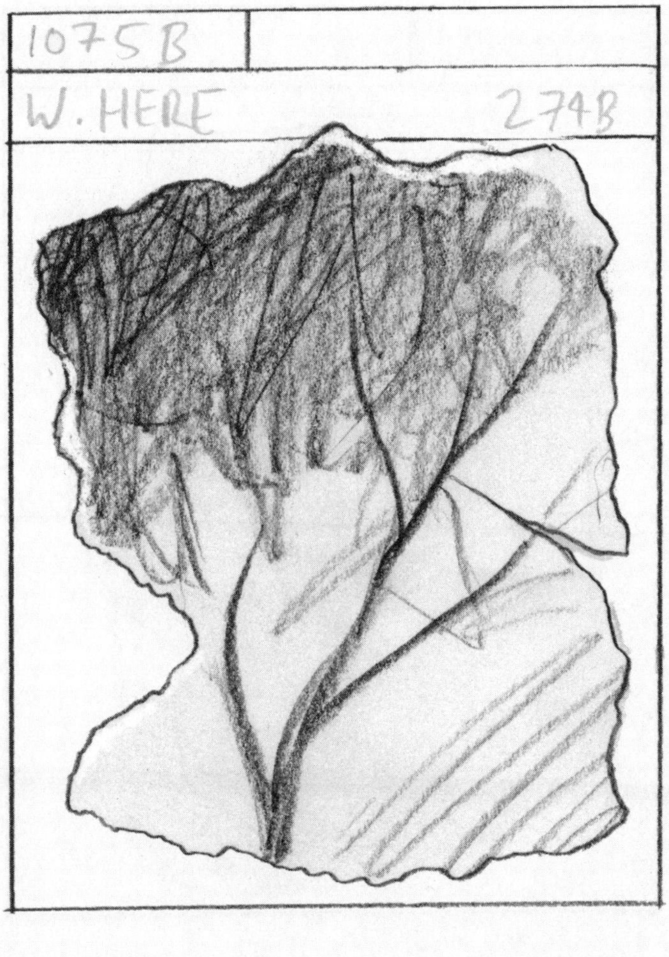
1075B
W. HERE
274B

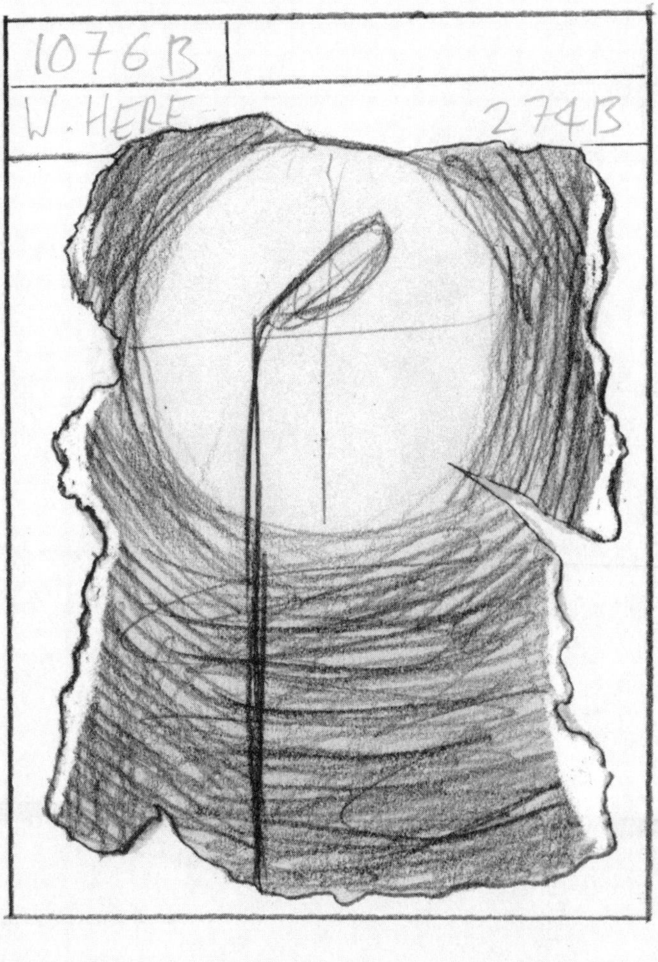
1076B
W. HERE
274B

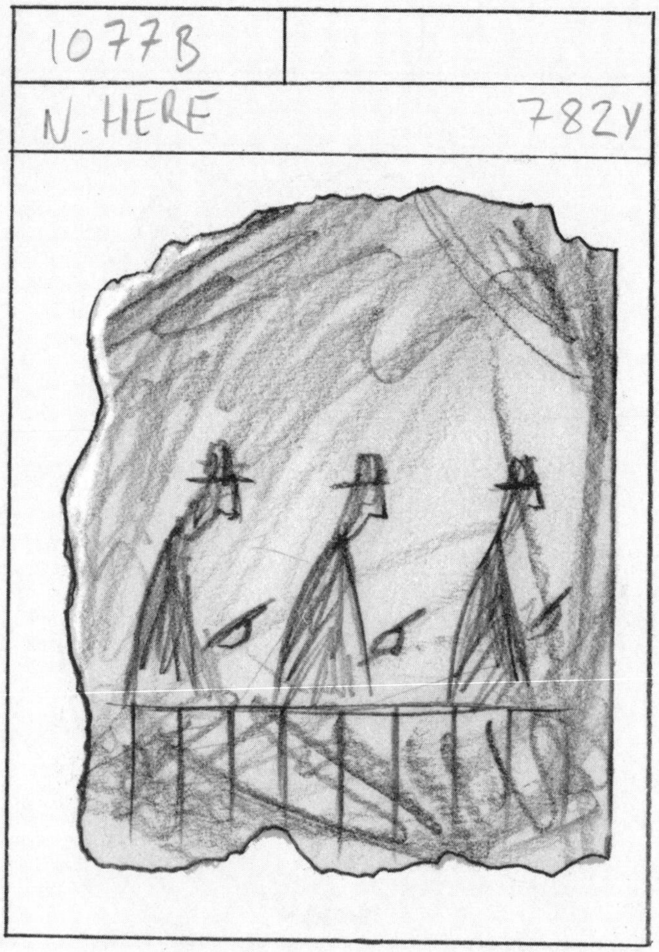
1077B
N. HERE
782Y

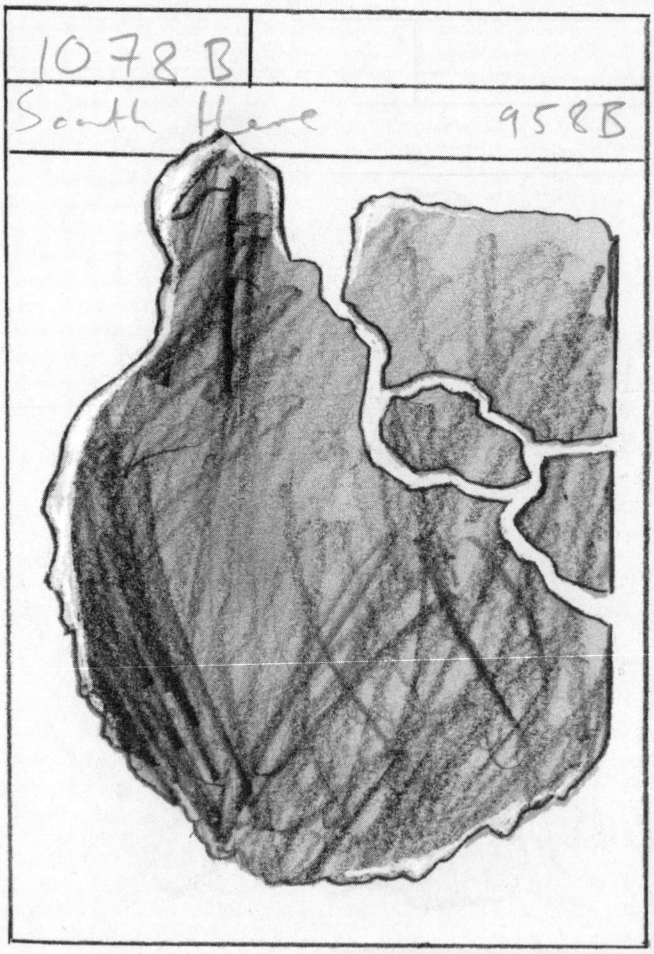
1078 B
South Here
958B

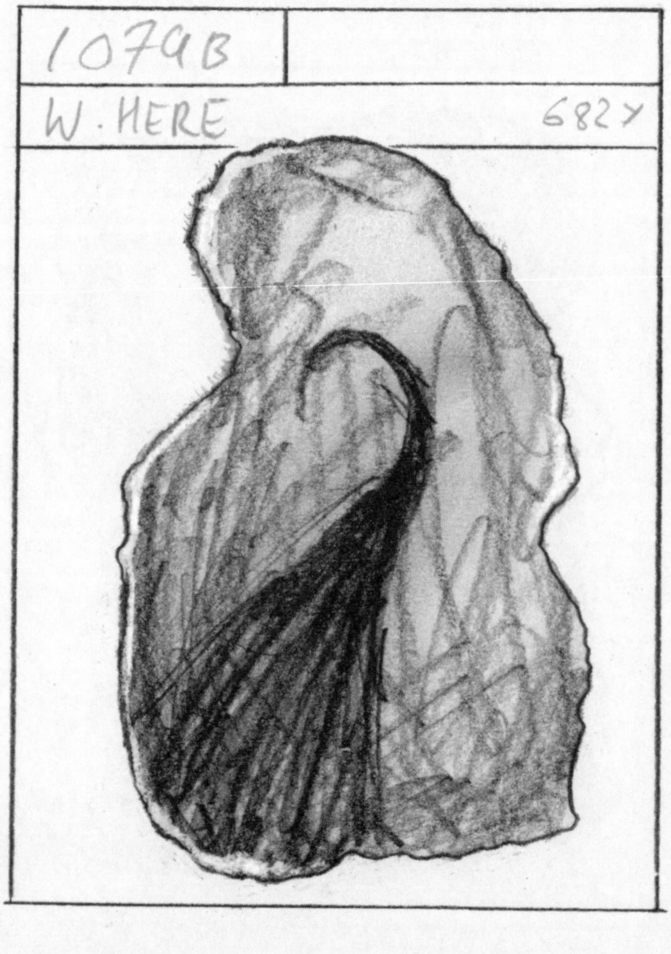
1079B
W. HERE
682Y

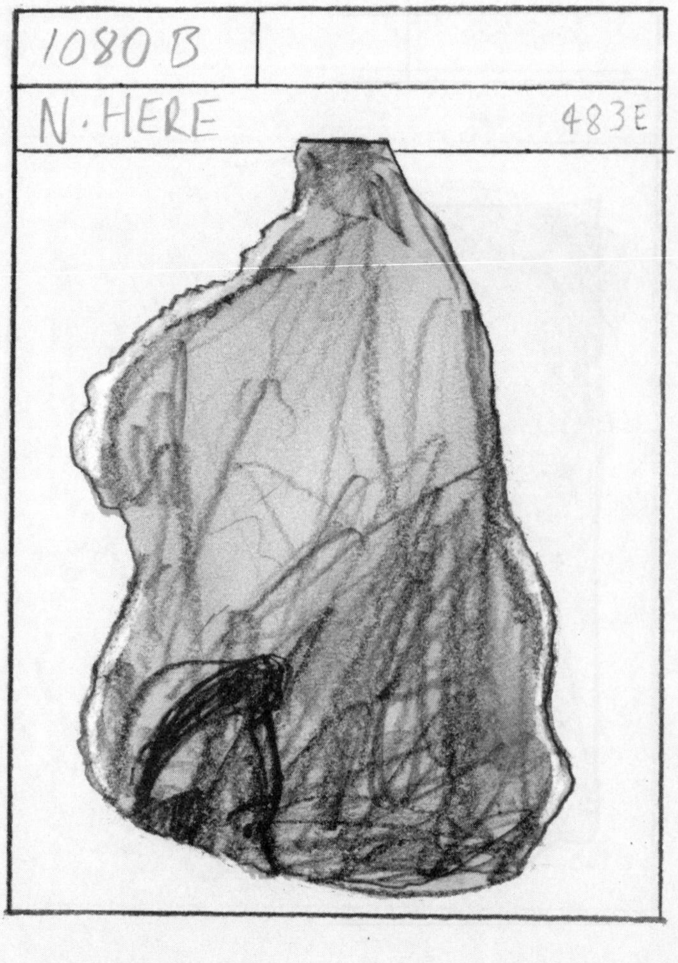
1080 B
N. HERE
483E

1081B	
WEST HERE	432Y

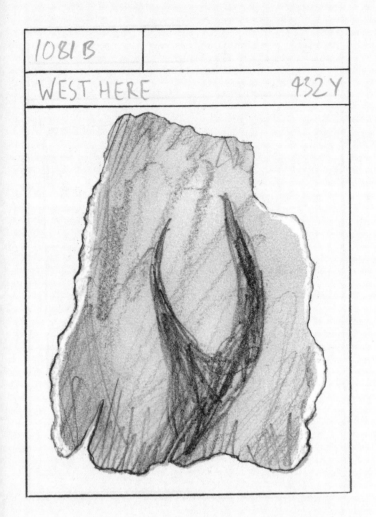

1082B	
E. HERE	241C

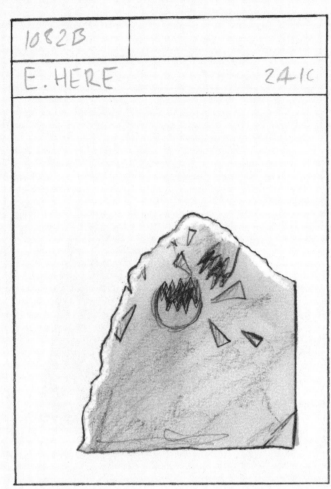

1083B	
EAST HERE	125E

1084B	
N. HERE	429E

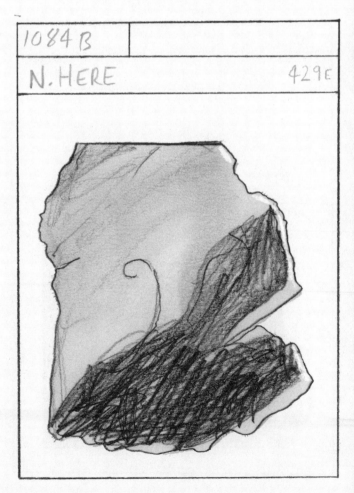

1085B	
W. Here	193y

1086B	
S. Here	128B

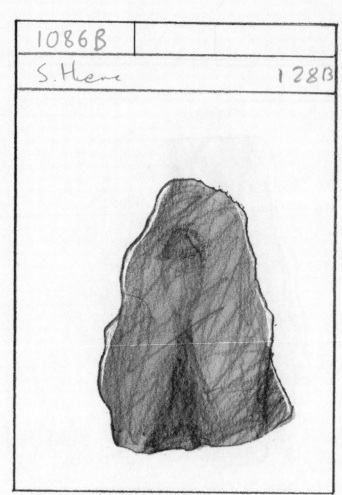

1087.B	
E. Here	149B

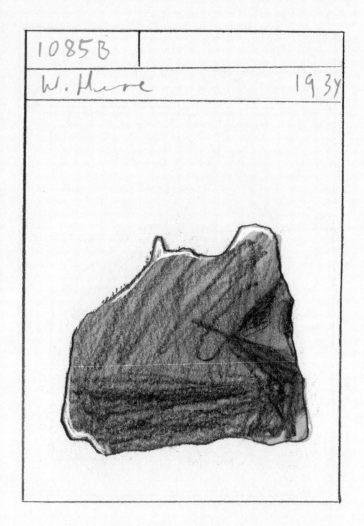

1088B	
E. Here	289B

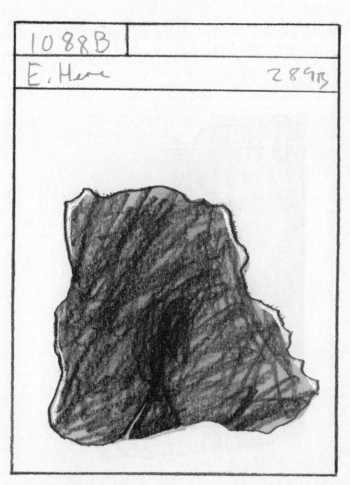

W. Here   193y

E. Here   289B

1089B	
S. Here	947B

1090B	
S. Here	432B

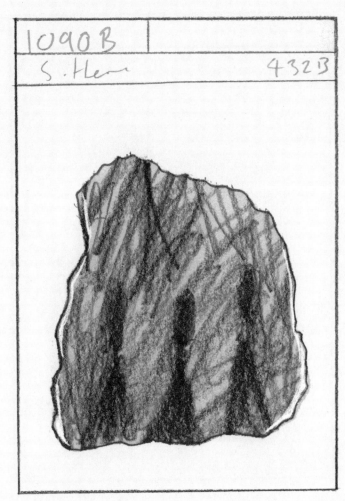

1091B	
West Here	459Y

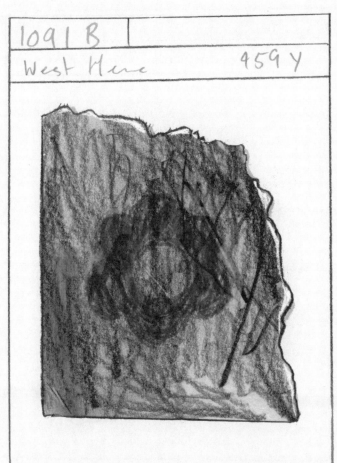

1092B	
W. Here	679Y

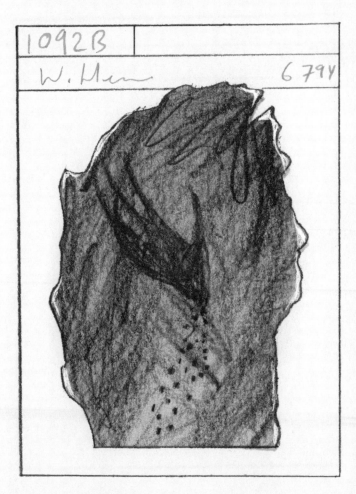

1093B	
W. Here	273Y

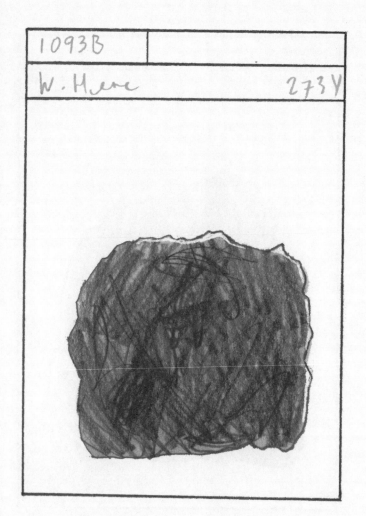

1094B	
W. Here	193Y

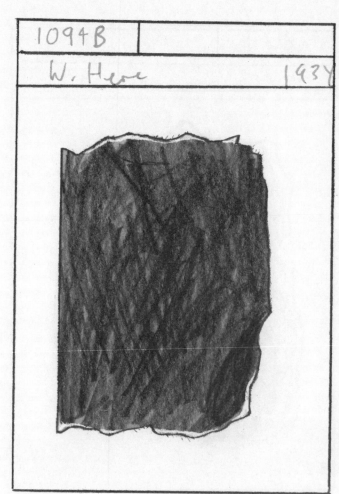

1095B	
E. Here	655Y

1096B	
North Here	556B

1097 B	
E. Here	249B

1098 B	
N. Here	658B

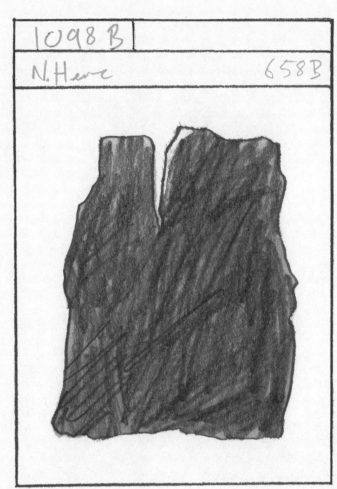

1099 B	
South Hem	199B

1100 B	
E Here	348B

Thank You

Alex Bowler and all at Jonathan Cape for
Beard-trimming and encouragement

Sam Copeland at RCW

My parents Margaret and Geoff Collins
for pretty much everything

Tony Illingworth and Maureen Rodger
for being inspirational teachers

Peter Brown, who commissioned my first cartoons
and encouraged me to keep at it

Tom Humberstone for showing me
what comics can do

Roger and Barbara Clarke
for letting me take over their office

And my wife Hannah - without
whose ideas, inspiration, editing,
support and endurance
this book would not exist.

Published by Jonathan Cape 2013

4 6 8 10 9 7 5 3

First published in Great Britain in 2013 by
Jonathan Cape

Random House, 20 Vauxhall Bridge Road,
London SW1V 2SA

www.capegraphicnovels.co.uk

Addresses for companies within The Random House Group Limited can be found at:
www.randomhouse.co.uk/offices.htm

The Random House Group Limited Reg. No. 954009

A CIP catalogue record for this book is available from the British Library

ISBN 9780224096287

The Random House Group Limited supports The Forest Stewardship Council (FSC®),
the leading international forest certification organisation. Our books carrying the FSC label
are printed on FSC® certified paper. FSC is the only forest certification scheme endorsed by
the leading environmental organisations, including Greenpeace. Our paper procurement
policy can be found at: www.randomhouse.co.uk/environment

Printed and bound in Great Britain by TJ International Ltd, Cornwall

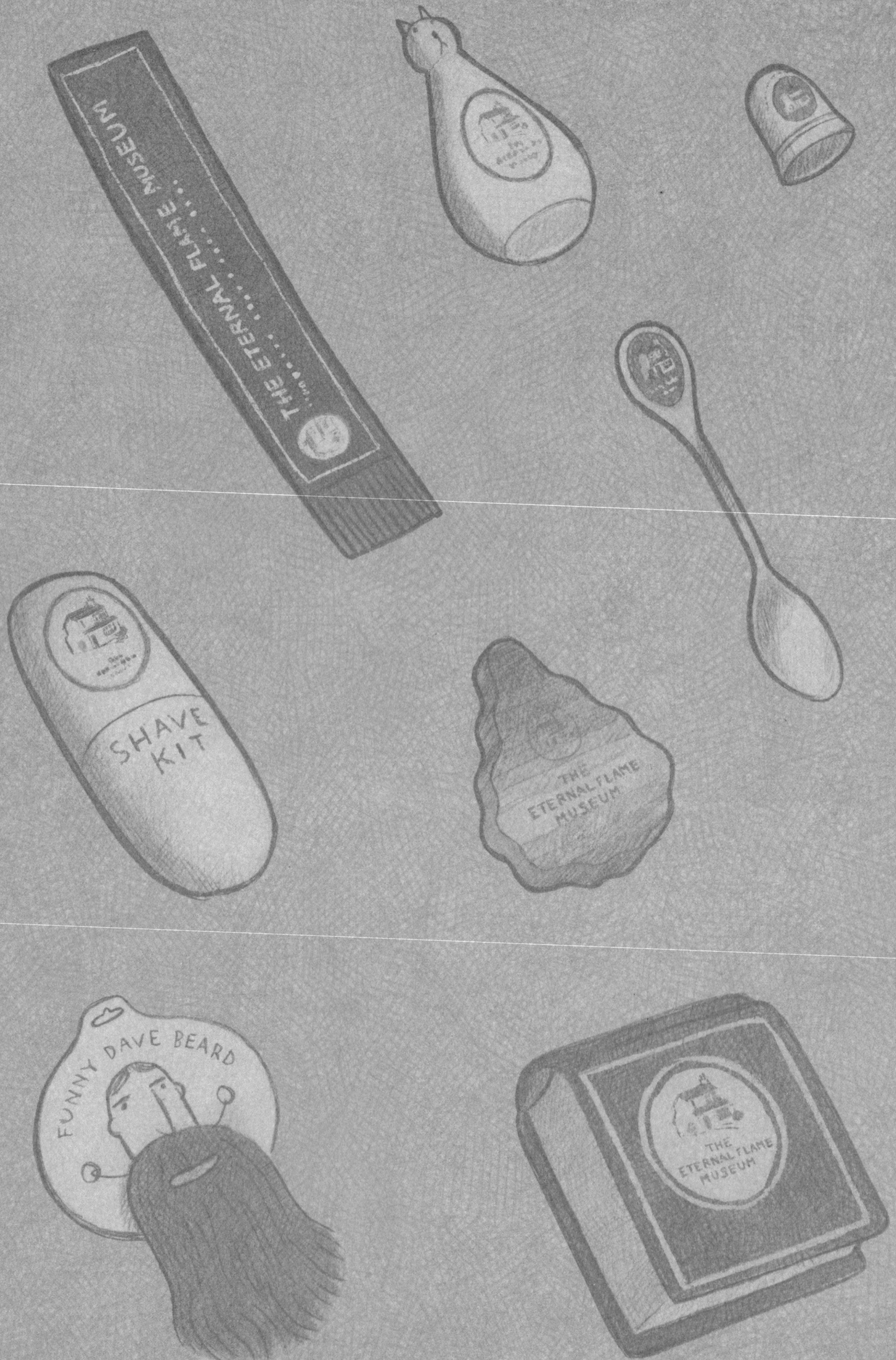
THE ETERNAL FLAME MUSEUM
SHAVE KIT
THE ETERNAL FLAME MUSEUM
FUNNY DAVE BEARD
THE ETERNAL FLAME MUSEUM